MANAGING SACRALITIES

Explorations in Heritage Studies

Series Editors:
Ali Mozaffari, *Deakin University*
David Charles Harvey, *Aarhus University*

Explorations in Heritage Studies responds directly to the rapid growth of heritage scholarship and recognizes the transdisciplinary nature of research in this area, as reflected in the wide-ranging fields, such as archaeology, geography, anthropology and ethnology, digital heritage, heritage management, conservation theory, physical science, architecture, history, tourism, and planning. With a blurring of boundaries between art and science, theory and practice, culture and nature, the volumes in the series balance theoretical and empirical research, and often challenge dominant assumptions in theory and practice.

Volume 6
Managing Sacralities: Competing and Converging Claims of Religious Heritage
Edited by Ernst van den Hemel, Oscar Salemink, and Irene Stengs

Volume 5
Heritage, Gentrification and Resistance in the Neoliberal City
Edited by Feras Hammami, Daniel Jewesbury, and Chiara Valli

Volume 4
Forging Architectural Tradition: National Narratives, Monument Preservation and Architectural Work in the Nineteenth Century
Edited by Dragan Damjanović and Aleksander Łupienko

Volume 3
Walls and Gateways: Contested Heritage in Dubrovnik
Celine Motzfeldt Loades

Volume 2
Heritage Movements in Asia: Cultural Heritage Activism, Politics, and Identity
Edited by Ali Mozaffari and Tod Jones

Volume 1
Politics of Scale: New Directions in Critical Heritage Studies
Edited by Tuuli Lähdesmäki, Suzie Thomas, and Yujie Zhu

MANAGING SACRALITIES
Competing and Converging Claims of Religious Heritage

Edited by
Ernst van den Hemel, Oscar Salemink, and Irene Stengs

First published in 2022 by
Berghahn Books
www.berghahnbooks.com

© 2022, 2024 Ernst van den Hemel, Oscar Salemink, and Irene Stengs
First paperback edition published in 2024

All rights reserved. Except for the quotation of short passages
for the purposes of criticism and review, no part of this book
may be reproduced in any form or by any means, electronic or
mechanical, including photocopying, recording, or any information
storage and retrieval system now known or to be invented,
without written permission of the publisher.

Library of Congress Cataloging-in-Publication Data
Names: Hemel, Ernst van den, editor. | Salemink, Oscar, editor. | Stengs, Irene, editor.
Title: Managing Sacralities: Competing and Converging Claims of Religious Heritage /
   edited by Ernst van den Hemel, Oscar Salemink, and Irene Stengs.
Description: [New York]: Berghahn Books, 2022. | Series: Explorations in Heritage
   Studies; volume 6 | Includes bibliographical references and index.
Identifiers: LCCN 2022025324 (print) | LCCN 2022025325 (ebook) |
   ISBN 9781800736177 (hardback) | ISBN 9781800738225 (open access ebook)
Subjects: LCSH: Cultural property—Protection—Europe—Religious aspects. | Sacred
   space—Conservation and restoration—Europe. | Historic preservation—Social
   aspects—Europe. | Religion and culture—Europe.
Classification: LCC CC135 .M3135 2022 (print) | LCC CC135 (ebook) |
   DDC 363.6/9094—dc23/eng/20220706
LC record available at https://lccn.loc.gov/2022025324
LC ebook record available at https://lccn.loc.gov/2022025325

British Library Cataloguing in Publication Data
A catalogue record for this book is available from the British Library

ISBN 978-1-80073-617-7 hardback
ISBN 978-1-80539-713-7 paperback
ISBN 978-1-80073-618-4 epub
ISBN 978-1-80073-822-5 web pdf

https://doi.org/10.316/9781800736177

The electronic open access publication of *Managing Sacralities* has been made
possible through the generous financial support of the Dutch National Research
Council (NWO), European Union's Horizon 2020 Research and Innovation
Programme, and the Meertens Institute.

This project has received funding from the Dutch National Research
Council (NWO) and the European Union's Horizon 2020 Research and
Innovation Programme under grant agreement No. 649307.

This work is published subject to a Creative Commons Attribution
Noncommercial No Derivatives 4.0 License. The terms of the license can
be found at http://creativecommons.org/licenses/by-nc-nd/4.0/. For
uses beyond those covered in the license contact Berghahn Books.

Contents

List of Illustrations — vii

Acknowledgments — ix

Introduction. Management of Religion, Sacralization of Heritage — 1
 Ernst van den Hemel, Oscar Salemink, and Irene Stengs

Part I. The Afterlives of Churches in the UK: Two East Anglian Case Studies

Chapter 1. The Redundant Church: Heritage Management of the Religious-Sacred-Secular Nexus — 21
 Clare Haynes

Chapter 2. "A Sense of Presence": The Significance of Spirituality in an English Heritage Regime — 44
 Ferdinand de Jong

Part II. The Management of National Religious Sites in Denmark

Chapter 3. Churches as Places of Worship, Cultural Heritage, and National Symbols: Centralism, Autonomy, and the Hybrid Nature of Church-State Relations in Denmark — 69
 Ulla Kjær and Poul Grinder-Hansen

Chapter 4. World-Heritagization, Bureaucratization, and Hybridization in Two Religious Heritage Sites in Denmark — 90
 Sofie Isager Ahl, Rasmus Rask Poulsen, and Oscar Salemink

Part III. The Religious Cityscape of Kraków, Poland

Chapter 5. Challenging or Confirming the National Sacred? Managing the Power Place at Wawel Hill in Kraków — 113
 Anna Niedźwiedź

Chapter 6. Playing the Game of Truth: The National Heritage Regime
in Poland and Contemporary Paganism   136
   Kamila Baraniecka-Olszewska

Part IV. Portuguese Heritages and Lusotropicalism

Chapter 7. Curating Culture and Religion: Lusotropicalism and
the Management of Heritage in Portugal   159
   Maria Cardeira da Silva and Clara Saraiva

Chapter 8. Between Catholic Nationalism and Inter-religious
Cosmopolitanism: Religious Heritage in Fátima and
Mouraria, Portugal   183
   Anna Fedele and José Mapril

Part V. Performances, Rituals, and Religious Heritage in the Netherlands

Chapter 9. To Applaud or Not to Applaud? Bach's *Saint Matthew
Passion* and Management of Sacrality in the Netherlands   205
   Ernst van den Hemel

Chapter 10. Moral Management and Secularized Religious
Heritage in the Netherlands: The Case of the Utrecht Saint Martin
Celebrations   228
   Welmoed Fenna Wagenaar

Afterword. Heritage as Management of Sacralities   249
   Oscar Salemink

Index   260

Illustrations

1.1. Postcard of Saint Peter Hungate, circa 1908. © collection Clare Haynes. — 29

1.2. Interior of Saint Peter Hungate, 2019. © Philip Sayer. — 37

2.1. View of the ruins of the Abbey of St Edmund, with the fenced tennis courts on the left, 2018. © Ferdinand de Jong. — 45

2.2. Tennis courts with the letter *E* for Edmund in the public gardens of Bury St Edmund. The second circle indicates the site of St Edmund's former shrine, 2018. © Steve Dawson. — 60

3.1. Almost all Danish churches have a flagpole, and the Danish flag will wave at each service. Aggersborg Church, Jylland, 2019. © Ulla Kjær. — 72

3.2. Aastrup Church, the island of Falster, Denmark, 2012. The medieval church in the middle of its neat and well-maintained churchyard. © Ulla Kjær. — 76

4.1. View of a field cleared of houses (left of the footpath) next to the northern mound, on a so-called Jelling Music Day, which brought together many spectators. In the distance one can see the white poles that follow the contours of the former palisade wall. © Sofie Isager Ahl, 2017. — 94

4.2. A special section cordoned off for religious worshipers in Roskilde Cathedral. © Oscar Salemink, 2018. — 101

5.1. Drawing energy at the roped-off wall at the Wawel castle courtyard, September 2016. © Anna Niedźwiedź. — 118

5.2. A group of tourists at the northwest corner of the Wawel castle courtyard and a person sitting and performing his meditation at the chakra spot. Next to him are the exhibition stands, rope, chain, and poles erected by the museum managers around the chakra site, June 2019. © Anna Niedźwiedź. 122

6.1. Saint Benedict church on the Lasota Hill, Rękawka, Kraków, 2018. © Kamila Baraniecka-Olszewska. 139

6.2. Weles with goddesses Marzanna and Dziewanna in Nawia—Slavic Netherworld, Rękawka, Kraków, 2018. © Kamila Baraniecka-Olszewska. 146

7.1. Tourists taking selfies in Sintra. © Left Hand Rotation. 165

7.2. Islamic Festival, 2019. © CRIA. 173

8.1. The statue of Our Lady of Fátima during the crowded procession for the celebration of the centenary of the apparitions on 13 October 2017. Note the crown made of gold donated by Portuguese women. © Anna Fedele. 190

8.2. The Baitul Mukarram Mosque in Mouraria on its inauguration day. © José Mapril. 196

9.1. Performance of the Sing-Along *Saint Matthew Passion*. Geertekerk Utrecht, 30 March 2018. © Ernst van den Hemel. 206

9.2. Performance of *Saint Matthew Passion*, Grote Kerk Naarden, 22 April 2011. Dutch prime minister Mark Rutte and other cabinet members in attendance in the first row. Public domain. 210

10.1. The light sculpture of Saint Martin, just before passing the cathedral Dom Tower in Utrecht, 2018. © Welmoed Fenna Wagenaar. 229

10.2. The light sculpture of Saint Martin, 2018: a soldier on horseback, deliberately without showing signs of Christianity. © Welmoed Fenna Wagenaar. 241

Acknowledgments

This volume is an outcome of the European research project "HERILIGION: Heritagization of Religion and the Sacralization of Heritage in Contemporary Europe." The project studied intertwining of processes of heritagization and sacralization against the backdrop of religious and secular dynamics in Denmark, the Netherlands, Poland, Portugal, and the United Kingdom (see www.heriligion.eu).

We would like to acknowledge the generous funding by Humanities in the European Research Area (HERA), the EU, and the contributing national research councils of Denmark, the Netherlands, Poland, Portugal, and the United Kingdom for their support for this project. In addition, we thank the Dutch Research Council (NWO) for its generous support to make this volume open access, and the Meertens Institute for taking care of the remaining deficit. Academics write to reach as many people as possible, and being able to publish this book in open access is hopefully a step toward a future that lowers boundaries of expression and circulation of academic work. We would also like to acknowledge the editors of Berghahn Books, for their kind support and expertise, and the anonymous peer reviewers, for their constructive feedback and kind words.

This volume is a testament to HERILIGION in that it allowed us to work closely with many affiliated researchers, heritage institutions, and engaged colleagues, students, and audiences. Their contributions to this volume greatly expanded the scope of this project. The topic of this volume, management of sacralities, arose in no small degree out of observations in the field and conversations with societal partners. In particular we would like to mention the institutions that we collaborated with (the so-called associate partners) over the course of HERILIGION: the National Museum of Denmark in Copenhagen; Museum Catharijneconvent in Utrecht, the Netherlands; the Ethnographic Museum and the Tygodnik Powszechny Foundation in Kraków, Poland; the National Museum of Ethnology, the Lisbon Museum—

Palácio Pimenta, and the ATUPO (Umbanda Temple Pai Oxalá Association) in Portugal; and Hungate Medieval Art, Norwich, United Kingdom.

Finally, we would also like to highlight an important source of academic work, namely pleasure and fun. While academic work is often seen as competitive, it can—and should—also be collaborative, predicated on open-ended dialogue, mutual respect, and therefore a dynamic process of human interaction. We remember with particular fondness how this volume came about not just in conference halls and in the pages of books, but also during walks, drinks, and animated, meandering conversations and travels. Especially since the beginning of the COVID-19 pandemic, the importance of such simple sociality has become crystal clear. Therefore, we dedicate this work to all of you who make research and writing fun. May we all meet again soon in good health.

INTRODUCTION

Management of Religion, Sacralization of Heritage

Ernst van den Hemel, Oscar Salemink, and Irene Stengs

Managing Religious Heritage

On 21 November 2019, in the Oude Kerk (Old Church) in Amsterdam, the art installation Poems for Earthlings *of Argentinian artist Adrián Villar Rojas was opened. The thirteenth-century Oude Kerk, the city's oldest building and parish church, is a listed national monument, including the church's collection of twenty-six hundred objects, around one hundred portraits and paintings, gravestones of historical public figures, the organs, and its bell tower. Today, the building is a location where, as the Oude Kerk website states, "heritage, museum, music, and, still on Sundays, churchgoers mingle."[1] In 1955, the church's present owner, the Stichting Oude Kerk (Foundation Old Church), was established, because of declining church membership and consequent serious financial and maintenance problems. In the last decade, the Old Church's outreach as a museum and cultural center grew to the extent that it not only houses exhibitions, but also invites global artists to use the church for site-specific art work. As a consequence of the latter policy, the members of the Protestant congregation regularly have to "re-arrange" their services for months in a row within a changed liturgical context where, depending on the installation, objects of the original interior may be taken out as well as new elements may be brought in. In the words of religious studies researcher Elza Kuyk (2018), "It is like the change of the décor in a theatre with (sometimes quick) adaption for the next scene."[2] But never before have the church's interior and atmosphere been so drastically transformed as during* Poems for Earthlings. *According to Kuyk, in a blog post a few days after the opening, "The church is darkened. The church is full of objects reminiscent of* barricades. *The fence-like positions refer to war zones and trenches. Parts of the permanent inventory (such as the votive ships at the high choir) have been temporarily removed. The large chandeliers do not hang in place, but are arranged in wooden crates.*"[3] Poems for Earthlings *stirred an emotional outcry among members of the congregation, the general public, and the members of the heritage foundation* Stichting ter behoud van de Oude Kerk *(Foundation for the Preservation of the Old Church). The latter foundation had been established earlier out of accumulating frustrations about what was considered the abuse and mismanagement of the church by the Foundation Old Church.*

In a nutshell, the case of the Amsterdam Old Church brings together many of the dilemmas, issues, and contestations that form the theme of this publication. *Managing Sacralities: Competing and Converging Claims of Religious Heritage* consists of ten detailed ethnographic and historical studies of the management of diverging and converging interests and expectations of different groups of people with various stakes in religious sites, objects, or practices that have been listed as cultural heritage within Europe.[4] Rather than presenting a management handbook of religious heritage sites and traditions, we explore the diverse and complicated ways religion and heritage are entangled, asking: What happens when sites, objects, and practices that are experienced and perceived as religious become cultural heritage? Who is involved in the management of religious heritage sites, objects, and practices? Which religious or secular sources of authority that validate and regulate religious heritage sites, objects, and practices do the so-called stakeholders mobilize or create? Since cultural heritage has become an increasingly popular and influential frame to think and valuate what is of importance and what is worth safeguarding for religious communities and others, these questions arise in diverse and challenging manners.

Recognition as heritage involves the organization of new expressions and configurations of value, but also financial interests and ideas about "stakeholdership," in the sense that the clergy and congregation now have to share their ownership, control, and management—to use the UNESCO term—with other "stakeholders": experts, conservation agencies, local and national authorities, artists, businesses, tourists, and other visitors. This informs and influences how a site functions, what a ceremony does, and which people are allowed or encouraged to visit or to participate. Signs, placards, information booths, and souvenir shops may provide framing and information about the site or the performance as not only religious but also as cultural heritage.

Heritagization, however, does not mean profanation in a Durkheimian sense, because to heritagize something means setting it apart from the everyday, for special contemplation, consideration, and protection, and hence imbuing it with well-nigh sacred characteristics (Durkheim 1965). As pointed out by Meyer and de Witte in "Heritage and the Sacred: Introduction," "Not unlike religion, heritage formation involves some kind of sacralization, through which cultural forms are lifted up and set apart so as to be able to speak of what is considered to be central to social life" (Meyer and de Witte 2013: 276). Therefore, heritagization also sacralizes heritage sites, objects, and practices, to the extent that heritage recognition renders them non-everyday and non-profane, to be separated from the everyday, treated with awe, and contemplated for their inherent values—what Walter Benjamin (2007: 221) called their "aura." The title of this volume, *Managing Sacralities*, indicates that heritagization, especially when it involves heritage that is connected to religion, often involves multiple forms of sacrality.

Much cultural heritage around the world is or was religious in nature: sites of extinct religions like the pyramids of Teotihuacán in Mexico; "abandoned" temples like (Buddhist) Borobudur and (Hindu) Prambanan in Muslim Java; or archaeological sites reappropriated as religious sites, like Angkor in Cambodia or Stonehenge in England. At the same time, many cultural heritage sites continue to be religious sites—like the Masjed-e Jāmé ("Friday mosque") of Isfahan or the many cathedral churches in Europe, such as Saint Peter's Basilica in Rome or the Roskilde Cathedral in Denmark. After the devastation of World War II, a discourse of cultural heritage as shared by humanity emerged and globalized, buttressed by UNESCO's 1972 and 2003 heritage conventions (Meskell 2013). A process of evaluating, authenticating, recognizing, and listing of religious sites, objects, and practices was initiated under the auspices of expert knowledge, against the backdrop of the simultaneous emergence of a visiting public through mass tourism (Kirshenblatt-Gimblett 1998; Hitchcock, King, and Parnwell 2010). After all, one "banal but not self-evident" feature of heritage is that it "can be visited" (Bernhard Tschofen in Macdonald 2013: 18). Religious sites, both those still in use and those that are derelict, are related to profound affects as well as particular localized affects and interests (cf. Smith, Wetherell, and Campbell 2018; Smith 2020).

Religious sites that are heritagized while still in use invite complex layers of meaning making, in connection with the different modalities of governing religion and cultural heritage, which implies very different conceptual and practical approaches. If a site, object, or practice is considered religious, then the dominant liberal ideology demands that the state must take a back seat, foregrounding the principle of freedom of religion. If the same object is recognized as cultural heritage, however, the state must take a front seat and assume responsibility for its protection. Within Europe, this has a particular material urgency in times when secularization has meant that religious piety, affiliation, and participation are a matter of choice (cf. Casanova 2009), often taking the form of declining numbers of active and paying churchgoers. The apparent disappearance of the "sacred canopy" (Berger 1967) and resulting "disenchantment" of the world (Weber 1965) as brought out in the withdrawal of classical forms of Christianity have enabled and stimulated the heritagization of religious buildings throughout Europe. As Coleman and Bowman (2019) have pointed out, monumental Anglican cathedrals in contemporary England are being put to increasingly diverse uses and for different audiences. Elsewhere in Europe this diversification of uses produces divergent effects. For example, the Church of Saint-Germain-des-Prés in Paris asks visitors for a financial contribution to its maintenance—but as *cultural heritage*, not as a Catholic church. In contrast, Granada's Cathedral of the Incarnation in Spain charges entry fees but uses the audio guides as a medium for religious propagation by consistently pointing out that the artworks, artists, and craftspeople were inspired by God.

The decline of certain previously dominant forms of organized religion within western Europe is also connected to deeper questions of identity and belonging in the twenty-first century. One only has to look at national politics in western Europe to see that the drive to protect national identity is often couched in terms of tradition, heritage, or roots. Contexts for anxiety about migration and narratives on cultural "others" further add to the specific, volatile mix of religion, secularity, and identity in contemporary Europe. More intellectualist anti-immigration discourses in Europe often predicate a celebratory narrative of the Enlightenment, as a historical European philosophical project, on Europe as a so-called Judeo-Christian civilization, thereby implying that Muslims are unable to achieve enlightenment and become European to the core. There has hardly been a European context that has not seen an electorally successful opposition between the "Judeo-Christian" West and "Islamic" other, pitting enlightened native "Judeo-Christians" against "Islamic newcomers" (van den Hemel 2014). But the current, postwar celebration of Judeo-Christian civilization is predicated on historical erasures, first of the historical presence of Muslims in various parts of southern and eastern Europe and second of Jews through the Holocaust and subsequent emigrations, which made the prefix "Judeo-" to "Christian" civilization politically possible. Under the pressure of the emotional need to protect identity, religious heritage is often allotted a special place even, or perhaps especially, in societies in which hitherto dominant religious frameworks are experienced as being on the wane. Religious heritage thus becomes implicated in narratives about who belongs and who does not, which religious sites and traditions should be funded, and who gets to decide what a cityscape has meant in the past, does mean in the present, and will mean in the future.

The heritagization of religious sites and practices, in short, involves complex and sometimes contradictory series of viewpoints, hierarchies of value, and policy traditions. Importantly, these processes play out differently at each site, for each object, for each practice, and in each moment of time on various levels and scales, as the chapters in this volume will illustrate. *Managing Sacralities: Competing and Converging Claims of Religious Heritage* presents ethnographic case studies that analyze the divergent interests, attachments, and emotions of the people involved and the ways these are managed at various, intersecting levels and scales when religious sites, objects, or practices are transformed into cultural heritage.

This book engages with often used, critical notions such as "heritage regime" (Bendix, Eggert, and Peselmann 2012; Geismar 2015) and "authorized heritage discourse" (Smith 2006) that draw attention to the disciplinary effects of heritagization on a global scale. But in order to do justice to the ethnographic complexities in each of the cases offered, we focus on "management" as a way of comprehending the multifarious relations that are not simply a top-down process at a local level. This allows us to pay attention to on-the-ground tensions and to show how various social actors at various levels manage these tensions. At the same time, "heritage" is not just a global category but has become a vernacular category that allows local groups and communities to use their voice, mobilize around their aims, and exercise their agency, as Michael Herzfeld showed in his studies of Rome (2009) and Bangkok (2016). But before we zoom in on how our case studies work bottom up with these questions in a variety of contexts in Europe, let us elaborate further on two premises for this book, namely the heritagization of religion and the concern for how its implications are managed locally.

Heritagization of Religion and Sacralization of Heritage

The category of heritage can be understood as part of the paradigm of secularization, understood in Talal Asad's way (2003). The global criteria for heritage recognition, as brought out in the UNESCO heritage conventions, are secular in nature in the sense of predicated on immanent, this-worldly cultural values—cultural, aesthetic, historical, ontological—but never directly on transcendental, religious values. Many World Heritage Sites are churches, cathedrals, temples, and other religious structures, but only a tiny minority of religious buildings are considered cultural heritage.[5] For instance, Roskilde Cathedral (Denmark) is a church, which is recognized as World Heritage not *because* it is a church, but because of its (art) historical, aesthetic, cultural, and ontological qualities as a church; as such, it is a culturally particularly important church of "outstanding universal value" beyond its immediate religious constituency. Because such valuation is based on nonreligious criteria, validating specific religious sites and objects as cultural heritage overlays such religious sites, objects, or practices with secular heritage values in a palimpsestic manner and hence, to some extent, secularizes them; it potentially desecrates such sites by capturing their sacred character and religious uses through a secular heritage gaze.

If heritagization involves a movement of "secular sacralization" (cf. Balkenhol, van den Hemel, and Stengs 2020), then it does not make sense to limit ourselves to a superficial definition of secularization as a one-directional withdrawal of religion when we call something heritage, as it brings along a whole host of associations and sentiments. This is not the place to rehash critiques of the secularization narrative, but let us offer a small number of considerations. In *Formations of the Secular*, Talal Asad (2003) argued that the ideas of religion and secularity historically emerged simultaneously and shifted the optics, experiences, and sensibilities regarding a wide range of issues, from pain and the body, to the idea of rights, often captured as a shift from a transcendental to an immanent frame. Since then, many discussions of secularization understand secularization not simply as a withdrawal or privatization of religion, but as an exploration of new forms of spirituality and meaning making and as an attribution of transcendent qualities to different political and cultural figures and phenomena (Turner 2006; Salemink 2009). It would perhaps be appropriate to speak not of the decline of religion, but rather of the partial "migration" of notions of the sacred to other realms than religion. This development, which John Bossy (1985) coined the "migration of the holy," makes it clear that notions of the sacred are taken up in new configurations and practices of meaning making. *The Religious Heritage Complex*, edited by Cyril Isnart and Nathalie Cerezales (2020), covers some of the same ground as this volume but seeks to refute the "migration of the holy" thesis by adopting the view that "the divorce between religion and cultural heritage is not a universal rule and the religious metaphor increasingly blurs this issue. Religious buildings, rituals, and objects do not always lose their original religious values and powers when entering the heritage realm" (Isnart and Cerezales 2020: 14). But their perception that religion and cultural heritage might overlap in practice does not constitute a convincing rebuttal that these two categories are aligned with and predicated on two different types of valuation.

Countries that are seen as providing the strongest illustration of secularization, like the Netherlands or Denmark, prove to be more of a challenge to common secularization narratives than a textbook illustration. Take the national church of Denmark, which, although the number of people who would state that they believe in the dogmas of the faith might be declining—Denmark is among the nations with the highest number of citizens who do not identify themselves as religious—retains a solid connection with Danish national identity. The Netherlands might have rapidly declining church numbers in mainstream Catholic and Protestant denominations, but Pentecostals, Evangelicals, and new forms of spirituality are on the rise. Moreover, the return of nationalism brought along a fiery debate about the importance of the religious past for defining present-day culture (Meyer 2019). Both the Netherlands and Denmark have had a significant rise of right-wing, nationalist movements proclaiming a desire to protect the religious identity of the nation. In a wider sense, in these countries the twenty-first-century decline in church attendance was paradoxically coupled with an emergent interest in protecting religious heritage. In other words, although the sacred might no longer be primarily located in holy books or the power of the church in public life, religion continues to influence, shape, and divide cultural identities in twenty-first-century Europe through the secular sacralization of religious attributes at the service of the ethno-nation.

We should also not forget that secularization understood as declining church attendance and the retreat of religion from society counts for only a very limited number of cases in northwestern Europe (and perhaps Canada and New Zealand), but that elsewhere in Europe contemporary configurations of religion are very different. Also, while some forms of religiosity are in numerical decline, other forms increase. In Portugal, for instance, mass attendance might be declining, but connections to Catholicism subsist in baptism numbers, religious education, pilgrimages, and the celebration of patron saint days in local communities. Poland provides a counterexample to the common secularization thesis, which is next to useless to describe the contemporary role of the Catholic church in that country. In short, if we connect the contemporary heritagization of religious sites, objects, and practices in Europe with secularization, we link the latter process with the adoption of an immanent frame rather than de-religionization as brought out in, for example, declining church attendance. Hence, when we use the term "secularization," we would do well to reject a one-size-fits-all understanding of it. Instead, if we want to analyze the heritagization of religious sites, objects, and practices in different European countries, we have to situate it in specific religiopolitical contexts.

This is perhaps clearly indicated by the debates around the heritage of religious minorities. In times of increasing use of religious heritage to delineate national identity, how do minority religions succeed in claiming heritage status? The holy has migrated not just to culture and heritage, but also to an increasing diversity of expressions of spirituality (cf. Heelas and Woodhead 2005). What determines how minority religions or spiritual practices are recognized as cultural heritage? Again, a situated approach is crucial here. Although it is undoubtedly the case that heritagization can further cement the power of dominant groups in a society, it can also provide platforms for subversion, by reworking what the roots of a national community are (Hall

1999; Macdonald 2003). One can think of debates around heritage of Islam or Judaism in Europe, but as Kamila Baraniecka-Olszewska argues in her chapter, also (Neo-)Pagans struggle for recognition within majority constructions of a *Leitkultur* through what Agnieszka Pasieka (2015) in her book on religious diversity in Poland terms hierarchical pluralism. Oscar Salemink has shown how the seemingly top-down criteria for recognition of heritage can be used to further as well as hamper minorities' rights, dependent on the force fields on the ground (Salemink 2016). How can diverse grassroots practices influence and shape processes of heritagization? How are debates concerning religious pluralism played out in the recognition of religious heritage? Which religions are considered part of the heritage of the nation, and how does this impact minority religions? The chapters by Maria Cardeira da Silva and Clara Saraiva, Anna Fedele and José Mapril, Anna Niedźwiedź, Kamila Baraniecka-Olszewska, and Welmoed Fenna Wagenaar investigate these questions in ethnographic detail.

It is these tensions of claiming and validating cultural heritage and concomitant processes of inclusion and exclusion that are at the heart of this volume. The subtitle of this volume, *Competing and Converging Claims of Religious Heritage*, indicates a dynamic focus on religious heritage: on the one hand, heritage can be claimed by people, but it also points to the inverse: heritage discourse has its own claims and thus pushes people to situate themselves in relation to it.

To clarify our position, a brief reflection on the notion of "heritage regime" is in order here. Heritage is not just there, to be assessed and recognized by experts and state agencies, but the process of heritage making or heritagization takes place in a contemporary context and, much like any other activity, involves specific interests, languages, rules, and regulations and, what Laurajane Smith (2006) calls, an "authorized heritage discourse." This discourse is part of a variety of heritage regimes that are linked up with a global heritage regime, or in the words of Regina Bendix et al., "The very effort to adopt a global heritage regime forces myriad adaptations to particular state and interstate modalities of building and managing heritage" (Bendix 2012: 11). The use of such terms as "discourse," "regime," and "force" denote a top-down architecture that is characteristic of conceptual approaches under the header of "heritage regimes" (Geismar 2015). And it has given an impetus to disenchant the naive belief in heritage as a natural expression of a community's history and present. Yet, at the same time, an overemphasis on the disciplinary force of heritage regimes runs the risk of occluding the ways in which heritage, much like any other discursive practice, should be seen as a performance, often initiated, enacted, promoted, and adapted by individuals, groups, and local communities to further their own agendas, as shown convincingly in the chapters by Kamila Baraniecka-Olszewska and Welmoed Fenna Wagenaar.

The goal of this volume is not to pass judgment on the category of heritage (cf. Brumann 2014), but to approach it as the object both of contemporary practices of state regulation and of practices of the self—playing an increasing role in people's subjectivities and affects (cf. Smith 2020; Smith et al. 2018). How is the regime of heritage appropriated, embedded, embodied, materialized, and enacted in the lives of communities and individuals and in sites and objects? The various chapters in this book show how often conflicting, overlapping dimensions in the heritagization of religion are experienced as emancipatory by some, but by others as contributing to the cementing of a majority cultural identity. Therefore, the question is not just how heritage is codified and enforced top-down, but also embraced, adapted, rejected, and reshaped bottom-up. How are such sites and objects managed and such practices enacted, with reference to their dual and often paradoxical religious and cultural heritage qualities? How are tensions mediated and conflicts resolved? This volume focuses on the intersections of religion and heritage but resists folding examples of heritagization into a larger regime or a stable discourse. Instead of a focus on regimes, with its concomitant emphasis on power, top-down implementation, and regulatory straightjackets, this book focuses on the management of the diverging interests and inevitable tensions surrounding religious heritage in contemporary Europe.

The Need for Ethnographies of the Management of Religion and Heritage

We focus on management of religious heritage, not as an instrumental aim but as a way to interrogate both the categories of heritage and religion. In this volume, we take note of the convincing critiques of the notion of heritage, as formulated by Regina Bendix (2009), Laurajane Smith (2006), and others, implied in the concepts of "heritage industry," "heritage regime," "authorized heritage discourse," and "heritagization." However, a critical deconstruction of heritagization might not suffice to *understand* the contemporary heritage fever (cf. Blumenfield and Silverman 2013), let alone to unpack the different interests and claims made through heritage work. The authority of UNESCO to appraise what is and what is not heritage has often been scrutinized, and some have highlighted that this implies that UNESCO is at the pinnacle of a global heritage regime that seeks to enforce a top-down application of global value (Askew 2010; Brumann 2017, 2019, 2021; Di Giovine 2009; Meskell 2013, 2018; Meskell and Brumann 2015). While participating in a UNESCO-led process of recognition of a religious site as cultural heritage might have unintended consequences for the religious constituency, this does not explain the willingness and indeed enthusiasm with which many local communities and religious congregations embrace heritage nomination. After all, heritage has gone global and has been vernacularized through a widely shared discursive language in which communities express values and recognition on different levels and scales (De Cesari 2012). Thus, it is pertinent to pay attention to how heritage regimes are instrumentalized, adapted, changed, hacked, and turned inside out by different groups and societal actors that claim to have a stake in the cultural heritage and its management. Through the process of heritagization, a dance ensues of interests and affects, of goals and tasks, of claims and repertoires of action, the outcome of which is not so certain. So while heritage invokes an authoritative discourse and a regime of power, it might not always be easy to answer the questions who manages what, whose interests are foregrounded, and who might be excluded. Precisely because the process of heritagization is not stable or predictable, the question of who manages what or whom and with what effect becomes of interest.

This is even more the case when speaking of sites, objects, or practices that are experienced and considered religious but that have become cultural heritage. The paradoxical movement of simultaneous religious and secular forms of sacralization creates tensions between different valuations, interests, expectations, and sensibilities, between different authoritative discourses and hierarchies of value, involving different groups of people with a stake in the specific religious heritage site, object, or practice. And where better to investigate the management of these tensions than in the European continent, where, on one hand, the discourses of religion and of the secular emerged; and, on the other hand, the modern idea and practice of heritage first took root (albeit sometimes also in colonial settings; cf. Betts and Ross 2015; Swenson and Mandler 2013)? From its broadest definition as those things a community will deem worthy of safeguarding for future use, the idea of cultural heritage involves in its core a commitment of care for the site, object, or practice labeled heritage (Geismar 2015: 78). This caretaking happens at different scales, from global codifications by UNESCO down to the individual level of a visitor or volunteer at a particular site, and involves the management of the site, object, or practice. As such, management does not relate only to the top level of the head of a committee or drafter of a charter, but has to do with concrete practices, affects, and repertoires in the entire chain of caretaking of the heritage.

In this book we understand management in, roughly, two senses. We focus on the organizational sense of management: How is a building maintained, an object displayed, a practice enacted, or access regulated? What is seen as sound management in regard to these issues? As the example of the Old Church in Amsterdam demonstrates, opinions on preservation and maintenance of religious heritage in terms of the building, as well as its congregation, may differ widely and even lead to emotional clashes. We understand management, therefore, in a broader sense. How are expectations and affects managed? What kinds of scripts are used, reused, adapted, and modified? Both heritage and religion depend on everyday commitments of volunteers and other nonprofessionals whose commitment impacts and is impacted by the religious and secular processes of sacralization as outlined above. Again, evoking the example of the Old Church, cultural heritage listing might help in maintaining a church building and increase its visibility and relevance for a broader public, but at the same time the resulting demands of institutions and visitors might interfere with the religious function or atmosphere of a building (which in turn impacts and shapes motivation of volunteers). How do top-down processes impact "heritage on the ground" (cf. Brumann and Berliner 2016)? And how do these two different types of management—the formal/organizational and the personal/affective—interact with and influence each other? The studies in this volume seek to address these questions in context and in ethnographic and historical detail.

Outline of the Volume

This book brings together ten chapters that analyze processes of nomination and validation of religious sites, objects, and practices as cultural heritage—what we in this volume call religious heritage—and the widely diverging ways in which such religious heritage is regulated and managed. It maps lines of top-down, bottom-up, and transversal claims, authorizations, and—ultimately—sacralizations, while seeking to protect the heritage sites, objects, and practices as either religious or cultural heritage objects or both at the same time. While focusing on the ways in which heritage is managed, regulated, enacted, and maintained, this focus is not limited to the institutional sides of heritage formation. Rather, the chapters investigate bottom-up production, regulation, and maintenance of heritage and the interactions and clashes of bottom-up and top-down perspectives. Since Europe is arguably the historical source of many universalizing discourses and practices of modernity as well as of postmodern, nostalgic yearnings that seek to preserve the past in the present under the rubric of heritage (cf. Macdonald 2013), the ten contributions will focus on Europe, in particular on the United Kingdom, Denmark, Poland, Portugal, and the Netherlands.

The first part, "The Afterlives of Churches in East Anglia, UK," addresses the management of religious and secular understandings of religious heritage in the contexts of the Church of England and heritage conservation practice. The opening chapter, by Clare Haynes, presents a case study from Norwich, the city with the highest density of medieval churches north of the Alps. In the 1930s, one of these—Saint Peter Hungate—became the first Church of England building to be put permanently to a nonreligious use. This innovation, heralding a new approach to religious heritage management in England, was achieved through local partnerships, not state or institutional direction. Repurposed as a civic museum of religious art, Haynes shows how Hungate's religious past has continued to influence how the building is managed and appreciated. Haynes argues that its value and validity as heritage depend on it being recognized, in multiple senses, as a sacred place. In the second chapter, Ferdinand de Jong examines how the ruins of a Benedictine abbey are managed in the market town Bury St Edmunds. The chapter focuses on the Heritage Partnership, a civic association set up to promote the conservation and interpretation of this religious heritage. Given that a strong spiritual interest remains in the ruins of the abbey, what place is given to religious belief when the remains of a monastic infrastructure are elevated to cultural heritage? What forms of belief are considered legitimate and appropriate in the current secular heritage regime? This chapter demonstrates that the authorization of religious heritage is a discriminatory practice that privileges some forms of spirituality over others.

In part II, "The Management of National Religious Sites in Denmark," the chapters focus on the status of culture and Christianity in Denmark. As a consequence of the non-separation of church and state in Denmark, all churches belonging to the Danish national church are overseen by both the Ministry of Religion, which sets the legal and economic framework for the national church, and the local bishops and dioceses, which have the authority to decide, among other things, all aspects concerning the Danish church buildings and their fittings, with the National Museum in a consultative role concerning the cultural heritage aspects. This implies that the materialized expression of state-mandated Christianity is officially viewed as cultural heritage in Denmark. Rejecting facile narratives of heritage and secularization, Ulla Kjær and Poul Grinder-Hansen highlight that the embrace of national religion as heritage involves a more complex position of religion in Danish society than is often assumed. Although a majority of Danes do not consider themselves religious, the intertwinement of national religion with Danish national identity remains strong. In a second chapter on the Danish context, Sofie Isager Ahl, Rasmus Rask Poulsen, and Oscar Salemink investigate the sentiments with regard to national religion and national belonging in ethnographic detail by describing how this narrative of national religion and heritage plays out in the management of two of the most important religious-cultural sites in Denmark. These multidimensional and multidirectional organizing principles in the management of two of Denmark's officially designated World Heritage Sites that include an explicit Christian aspect, namely Jelling and Roskilde, are complicated by the overlaying of another layer of governance in what they call "World-Heritagization."

A third part, "The Religious Cityscape of Kraków, Poland", focuses on how religious pluralism shapes and is shaped by the architecture of the city. Anna Niedźwiedź analyzes the management of a chakra that is believed to be located in the city's most sacred heritage site, namely Wawel Hill, with its castle and cathedral. Focusing on visitors, tour guides, and heritage managers, she describes how the management of religious heritage is used to exclude devotional and affective practices by chakra believers as unwelcome superstition. This process is highlighted from a different angle in a second chapter on Kraków's heritagization of religious heritage. Kamila Baraniecka-Olszewska discusses two competing celebrations in Kraków. The first one is a re-enactment of tenth-century Slavic Pagan rites on the Krakus Mound, and the second a Roman Catholic festivity (an indulgence feast) held on a nearby hill. Both events are referred to as Rękawka; both are perceived and advertised (respectively by the city authorities and by the Catholic parish in the district where the whole event takes place) as traditional and as a recognized part of Kraków's heritage. Baraniecka-Olszewska argues that contemporary Pagans use the heritage status of the re-enactments as an embodied claim to public space for their religion, thereby shedding light on mutual entanglement of the secular and the religious, as well as on the place of religions in the process of heritage building in Poland.

A fourth part, "Portuguese Heritages and Lusotropicalism," covers the diverse processes of curating religious diversity in various religious and heritage sites in Portugal against the backdrop of migration. Maria Cardeira da Silva and Clara Saraiva investigate the histories and management of diverse religious affects in the World Heritage Site of Sintra and the old town of Mértola with reference to the notion of lusotropicalism, which was developed in Brazil to denote the supposedly more inclusive and tolerant colonial enterprise of Portugal and which was adopted by successive—dictatorial and democratic—regimes in Portugal. Even when academics have criticized lusotropicalism as a whitewash of Portuguese imperialism, elements of this kind of thinking—which the authors dub "lusotropes"—inform both official policies and public perceptions, creating space for diversity against a Christocentric historical narrative. Anna Fedele and José Mapril investigate the sometimes surprising interaction between Catholic nationalism and inter-religious cosmopolitanism in the Catholic pilgrimage site of Fátima and the Mouraria neighborhood in Lisbon. They show how ideas about Portuguese religious heritage inform processes of (re)imagining national identity and belonging and how non-Christian groups are domesticated through the creation of the "proper" places for religious minorities besides the (Catholic) religious majority.

Part V, "Performances, Rituals, and Religious Heritage in the Netherlands," focuses on how performances and rituals convey new affects and identity formations in the Netherlands. Both the backdrop of rapid deconfessionalization and "de-churching" in the Netherlands and a profound national debate about "Dutchness" and the role of the religious past therein generate another European context in which heritage is pressured into national prominence. National rituals and recurring performances are particularly apt platforms for displaying and negotiating affects relating to religious heritage and community. Ernst van den Hemel analyzes the popularity of Johann Sebastian Bach's *Saint Matthew Passion* in the Netherlands, where attending performances during Lent have become a widespread tradition that took hold early in the twentieth century but came to a crescendo at the beginning of the twenty-first century. He focuses on the recurring debate about how these performances should be managed—whether to hold them in a concert hall or in a church, whether one should applaud or not. He describes how these expectations and practices get a new twist in a contemporary innovative form of staging the *Saint Matthew Passion*: the "Sing-Along *Saint Matthew Passion*." In an ethnographic description of one of these participatory performances, he lays bare the entanglements and disentanglements of religious and secular appreciations and sacralizations of the *Saint Matthew Passion*. In her analysis of the Saint Martin celebrations in the city of Utrecht, Welmoed Fenna Wagenaar highlights the significance of management in making a celebration like Saint Martin be recognized and appreciated as heritage. This annual city celebration has grown in length and importance in the twenty-first century, even being inscribed on the UNESCO-associated Inventory Intangible Cultural Heritage in the Netherlands in 2012. The parties and organizations involved place their initiatives within a moral framework that seeks its inspiration from Saint Martin's generosity. In order for the feast to be acknowledged as a socially inclusive practice in a plural society, however, this framework should by no means be understood as religious, as the heritage custodians make great efforts to ensure. Herewith, Wagenaar addresses a remarkable development: the difficulty of managing religion in a ritual performance that has come to be widely perceived as secular.

Taken together, the ten chapters in this volume covering five European countries paint a detailed picture of the complex intersection and interaction between two different types of valuation, two types of claims, two constituencies ("communities of care"), two types of sovereignty, and two management regimes: the religious pole has a transcendental dimension, while the cultural heritage pole is rooted in a set of secular assumptions within an immanent frame. By situating the case studies in Europe, where the secularist frame is more widespread and widely accepted than in many other parts of the world, we can show the validity of this analytical distinction in empirical practice. Overall, the case studies show that there may be tension but also much overlap between the religious and heritage poles: sometimes the religious frame is instrumentalized for secular purposes, while at other times cultural heritage discourse is used to further religious agendas. By making a clear analytical distinction, we can get better insight into the exact ways in which religion and cultural heritage intersect in empirical practice, namely through the management of the sites, objects, and practices that are simultaneously considered religion and heritage.

Ernst van den Hemel is a researcher at the Meertens Institute. He defended his dissertation about Calvinism and political emotions at the University of Amsterdam in 2011. He was postdoctoral researcher in the HERA-funded HERILIGION: The Heritagization of Religion and the Sacralization of Heritage in Contemporary Europe project. In 2019 he joined the interdisciplinary research group NL-Lab, at the Humanities Cluster of the Royal Netherlands Academy of Arts and Sciences. In his research, he combines ethnographic fieldwork, social media analysis, and historiography and focuses on religion, heritage, and national identity. His publications include *The Secular Sacred: Emotions of Belonging and the Perils of Nation and Religion* (Palgrave, 2020; coeditors Markus Balkenhol and Irene Stengs).

Oscar Salemink is professor of anthropology at the University of Copenhagen. Between 2001 and 2011 he worked at Vrije Universiteit Amsterdam, from 2005 as professor of social anthropology, and from 1996 through 2001 he was responsible for Ford Foundation grant portfolios in social sciences and arts and culture in Thailand and Vietnam. He received his doctoral degree from the University of Amsterdam, based on research on Vietnam's Central Highlands. He is currently working on global projects on heritage and contemporary arts. He has published two monographs, ten edited volumes, and eight themed issues of journals.

Irene Stengs is senior researcher at the Meertens Institute and professor by special appointment "Anthropology of Ritual and Popular Culture" at the Vrije Universiteit Amsterdam. Her research in the Netherlands and Thailand focuses on popular religiosity, material culture, commemorative ritual, and processes of heritage formation. She is the author of *Worshipping the Great Moderniser: King Chulalongkorn, Patron Saint of the Thai Middle Class* (2009, NUS Press, Singapore) and coeditor of *The Secular Sacred: Emotions of Belonging and the Perils of Nation and Religion* (Palgrave, 2020; coeditors Markus Balkenhol and Ernst van den Hemel).

NOTES

1. https://oudekerk.nl (accessed 23 September 2021, translation by the authors).
2. https://religiousmatters.nl/living-in-an-exhibition-in-a-church/ (accessed 23 September 2021).
3. https://religiousmatters.nl/wie-beschermt-de-oude-kerk-in-amsterdam/ (accessed 23 September 2021, translation by the authors). For more on Kuyk's research on "multiple used churches," see https://religiousmatters.nl/author/elza-kuyk/ (accessed 23 September 2021).
4. This volume is a collective output from the Humanities in the European Research Area (HERA) JRP *Uses of the Past* funded project HERILIGON: The Heritagization of Religion and Sacralization of Heritage in Contemporary Europe (2016–20), grant # 5087-00505A, involving teams of researchers in Denmark, the Netherlands, Poland, Portugal, and the United Kingdom.
5. One exception is Denmark, where the vast majority of churches belonging to the Danish Lutheran Church date from the Middle Ages and are officially regarded as national heritage.

REFERENCES

Asad, Talal. 2003. *Formations of the Secular: Christianity, Islam, Modernity*. Stanford, CA: Stanford University Press.

Askew, Marc. 2010. "The Magic List of Global Dtatus: UNESCO, World Heritage and the Agendas of States," in Sophia Labadi and Colin Long (eds.), *Heritage and Globalization*. London: Routledge, pp. 19–44.

Balkenhol, Markus, Ernst van den Hemel, and Irene Stengs (eds.). 2020. *The Secular Sacred: Emotions of Belonging and the Perils of Nation and Religion*. Cham: Palgrave Macmillan.

Bendix, Regina. 2009. "Heritage between Economy and Politics: An Assessment from the Perspective of Cultural Anthropology," in Laurajane Smith and Natsuko Akagawa (eds.), *Intangible Heritage*. London and New York: Routledge, pp. 253–69.

Bendix, Regina, Aditya Eggert, and Arnika Peselmann (eds.). 2012. *Heritage Regimes and the State*. Göttingen: Universitätsverlag Göttingen.

Benjamin, Walter. 2007 [or. 1955]. *Illuminations*. New York: Schocken Books.

Berger, Peter. 1967. *The Sacred Canopy: Elements of a Sociological Theory of Religion*. Garden City, NY: Doubleday.

Betts, Paul, and Corey Ross. 2015. "Modern Historical Preservation—towards a Global Perspective," *Past and Present*, Supplement 10: 7–26.

Blumenfield, Tami, and Helaine Silverman (eds.). 2013. *Cultural Heritage Politics in China*. New York and Heidelberg: Springer.

Bossy, John. 1985. *Christianity in the West, 1400–1700*. Oxford: Oxford University Press.

Brumann, Christoph. 2014. "Heritage Agnosticism: A Third Path for the Study of Cultural Heritage," *Social Anthropology* 22(2): 173–88.

Brumann, Christoph. 2017. "How to Be Authentic in the UNESCO World Heritage System: Copies, Replicas, Reconstructions, and Renovations in a Global Conservation Arena," in Corinna Forberg and Philipp W. Stockhammer (eds.), *The Transformative*

Power of the Copy: A Transcultural and Interdisciplinary Approach. Heidelberg: Heidelberg University Publishing, pp. 269–88.
Brumann, Christoph. 2019. "Slag Heaps and Time Lags: Undermining Southern Solidarity in the UNESCO World Heritage Committee," *Ethnos* 84(4): 719–38.
Brumann, Christoph. 2021. *The Best We Share: Nation, Culture and World-Making in the UNESCO World Heritage Arena*. New York and Oxford: Berghahn Books.
Brumann, Christoph, and David Berliner (eds.). 2016. *World Heritage on the Ground: Ethnographic Perspectives*. Oxford and New York: Berghahn Books.
Casanova, José. 2009. "The Secular and Secularisms," *Social Research* 76(4): 1049–66.
Coleman, Simon, and Marion Bowman. 2019. "Religion in Cathedrals: Pilgrimage, Heritage, Adjacency, and the Politics of Replication in Northern Europe," *Religion* 49(1): 1–23.
De Cesari, Chiara. 2012. "Thinking through Heritage Regimes," in Regina F. Bendix, Aditya Eggert, and Arnika Peselmann (eds.), *Heritage Regimes and the State*. Göttingen: Universitätsverlag Göttingen, pp. 399–413.
Di Giovine, Michael A. 2009. *The Heritage-scape: UNESCO, World Heritage, and Tourism*. Lanham, MD: Lexington Books.
Durkheim, Emile. 1965. *The Elementary Forms of the Religious Life*. New York: Free Press.
Geismar, Haidy. 2015. "Anthropology and Heritage Regimes," *Annual Review of Anthropology* 44: 71–85.
Hall, Stuart. 1999. "Un-settling 'the Heritage,' Re-imagining the Post-nation: Whose Heritage?," *Third Text* 13(49): 3–13.
Heelas, Paul, and Linda Woodhead. 2005. *The Spiritual Revolution: Why Religion Is Giving Way to Spirituality*. Oxford: Blackwell.
Hemel, Ernst van den. 2014. "(Pro)claiming Tradition: The 'Judeo-Christian' Roots of Dutch Society and the Rise of Conservative Nationalism," in Rosi Braidotti, Bolette Blaagaard, Tobijn de Graauw, and Eva Midden (eds.), *Transformations of Religion and the Public Sphere*. London: Palgrave Macmillan, pp. 53–76.
Herzfeld, Michael. 2009. *Evicted from Eternity: The Restructuring of Modern Rome*. Chicago and London: University of Chicago Press.
Herzfeld, Michael. 2016. *Siege of the Spirits: Community and Polity in Bangkok*. Chicago and London: University of Chicago Press.
Hitchcock, Michael, Victor T. King, and Mike Parnwell (eds.). 2010. *Heritage Tourism in Southeast Asia*. Honolulu: University of Hawai'i Press.
Isnart, Cyril, and Nathalie Cerezales (eds.). 2020. *The Religious Heritage Complex: Legacy, Conservation, and Christianity*. London: Bloomsbury.
Kirshenblatt-Gimblett, Barbara. 1998. *Destination Culture: Tourism, Museums, and Heritage*. University of California Press.
Macdonald, Sharon. 2003. "Museums, National, Postnational and Transcultural Identities," *Museum and Society* 1(1): 1–16.
Macdonald, Sharon. 2013. *Memorylands: Heritage and Identity in Europe Today*. London: Routledge.
Meskell, Lynn. 2013. "UNESCO's World Heritage Convention at 40: Challenging the Economic and Political Order of International Heritage Conservation," *Current Anthropology* 54(4): 483–94.
Meskell, Lynn. 2015. "Transacting UNESCO World Heritage: Gifts and Exchanges on a Global Stage," *Social Anthropology* 23(1): 3–21.

Meskell, Lynn. 2018. *A Future in Ruins: UNESCO, World Heritage, and the Dream of Peace*. Oxford and New York: Oxford University Press.

Meskell, Lynn, and Christoph Brumann. 2015. "UNESCO and New World Orders," in Lynn Meskell (ed.), *Global Heritage: A Reader*. London: Wiley, pp. 22–42.

Meyer, Birgit. 2019. "Recycling the Christian Past: The Heritization of Christianity and National Identity in the Netherlands," in Rosemarie Buikema, Antoine Buys, and Ton Robben (eds.), *Culture, Citizenship and Human Rights*. London and New York: Routledge, pp. 64–88.

Meyer, Birgit, and Marleen de Witte. 2013. "Heritage and the Sacred: Introduction," *Material Religion* 9(3): 275–80.

Pasieka, Agnieszka. 2015. *Hierarchy and Pluralism: Living Religious Difference in Catholic Poland*. London and New York: Palgrave Macmillan.

Salemink, Oscar. 2009. "Afterword: Questioning Faiths? Casting Doubts," in Thomas D. DuBois (ed.), *Casting Faiths: Imperialism, Technology and the Transformation of Religion in East and Southeast Asia*. Basingstoke and New York: Palgrave Macmillan, pp. 257–63.

Salemink, Oscar (ed.). 2016. "Scholarship, Expertise and the Regional Politics of Heritage," in *Scholarship and Engagement in Mainland Southeast Asia: A Festschrift in Honor of Achan Chayan Vaddhanaphuti*. Silkworm Books, pp. 167–95.

Smith, Laurajane. 2006. *Uses of Heritage*. London and New York: Routledge.

Smith, Laurajane. 2020. *Emotional Heritage: Visitor Engagement at Museums and Heritage Sites*. London: Routledge.

Smith, Laurajane, Margaret Wetherell, and Gary Campbell (eds.). 2018. *Emotion, Affective Practices, and the Past in the Present*. London: Routledge.

Swenson, Astrid, and Peter Mandler (eds.). 2013. *From Plunder to Preservation: Britain and the Heritage of Empire, c. 1800–1940*. Oxford: Oxford University Press.

Turner, Bryan S. 2006. "Religion and Politics: Nationalism, Globalisation and Empire," *Asian Journal of Social Science* 34(2): 209–24.

Weber, Max. 1965. *The Sociology of Religion*. London: Methuen.

PART I

THE AFTERLIVES OF CHURCHES IN THE UK
TWO EAST ANGLIAN CASE STUDIES

CHAPTER 1

The Redundant Church
Heritage Management of the Religious-Sacred-Secular Nexus
Clare Haynes

Introduction

This chapter focuses on three episodes in the history of one small medieval church, which was made redundant (closed for worship) in the 1930s. It explores how the religious, sacred, and secular have been managed there at key moments in its history. As a case study, Saint Peter Hungate, Norwich is richly illustrative of the negotiations that have taken place over the management of redundant church buildings in England since the nineteenth century. In 1933, for example, Hungate became the first church in the country to be put to a permanent nonreligious use, when it became a museum of ecclesiastical art, run not by the Church of England but by local government. This was a groundbreaking moment in the development of religious heritage practice. Hungate also exemplifies how significant the presence and production of the sacred are to heritage management and demonstrates the intimate entanglements that develop with both the religious and secular.[1] Before we turn to consider the first episode, an introduction to some relevant aspects of the history of UK religious heritage management may be useful to the reader.

The Development of Religious Heritage Management in England

Heritage, as a way of thinking, can be said to have developed in the British Isles as a response to the tumult of the Reformation.[2] Britain's Reformation was long, so that the English Civil Wars of the mid-seventeenth century between Royalists and Parliamentarians were also religious wars. Iconoclasm continued and gained momentum in the 1640s and '50s as a significant part of the Parliamentary campaign to establish a Puritan settlement. Against this background of destruction, a new sense of the past began to develop when, in 1688–89, the monarchy was restored and the Church of England re-established. As the forerunners of modern historians, archaeologists, and art historians, antiquarians began to focus in new ways on historical sites, buildings, material culture, as well as texts. These early antiquarians, many of whom were churchmen, were all amateurs. They studied churches less as architecture and more as sites of historical Christian association and social and family history, where events, property, and customary rights were recorded in monuments and church documents. They narrated the history of these buildings and their parishes, binding the fractures of the Reformation and the Civil Wars into long narratives that offered a vision of continuity. Their writings and collections are still fundamental to heritage practice, but more than that, the value they placed on recording and collecting the past and, later, preserving it established the foundation stones of heritage thinking (Jokilehto 1999; Sweet 2004; Swenson 2013).

Over the course of the eighteenth century, ecclesiastical architecture began to be studied more attentively by antiquarians, for its form and style, as well as its uses. The field was given greater impetus in the late eighteenth century by the development of Romanticism, as well as a growing nationalism. Whereas before, Gothic architecture had been disparaged as barbarous and representative of monkish superstition, in the late eighteenth century it began to be valued as picturesque and potentially sublime. Gradually losing its negative associations with Catholicism, Gothic became established as the authentic native English style (as opposed to Classicism, which came to be regarded as a foreign import) (Brooks 1999).

In the same period, huge social and political changes brought by the Industrial Revolution created new challenges for the established church, the Church of England (known more informally as the Anglican Church). A breakdown of traditional social structures accompanied huge demographic shifts from rural areas to new towns and cities. In addition, the development of suburbs, with new transport systems, led to the depopulation of city centers. Many ancient rural and inner-city parishes were left with small, poor congregations, and newly populated areas might not have a church at all. There was widespread fear of de-Christianization. In addition, religious dissenters were clamoring for and securing the removal of their civil disabilities. On all sides, the Church of England seemed to be losing its position in the nation's civic and religious life. There was a crisis of both management and mission (Brooks and Saint 1995; Knight 1995).

In these circumstances, a conservative movement of churchmanship arose that looked back to the medieval church for inspiration, regarding it as continuous with the apostolic era and thus having greater religious and social integrity. It became, in complex ways, a resource for dealing with the rapid changes of the nineteenth century. This movement was accompanied by a revolution in church building and restoration. Gothic became the sign of a purer, more authentic national church, and thousands of churches were built, rebuilt, and restored in an idealized Gothic manner. New vestments, stained glass, furnishings, and liturgical practices patterned on medieval models were also introduced. This was not simply a style revival; it was a form of heritage movement, which sought to mobilize the past to change the present. The Gothic Revival, as it became known, was a pan-European phenomenon (Brooks 1999; Jokilehto 1999; Lofgren and Wetterberg 2020). Remarkably, the Romantic and picturesque vision of "a church as it should be," essentially rural, still dominates popular perceptions and continues to influence the presentation of churches in Britain (Webster and Elliott 2000).

This revolution in church building was governed by a system of largely pre-Reformation ecclesiastical law, which was managed at the diocesan level. It was based on the principle of ensuring that buildings were fit for contemporary worship needs. Fired by a new sense of mission, renewal, not conservation, was the priority (Dellheim 1982: 112–30; Miele 1995; Pevsner 1976). Many buildings underwent what became seen as drastic "restorations" in the search to rebuild the ideal, causing loss and damage that has been calculated to have been worse than that of the Civil Wars (Cocke 1987: 190). Substantial numbers of genuine medieval features were lost, along with post-Reformation interventions. In addition, buildings that were too derelict or in places where the population had moved away were regarded as having outlived their purpose—to be redundant. In ecclesiastical law, as it then stood, churches could not be used for secular purposes. When no religious use could be found (as, for example, a mission hall or parish room), they would be dilapidated, in order that funds could be redirected to places where new or larger churches were required to serve growing populations. Dilapidation might involve simply removing the roof and letting the building rot, taking the building away completely so that the land could be sold, or reducing it to a picturesque ruin set in a churchyard garden. In managing their approximately ten thousand church buildings, of which at least eighty-five hundred were medieval, the heritage of the pre-Reformation church had become a tool of mission for the Church of England but one that did not yet imply an obligation to preserve.

Although there had been scattered voices of opposition to restoration and dilapidation in the eighteenth century, it was not until the late 1870s that these began to coalesce into a movement, which focused on the merits of preservation over restoration (Fawcett 1976; Hunter 1996). By this point, unlike in some other European countries, there was no state-led heritage apparatus either for registering or protecting the built heritage in Britain (Glendinning 2013; Jokilehto 1999; Swenson 2013). Any work in this direction was done in informal, voluntary associations or by individual amateurs. Volunteerism remains a significant aspect of British heritage management, as will be discussed. Perhaps the first, most important, step was the founding of the Society for the Protection of Ancient Buildings (SPAB) in 1877 (Glendinning 2013: 121–28; Miele 1996). William Morris (1834–96), the designer and socialist activist, and Phillip Webb (1831–1915), architect and designer, developed a manifesto of preservation, strongly influenced by the work of the art and social critic John Ruskin (1819–1900). Church restoration was their primary target. As Morris wrote, "Our ancient buildings are not mere ecclesiastical toys, but sacred monuments of the nation's growth and hope" (Pevsner 1976: 51). While their aims were certainly not religious, their language often suggested the sacred. As the text of their famous *Manifesto* concluded, their aims were to protect ancient buildings, so that they could be handed down "instructive and venerable to those that come after us."[3]

The SPAB's early successes revealed that their views were widely shared, including among churchmen, who joined the society in large numbers. The British Parliament made a first gesture toward heritage protection in 1882 by passing the Ancient Monuments Act, which listed fifty prehistoric sites that had to be offered to the government if the owners wanted to sell them. Further legislation came slowly, accelerating after World War II (Glendinning 2013; Hunter 1996; Thurley 2015). However, the Church of England was largely exempted from legal measures, and it bolstered its claim to independence by developing its own heritage management framework. The first substantial acknowledgment of its responsibilities came in 1914 with the establishment of the Ancient Monuments (Churches) Committee, which sought to respond to ever louder criticism that the church was lax in its building control where heritage buildings and fittings were concerned. It took decades to bring the church under any kind of state heritage framework, and it still retains a degree of exemption from planning legislation, on the basis of the rigor of its own system of regulation (Delafons 1997; Mynors 2006; Mynors 2009). Most Church of England buildings are registered or "listed" by the governmental body Historic England. This system entails a measure of planning and use oversight, at both local and national levels. The church's own legal framework has also developed considerably to direct the heritage management of its buildings. Alongside this, it has begun to pursue a considerable amount of heritage policy research and innovation, usually in partnership with heritage organizations. Driven by financial considerations, a changing heritage funding climate, and a continuing desire for institutional self-determination, the church commissioned reports such as *Heritage and Renewal* (1994) and *Spiritual Capital* (Theos and the Grubb Institute 2012) on cathedrals. Most recently they have participated, as a major stakeholder, in the government-commissioned Taylor Review and subsequent pilot scheme on parish churches and cathedrals. In each case the church has encouraged an image of integration in national (state and NGO) heritage management frameworks and simultaneously a significant measure of independence from them (Coleman 2019: 123, 139; Coleman and Bowman 2018: 12).[4]

In relation to redundant churches, the main focus of this essay, the Church of England has also moved substantially. For example, under the terms of the 1968 Pastoral Measure, it became possible for the church to dispose of church buildings for nonreligious purposes, and uses such as domestic accommodation, arts centers, shops, offices, and so on have since become common. An endowed trust established by the same legislation, now known as the Churches Conservation Trust (CCT), maintains some 350 churches of architectural or historical significance as heritage buildings. With limited funds, the CCT's work is supplemented by many voluntary bodies that have grown up to look after individual churches or groups of churches, whether closed or open. On closure and disposal, redundant churches become subject to state heritage governance. It is worth noting that Church of England buildings were not (and still are not) deconsecrated when they become disused for worship purposes. Consecration, in the post-Reformation Church of England, can be understood best as a service of dedication. In contrast to the Roman Catholic Church, the building is only set apart for the purposes of worship; it is not religiously sacred in and of itself. Although attitudes vary considerably on this point within the Anglican Church (and have done since the mid-nineteenth century), a church building is in some sense religiously sacred only in its association with worship and the sacraments. Once worship ceases, that tie is simply broken and thus deconsecration is unnecessary. As we shall see, state governance and disuse do not, in fact, necessarily extinguish the sacred potential of these buildings.

This all too cursory introduction to the UK framework of religious heritage management must serve to contextualize the case study that follows. Further details will be added as they become relevant. Two distinctive aspects to the UK system have been noted. First, the established position of the Church of England enabled it to maintain for a long time a separate system of planning and heritage governance that was subsidiary to its mission goals. The state and ecclesiastical systems are now much more closely connected. For example, Historic England retains specialists who work on ecclesiastical buildings, and they must be consulted over proposed changes.

They offer expertise and guidance to individual parishes, which supplements the work of the church's own system of heritage management. This was a significant focus of the "Taylor Review Pilot."[5] Second, amateurs and independent voluntary and professional bodies continue to play an important role in heritage management at local and national levels, to the extent that some NGOs must by law be consulted before any significant change to a building is made.[6] Thus, heritage management in the UK remains a system of cooperation, born out of networks of association, amateur and professional, mixed with robust legal constraints. We can now turn to the consideration of Saint Peter Hungate and the terms on which heritage management requires and endeavors to ensure that the sacred persists.

Saint Peter Hungate: Introduction

Saint Peter Hungate is a small late-medieval church in the City of Norwich. Situated at the junction of three streets, its tower rises up over a rich heritage landscape. For much of the medieval and early-modern period, Norwich was England's second largest city, a place of great wealth based on wool and textile manufacturing. Elm Hill, for example, to the north of the church, was a street of considerable trading activity. With ready access to the river, it became the site of the homes, workshops, and warehouses of wealthy merchants (Ayers 1994; Rawcliffe and Wilson 2004). Indeed, the church, as we see it today, was rebuilt in the mid-fifteenth century by parishioners who were some of the wealthiest people in the region. Its heritage significance lies in these historical associations and its architecture: the extraordinary angel roof covering the nave and transepts, the sheer size of its windows, and the remains of the medieval Norwich School stained glass, which once filled them (Ayers 1994: 116; Pevsner and Wilson 1997: 247).

Saint Peter Hungate is one of thirty-one surviving medieval churches in Norwich, thirty of which continued to be used by the established church (the Church of England) after the Reformation. The density of church provision in Norwich is remarkable, and significant to Hungate's story. No other town or city north of the Alps has so many medieval churches, and they have long been recognized as key not only to the city's topography but also to its distinctiveness (Betjeman 1974; Harvey 1972: 76). For example, visitors in the late seventeenth century were encouraged to climb the mound of the Norman Castle to survey the circumference of the city's walls and the towers of the thirty-six churches then standing within them. In the eighteenth century, the first comprehensive history of the city was written, which treated the churches as places of personal and civic memory, of local governance and charity, as well as of public worship (Blomefield 1805–10, vols. 3–4). In the mid-nineteenth century, photographers succeeded topographical artists in continuing to record and publish views of Norwich's churches (Haynes 2017). Thus, by the mid-nineteenth century, these buildings had been regarded as worthy of observation, record, and historical interest for nearly two hundred years.

Furthermore, Norwich's citizens had long had a strong sense of parochial identity and investment. Beyond collective worship, from which many did dissent, civic responsibilities and rights were tied to the parish and had been both before and after the Reformation. In times of trouble, individuals might rely on the charities and poor relief, which were collected and distributed from their church. Vestries also undertook the maintenance of civic amenities. At Hungate, for example, the vestry provided and repaired the public water pump and cared for the famous tree on the street that gave Elm Hill its name.[7] The church building, its clergy and officers, and its fixtures and fittings had long been maintained largely through benefactions and a parish rate. Church and community were closely identified. Thus, as a place to be studied and visited, and at the heart of the local community, Saint Peter Hungate had long been viewed as an inheritance to be valued and passed on. It was in these respects already heritagized *avant la lettre* in the eighteenth century. It had also long been a place of both sacred and secular amenity.

Episode 1: 1905—On the Brink of Destruction

As has been discussed, the politico-religious landscape of Britain changed considerably over the course of the nineteenth century. The Church of England was shorn of some of its privileges and civic responsibilities, largely because of the removal of civil penalties against Nonconformists (Brooks 1995). For example, from 1868, almost all its buildings had to be maintained by voluntary contributions and not by a compulsory rate on local property owners, as had been the case (Piggott 2016). In addition, the demographic and economic changes mentioned above led to the depopulation of town and city centers and the rapid development of new suburbs, linked to the city by transport systems of railways, buses, and trams. In Norwich, this meant that small parishes like Saint Peter Hungate struggled not only to maintain an active congregation but to pay for even the most basic maintenance of their decaying building as well. Theirs was not a unique problem; similar situations existed in other "over-churched" places such as York and London (Dellheim 1982: 112–30; Weinstein 2014).

By the end of the century, the condition of Saint Peter Hungate was a matter of increasing concern. Money had been found in the 1880s to fix, in the cheapest way possible, its crumbling tower, because it threatened to fall on passersby, but little else had been managed. By 1897, the state of the building was dire. A local newspaper reported that the roof of the chancel had been covered by a tarpaulin for two years, the medieval stained glass in the east window had been removed for safety, and weekly worship appeared to have ceased because of the building's condition. As was common in these cases, the parish was united with one of its neighbors, and by the beginning of 1905, with little likelihood of sufficient funds being forthcoming or a sustainable religious use identified, proceedings got underway to declare the church redundant and for it to be partially demolished. The city's museum asked for the bells and the roof, while the font and other furnishings were earmarked for distribution to new churches in the suburbs. The churchyard was to be adapted to provide a green space in the city.[8] In some respects, this was a routine administrative procedure, one that had been undertaken in Norwich twenty years before, when the church of Saint Peter Southgate had been made redundant and partially demolished. In the interval, however, the context in which such decisions were made had changed considerably.

Where few voices had been raised in public to protest the dilapidation of Saint Peter Southgate in the mid-1880s, in 1905 there was a clamor in support of Hungate's preservation. Those who spoke up included local antiquarians but also churchmen. The rector described it as a public scandal if the church were "abolished." Similarly, the archdeacon of Norwich (the diocesan official responsible for the fabric of Norwich churches) also wrote to a local newspaper to garner support, describing the church as "an exceedingly interesting monument of antiquity."[9] In 1905, an agenda of preservation was shared much more widely. Nevertheless, the Church of England's institutional priorities were unchanged: its mission could only be served, morally and financially, by buildings with sustainable religious uses. If money and a religious use could not be found, the building had to be dilapidated.

At the eleventh hour, a prominent and highly placed local layperson intervened. Prince Duleep Singh (1868–1926) was a man with wide antiquarian interests, a member of the Norfolk and Norwich Archaeological Society (NNAS) and the SPAB. Acting as an intermediary, he secured the interest and backing of the SPAB, who agreed to support and promote the scheme, so long as their own architect, working to the society's principles, was employed to direct the restoration.[10] This was agreed and, through the promotion of the SPAB and Prince Duleep Singh's efforts, sufficient funds were forthcoming to restore the church. Duleep Singh kept a watchful eye on the architect's plans and decisions, which were also scrutinized by the diocese. The work of preserving the church was thus a partnership between the Church of England, individuals, and voluntary organizations.

However, Hungate's future had not been secured. In 1908, it was reopened for services, but it was not long before these had ceased again and other

Figure 1.1. Postcard of Saint Peter Hungate, circa 1908. © collection Clare Haynes.

religious roles were sought for the building. While ideas were forthcoming that it could be used as a parish room or mission hall, these came to nothing because provision already existed in the parish or in neighboring parishes. The only sustained use of the building that was found was as a drill hall for the Church Lad's Brigade, a national Christian organization for boys, akin to the Boy Scouts. However, by the late 1920s, Hungate was again in immediate need of repair.[11] No systematic program of maintenance or management had resulted from the heritage partnership, and of course, the preservation lobby had no control over the ongoing upkeep of the church's fabric. The rules of the Church of England and Hungate's financial difficulties in an overchurched city were still dictating its fate.

Nevertheless, Hungate's heritage status had changed. The significance of the building, in architectural and historical terms, had been widely asserted and accepted. It had been preserved by a voluntary community of local people and antiquarians and with the support of a national society, not by the Church of England. Hungate remained a religious space; it was not secularized as a result of this intervention. Worship did continue for a time before it was used for the promotion of ideals of Christian masculinity and prayer. An increasingly vocal and active lobby in Norwich intent on preserving the historic fabric of the city kept a watching brief on the building. So, for example, in 1929, the parish borrowed money from the NNAS to buy wire guards to protect the remaining stained glass. Under pressure it seems from the NNAS, the bishop insisted that the Lad's Brigade was not to use the building any longer, in order to preserve the fabric.[12] Significantly, an expectation had developed that the preservation of Hungate, as a building without a suitable religious function, had become, at least partially, the responsibility not of the Church of England but of "the enthusiasts and lovers of archaeology."[13] It could be argued that secularization took place with the expulsion of the Lad's Brigade, as the only sustainable religious use that had been found had become unsuitable on heritage grounds. Hungate's religious value would seem to have reached zero as its heritage value had risen.

Episode 2: 1933—A Way Out?

By the late 1920s, what had seemed obvious to some in 1905 became fully apparent: Hungate had no viable future within the Church of England. The City of Norwich was simply over-churched. While preservationists had come to the rescue of the Church of England since the 1870s, they had dictated their terms, and a new value—heritage value—had had to be accepted. The Church of England was caught: its legal position had not changed, but the moral authority of the heritage lobby had become impossible to ignore (Delafons 1997: 119–22). In this, Hungate's situation exemplifies the much larger crisis that was confronting the Church of England. On the one hand, it faced changes to its established status, decreasing congregations, and shifting populations, which reduced the religious value of many of its buildings. On the other, the heritage lobby was arguing, increasingly insistently, that the Church of England was morally responsible for the preservation of churches, not according to its own priorities but for the benefit of all (Binney and Burman 1977).

Nevertheless, dilapidation still remained the most likely outcome for Hungate, even with the support and oversight of local groups. Other churches in the city were struggling to stay open, and the burden of maintenance was getting heavier. As late as the 1960s, a diocesan proposal to make twenty-five of Norwich's medieval churches redundant was accompanied by the threat of demolition (Groves 2016: 50–51). In the late 1920s, however, Hungate's difficulties were perhaps compounded by the city's campaign of modernization and development, which included slum clearance. Even Elm Hill, the medieval street to the north of Hungate, now a jewel in Norwich's heritage crown, came very close to being pulled down in order to make way for new homes and businesses.

Instead, Hungate was saved again by an unprecedented alliance of antiquarians, the City Council, and the diocese, who gathered to support the conservationist cause. Their co-operation, as well as its result, was new not just in local but in national terms. It arose from the overlapping circles of society, civic volunteerism, and business that are characteristic of a small city like Norwich (Pendlebury and Hewitt 2018). Despite tensions between them over their priorities in the past, between modernization and conservation, this group found common cause and produced a plan to put Hungate to an entirely new use: it was to be the first museum of ecclesiastical art in the country. The idea may well have been inspired by a trip to Paris that Frank Leney, the curator of Norwich's main museum (the Castle Museum), had made in 1921 with the Museums Association (a national body founded in 1889). It is likely he visited at least one of the city's churches that were put to different uses after the French Revolution, such as the Musée des Arts et Métiers.[14]

To found an ecclesiastical museum might seem a small shift in purpose now, as we are used to the idea that churches can be made into homes or restaurants, circus schools or art galleries, but in the 1920s this was a radical departure (Saxby 2016). The civic authority was to lease the church, keep it in repair, and manage it, subject to one or two minor restrictions, according to its own lights. The Ecclesiastical Commissioners, the body responsible for the Church of England's financial and property matters, was persuaded that a liberal interpretation of the current legislation could be interpreted to cover the plan, and after five years or more of negotiation, planning, and fund-raising, the Saint Peter Hungate Museum of Ecclesiastical Art was opened finally on 27 June 1933. The event was widely heralded in the local and national press. For example, an editorial published in *The Listener*, a magazine of cultural record, offers an insight into how significant the plans for Hungate were recognized to be:

> An interesting and highly practical solution of the problem of utilising city churches in areas where there are too many, or where the population has moved, comes from Norwich, where the Church of St. Peter, Hungate, is to be transferred to the City Corporation for use as an ecclesiastical museum. Within the boundaries of the City of Norwich are something over fifty churches, many of them planned on the most ambitious scale. As the city becomes more and more of a business centre and workers tend to live on the fringe, a number of these churches (as is the case in London and other big cities) are naturally becoming redundant. The churches, many of which stand on land which has increased in value, all too frequently fall into the hands of the house-breaker to make way for palatial blocks of offices. Every big city has many ecclesiastical treasures which cannot satisfactorily be exhibited in the churches to which they belong. A building such as that in Norwich, in which they can be shown successfully in their traditional surroundings, will therefore be serving an excellent purpose. As an alternative to demolition there must be many uses to which these buildings can be put to provide practical justification (if that be needed) for saving them, and

their use, too, for a purpose such as that in Norwich must serve to invest them with a new interest in the eyes of many to whom perhaps they have become so familiar as to be barely noticed.[15]

The precedent that Norwich was setting for much wider uses of redundant churches was patently clear to the writer, but the choice of the phrase "traditional surroundings" begs a question that has been raised already: was such a transformation perceived as secularization? We can begin to address this by exploring what some of the participants in the process thought about what they were doing.

At the opening ceremony of the museum, the bishop of Norwich, Bertram Pollock, gave a remarkable speech. He is reported to have begun by saying:

> There are three avenues, commonly speaking, which lead men and women to God. . . . These three roads are the ways of Goodness, Truth, and Beauty. We may look upon them as ultimate realities. . . . The contemplation of beautiful forms in nature and in art quickens our appreciation of beauty, and our devotion to it; Goethe said one ought to behold one thing of beauty every day. So are we drawn to God, who is the source of beauty, and once again we are led upwards to worship.
>
> I do not . . . consider that this little gem of a church is being divorced from its original purpose when it is being constituted a repository of ecclesiastical art. Let us not say to ourselves, "The city-dwelling population is so much reduced that these churches can go. What a capital idea to find some use for a derelict place of worship." We will rather hope that in a new way it will do some of its former spiritual work. We will ask that it may be still a House of God, teaching the things of God through the eye if no longer through the ear.

At the end of his speech, in a piece of drama, rich in symbolism, it was reported, "The Bishop vacated the chair and the remainder of the ceremony was presided over by Col. Bulwer."[16] Bulwer was a significant intermediary in the scheme, a Norfolk lawyer, landowner, and antiquarian, who sat on the Museum Committee of the Town Council. For the bishop, nevertheless, the museum was a place that still had a religious function, albeit one now directed by the secular authorities.

For the Lord Mayor of Norwich, Henry Holmes, who also addressed the audience on that day, something slightly different was happening. After describing the groundbreaking nature of the project and how it had come to pass, he observed in conclusion that "in time, this building should become a rich treasure house . . . , for let it never be forgotten that it was the Church which fostered every form of true art in the past."[17] For the mayor, then, this was a historical endeavor, one rooted in the past and entirely secular—it was a museum of art. These two visions of the new museum may seem, at first, to be at odds.

A different perspective on Hungate's transformation was offered by someone else present that day: Eric Maclagan, the director of the Victoria and Albert Museum, London, who had long been a supporter of the scheme. In 1934, attending another opening at Hungate for an exhibition of ecclesiastical pewter, Maclagan gave a speech, in which he argued:

> In adapting [the] church so perfectly as a museum of ecclesiastical art Norwich has set an example.... It might be true that the church was not serving precisely the purpose for which it was destined by its pious builders, but it still testified to the glory of God, just as it did when it was used as a place of public worship. Museums were not places which were to be regarded as wholly secular and divorced from the honour of the Creator.[18]

Maclagan was a practicing Christian, the son of an archbishop, as well as a leading figure on the Central Council for the Care of Churches (the Church of England body founded in 1917 charged with advising on restoration and reordering). For Maclagan, like Bishop Pollock, Hungate was still a religious building, but as a museum professional, he was also heir to a tradition of thinking of museums as, in some sense, sacred places. Just as Pollock had quoted Goethe, Maclagan may well have had his ideas in mind or those of the English writer and critic William Hazlitt (1778–1830), who also wrote a great deal about the new art galleries of the first quarter of the nineteenth century. Both Goethe and Hazlitt engaged with museums as places "consecrated to the holy ends of art," albeit from different religious positions. Maclagan's formulation of museums as not "wholly secular" seems perhaps closest to Goethe's recognition of a museum as capable of producing an emotion "akin (to that) ... experienced upon entering a House of God" (Goethe, quoted in Duncan 1995: 14–15; Cheeke 2007). The museum was a place to experience the sublime.

We can pursue this further by considering the ways in which the museum studies scholar Carol Duncan used both Goethe and Hazlitt in considering museums as places of secular ritual. She observed, inter alia, "the beneficial outcome that museum rituals are supposed to produce can sound very like claims made for traditional, religious rituals ... such as a sense of enlightenment, or a feeling of having been spiritually nourished" (Duncan 1995: 13). The potential of museums to act in this way was recognized early in the history of public museums. Soon after the French Revolution and the ensuing Napoleonic Wars, critics such as Quatremère de Quincy began to notice, and in his case, regret, that art and its museums had the potential to be secular substitutes for religion (Cheeke 2007). In works of art being removed from their sacred settings and moved into the museum, they were torn from their functions and "the beliefs that created them" (Cheeke 2007: 115). It is in this light that we might choose to regard the phrase "traditional surroundings" in *The Listener* editorial above. Indeed, when the museum idea was first mooted, the argument was made that the church would be a more "appropriate" place to exhibit "sacred" objects than the city's own museum in Norwich Castle.[19] The building's religious past offered a more authentic context in which to view the objects. So, for Maclagan, Hungate was perhaps doubly sacred, as church and museum. Of course, these two denominations of the sacred are not identical, nor do they necessarily have the same referent, as will be discussed.

It is surely significant for our understanding of the heritagization of religious buildings that while Hungate's heritage status was confirmed by its transformation into a museum, its religious value was also seen to increase. From a building without function, without future, it had been made to speak again of religious matters. This was despite the fact that in management terms, it had been transferred to the control of a secular authority. It is worthy of notice that each of the managers in the process—bishop, mayor, and curator—invoked, in quite different ways, the sacred.

Episode 3: 2007—Hungate Medieval Art

For nearly seventy years Saint Peter Hungate was used as a museum (Haynes 2021; Young 1975). In 2001 it was closed, against some opposition, because of local government budget cuts. In a letter to the leading regional newspaper, one of the local councilors involved in making the decision argued that low attendance figures and the need to update exhibits and facilities were the main factors.[20] It seems that Hungate was less well regarded than it had been, and in straitened times funds were not available to support four museums in the city. The Hungate collection, which had been built up over the previous sixty years from donations, purchases, and loans, was divided up among Norfolk's museums, and some objects were returned to their lenders. Others, including some rare medieval religious textiles, were retained by the museum service for safekeeping because the parishes to which they belonged were unable to take care of them.

The building, which in 1995 had been vested in a new independent trust, the Norwich Historic Churches Trust (NHCT), did for some time receive support from the City Council; however, yet again, it faced another period of uncertainty (Groves 2016). After a number of short-term uses, a voluntary trust was founded to lease Hungate from the NHCT to use as a center to encourage engagement with the region's rich culture of medieval art. The church's fate was again in the hands of volunteers, albeit now constrained by state conservation legislation, the requirements of the NHCT's lease, and the terms of their insurance. Hungate Medieval Art opened in 2007, a name that seems indicative of further secularization, as the church's dedication to Saint Peter was omitted. After a successful bid to the Heritage Lottery Fund, Hungate opened by focusing on stained glass and offering lots of information, including trail leaflets, about medieval art in Norfolk's churches. They hired a member of staff to manage their offering. Unfortunately, the money ran out, and so they had to depend entirely on volunteers and donations, both to manage and run the building and its activities.

Contemporary art shows as well as historical exhibitions began to be offered. Most of these, but not all, responded to the theme of medieval art in some way, and the volunteers have also mounted small shows about the history of the parish and the church. In 2017, for example, *Vanishing Point* featured photographs of World War I landscapes and the stories of some of the men who fought in them and *Epoche: Suspension of Judgment* was displayed, a single-work art show of a large installation made of threads suspended along the length of the nave. The following year, a historical exhibition about the famous medieval family the Pastons, who contributed to the rebuilding of Saint Peter Hungate, was held. In 2019, the HERILIGION project put on a historical exhibition and a series of four contemporary art exhibitions responding to the project's research questions, called *Sacred and/or Secular*. Each of these exhibitions came about through the working of overlapping circles of the University of East Anglia, Norwich University of the Arts, and heritage bodies in the city. Most of the trustees and volunteers study, work, or have worked at one of these institutions. Again, it is worth noting the circles of association and volunteerism that are essential to heritage management in the UK. Alongside these exhibitions, Hungate Medieval Art's other activities have continued: visitors coming to see the building for its own sake, educational outreach activities, as well as participation in heritage festivals, such as the national scheme of Heritage Open Days.

So, eighty-five or so years after it was last used for public worship, what kind of institution is Hungate now? Not subject to any control by the Church of England, governed instead by the requirements of state heritage preservation legislation, as well as those of its landlords and the NHCT, and managed by a group of heritage volunteers, Hungate may appear, at first glance, to be a secular organization. However, when we look closer, certain details of the practices of management and the responses of users suggest that the building retains a dual identity, that it remains both sacred and secular and indebted to the religious.

This is perhaps most obvious in the operation of a largely unspoken system of decorum at Hungate, which acknowledges the building's past as a place of Christian worship. Thus, the trustees observe their own feelings, and the possible sensitivities of visitors, in choosing programming. While there was not the means to examine beliefs, attitudes, and responses scientifically during the HERILIGION season (spring–summer 2019), it was striking how often visitors invoked a sense of what was appropriate or not. One work in the final show of *Sacred and/or Secular*, which was placed at the east end of the building, caused some unease because of an interpretation that visitors might have made of its form.[21] Shaped with a deliberate ambiguity, the figure could appear from a distance as a pair of legs widely splayed, apparently drawing attention to the genitalia. A closer viewing revealed a complicated lack of realism, which seemed to propose, in addition, a pair of shoulders with a head pushing down or up through the floor. In addition to the exhibition leaflet, a text was provided for the guidance of volunteers, which offered an interpretation of the work and encouraged closer examination, in order to allay the anxieties that were expressed or at least to complicate them. The book in which visitors may leave comments (only a tiny proportion actually do) provides some further evidence of Hungate's interior being policed by some on the basis of it having a continuing religious identity. A visitor described a sound work as "cacophonous" and "not conducive to meditation," while another described the final visual exhibition as "a fitting use for this lovely church." Commenting on the same exhibition, one visitor, expressing sentiments that were shared by several others, wrote that the church was very "peaceful and beautiful. The statue at the altar is offensive and should be removed."[22]

Significantly many of the trustees, volunteers, artists, and visitors expressed, both in writing and verbally, a recognition of the sacred, as well as a sense of spiritual uplift that they gained from being in the building and from some of the exhibitions. One spoke, for example, of Hungate as a place of "spiritual resonance" (anon. personal communication). These responses are perhaps not always distinguishable from reactions to its past use or its long history, although visitors do speak of the aesthetic qualities of the building or the works of art: the beauty of the space, its architectural form, the quality of the light, and the stained glass. These kinds of responses have been surveyed at "living" (or open) cathedrals and churches in Britain in relation to tourism, but the analysis can be hampered by a rather rigid, if graduated, dichotomy between the secular and the religious (Hughes, Bond, and Ballantyne 2013: 211; however, see Coleman and Bowman 2019). Such an approach is not applicable in accounting for what happens at Hungate, as evidence of any religious response to Hungate is negligible. Rather we might consider a much broader sense of the sacred as being relevant. As Isnart and Cerezales put it, "[As all that is] separated and protected from . . . daily life by an acknowledged interdiction . . . sacredness lies at the heart of society, as a foundational linking force that is not essentially religious, but is more generally

Figure 1.2. Interior of Saint Peter Hungate, 2019. © Philip Sayer.

social and distributed among various fields of human life" (2020: 3; see also Knott 2013). We will return to this point shortly.

The building does nevertheless continue to speak, through its architecture and iconography, of its Christian past. The Church of England's guidance on the closure of churches and their future uses now recognizes this, declaring:

> Central to the Christian faith is the unique revelation of God in Jesus Christ and the restoration of humankind's relationship with God through Christ. Any consideration of suitable alternative uses (for church buildings) must be placed in this context. Moreover, ecclesiastical buildings and consecrated places bear enduring public witness to the faith and values of the Christian community.[23]

As we have seen, this is clearly the case at Hungate, as visitors judge Hungate's exhibitions not in terms of the stated aim of encouraging engagement with medieval art, but largely in the use of the building as a historic religious space. However long ago it was that it was last used for religious services, that past lingers and determines the present. It could thus be argued that heritage at Hungate sustains or buttresses religion now, just as it did in 1933.[24]

Another interpretation is possible: that it is not Christianity that is being borne up precisely, but a looser, more capacious sense of the sacred. It is Isnart and Cerezales's "foundational linking force" that is still being guarded and produced at Hungate and sought by visitors. Heritage is not iconoclastic, neither destructive nor ultimately substitutive; it requires the signs of the past to be present for the sake of that fundamental and, one could argue, sacred heritage value—authenticity.[25] The religious past is appropriated, and the sacred tacitly unbound from the grasp of religion. Religion is part of the story the building must tell, neither denied nor affirmed but always present as an image or a memory.

The sacred encouraged by the heritage management system can even appear as a close simulacrum of religion. The building is set apart, managed, and maintained for edification and communion, with practices that adhere to a shared sense of decorum, purpose, and understanding. It is sacred and it has its affects: spiritual transcendence, a heightened sense of meaning, or, to refer to the famous poem by Philip Larkin (1922–85), "Church Going," a kind of "seriousness" (Larkin 2016). However, these are the characteristics of the *secular* sacred (i.e., both secular and sacred) that is complexly indebted to the religious past and certainly in some relation to the religious present but distinguishable from it. Does heritage sacralize or simply provide the means to acknowledge the sacred, if on changing terms? It is certainly true that in its spiritual, rather than religious or secular, value to the individual and community, it can easily be misunderstood as in some sense quasi-religious (Huss 2014; Isnart and Cerezales 2020: 3–7).

Conclusion

Neither "wholly secular," as Eric Maclagan put it in 1933, nor indeed never wholly religious, as was noted in the introduction, Hungate is a sacred place now, as it has always been. We must conclude that Hungate has never been secularized if by that word we imply an opposition to all forms of spirituality. Over the past hundred years, Saint Peter Hungate has retained its designation as a building of historical significance and aesthetic value; it remains a "sacred monument," as the SPAB put it. Set apart and protected, the building retains the power to enchant, and the works of art that are introduced to it may do too (Haynes 2020). It also remains entailed to the religion that built and sustained it, as its architecture and ornament speak of the past and resound with religious associations. Hungate's "church-ness" has been preserved, and present-day visitors are still offered, as they were in 1905 and 1933, an image of the religious sacred, albeit an attenuated one. The ways in which Hungate has been managed, as church, museum, and art center, with continuous and decorous acknowledgment of its original religious function has ensured that. Furthermore, visitors continue to be offered a space in which they can pursue, if they choose, forms of religious or spiritual transcendence. Without this, of course, its authenticity could, in one sense at least, be denied.

Clare Haynes is an art historian who writes about anti-Catholicism, the religious history and art of the eighteenth-century Church of England, the history of museums, and the representation of church buildings and fittings in antiquarian and archaeological illustrations. She is a fellow of the Society of Antiquaries of London.

NOTES

The author is very grateful to the trustees and volunteers of Hungate Medieval Art for their co-operation, and her colleagues on the HERILIGION team for their feedback on an earlier draft of this essay. The research was conducted as a part of the HERILIGION research project The Heritagization of Religion and Sacralization of Heritage in Contemporary Europe, funded by Humanities in the European Research Area (HERA) grant # 5087–00505A.

1. The idea of a nexus was devised before the publication of the work by Isnart and Cerezales (2020) on the religious heritage complex, to which the reader is referred.
2. This chapter focuses on the Church of England, and it must be noted that England and Britain are not interchangeable terms. The other nations of the United Kingdom have separate systems of heritage management and church-state relations. There are, nevertheless, strong similarities between them.

3. "Manifesto," SPAB, 1877, https://www.spab.org.uk/about-us/spab-manifesto (accessed 8 September 2020).
4. See also "The Taylor Review: Sustainability of English Churches and Cathedrals," HM Government, 2020, https://www.gov.uk/government/publications/the-taylor-review-sustainability-of-english-churches-and-cathedrals (accessed 8 October 2020).
5. "Taylor Review Pilot: Final Evaluation," HM Government, 2020, https://www.gov.uk/government/publications/the-taylor-review-pilot-final-evaluation (accessed 8 October 2020).
6. "Amenity Societies and Other Voluntary Bodies," Historic England, 2020, https://historicengland.org.uk/advice/hpg/publicandheritagebodies/amenitysocieties/ (accessed 8 September 2020).
7. *Churchwardens' Accounts and Vestry Minutes of St Peter Hungate, 1789–1890* [ms.], Norfolk Record Office, PD 61/32, Archive Centre, Norwich.
8. Tillett MS 21 (n.d.), *St Michael at Plea and St Peter Hungate*, Norfolk Heritage Centre, MS 396, Millennium Library, Norwich.
9. Tillett MS 21 (n.d.), *St Michael at Plea and St Peter Hungate*, Norfolk Heritage Centre, MS 396, Millennium Library, Norwich.
10. Tillett MS 21 (n.d.), *St Michael at Plea and St Peter Hungate*, Norfolk Heritage Centre, MS 396, Millennium Library, Norwich; *St Peter Hungate*, n.d., SPAB archives, London.
11. *Parochial Church Council Minutes of St Michael at Plea and St Peter Hungate*, 1926–1940, Norfolk Record Office, PD 66/89, Archive Centre, Norwich.
12. *Parochial Church Council Minutes of St Michael at Plea and St Peter Hungate*, 1926–1940, Norfolk Record Office, PD 66/89, Archive Centre, Norwich.
13. *Vestry Minutes of St Peter Hungate*, 1904–1905, Norfolk Record Office, PD 66/61, Archive Centre, Norwich.
14. *Cuttings relative to St Peter Hungate*, n.d., Bolingbroke Collection, Norwich Heritage Centre, Millennium Library, Norwich.
15. *Acquisition by the Corporation of St Peter Hungate Church for use as an ecclesiastical museum*, 1936, Norfolk Record Office, N/TC 52/35, Archive Centre, Norwich.
16. *Cuttings relative to St Peter Hungate*, n.d., Bolingbroke Collection, Norwich Heritage Centre, Millennium Library, Norwich.
17. *Cuttings relative to St Peter Hungate*, n.d., Bolingbroke Collection, Norwich Heritage Centre, Millennium Library, Norwich.
18. *Cuttings relative to St Peter Hungate*, n.d., Bolingbroke Collection, Norwich Heritage Centre, Millennium Library, Norwich.
19. *Acquisition by the Corporation of St Peter Hungate Church for use as an ecclesiastical museum*, 1936, Norfolk Record Office, N/TC 52/35, Archive Centre, Norwich.
20. Felicity Hartley, "Decision Was Far from Easy," *Eastern Daily Press*, 14 February 2001, 5.
21. For a discussion of *Sacred and/or Secular* and the works of art that were displayed in the series, see Haynes 2020.
22. *St Peter Hungate Visitors' Book*, 2019–, Hungate Medieval Art, Norwich.
23. "Code of Recommended Practice, Mission and Pastoral Measure," Church of England, 2011, https://www.churchofengland.org/sites/default/files/2017-10/mission_and_pastoral_measure_2011_-_volume_2.pdf (accessed 25 October 2019).

24. For the closely related idea of "sacred residue," see Beekers 2016.
25. For a useful discussion of authenticity in heritage management, see Jones 2009.

REFERENCES

Ayers, Brian. 1994. *Norwich*. London: English Heritage and B. T. Batsford.
Beekers, Dan. 2016. "Sacred Residue," in S. Lanwerd (ed.), *The Urban Sacred: How Religion Makes and Takes Place in Amsterdam, Berlin and London*. Berlin: Metropol, pp. 39–41.
Betjeman, John. 1974. *A Passion for Churches*. BBC Films.
Binney, Marcus, and Peter Burman (eds.). 1977. *Change and Decay: The Future of Our Churches*. London: Studio Vista.
Blomefield, Francis. 1805–10. *An Essay towards a Topographical History of the County of Norfolk*. 2nd edn. London: William Miller.
Brooks, Chris. 1999. *The Gothic Revival*. London: Phaidon Press.
Brooks, Chris, and Andrew Saint (eds.). 1995. *The Victorian Church: Architecture and Society*. Manchester: Manchester University Press.
Cheeke, Stephen. 2007. "Hazlitt and the Louvre," *Keats-Shelley Journal* 56: 111–35.
Cocke, Thomas. 1987. "The Wheel of Fortune: The Appreciation of Gothic since the Middle Ages," in J. Alexander and P. Binski (eds.), *The Age of Chivalry: Art in Plantagenet England 1200–1400*. London: Royal Academy of Arts in association with Weidenfeld and Nicolson, pp. 183–91.
Coleman, Simon. 2019. "On Praying in an Old Country: Ritual, Replication, Heritage, and Powers of Adjacency in English Cathedrals," *Religion* 49(1): 120–41.
Coleman, Simon, and Marion Bowman. 2019. "Religion in Cathedrals: Pilgrimage, Heritage, Adjacency, and the Politics of Replication in Northern Europe," *Religion* 49(1): 1–23.
Delafons, John. 1997. *Politics and Preservation: A Policy History of the Built Heritage 1882–1996*. London: E & F N Spon.
Dellheim, Charles. 1982. *The Face of the Past: The Preservation of the Medieval Inheritance in Victorian England*. Cambridge: Cambridge University Press.
Duncan, Carol. 1995. *Civilizing Rituals inside Public Art Museums*. London: Routledge.
Fawcett, Jane (ed.). 1976. *The Future of the Past: Attitudes to Conservation 1147–1974*. London: Thames and Hudson.
Glendinning, Miles. 2013. *The Conservation Movement: A History of Architectural Preservation Antiquity to Modernity*. London: Routledge.
Groves, Nichola. 2016. "'With concern, but not without hope': An overview of the Norwich Historic Churches Trust," in N. Groves (ed.), *Redundancy and Renewal: Maintaining and Using Historic Churches*. Norwich: Lasse Press, pp. 48–60.
Harvey, John. 1972. *Conservation of Buildings*. London: John Baker.
Haynes, Clare. 2017. *Drawing in the Archive: The Visual Record of Norwich's Medieval Churches 1700–2017*. Norwich.
Haynes, Clare. 2020. "Between-ness: Art and Piety in Religious Heritage Space," *Anthropological Notebooks* 26(3): 17–39.
Haynes, Clare. 2021. *St Peter Hungate Guidebook*. Norwich: Hungate Medieval Art.

Hughes, Karen, Nigel Bond, and Roy Ballantyne. 2013. "Designing and Managing Interpretive Experiences at Religious Sites: Visitors' Perceptions of Canterbury Cathedral," *Tourism Management* 36: 210–20.
Hunter, Michael. (ed.). 1996. *Preserving the Past: The Rise of Heritage in Modern Britain*. Stroud: Alan Sutton.
Huss, Boaz. 2014. "Spirituality: The Emergence of a New Cultural Category and Its Challenge to the Religious and the Secular," *Journal of Contemporary Religion* 29(1): 47–60.
Isnart, Cyril, and Nathalie Cerezales (eds.). 2020. *The Religious Heritage Complex: Legacy, Conservation, and Christianity*. London: Bloomsbury Academic.
Jokilehto, Jukka. 1999. *A History of Architectural Conservation*. Oxford: Butterworth-Heinemann.
Jones, Sian. 2009. "Experiencing Authenticity at Heritage Sites: Some Implications for Heritage Management and Conservation," *Conservation and Management of Archaeological Sites* 11(2): 133–47.
Knight, Frances. 1995. *The Nineteenth-Century Church and English Society*. Cambridge: Cambridge University Press.
Knott, Kim. 2013. "The Secular Sacred: In-Between or Both/And," in A. Day et al. (eds.), *Social Identities between Secular and Sacred*. Aldershot: Ashgate, pp. 145–60.
Larkin, Philip. 2016. "Church Going," in K. J. Gardner, (ed.), *Building Jerusalem: Elegies on Parish Churches*. London and New York: Bloomsbury Continuum, pp. 98–100.
Lofgren, Eva, and Ola Wetterberg. 2020. "The Church Building as a Practiced Duality of Religion and Heritage," in Cyril Isnart, and Nathalie Cerezales (eds.), *The Religious Heritage Complex: Legacy, Conservation, and Christianity*. London: Bloomsbury Academic, pp. 15–36.
Miele, Chris. 1995. "'Their Interest and Habit': Professionalism and the Restoration of Medieval Churches, 1837–1877," in C. Brooks and A. Saint (eds.), *The Victorian Church: Architecture and Society*. Manchester: Manchester University Press, pp. 151–72.
Miele, Chris. 1996. "The First Conservation Militants: William Morris and the Society for the Protection of Ancient Buildings," in M. Hunter (ed.), *Preserving the Past: The Rise of Heritage in Modern Britain*. Stroud: Alan Sutton, pp. 17–37.
Mynors, Charles. 2006. *Listed Buildings, Conservation Areas and Monuments*. London: Sweet and Maxwell.
Mynors, Charles. 2009. "Ecclesiastical Buildings: Constraints and Opportunities," *Ecclesiastical Law Journal* 11: 266–83.
Pendlebury, John, and Lucy Hewitt. 2018. "Place and Voluntary Activity in Inter-war England: Topophilia and Professionalization," *Urban History* 45(3): 453–70.
Pevsner, N. 1976. "Scrape and Anti-scrape," in J. Fawcett (ed.), *The Future of the Past: Attitudes to Conservation 1147–1974*. London: Trustees of the Victorian Society, pp. 35–53.
Pevsner, Nikolaus, and Bill Wilson. 1997. *Norfolk 1: Norwich and North East*. The Buildings of England. 2nd edn. London: Yale University Press.
Piggott, Robert. 2016. "Historic Churches: Heritage and Voluntary Action," in N. Groves (ed.), *Redundancy and Renewal: Maintaining and Using Historic Churches*. Norwich: Lasse Press, pp. 1–18.

Rawcliffe, Carole, and Richard Wilson (eds.). 2004. *Medieval Norwich*. London: Hambledon and London.

Saxby, Stephen. 2016. "The Use, Reuse and Abuse of 'Alternative Use': A Historical Perspective on the Re-appropriation of Urban Closed Churches for Other Purposes," in N. Groves (ed.), *Redundancy and Renewal: Maintaining and Using Historic Churches*. Norwich: Lasse Press, pp. 19–40.

Sweet, Rosemary. 2004. *Antiquaries: The Discovery of the Past in Eighteenth-Century Britain*. London: Hambledon Press.

Swenson, Astrid. 2013. *The Rise of Heritage: Preserving the Past in France, Germany and England, 1789–1914*. Cambridge: Cambridge University Press.

Thurley, Simon. 2015. *Men From the Ministry: How Britain Saved Its Heritage*. New Haven and London: Yale University Press.

Webster, Christopher, and John Elliott (eds.). 2000. *"A Church as It Should Be": The Cambridge Camden Society and Its Influence*. Stamford: Shaun Tyas.

Weinstein, Ben. 2014. "Questioning a Late Victorian 'dyad': Preservationism, Demolitionism, and the City of London Churches, 1860–1904," *Journal of British Studies* 53: 400–425.

Young, Rachel. 1975. *Guide to the St Peter Hungate Church Museum*. Norwich: Norfolk Museums Service.

CHAPTER 2

"A Sense of Presence"
The Significance of Spirituality in an English Heritage Regime
Ferdinand de Jong

Introduction

In 2012 archaeologists found the physical remains of Richard III—the last Plantagenet king of England, immortalized by Shakespeare—under a parking lot in Leicester (Buckley et al. 2013). The publicity surrounding this spectacular find, the identification of the bones, and their subsequent reburial in a purpose-built monument in Leicester Cathedral rekindled a rumor in Bury St Edmunds that the remains of Saint Edmund might be buried under some derelict tennis courts situated in the ruins of the town's former Benedictine abbey (see figure 2.1). Shortly after a surge in interest in the rumor, several stakeholders set up the Abbey of St Edmund Heritage Partnership. Since 2016, the St Edmundsbury Heritage Partnership has worked toward the conservation and interpretation of the ruins of the St Edmundsbury Abbey and the public gardens in which they are situated.

The Heritage Partnership promotes and cares for this religious heritage in the context of a secular, national heritage legislation. This raises the question how this religious heritage is validated in a society in which different forms of religiosity coexist within an immanent frame of the secular (Taylor 2007). This coexistence of the sacred and the secular has been subject to considerable academic debate since religion regained its prominence in the public sphere of countries that were thought to be secularized. In this debate Talal Asad (2003) argued that secularism should be understood not as mere absence of religion, but as shaping religion in a secular frame. This led Craig Calhoun (2010: 35) to observe that secular orientations may shape

Figure 2.1. View of the ruins of the Abbey of St Edmund, with the fenced tennis courts on the left, 2018. © Ferdinand de Jong.

the sacred or transcendent. The subsequent debate around secularism has examined the different ways in which secularism shapes religion and religion shapes secularism (Mapril et al. 2017). Hence, in the immanent frame of secularity, "the question becomes whether or not belief—in transcendence in particular—is any longer what it once was" (Rectenwald and Almeida 2017: 5). For our case, this raises the following questions: When the remains of a monastic infrastructure are presented as cultural heritage, what significance is attributed to belief? In the current secular heritage regime in England, what forms of belief are considered appropriate and legitimate in an assessment of monastic heritage? These questions take on added relevance in a context in which the grounds of religiosity are shifting and established forms of belief are giving way to new forms of spirituality (Davie 1994; Heelas and Woodhead 2005; Engelke 2012; Woodhead and Catto 2012).

With the global recognition of intangible cultural heritage, the range of values associated with heritage has significantly expanded.[1] Although the United Kingdom has not ratified the 2013 UNESCO Convention for the Safeguarding of the Intangible Cultural Heritage, national heritage organizations such as English Heritage, Historic England and the National Lottery Heritage Fund do acknowledge spirituality as a heritage value.[2] This raises the question how religious referents associated with the Abbey of St Edmund—bones, monuments, spirituality—are valued in its heritage assessment. In the first instance, the process of "heritagization" of the Abbey of St Edmund focused on the material remains of its historic fabric. It entailed an assessment of the heritage value of the abbey ruins by heritage experts commissioned for this purpose. But in subsequent discussions about heritage values, the Heritage Partnership was quite willing to involve representatives of different forms of spirituality. Building on recent discussions of processes of authentication and authorization of heritage (Meyer and van de Port 2018), this chapter examines how the Heritage Partnership has authorized (and de-authorized) different aspects of religious heritage in a wider context of changing religiosities and an increasing acknowledgment of spirituality in England's secular heritage regime.

The Heritage Partnership

Monastic sites have been the object of a monarchical suppression, known as the Suppression of the Monasteries, that haunts England's religious imagination to this day. In 1534, King Henry VIII became the Supreme Head of the Church in England, thus separating England from papal authority. In a bid to appropriate the income of religious houses in England and Ireland, through a set of legal and administrative procedures adopted between 1536 and 1541, Henry VIII initiated the so-called Dissolution of the Monasteries. It took place in the political context of other attacks on the ecclesiastical institutions of Western Roman Catholicism, which had been under way for some time. In a complex fashion the Dissolution was part of the wider European Reformation, but with distinct national inflections and consequences.

Throughout the history of the Church of England, several movements have called for the restoration of pre-Reformation architecture, liturgy, and music. These movements have not made the Reformation undone, but they have rendered the Catholic legacy itself a project of restoration, resulting in a peculiar national heritage complex in which religion and heritage are entangled (cf. Isnart and Cerezales 2020). It need not surprise us, then, that the heritagization of religious sites results in conversations that recall and resonate with earlier conversations on religious pluralism, entangling the heritagization of monastic remains in ongoing processes of religious transformation, secularization, and re-sacralization. In order to assess how religion and heritage intersect in our case study, it is imperative to recognize that the relationship between religion and heritage is very much determined by the national historical context (Wohlrab-Sahr and Burchardt 2012; Astor, Burchardt, and Griera 2017).

The legend of Saint Edmund that is celebrated in Bury St Edmund also has distinct national resonance and revolves around his martyrdom. Born in 841 AD, Edmund succeeded to the throne of East Anglia in 856. A Christian from birth, he fought alongside King Alfred of Wessex against the pagan Viking invaders until 869, when his forces were defeated and Edmund was captured by the Vikings. They ordered him to renounce his faith and share power with the pagan Vikings, but the Christian king refused. According to a tenth-century account of the saint's life, the *Passio Sancti Eadmundii* (*The Passion of Saint Edmund*) by Abbo of Fleury (2018), Edmund was then bound to a tree, shot through by arrows, and beheaded. To prevent a Christian burial of Edmund's body, his killers threw his head in the undergrowth. Searching for his head, Edmund's followers were guided by the king's words as his head called, "Here, here, here." They found the head lying between the paws of a wolf, who protected it against other wild animals. Once they returned the head to the body, the head and body miraculously reunited.

Initially kept at the place of his martyrdom, Edmund's body was subsequently taken to Beodricesworth, a town later renamed Bury St Edmunds in his honor. In the tenth century, the secular monks who cared for the body were replaced by Benedictine monks, who built the Romanesque abbey church, one of the largest in the country. This church became a major medieval pilgrimage destination focused on Edmund's "incorrupt" body, until Henry VIII dissolved the abbey in 1539 and the townspeople wrought its destruction.[3] This destruction did not mean the end of the Catholic faith in Bury St Edmund, and for a short spell Jesuits erected a school in the Abbot's Palace (Young 2016: 162), but while Catholics maintained a presence in a church in town, the monastic site nonetheless fell into ruin. An antiquarian interest in the ruins emerged in the eighteenth century. The process of heritagization of the ruins, resulting in a site with multiple heritage designations, took effect in the nineteenth century.[4] Today several elements of the abbey church, such as the crypt, the nave, and the crossing, are still recognizable in the ruins, while much of the remaining demolition rubble now makes up a thick layer of unexplored archaeology.

Bury St Edmunds is a small market town that prospered due to the Benedictine abbey. Although a small settlement already existed when the Benedictine monastery was founded, the town was effectively designed, laid out, and tightly controlled by the abbey until the Dissolution, at which point it effectively broke free.[5] Today, many of its inhabitants remember the town's historical relations with the abbey in terms of domination and exploitation of the townspeople by the wealthy abbots and monks. Nonetheless, after the discovery of the remains of King Richard III under a parking lot in Leicester in 2012, the rumor that the bones of St Edmund might be buried in the abbey ruins has reanimated the public imagination of the town's patron saint.

The rumor set the context for the contemporary title holders of the large abbey precinct to join forces in a partnership comprising St Edmundsbury Cathedral, St Edmundsbury Borough Council (later subsumed in West Suffolk Council), the Town Council, the University of East Anglia, and the Bury Society. The partnership enjoys the support of respected local architects, planners, historians, and archaeologists.[6] As reported in the *East Anglian Daily Times*, the Heritage Partnership was formally established on 13 September 2016.[7] The official mission of the partnership was formulated to "deepen public understanding of the life and times of St Edmund and the medieval abbey at Bury St Edmunds and to encourage people of all ages, beliefs and interests to experience the spiritual, historical and environmental significance of the abbey ruins and the abbey gardens in the modern world."[8]

It is important to signal that the Heritage Partnership includes both the religious and temporal custodians of the abbey ruins situated in the former precinct: St Edmundsbury Cathedral and St Edmundsbury Borough Council (now part of West Suffolk Council). The latter is the sole owner of the vast abbey gardens, which the borough council had purchased in 1951 (Richard Hoggett Heritage 2018: 237–41). The abbey gardens are managed by the West Suffolk Council, and they constitute the principal attraction of Bury St Edmunds, competing annually for the Britain in Bloom award and attracting more than one million visitors per year. As owner of the gardens in which the ruins of the abbey are situated, the council has also been responsible for the management of the ruins, jointly with English Heritage, under whose guardianship the abbey ruins are placed.[9] In the Heritage Partnership, the council acknowledges St Edmundsbury Cathedral as its counterpart even though it does not own the ruins. This Anglican cathedral, housed in what was once one of three parish churches in the precinct of the abbey, was originally dedicated to Saint James and has recently been dedicated to Saint Edmund as well, thereby assuming the legacy of the saint. Hence, the establishment of the Heritage Partnership signals a shift in the custodianship of the town's heritage, whereby West Suffolk Council has agreed to share custodianship of the abbey ruins with the cathedral, and the cathedral has reclaimed the saint's legacy. This latter move should be understood as part of a wider trend within the Church of England to reclaim its pre-Reformation legacies.

Within the Heritage Partnership, West Suffolk Council and St Edmundsbury Cathedral constitute the most important landowners, whose mission it is to formulate a joint vision for the management of the ruins and the wider precinct. At my first meeting with the cathedral's canon pastor, who is chair of the Heritage Partnership, and the Heritage Partnership's co-ordinator, a retired town planner and member of the Anglican Church, they made it very clear that the different authorities had different visions. They informed me that West Suffolk Borough Council perceives the ruins as a secular feature in a public park, which it manages in a nondenominational manner. In contrast, the cathedral perceives the ruins as a sacred site and would like the religious significance of the site to be acknowledged. It was remarkable how outspoken the canon was about the site as a "sacred" place. The co-ordinator also held strong views on the significance of the site and conveyed the seniority of St Edmund's claims to the site by stating, "St Edmund was here before the Borough Council." The canon and the co-ordinator agreed that any dissonant views on the future interpretation of the site should not be addressed in the early stages of the collaboration and expected that any differences of opinion between the cathedral and the council could be resolved in due course. Questions about the secular or sacred significance of the Abbey of St Edmund area have indeed come up during the preparation of the *Heritage Assessment* and the *Conservation Plan* but have not been a cause of conflict.

The membership of the Heritage Partnership comprises representatives of different institutions. They are mainly male, middle-class, and over fifty years old, if not retired. In fact, the composition of the membership is interesting for what it tells us about the heritage sector in the United Kingdom. Although some of the members are professionals who represent their institutional employer, quite a few of the members are volunteers, including the co-ordinator, who spends a substantial amount of his time on the Heritage Partnership. Indeed, most of the volunteers are quite busy people. Although one of them joked to me that his volunteer work served "to stave off dementia," the volunteers take their volunteer jobs very seriously indeed and prepare accordingly for the regular meetings. Their membership in the Heritage Partnership is the result of a discreet selection process by which prospective members with promising capacities and contacts are invited to get involved. Most of the volunteers have had impressive careers as archaeologists, heritage architects, town planners, or financial advisers and have spent their working lives in London before retiring to Bury St Edmunds. Currently, about a third of the members of the Heritage Partnership are practicing Christians, while the rest wear their agnosticism on their sleeves. Several members of the Heritage Partnership meet each other in church, but their shared interest in the work of the Heritage Partnership is not so much in religion as in the archaeological, historical, and architectural heritage of the abbey. All members of the Heritage Partnership display a keen interest in civic matters; that the Heritage Partnership works so well is indeed indicative of the thriving civic culture of this English market town.

The *Heritage Assessment* and the *Conservation Plan*

At the launch of the Heritage Partnership, the council received a development grant of £40,000 from Historic England and the St Edmundsbury Borough Council to carry out heritage research and conservation planning.

In a formal tender process, briefs stipulated the aims and objectives for the Heritage Assessment and the Conservation Plan. These briefs clearly set out that the *Heritage Assessment* (HA) was to provide an inventory of the historical and archaeological information available on the site and to serve as "baseline" for the preparation of a *Conservation Management Plan* (CMP, later renamed *Conservation Plan*): "The HA should include sufficient historical information to understand the background and relevance of the project area and provide the context upon which its heritage values and their significance can be assessed in the CMP" (ibid., 4). Clearly, the two documents were meant to accomplish different tasks, but the *Conservation Plan* would be based on the *Heritage Assessment*. Through transparent selection procedures, a freelance archaeologist and heritage consultant was commissioned to write the *Heritage Assessment*, while the international heritage consultants firm Purcell was commissioned to produce the *Conservation Plan*. In this section, I examine how these two research documents were produced and what place they accorded to spiritual values.

As might be expected from a research report that provides an inventory of the historical and archaeological research conducted on the site, the *Heritage Assessment* does not include an assessment of its current religious significance, although it does at various points establish how historically the abbey precinct was divided into a "secular" part, including a court for temporal transactions, and a "sacred" part including the abbey church, cloister, and great churchyard. Through a series of presentations, the archaeologist in charge of the *Heritage Assessment*, in consultation with the members of the Heritage Partnership, established the principal lines of inquiry of the assessment (Richard Hoggett Heritage 2018). At a presentation of the *Heritage Assessment* to the members of the Heritage Partnership, the consultant took the members out on a walk through the precinct, leading them to a scale model of the abbey complex that stands near the ruins. Speaking, gesturing, and pointing at the model, he reiterated the distinction between the sacred and secular realms in the historical abbey. The diminutive scale of the model facilitated a spatial understanding of the ruins scattered and strewn across the precinct.

Although this was not part of the remit of the *Heritage Assessment*, during one of its progress meetings the chairman of the committee had raised the subject of the site's significance. As this was the first occasion for the members of the Heritage Partnership to speak up and articulate their points of view on what for many of them constitutes the heart of the town, the members of the Heritage Partnership responded immediately, and their views differed markedly. One person explicitly addressed the sacredness of the site, when she confessed that it hurt her to see kids kicking around footballs in the remains of the crypt. While most members empathized with her veneration of the sacred site, the idea that kids should be forbidden to play in the ruins—in spite of the damage to the ruins they could cause—was one that nobody was prepared to articulate. That the site was sacred went undisputed—although some members of the Heritage Partnership might have different views on that—but that its protection might require a policy to set it apart and make it inaccessible was a sacrifice most members of the Heritage Partnership seemed not prepared to make. Some people remembered that the ruins had once been fenced off, and they regretted that policy. Clearly, the debate veered toward the greater good of public accessibility, a value most members seemed to hold above the sacred significance the site might have for those for whom its sacredness required protection.

The results of this debate were not related in the *Heritage Assessment*, but the subject was raised again in several meetings held in the preparation of the *Conservation Plan*, for which the brief stated the following rationality:

> This CMP is being commissioned to demonstrate the heritage value and significance of the project area and to develop a strategic approach to the sustainable conservation management of the heritage assets it contains. It should provide objective background material to inform conservation, management and the assessment of any future proposals for change to the historic assets. (Consultancy Brief for a Conservation Management Plan, 2)

As the *Conservation Plan* and the *Heritage Assessment* were commissioned at the same time, the Purcell heritage consultant who had been contracted to draft the *Conservation Management Plan* had attended most of the progress meetings on the *Heritage Assessment* and was well prepared to start the work on the *Conservation Plan* once the assessment was completed. As stipulated in the brief, she drew on the archaeological and historical information presented in the *Heritage Assessment* but also conducted considerable research of her own, consulting numerous documents, property owners, and stakeholders. To determine the heritage significance of the site, the consultant worked within the National Lottery Heritage Fund and Historic England guidelines to establish the historical, communal, aesthetic, and evidential value of each subarea of the site (Wood 2018: 59–76, 94–128). The consultant received ample assistance from members of the Heritage Partnership, paid staff of the St Edmundsbury Borough Council, and other institutions on site.[10]

In its introduction, the *Conservation Plan* acknowledges that the abbey of St Edmund "is valued locally and regionally as a green space and a spiritual place" (Wood 2018: 8). In its criteria for the assessment of heritage significance, it acknowledges the "spiritual value" as a part of the "communal value" of the heritage asset (Wood 2018: 60). The "Summary Statement of Significance" states:

> The area as a whole encompasses spaces that are valued by the community as a place of leisure, a place for community events and a place for quiet and reflection. The spiritual value extends beyond that associated with the places of worship to encompass the wider spiritual value of the green, open space of the Abbey Gardens as a place of inward renewal. The Abbey ruins also remain a place of spiritual value for some Christians whilst the site is also valued as part of other spiritual beliefs. (Wood 2018: 61)

The report thus acknowledges that spiritual value may exist in places not associated with the abbey church, a sacred place for Christians. It also acknowledges that the place may have spiritual value for non-Christians. Interestingly, while the Heritage Assessment conceptualized the space of the abbey precinct as composed of sacred and secular components, presenting the southern section comprising the abbey church and great churchyard as "sacred" while designating the northern section for temporal transactions as "secular," the *Conservation Plan* takes a very different approach by not employing the terms "sacred" or "secular," but designating relatively diffuse spaces as "spiritual." In her assessment of the spiritual significance of the site, the heritage consultant had followed the recent Historic England guidelines but had also been informed by a meeting to discuss the site's spirituality that had been convened by the chair of the Heritage Partnership.[11]

The Spiritual Significance Consultation

To provide the heritage consultant with a view on the spiritual significance of the site, the chairman and the co-ordinator of the Heritage Partnership convened a meeting to which they invited ten people for whom the site holds spiritual significance. As the meeting minutes state, the participants included "people of faith, multi-faith and no faith, people from different religious denominations and spiritual traditions and people with parallel interests such as *feng shui, tai chi,* earth energies and geomancy."[12] All participants were white, English, and most over fifty years old. There was equal distribution in terms of gender. The meeting enabled people to speak about their privately held views on the site's spiritual significance. As observer I was allowed to attend and record the meeting, which was a privilege, for the widely held view that religious beliefs should be held private is routinely observed with much discretion in the United Kingdom. The discussion was organized around a questionnaire previously circulated by email, including questions such as the following: Why do people value the abbey site? What is the religious significance of the abbey site today? What is the spiritual significance of the abbey site today? Are people aware of the religious history and layout of the abbey site? Does that affect their sense of its spiritual significance? The resulting conversation was structured and did not veer off into discussions on the meaning of spirituality. The participants were free in the expression of their convictions, but it is important to acknowledge that the meeting had an instrumental purpose, and the exchange of views that took place was carefully chaired so that alternative views could be articulated without inhibition. The meeting resulted in minutes that the heritage consultant could translate in statements on spiritual significance in the *Conservation Plan*.

It is interesting that the coordination of this spiritual significance consultation was undertaken by the Heritage Partnership. As one of its constituent members, the cathedral thus helped create the conditions for a conversation among people with spiritual interests in the ruins. This confirms the view that the Church of England assumes the authority to lead conversations in matters of spirituality and extends this authority to debates about religious heritage (cf. Lehmann 2013). The institutional framing of this debate was aimed at consultations, but not entirely without interests. For one, it turned out that all participants were aware of the challenges of preservation. One speaker with an important function in the Heritage Partnership pointed out, "The concept of significance is almost *hallowed* by the heritage sector as the thing that everything, all of their work, revolves around" [my emphasis]. Framing the conversation on significance as contributing to the sacralization of heritage, the speaker went on to note that the Quebec Declaration of ICOMOS spoke about the "spirit of place" and that this notion had unfortunately been removed from any guidelines produced by Historic England and the National Planning and Policy Framework. Regretting the loss of this acknowledgment of the spirituality of place, he hoped to get this notion back on the agenda. This confirms that some of the participants were well versed in the discourse of heritage management and willing to engage with its terminology in critical ways. This also appeared from an intervention by the tourism manager of the council, who argued that the site—whatever one wished to do with it—"should not become an archive of religion, it should be a continuation." Another heritage specialist concurred by referencing John Berger's influential *Ways of Seeing* (1973), which accompanied the popular eponymous BBC series, stating that without understanding of the historical context, one would slide into becoming a mere specialist of relics. Rather than preserve the site for antiquarian purposes, these speakers proposed to maintain it as a site of living religion. Clearly, these participants were familiar with the risks of the reification of religion into an object of antiquarian interest: they spoke out in favor of new and renewed forms of spirituality.

In a recent contribution on debates on contemporary religion, Huss (2014) has argued that spirituality has displaced the modern opposition of the sacred and the secular with an opposition of spirituality to the religious. This position is widely popularized in the phrase "spiritual, but not religious," a phrase that was explicitly used by some of the participants in the spiritual significance group meeting. Huss's observation was largely corroborated within the context of this discussion, but his opposition between religion and spirituality acquired quite specific semantic connotations. The opposition seemed to surface in some discussions but ignored in others, suggesting that context-specific code switching was taking place. One question discussed at the meeting was "Are people aware of the religious history and layout of the abbey site and does that affect their sense of spiritual significance?" One Catholic attendant reminded everyone that this was the site of a Benedictine abbey and—referencing the text of the *Heritage Assessment*—that monasticism was not very well understood these days. She held the site sacred because of the many prayers said there—which, indeed, constitutes a conventional understanding of the sacredness of a site. Interestingly, by referencing both the history of monasticism and the prayers said in this monastic site, this speaker made both a secular and a religious argument to frame the site as essentially monastic. In response to this, and echoing an argument made earlier, someone else argued that monasticism should not be preserved as a relic. In another muted reference to the *Heritage Assessment* that had acknowledged the site's pre-Christian history, it was suggested that the site should be understood as layered; had this place not been a Pagan site before it was Christian?[13] This turn of phrase enabled another participant to compare the site to Avebury and Glastonbury and to speak of earth and dragon energies. Concluding that this was once a "Pagan place of worship," this speaker took the conversation about the significance of the Benedictine abbey to an argument about energy lines that he believed had been in existence since prehistoric times.

In these discussions "the sacred" and "the spiritual" were often conflated and used without distinction. As all participants seemed well attuned to their different connotations, their employment supported subtle distinctions between utterances without causing confusion. The extent to which the denotations and connotations of different terms were stretched and appropriated without any offense given or taken was striking evidence of a shared sense of idiom in spite of obvious religious differences among the participants. The terms "sacred" and "spiritual" could be conflated as long as they served to articulate a common sense of spirituality. But this shared sense of spirituality was fragile. When the discussion focused on the question whether the site is "sacred" and someone answered that question in the affirmative, this immediately provoked a response from a speaker who confessed to being "uneasy with the term 'sacred,'" preferring the term "magnetism" instead. Others chimed in to claim that the site afforded health and well-being, even harmony. This suggests that in this meeting the concept of "spirituality" was open-ended and served the purpose of creating a coherent majority because the term covered a wide semantic field *and* could be mobilized against "the sacred"—the concept used to claim ownership of the site by established religions. Interestingly, the Church of England, represented at the meeting by the chair and the coordinator, did not oppose the preference of the majority for the concept of spirituality.

The current spiritual significance of religious heritage is perhaps less opposed to materiality than spirituality historically was (cf. Huss 2014, 2018), but also less prescriptively mediated by the materiality of places conventionally associated with the sacred—such as the crypt, the nave, or the crossing, features of the abbey church still recognizable in the ruins and highlighted in discourses on the site's sacredness. But even when such conventional forms of materiality mediate different forms of spirituality, during the meeting the site was clearly appropriated for spiritual and sacred uses in opposition to "the secular." One multi-faith participant considered the placement of the tennis courts so close to the shrine of St Edmund—which has been defunct for almost five hundred years—"an incredible affront to any sense of spirituality." Defining the shrine as pivotal to the "spirituality" of the site, this speaker mobilized the term "spirituality" in opposition to the secular. Indeed, although Huss (2014: 50) argues that "in contemporary definitions and uses of the term, the dichotomy between spirituality and corporality/materiality is much less distinct," the meeting on spiritual significance suggested that materiality still matters a great deal in the spiritual experience of the ruins today. In fact, no matter how divergent or convergent current persuasions in relation to spirituality in other regards, different attitudes toward the material seemed to (re)produce ancient bones of contention. Quite deliberately speaking as the devil's advocate, one speaker claimed that as houses in the old town are built with stones taken from the rubble of the abbey, some citizens of Bury St Edmunds happily enjoy the benefits of the Dissolution to this day. Throughout my fieldwork, I had observed that the legacy of the Dissolution indeed produces in the inhabitants of Bury an embodied historical sensation, rather than a detached historical understanding. Affects vis-à-vis the building blocks of one's house convey one's position with regard to the Dissolution, even today. When addressing the occasional and relatively minor vandalism on the site of the abbey church, one speaker put it like this: "It seems like a continuous and ongoing violation of a sacred place."[14] Such feelings toward the enduring material legacy of the Dissolution are not so easily effaced by the recent trend toward spirituality and signal that ancient affects for the sacred can be compatible with relatively new forms of spirituality—and even support new sensibilities (see De Jong 2023).

Participants in the meeting felt that a spiritual counterpart to a secular experience of the site was needed and that heritage interpretation was the way to achieve this. If the people attending the meeting credited the site with a rather diffuse spirituality, they were unexpectedly united on how the site should be interpreted. The minutes stated:

> There was general agreement that heritage interpretation and education programmes should all be multi-cultural and appeal to schools and young people as well as to growing families, adults and the elderly. They should make use of a variety of conventional and technological presentation media and offer a focal point for the heritage story of the town. They should provide a spiritual counterpart to various mass events in the Abbey Gardens such as popular concerts and firework displays. There was general unease about the retention of caged birds in the aviary although it was recognised that they are part of the attraction to children.[15]

This quotation conveys how the discussion on spirituality fed into the information gathered for and communicated to the author of the *Conservation Plan*. Indeed, the secular heritage regime enabled discussions about religiosity and spirituality but in its official documentation suppressed the divergence of views in relation to faith and spirituality. During the spirituality meeting, the chairman intervened and moved the discussion along whenever it invoked the Dissolution. Conflicts of interpretation of the sacred and the spiritual were successfully circumvented, and consensus revolved around a shared belief in middle-class values. Speaking about the general public in the abbey ruins, someone said, "They don't understand, they just do not understand that area, and I think that is where interpretation and information would be crucial to respect." Time and again, the irreverential behavior of visitors to the abbey ruins was attributed to a "lack of understanding," and "interpretation" and "information" were presented as the panacea.[16] One cannot escape the impression that the shared stance on education of the public simultaneously concealed conflicting views on the sacred and spiritual. Indeed, such conflicting views were disavowed in the diplomatic formulas on the "spiritual significance" of the site in the *Conservation Plan*. The heritagization of the site and the public discussions it afforded on the sacred and the spiritual seemed to overcome such conflicting views by creating a shared focus on an ambient sense of spirituality and on heritage interpretation as an instrument to realize the conditions of its experience.

"A Sense of Presence"

In the spirituality meeting, we observed a constant slippage between the terms "sacred" and "spirituality," which, according to Huss (2014), are incompatible concepts. Nonetheless, various speakers derived from the generic concept of spirituality the authority to speak and used the concept to rank places or practices. The meeting on spirituality was instrumental in establishing the "significance" of spirituality and attributed value to certain forms of spirituality while disavowing others. Remarkably, during the entire meeting St Edmund was mentioned only twice. At the start, a prominent member of the Heritage Partnership said he experienced "a sense of presence of Edmund in the abbey." And toward the end of the meeting another speaker suggested, "It's easy to dismiss the public frenzy about the location of Edmund's remains as frenzy newspapers going mad and all the rest of it," but he believed that through their interest in Edmund's remains the public might express a *spiritual* interest. The speaker was aware that others might not recognize the interest in "the bones" as a form of spirituality worthy of attention, and indeed, the discussion moved on to other matters.

It is not surprising that Edmund's remains were not considered as an item at the spirituality meeting. Ever since the Heritage Partnership was set up, it treated the rumor on Edmund's remains with caution—acknowledging the uncertainty surrounding their location under the tennis courts. One reason for this was that most members of the Heritage Partnership do not believe in rumors based on scanty evidence, and the rumor of the bones certainly lacked robust evidence. Moreover, the members of the Heritage Partnership who are practicing Anglicans have little affinity with relics. Since the Dissolution, the status of miracles, saints, and their relics has been an issue of complex sensibilities in the Anglican Church, although the nineteenth-century Oxford Movement, which aimed to restore Catholic liturgy within the Anglican Church, succeeded in making the worship of saints acceptable again (Cunningham 2005: 96–101). The interest in the remains of St Edmund cannot be ignored by the Heritage Partnership, as the rumor causes the public interest in the ruins to thrive, and an attempt to dismiss the rumor would not be received positively (see De Jong 2023).

Since the Dissolution, the whereabouts of the body of St Edmund have been an enigma, replicating the original legend of the "loss" of his head in an enduring absence and promise of his return. After the Reformation, the great basilica Saint-Sernin in Toulouse claimed to possess the relics after their successful theft from the Abbey of St Edmund in 1216, a claim disputed by several English historians. In response to the actions of a Catholic priest in Bury, the bones were allegedly returned to the United Kingdom in the early twentieth century, but on close inspection they turned out to be inauthentic (Young 2018: 132–39). In the subsequent search for Edmund's remains, adepts have had recourse to mediums, ghosts, and psychic archaeology, a whole range of spiritual methods to locate the bones in the ruins or elsewhere in the county (Young 2014). Since 2012, rumors have circulated that the remains of St Edmund may be found under the tennis courts in the abbey ruins. The local press has a keen interest in the matter and always associates the work of the Heritage Partnership with the possibility of archaeological excavations of the bones.

Because the rumor generated popular interest in the archaeology of the abbey, it contributed to the making of the Heritage Partnership. From its inception, Francis Young was a member of the Heritage Partnership. Young is a historian with an interest in Counter-Reformation culture and popular religion in England. Born in Bury St Edmunds and educated at the University of Cambridge, Young is a prolific author. He has published more than ten books, many of them on Catholicism and more specifically on St Edmund. Without formal university position, he publishes his works with an eye toward the popular market. But it is not just with commercial motivation that he published several books on St Edmund; as an Anglican with leanings toward Catholicism, he is driven by devotion. His *Edmund: In Search of England's Lost King* (2018) makes the case that St Edmund was England's first patron saint. Local pressure groups have made this argument for some time, and it has some credibility. As an excellent public speaker, Young has been invited to speak on the subject on numerous occasions. Nonetheless, it seems unlikely that his thesis on St Edmund's status as first English patron saint will be validated by his peers.

Young's 2018 book also suggests that the bones can be found under the tennis courts, a claim supported by an oral tradition that alleged a secret burial of the saint's body in an iron chest. The evidence is slight, as the source of the oral tradition appeared to suffer from amnesia and did not recollect the story when pressed to recall it again in 1710 by a monk of St Edmund's who reported that the man's memory was "quite lost and gone" (the monk Hugh Frankland, quoted in Young 2018: 146). But avid readers of Young's work have found in this a firm indication that an "iron chest" containing the saint's body might indeed have been buried in the monks' cemetery. As a hypothesis, Young argues, it requires testing. While the Heritage Partnership has always entertained the possibility of noninvasive archaeology, the leaders of the local dowsing group Dowsing Anglia claim they have already tested the hypothesis and established the evidence. On 6 May 2018, the *East Anglian Daily Press* published an online article in which it reported on an International Dowsing Day in the abbey gardens. The newspaper presented the group's claim that St Edmund's remains are located under the tennis courts and that "they have known this for more than 20 years." The newspaper goes on to quote Steve Dawson, cofounder of the group, as stating, "We're confident he's there."[17]

To find out more about the dowsing group, I contacted Steve Dawson. He and his wife, Ann Dawson, agreed to meet me at the abbey gardens. We first talked extensively about their practices and beliefs. It turned out that Steve Dawson had learned dowsing while working for the British army in

Yemen, from the "Arabs," who he claimed dowse with their feet. "Dowsing is a technology that enables us to feel energies to which we were once more sensitive," Dawson explained, "but today we need technological aids such as rods."[18] I learned that there are different energy lines, which can be classified in different categories. Steve and Ann used various idioms to speak about the energy lines. Sometimes they anthropomorphized the energy lines, or they presented them in mechanical terms such as "cables" or "infrastructure"; at other times they referred to them in spiritual terms. Whichever way the lines were denoted, they were understood to be material, to have volume, to grow and shrink, to connect and be entangled in nodes, and to extend across the world. They respond to human engagement, and whenever one sings on a line, it expands. Moreover, the lines can be mapped, and much of the work of the dowsing group seemed to consist of mapping these energy lines. Where lines meet at nodes, good energy can be tapped. Incidentally, at the site of the Benedictine monastery in Bury St Edmunds, the Michael and Mary lines that run through Britain meet and "kiss" just a few meters from the site where St Edmund's shrine used to be. The Dawsons presented a theory that explained why the crossing of the lines has historically determined the site of the Benedictine abbey.

After I had been introduced to the basics of dowsing, the Dawsons demonstrated how they dowsed for Edmund. In fact, they brought with them a laminated A4 sheet on which the letter *E* was printed, which they were going to place at the very location of Edmund's remains (see figure 2.2). Unfortunately, that day the park rangers did not show up, and we could not get the key to unlock the fence that surrounds the tennis courts. This turned out not to be as much of a problem as I thought it would be. Steve explained that one could also "dowse by transit." Standing at the fence, his rods pointed in the direction of the location they had previously identified as the place where Edmund's bones rest. He then walked around the corner and pointed his rods in the same direction, but from another angle. I was told that the lines crossed at the resting place of Edmund's bones.[19]

Dowsing is about the identification of lines and the tracing of their trajectories; it is an exercise in which spiritual energies can be mapped on the land. This exercise is not merely imaginative but communicative, and the communication of shared understandings is facilitated by the plotting of lines on maps. The Dawsons keep a Dropbox with numerous files that document the results of their dowsing exercises. But although their work on the abbey site was recognized in the news item in the *East Anglian Daily Times*, they were not invited to attend the spirituality meeting. Although one of the invited attendants of the spiritual significance meeting was a dowser himself, he did not mention his dowsing practice. Likewise, although the *Conservation Plan* acknowledges the "kiss" of the Michael and Mary lines, the report

Figure 2.2. Tennis courts with the letter *E* for "Edmund" in the public gardens of Bury St Edmund. The second circle indicates the site of St Edmund's former shrine, 2018. © Steve Dawson.

does not mention dowsing as a form of spirituality. This suggests that when it comes to the valuation of spirituality, the spiritualities that privilege forms of transcendence compatible with the secular heritage regime seemed to be recognized over, and to the detriment of, forms of spirituality that point to the existence of the bones. In the absence of archaeological evidence, spiritualities that claim to identify the location of the bones are not as likely to be recognized in the valuation process.

Of course, none of the forms of spirituality recognized in the process of establishing "spiritual" value was vetted for material evidence. This raises the question why the enigma of St Edmund's remains, which generates so much interest in the town and is relevant to any archaeological inventory, should not be recognized. The local newspaper acknowledged the claim of the local dowsers as a form of knowledge about the location of the bones. Several members of the Heritage Partnership were as excited about the prospect of finding the bones as any other citizen in Bury, but many were skeptical of claims to the location of the bones and on the basis of secular calculations of probability did not expect the rumor of the bones to be confirmed. Such doubt did not affect the dowsers. The Dawsons told me that they had attended a lecture by Philippa Langley at Leicester University, the woman they claimed had been the first person to have "sensed" the presence of Richard III under the parking lot. When the Dawsons returned from Leicester, they decided that "we can do better than that." Of course, the competitive nature of their form of spirituality compromises their claim, as it can be discounted if the material evidence is found to be lacking. The energy that Edmund's remains radiate is too immaterial; it references a materiality that can be falsified when archaeological research finds no traces of the saint. Moreover, it presents a PR risk to the Heritage Partnership. It is most likely that the Heritage Partnership has calculated that rumors on the remains should be excluded from the *Conservation Plan* so as not to compromise its authority—and that of the Heritage Partnership.

Conclusion

In her article on relics in the post-Reformation era, Walsham (2010) shows that in this period—in spite of opposition to the localization and materialization of the holy by Reformation scholars—many relics and skeletons were reinterred in cemeteries in the hope of their resurrection. The "charisma" attributed to the relics that were preserved was spiritual and emotional, rather than material and miraculous. Subsequently subjected to secularization, relics migrated into the category of the historic artifact. Having lost their sacramental function, relics were increasingly seen and treated as souvenirs. But even though the sacrament and the souvenir seemed mutually exclusive categories, there were frequent slippages in the ways these categories were applied to the objects themselves. Likewise, the abbey ruins and the remains of St Edmund seem subject to shifting categorizations today. But irrespective of an acknowledgment of new forms of spirituality, the distaste for sacred immanence rooted in the Reformation is remembered in today's heritage regime that renders St Edmund as a spiritual and immaterial presence. Post-Reformation and post-secular heritage sensibilities seem to agree on the materiality of relics and are apprehensive regarding their spirituality.

The remains of Edmund's body—even if not venerated as relics—are on everyone's mind in today's Bury St Edmunds. However, because the presence of the bones is merely speculative and subject to archaeological verification, the spiritual significance of this sacred absence cannot be recognized and accorded a designated heritage "value." Even as a promise, the remains of Edmund cannot be accommodated in the current heritage regime that privileges an ambient spirituality over uncertified material remains. Likewise, ghost tours organized by the town guides that visit the charnel house in the great churchyard are not considered in the *Conservation Plan*. Only certain forms of spirituality are recognized and "valued," not the specters of the dark histories that haunt the ruins of the abbey. The heritage regime dismisses the haunting specters of a history of violence in favor of a spirituality of repair focused on "peace" and "quiet." Spirituality and heritage are different projects that attribute their own values to the abbey ruins, but this chapter demonstrates that heritage and spiritual projects do share some of these values.

That said, the current conceptualization of the spiritual in the *Conservation Plan* produced for the Heritage Partnership is as open as it could be given the demands and expectations placed on such documents for the identification and authorization of heritage "value." By and large in line with Huss's assertion that the concept of the sacred is giving way to the spiritual, the *Conservation Plan* recognizes the spiritual significance of the site. The document acknowledges that "the spiritual value extends beyond that associated with the places of worship" and that it affords different forms of "inward renewal." The *Conservation Plan* thereby accepts a definition of "the spiritual" alongside the sacred, transforming the site of the former Benedictine abbey into a more inclusive space for spiritual renewal. Indeed, the spirituality associated with the abbey might well be conceived as the contemporary "intangible" heritage of the ruins as the heritage regime is conceived by all as a way of protecting the spirituality of the site. In this instance, heritage regime and believers in spiritual renewal really sing from the same hymn sheet.

Ferdinand de Jong (PhD, University of Amsterdam) is associate professor in anthropology at the University of East Anglia, where he teaches African art, anthropology, and cultural heritage. He is the author of *Masquerades of Modernity: Power and Secrecy in Casamance, Senegal* (2007) and coeditor, with Michael Rowlands, of *Reclaiming Heritage: Alternative Imaginaries of Memory in West Africa* (2007). His latest book, *Decolonizing Heritage: Time to Repair in Senegal,* is published by Cambridge University Press (2022).

NOTES

This chapter is based on three years of research starting in September 2016 and a stint of six months of fieldwork in Bury St Edmunds in 2018. The research was conducted in the context of the HERILIGION: The Heritagization of Religion and the Sacralization of Heritage in Contemporary Europe project funded by HERA (Humanities in the European Research Area, grant # 5087–00505A). Throughout my research I have enjoyed the hospitality and generosity of the Heritage Partnership, which has allowed me to conduct research on the process of its formation and operations. I have been able to attend meetings, record the proceedings, and access the meeting minutes and various other documents. Moreover, all members have allowed me to interview them. I am extremely grateful for the trust that the members of the Heritage Partnership have put in me and would like to extend my heartfelt thanks to each and all of them for their collaboration. I would also like to thank Canon Pastor Matthew Vernon as chair of the Heritage Partnership and its coordinator Richard Summers, as well as Canon Librarian Peter Doll, Richard Hoggett, Oscar Salemink, Irene Stengs, and Steven Brindle (English Heritage Trust) for their constructive comments and helpful suggestions for improvement of this text. However, as its author I retain full responsibility for its contents.

1. The process of heritagization entails the discriminate placing of "value" on sites, objects, or performances. UNESCO arbitrates selection of proposals to its lists on the basis of outstanding universal value (Labadi 2013; Titchen 1996). Since valuation is critical to heritage discourse and increasingly contested, it has been subjected to conceptual debate and bureaucratic arbitration within UNESCO. Academic evaluations that critically examine values defined by different heritage organizations reveal a wide diversity and a lack of coherence, while signaling wide discrepancies between state and community valuations (De la Torre 2013; Fredheim and Khalaf 2016; Mydland and Grahn 2012).
2. See the Historic England document "Conservation Principles, Policies and Guidance for the Sustainable Development of the Historic Environment," 2008, https://historicengland.org.uk/advice/constructive-conservation/conservation-principles (accessed 15 July 2020). Although published by English Heritage in 2008, this document still expressed the views of its successor Historic England in 2015. This document informed the work by the firm Purcell that produced the Conservation Plan. In 2019, Historic England published a new document that substantially revises the earlier document: "Historic England 2019 Statement of Heritage Significance: Analysing Significance in Heritage Assets Historic England Advice Note 12," https://historicengland.org.uk/images-books/publications/statements-heritage-significance-advice-note-12/ (accessed 18 June 2022).
3. There are debates on the exact chronology of the foundation of a monastic community, the year of translation of the body of Saint Edmund to Beodricesworth, the building of a new or enlarged church by King Cnut, the motivations for a Danish king to facilitate the making of a cult for an English king martyred by the Danes, and the motivations of the Normans to accept a cult around an English saint. These matters pose a problem to historians because the documentation is scant and the available documents are often forgeries. See Gransden 1985; Gransden 2015; Licence 2014; Young 2014.
4. National legislation governs the preservation of these monuments and what changes can be undertaken in the built environment, irrespective of who owns them. The abbey gardens and the great churchyard are owned by West Suffolk Borough Council. The council also owns most of the ruins and the abbey gate, but these are managed by English Heritage Trust (Wood 2018: 28). The remains of the abbey and the chapel of the Charnel House are scheduled monuments. Alongside these, stand 21 Grade I listed buildings, 3 Grade II listed buildings and 115 Grade II listed structures, of which 100 are memorials in the great churchyard. See Wood (2018: 16–28).
5. I am indebted to Richard Hoggett for pointing this out to me.
6. In April 2019, the St Edmundsbury Borough Council was merged with Forest Heath District to form West Suffolk Council.
7. *East Anglian Daily Times*, 14 September 2016.

8. *East Anglian Daily Times*, 14 September 2016. This mission has since been reformulated as follows: "The mission of the Heritage Partnership is to encourage people to experience the international significance of St Edmund and the historic Abbey."
9. The English Heritage Trust is a charity, which exercises responsibility for the care of around 420 historic sites on behalf of the Crown, represented by the secretary of state for culture, media, and sport. The abbey ruins at Bury St Edmunds were placed in guardianship by their owners, the local authority, in the 1950s. The placing of the ruins in guardianship was followed by a long campaign of excavation and consolidation of the ruins, by the Ancient Monuments Branch of the Ministry of Works—the predecessors to the current trust. The Department of the Environment and (from 1984) English Heritage have carried out the archaeological excavation, consolidation, and presentation of the site in question. English Heritage remains the official guardian of the abbey ruins and has financial responsibility for their maintenance (email to author from Steven Brindle, senior properties historian, Curatorial Department, English Heritage Trust, 14 May 2022). English Heritage is currently designing new interpretation panels for the site in close collaboration with members of the Heritage Partnership. This work will be the subject of another paper.
10. The Purcell employee commissioned to draft the report allowed me to attend a day of her work, in which we visited the Norman tower, Saint Mary's church, and the abbey gardens, where we spoke to the cathedral's outreach officer, the volunteers running the church, the horticulturalists working in the gardens, and a retired gardens manager. I am grateful for her permission to second her for the day. The methodology followed the Historic England guidelines on the matter: "Historic England 2019 Statement of Heritage Significance: Analysing Significance in Heritage Assets Historic England Advice Note 12." See https://historicengland.org.uk/images-books/publications/statements-heritage-significance-advice-note-12/ (accessed 18 June 2022).
11. The Historic England guidance still current at the moment of writing is clear on its inclusiveness: "Spiritual value attached to places can emanate from the beliefs and teachings of an organised religion, or reflect past or present-day perceptions of the spirit of place. It includes the sense of inspiration and wonder that can arise from personal contact with places long revered, or newly revealed." See "Conservation Principles, Policies and Guidance for the Sustainable Development of the Historic Environment," 32, https://historicengland.org.uk/images-books/publications/conservation-principles-sustainable-management-historic-environment/conservationprinciplespoliciesandguidanceapril08web/ (accessed 18 June 2022).
12. Notes Spiritual Significance Group Discussion, 19 July 2018.
13. I should note that the *Heritage Assessment* does not state that the site's pre-Christian history involved a Pagan site or Pagan worship. The intervention made at the meeting therefore already signaled an appropriation of its pre-Christian history.
14. On the interesting etymology of the term "vandalism" that references the violence employed by the Vandals in the early medieval period and its secular employment in the aftermath of the French Revolution, see Merrills (2009).
15. Notes Spiritual Significance Group Discussion, 19 July 2018.
16. These discussions echoed nineteenth-century discourses on the benefits of museum visits to the working classes (Bennett 1995), in which the museum operated as an instrument of disciplinary regimes.

17. "Dowsing Group Confident of St Edmund's Burial Ground Location," *East Anglian Daily Times*, 6 May 2018, https://www.eadt.co.uk/news/xx-2451786 (accessed 18 May 2022).
18. For reasons of space, I refrain from contextualizing this primitivist allegation on Arab sensibility, but it goes without saying that it sits in a long history of Orientalism.
19. In an insightful article, Woolley (2018) examines how dowsing tools work as divinatory methodology to convey the dowser's environmental knowledge.

REFERENCES

Abbo of Fleury. 2018. *The Passion of Saint Edmund*. Translated by Francis Hervey. Durham: The Langley Press.

Asad, Talal. 2003. *Formations of the Secular: Christianity, Islam, Modernity*. Stanford, CA: Stanford University Press.

Astor, Avi, Marian Burchardt, and Mar Griera. 2017. "The Politics of Religious Heritage: Framing Claims to Religion as Culture in Spain," *Journal for the Scientific Study of Religion* 56(1): 126–42.

Bennett, Tony. 1995. *The Birth of the Museum: History, Theory, Politics*. London and New York: Taylors & Francis.

Buckley, Richard, Mathew Morris, Jo Appleby, Turi King, Deidre O'Sullivan, and Lin Foxhall. 2013. "'The King in the Car Park': New Light on the Death and Burial of Richard III in the Grey Friars Church, Leicester, in 1485," *Antiquity* 87: 519–38.

Calhoun, Craig. 2010. "Rethinking Secularism," *Hedgehog Review* 12(3): 35–48.

Consultancy Brief for a Conservation Management Plan for the site of Bury St Edmunds Abbey, Abbey Gardens and Precincts. St Edmundsbury Borough Council, Bury St Edmunds, August 2017.

Cunningham, Lawrence S. 2005. *A Brief History of Saints*. Oxford and Malden: Blackwell.

Davie, Grace. 1994. *Religion in Britain Since 1945: Believing without Belonging*. Oxford and Malden: Blackwell.

De Jong, Ferdinand. 2023. "Traces of the Sacred: Loss, Hope, and Potentiality in Religious Heritage," in Ferdinand de Jong and José Mapril (eds.), *The Future of Religious Heritage: Temporalities of the Sacred and the Secular*. New York: Routledge.

De la Torre, Marta. 2013. "Values and Heritage Construction," *Heritage & Society* 60(2): 155–66.

Engelke Matthew. 2012. "Angels in Swindon: Public Religion and Ambient Faith in England," *American Ethnologist* 39(1): 155–70.

Fredheim, L. Harald, and Manal Khalaf. 2016. "The Significance of Values: Heritage Value Typologies Re-examined," *International Journal of Heritage Studies* 22(6): 466–81.

Gransden, Antonia. 1985. "The Legends and Traditions Concerning the Origins of the Abbey of Bury St Edmunds," *English Historical Review* 100(394): 1–24.

Gransden, Antonia. 2015. *A History of the Abbey of Bury St Edmunds, 1257–1301*. Woodbridge.

Heelas, Paul, and Linda Woodhead, with Benjamin Seel, Bronislaw Szerszynski, and Karin Tusting. 2005. *The Spiritual Revolution: Why Religion Is Giving Way to Spirituality*. Oxford and Malden: Blackwell.

Huss, Boaz. 2014. "Spirituality: The Emergence of a New Cultural Category and Its Challenge to the Religious and the Secular," *Journal of Contemporary Religion* 29(1): 47–60.
Huss, Boaz. 2018. "Spiritual, but Not Religious, but Not Secular: Spirituality and Its New Cultural Formations." Paper presented at the European University, Saint Petersburgh, 17 November 2018.
Isnart, Cyril, and Nathalie Cerezales (eds.). 2020. *The Religious Heritage Complex: Legacy, Conservation, and Christianity*. London: Bloomsbury.
Labadi, Sophia. 2013. *UNESCO, Cultural Heritage and Outstanding Universal Value: Value-Based Analyses of the World Heritage and Intangible Cultural Heritage Conventions*. Lanham, MD: AltaMira Press.
Lehmann, David. 2013. "Religion as Heritage, Religion as Belief: Shifting Frontiers of Secularism in Europe, the USA and Brazil," *International Sociology* 28(6): 645–62.
Licence, Tom (ed.). 2014. *Bury St Edmunds and the Norman Conquest*. Woodbridge.
Mapril, José, Ruy Blanes, Emerson Giumbelli, and Erin K. Wilson (eds.). 2017. *Secularisms in a Postsecular Age? Religiosities and Subjectivities in Comparative Perspective*. Palgrave Macmillan.
Merrills, A. H. 2009. "The Origins of 'Vandalism,'" *International Journal of the Classical Tradition* 16(2): 155–75.
Meyer, Birgit, and Mattijs van de Port (eds.). 2018. *Sense and Essence: Heritage and the Cultural Production of the Real*. Oxford: Berghahn Books.
Mydland, Leidulf, and Wera Grahn. 2012. "Identifying Heritage Values in Local Communities," *International Journal of Heritage Studies* 18(6): 564–87.
Rectenwald, Michael, and Rochelle Almeida. 2017. "Introduction: Global Secularisms in a Post-Secular Age," in Michael Rectenwald, Rochelle Almeida, and George Levine (eds.), *Global Secularisms in a Post-secular Age*. Boston and Berlin: De Gruyter, pp. 1–24.
Richard Hoggett Heritage. 2018. *The Abbey of St Edmund: Heritage Assessment*.
Taylor, Charles. 2007. *A Secular Age*. Cambridge, MA: The Belknap Press of Harvard University Press.
Titchen, Sarah M. 1996. "On the Construction of 'Outstanding Universal Value': Some Comments on the Implementation of the 1972 UNESCO World Heritage Convention," *Conservation and Management of Archaeological Sites* 1(4): 235–42.
Walsham, Alexandra. 2010. "Skeletons in the Cupboard: Relics after the English Reformation," *Past and Present*, Supplement 5: 121–43.
Wohlrab-Sahr, Monika, and Marian Burchardt. 2012. "Multiple Secularities: Toward a Cultural Sociology of Secular Modernities," *Comparative Sociology* 11: 875–909.
Wood, Rowenna. 2018. *Abbey of St Edmund: Conservation Plan*. Purcell.
Woodhead, Linda, and Rebecca Catto (eds.). 2012. *Religion and Change in Modern Britain*. New York: Taylor and Francis.
Woolley, Jonathan. 2018. "The Wires Crossed: What Dowsing Reveals about Environmental Knowledge in Britain," *Anthropology Today* 34 (4): 22–25.
Young, Francis. 2014. *Where Is St Edmund? The Search for East Anglia's Martyr King*. Ely: East Anglian Catholic History Centre
Young, Francis. 2016. *The Abbey of Bury St Edmunds: History, Legacy and Discovery*. Norwich: The Lasse Press
Young, Francis. 2018. *Edmund: In Search of England's Lost King*. London: I.B. Taurus.

PART II

THE MANAGEMENT OF NATIONAL RELIGIOUS SITES IN DENMARK

 CHAPTER 3

Churches as Places of Worship, Cultural Heritage, and National Symbols
Centralism, Autonomy, and the Hybrid Nature of Church-State Relations in Denmark
Ulla Kjær and Poul Grinder-Hansen

Introduction

In 1694, Robert Molesworth, who had earlier served as British ambassador to Denmark, published a book about Denmark and the Danes: *An Account of Denmark as It Was in the Year 1692*. Much of what he wrote was discussed and contested in Denmark, but there was one point that the Danes apparently found to be justified—namely, that no Dane stood out among the others. According to Molesworth, all were mediocre and all held the same opinions: "A certain equality of Understanding reigns among them: everyone keeps the ordinary beaten road of Sence, which in this country is neither the fairest nor the foulest, without deviating to the right or left" (Molesworth 1694: 235; Olden-Jørgensen 2005). Very similar judgments are also to be found in recent studies: Danes are described as a tribe where all are alike and where people from outside can only be admitted once they have acquired the same unspecified Danish way of thinking and behaving (Mellon 1992; Jespersen 2011). The traditions upheld by the homogeneous Danish population in the last half of the nineteenth and most of the twentieth century have not lost their relevance in spite of the challenges of immigration from other cultural spheres (Østergaard 2012). Part of this well-established Danish self-concept is the idea that real Danes maintain middle-of-the-road positions while combining seemingly quite opposing qualities; they are both exclusive and inclusive, royalist Republicans and atheist believers in chosen values (Hauge 2013: 43–8).

The Danish Royal House is more than a thousand years old, and Christian culture within Denmark has a similar age. Both have been quietly, thoroughly, and deeply incorporated into traditional Danish identity, and as a consequence all church buildings of the Danish Lutheran state church are officially regarded both as the setting for Christian ceremonies and as national heritage.

This double role assumed by Danish churches is a central topic of this chapter, which discusses the relationship between the cultural preservation of Christian churches in Denmark and their use as religious buildings and explains the historical background to the Danish legislation concerning churches and the present-day practical consequences of that legislation. In particular we aim to show how a peculiar hybrid administrative structure regarding the management of the church buildings of the Danish state church goes hand in hand with a specific idea of the nation that has its roots in the nineteenth century. Such a *longue durée* historicization of a church-royalty-state relational nexus that incorporates discourses and affects of nation and heritage prepares the ground for understanding the complex engagement of religion and heritage in Denmark and, even further afoot, in Europe.

Danish Churches and Christianity

Denmark has been a Christian state since the second half of the tenth century, for the first approximately 575 years as a part of the Roman Catholic Church and since the Reformation in 1536 as a Protestant Lutheran country. The huge role that the medieval Catholic Church played, religiously, politically, and also culturally is well-documented, but as is evident from the analysis below, the Danish Lutheran Church had an equally far-reaching yet different impact on the lives of Danes and the Danish way of thinking. The national and later social revival in nineteenth-century Denmark unfolded in concord (and sometimes in conflict) with Christian revival movements. Even in modern Danish society, which in many ways seems secularized and which in recent decades has come to include many people with other religious and cultural backgrounds, a culture based on Christian values and traditions is encapsulated in several aspects of daily life, institutions, social conventions, philosophy, and ethics (Østergaard 2012; Holm 2017).

Most of the Danish church buildings originate from the twelfth and thirteenth centuries. They were built after approximately the same model, consisting of a chancel and a nave, a porch and maybe a tower, a vestry and one or more chapels. Yet no two of them are identical, since they have all been influenced by their surroundings. Their building materials depend on geological and climatic conditions, and their design and furnishings have been decided by the people who have used them and been responsible for their embellishment. In spite of all the resemblances between the many originally Romanesque churches, there is a great difference in appearance between a granite ashlar church like Hover on the windswept fields of Western Jutland, with no tower and with a flat wooden ceiling, compared to a neat, whitewashed church like Herfølge, situated in a rich agricultural district in East Denmark, gothicized with brick-built bell tower, vestry, vaults, and corbie-step gables. Besides that, the interior of each Danish church is typically a mix from various periods—for example, with a font from the thirteenth century, an altarpiece from the fifteenth century, a pulpit from the seventeenth century, benches from the nineteenth century, and an organ from the twentieth century. All old churches stand as living testimony to local history, mirroring it in their walls, mural paintings, furnishings, and memorials to the dead.

From State Church to the Danish People's Church

The Lutheran Reformation in Denmark was carried through in 1536 on the initiative of King Christian III (1534–59), who had become a follower of Luther's beliefs since, as a young duke, he had witnessed in person how Martin Luther stood firm at the Reichstag in Worms in 1521. King Christian imprisoned the Catholic bishops and confiscated their estates; he appointed so-called superintendents to be the new heads of the old dioceses and assigned to them the duty of establishing a true Lutheran church order in the dual monarchy of Denmark-Norway. All in all the Danish Reformation was a rather peaceful and gradual change, which nonetheless had a great impact on Danish society. Denmark remained a stable Lutheran state and played a leading role on behalf of the Protestant countries on the European religious and political scene during the reigns of Christian III's son, Frederik II (1559–88) and his grandson, Christian IV (1588–1648) (Lockhart 2007: 58–82).

The king himself was also the head of the church, and there was no leading religious figure, such as an archbishop, who could talk on behalf of the new Danish church. After the Reformation the clergy were state appointed, and for centuries they acted as representatives of the state and as living channels of information who could reach each and every parishioner in the realm. Official announcements from the state to its citizens were read from the pulpit during Sunday services, and the churches accordingly came to occupy a position that included functional ties to the state. Since the state upheld a strong church discipline and made it an obligation for all citizens to take part in Sunday services until the second half of the eighteenth century, the churches became the rallying ground and natural focal point of life in the parishes.

After the introduction of absolutism in 1660, the Danish kings ruled as representatives of God and with a clear obligation to support and consol-

Figure 3.1. Almost all Danish churches have a flagpole, and the Danish flag will wave at each service. Aggersborg Church, Jylland, 2019. © Ulla Kjær.

idate the Lutheran churches. The democratic Constitution from 1849 introduced freedom of worship but upheld the bond between the state and the Lutheran Church, which then acquired the name "the Danish People's Church" (Den danske Folkekirke). The significance of the descriptive *folke* (i.e., the people's) in the name of central Danish institutions like the public school system (Folkeskolen), the public libraries (Folkebiblioteker), and the parliament (Folketinget), in parallel with the national church (Folkekirken), reveals how closely people, nation, and state are symbolically coupled in Denmark (Korsgaard 2004: 13). Successive democratically elected Danish governments have always included a minister of ecclesiastical affairs. Section 66 of the Constitution states that a constitution for the church will be arranged by law in the future, but this has never happened. On the official English homepage of the state Church of Denmark, the relation between church and state is explained in these words:

> As "official national church" the Danish monarch is the supreme authority when it comes to organization, liturgy etc., whereas the national parliament (*Folketinget*) is the de facto deciding body with regard to church legislation. Thus, when female theologians were allowed to join the clergy, it was the national parliament

that took the decision. The Evangelical Lutheran Church in Denmark is not regulated by a synod (a national church council) as is the case with most other Lutheran churches.[1]

The church assumes a special role in relation to all Danes, whether they are Christians, Muslims, agnostics, or atheists, since the registration of all births takes place by means of the health authorities reporting them directly to the home parish of the mother, where the administration digitally records the information on behalf of the state. Only in the southern part of Jutland, which belonged to Germany from 1864 to 1920, are the records of births kept by the local civil municipality as a continuation of German administrative practices. In a similar way all deaths must also be recorded through the parish of the deceased.

The Evangelical-Lutheran Church in Denmark

About three-quarters of Denmark's population of almost six million have been baptized in a Danish Lutheran church and are thus counted as members of the Church of Denmark, even if many of them could be described as "passive members," since they are not outwardly practicing. They remain members until they actively choose to sign out.[2] The members are spread out over 2,158 parishes, each of them with at least one church, but in some cases more, so that Denmark has all in all 2,339 Lutheran church buildings. A little over 70 percent are medieval and were erected before the Reformation in 1536. There are also about 2,100 churchyards, most in close proximity to the churches.

Within the last hundred years all the churches of the Folkekirke have become self-governing. All of them are managed by the parish council as representatives of the church members in the parish. Each parish council consists of between five and fifteen members, who are elected every fourth year by all members of the congregation over eighteen years of age.[3] The parish council manages the daily activities of the churches and acts as employer of all staff (organists, sextons, churchyard administrators, etc.), except for the pastors. It also elects a warden for each church, with the task of tending to the church building, the churchyard, and other buildings owned by the church. The Danish parishes are grouped into 107 geographically defined deaneries, each managed by a dean (*provst*), who usually also serves as a pastor in one of the deanery's churches. The dean is the head of all pastors in the deanery and must supervise the discharge of their duties. The dean must also secure a fair distribution of the economic resources and a proper economic administration in each parish council. In each deanery there is a board of four to eight members elected from the parish councils, plus a pastor and the dean. These deanery boards are required to approve many categories of decisions taken by the parish councils, especially those with economic aspects, but in some cases also decisions concerning the physical surroundings of the churches.

The deaneries are grouped in dioceses: one semi-independent diocese that covers Greenland, which is a self-governing part of the Kingdom of Denmark, and ten within Denmark proper, each of them with its own cathedral. Each Danish diocese is managed by a bishop, who is democratically elected by all the pastors and all members of the parish councils in the diocese. Together with a representative of the state (with the symbolic title *stiftsamtmand*), the bishop constitutes the head of the diocese (*stiftsøvrighed*). Each diocese is thus a construction involving church and state, officially on an equal level. All administrative matters concerning the churches of the diocese are run by a diocese administration managed by an assistant secretary. This administration on behalf of the bishop is the authority in a range of church matters, such as applications from parish councils concerning restorations or permanent changes to or within the churches. Each diocese has its own board managing the funds of the churches and the pastors, composed of a broad representation of laypersons from the parish councils, pastors, one dean, and the bishop, and they elect their chairman and deputy chairman from among the representatives of the parish councils. Every year the condition of the churches and their surroundings is subject to inspection by the warden and members of the parish council together with a building expert, and every fourth year the dean, again with a building expert, also takes part in the inspection. When a parish council faces a costly task like a major renovation, the diocese board may grant a loan from the fund based on income from the sale of burial plots in churchyards, among other things.

According to the Danish Constitution, the monarch is the supreme authority over the Lutheran Church, but in fact it is parliament that decides all aspects of legislation concerning the Folkekirke. The minister of ecclesiastical affairs acts as the real administrative but not theological authority over the Danish Lutheran Church. The ministry can be considered to be part of the church organization, which is run not by theologians but by laypersons, and could be compared to the parish councils, which similarly consist of laypersons who are willing to work for the good of the church. The minister decides the overall economic framework of the common fund (*Fællesfonden*) of the Folkekirke, which is otherwise managed by the bishops and which pays all salaries and wages in connection with the operations of the churches. The primary income of this fund comes from taxes (*kirkeskat*) collected within the national tax system and paid by all those who are officially members of the state church. In addition to this, however, the state also provides a grant that comes from the general taxation paid by all Danes, which contributes to wages as well as to repairs and renovations.

In short, the management of the church buildings of the Folkekirke is done through a hybrid interwoven structure involving both (religious) church and (secular) state authorities, with simultaneous grassroots self-governance by local congregations and top-down oversight and funding on behalf of the central state.

Among the challenges confronting the Folkekirke is the fact that there is a very uneven relation between the distribution of churches and the distribution of the population. One-third of Danish rural parishes have under five hundred congregation members, and several hundred parishes have under two hundred members. Some urban parishes have several thousand members, and a few have more than twenty thousand members. On the other hand, some of the largest Danish towns have a comparatively low level of membership of the church, partly due to a high number of inhabitants with a non-European background. In this context, a handful of nineteenth- and twentieth-century churches in Copenhagen have been closed down and sold for other purposes. There has been discussion about whether churches in the smallest rural parishes should also be completely closed down, but that has proved extremely difficult (Kjær 2014). If a medieval church were to be taken out of religious use, it would automatically be listed as a historically important building under present-day heritage protection. It would therefore have to be preserved with the obvious next question: what could such a large stone building in a neighborhood with a few hundred inhabitants be used for—except as a church? In such areas the church building is typically of huge importance to the sense of identity of the community. A few churches have received the status of "occasional churches" (*lejlighedskirker*). They remain part of the Danish Lutheran Church and can still be used for baptisms, weddings, and funerals, but no regular services are held, except possibly for Christmas, so they are taken out of daily use, while their physical maintenance is upheld.

Danish Churches as a Special Category of Heritage

Chapter 2, §4 in the Danish law for protection of historic buildings states that "buildings older than 1536 are without any further decisions automatically protected by this law." But §5 adds that this law does not concern church buildings "as long as they are subject to the law concerning the Danish People's Church." This means that in contrast to all other medieval buildings in Denmark, the medieval church buildings—some 1,750 of them—are not listed as protected buildings under the legislation for cultural heritage, because they are defined as being in living use in accordance with their original purpose and because they are deemed sufficiently protected by the church organization itself. Considering this in an international context, it is an unusual circumstance that calls for explanation.

In the first law for the protection of historic buildings, issued on 12 March 1918, there is no mention of the churches being exempt from the law. Nonetheless, no churches and only a few rectories were entered on the first lists of protected buildings. There was a historical reason for omitting the churches: they were already covered by a protective law with its own history. Since the High Middle Ages, the congregations had paid tithes so that the churches could serve as suitable spaces for religious ceremonies. After the Reformation, the king took over most of the former ecclesiastical estates, including the churches, and during the following centuries these buildings, or more precisely the rights to manage their economy, were to a large extent sold to private persons. Most "church-owners" were diligent in keeping up their churches with repairs, new furnishings, and in many cases new sepulchral monuments for themselves and their families. Some, however, collected the tithes and lined their own pockets, neglecting the churches. A financial cri-

Figure 3.2. Aastrup Church, the island of Falster, Denmark, 2012. The medieval church in the middle of its neat and well-maintained churchyard. © Ulla Kjær.

sis in the first half of the nineteenth century made it tempting to cut down expenses on preservation of the churches, and some owners even started selling church furniture at auctions, where it was bought by private persons looking for reusable materials. But at the same time, an understanding of the importance of these buildings and the need for their protection developed, as part of a growing Romanticist nationalism (Iversen 2015).

Since the end of the eighteenth century, there had been an ideal of a functional art with local roots that could help improve society. Artists began to take an interest in the traditional styles of their region, which in northern Europe first of all meant the Gothic style. Gothic signified church architecture; it was the magnificent style of the ancestors and was mimicked in architecture in such a painstaking form that veritable pastiches came to be created (Sværke 2010: 79–81; Salling 1975: 97–98, with fig. XXXIII). The idealization of the medieval style became trendsetting for contemporary, often somewhat romantic restorations. Many architects were ideologically inspired by the French architect Viollet-le-Duc, whose ideal of a restoration was the re-creation of the building in its original, perfect shape. On the one hand, such a restoration demanded careful archaeological investigations to find out what the building originally looked like; on the other hand, it was a question of revealing and revitalizing the nature and spirit of the building (Kryger 1977).

In Denmark such thoughts about restoration were launched by the first art historian of the country, Niels Lauritz Høyen (1798–1870). On his travels through Denmark in the years 1829–33, he systematically examined churches but also manors and town houses. He noted a prevalence of decay and became a zealous advocate for the restoration of historical monuments. In the mid-nineteenth century, conditions had become favorable for implementing such ideals; national finances had improved, democracy had been introduced, and nationalism was on the upsurge. Restorations thrived, and Høyen had huge influence through his position as professor of art history at the Danish Academy of Art and Architecture. He was a gifted and inspired man, but his views on art were so colored by nationalism that this affected his professional judgment. His stylistic classificatory model was influenced by the then common European tendency to look for defining traits of each nation and thus contained strong elements of national historical ideology. In his stylistic chronology for medieval Danish architecture, Høyen preferred to focus on the Romanesque style that constitutes the core of most Danish churches instead of the international Gothic style (Agerbæk 1984: 467–70).

Partly inspired by Høyen, a wave of church restorations swept over Denmark in the second half of the nineteenth century, typically on the basis of careful architectural and stylistic studies seeking to re-establish the style of medieval churches that had over time lost their original appearance as a result of repairs and renovations. The method meant that many historically important details and, in some cases, whole elements were replaced by well-intended but sometimes erroneous or non-original reconstructions aimed at creating more "historical" church buildings (Smidt 2018). A glaring example is Viborg Cathedral, which in the years 1863–76 was torn down and re-erected in a style that imitated the famous Romanesque cathedrals of the Rhine area, which Høyen assumed to be the source of inspiration for Danish medieval church buildings (Vellev 1981a, 1981b). In Roskilde, Steen Friis, the churchwarden of the cathedral, tried to secure money for his own church but complained that Høyen spent all available funds "for the copy of the old cathedral in Viborg for which he so recklessly and baselessly seeks money to execute" (Kjær 2013: 319; Kjærbøl 2005). The painter Joakim Skovgaard, who was given the task of decorating the new cathedral, gave precise expression to the consequences of Høyen's ideals in a letter to his brother Niels in 1874. He wrote that that day he had had to draw a Lamb of God, and it had not been an easy task since the lamb should be from the twelfth century (Vellev 1987: 8).

The discussion preceding the restoration in Viborg became one of the reasons for the issuing of a new revised law about yearly inspections of churches, passed on 19 February 1861. In this law, churches were for the first time considered both as houses of Christian worship and as historical monuments (Smidt 2018; Agerbæk 1984: 365; Madsen 1983: 87). Any defects of the buildings or the furnishings should be repaired, and it was stressed, quite in the spirit of Høyen, that a restoration should as far as possible restore the building to its original style. If an inspection did not give an appreciative evaluation of the style of the church, then that was not a sufficient cause for changes. If defects were not repaired, it was possible to fine the responsible persons. The law was thorough and included guidance from the ministry with occasional advice from the National (then Oldnordisk) Museum, leading to the conclusion in the aforementioned law of 1918 that church buildings were sufficiently protected by the church authorities. This concept was maintained in the revised law of church inspections from 1922, when the great majority of Danish churches became self-governing under the local management of parish councils, as is still the case today. Thus, the management of the heritage of the Folkekirke remains the responsibility of the ecclesiastical authorities at various levels.

The National Museum and the Churches

In 1807 the king approved a Royal Commission for the Keeping of Antiquities (Den kongelige Kommission til Oldsagers Opbevaring), the humble beginnings of the later National Museum of Denmark. The commission took an interest in various remains from the past, including church furnishings from the Catholic times and other church monuments. The focus was mostly on objects that could become part of a museum collection. Later the new museum would also become engaged in the preservation of historic monuments throughout the country. On 20 March 1848, curator J. J. A. Worsaae from the Oldnordisk Museum in Copenhagen (after 1892 the National Museum of Denmark) was tasked with surveying the protection and preservation of the most important antiquarian sites and objects of the kingdom and the duchies of Schleswig, Holstein, and Lauenburg: stone settings, megalithic tombs, barrows, runic stones, castle mounds, ruins of castles and palaces, old churches, and similar architectural monuments. A supplementary decree stated that he should inform the rural deans as to which church objects were worth protecting, so that they could be taken into consideration during church inspections.[4]

Worsaae, however, had no possible means of securing the preservation of all these monuments, including churches. In January 1861 the librarian G. Burman Becker sent Worsaae a newspaper article he had written under the heading "vandalism," to inform him of recent paper advertisements of three auctions selling furniture, fixtures, and paraments from Ørum Church in Sønderlyng district [*herred*] in Jutland. The objects would be sold to private persons, who would reuse the materials for various purposes without any thought of conservation.[5] When you read such advertisements, Becker wrote, you clearly see how erroneous the common notion is that a person who has acquired the right to receive the tithes for a church should also have the right to dispose of its decorations and fixtures: chalice and paten, baptismal font, etc. You also realize, he continued, how badly the maintenance and continued existence of medieval monuments are protected. Worsaae only had 300 rigsdaler a year to spend on antiquarian protection, which was quite insufficient. Besides, the curator who had once been a representative of the absolutist king was now merely a common public servant. Therefore, it was necessary to make a revision of the law so that more staff could be employed for inspections all over the country. Experts from the museum began to travel all over Denmark on antiquarian inspections, and an important part of the task was to visit and describe all churches (Kjær 2007a, 2007b, 2007c). Through the years the museum has established a very solid knowledge of the material state of Danish churches (Mollerup 1908: 98–100).

Currently, the National Museum has a statutory obligation to act as consultant for the Danish dioceses with regard to the preservation of the cultural heritage in the churches of the Folkekirke (excluding non-state churches), and the National Museum works with Folkekirke churches on several levels. Important parts of the museum's medieval and Renaissance collections originate from churches. The archives of the museum contain information about all Danish churches and document all restorations and investigations covering more than one hundred years. Since the 1930s, the museum has published a systematic topographic documentation of each Danish church in the shape of the huge work *Danmarks Kirker*, which is now also digitally accessible. The museum has been the leading force behind the uncovering and restoration of mural paintings since the mid-nineteenth century and of church archaeology since the 1950s. Due to these basic activities, the National Museum holds a unique position with regard to all information and tools for transversal and in-depth studies of Christianity and the Christian institutions in their interaction with other elements of Danish society, where the church buildings serve as obvious indicators of tendencies at different times—albeit only for the buildings of the Folkekirke.

Protecting Religious Heritage: Inspectors and Curators

As previously mentioned, each local parish council has the responsibility for managing its church, including the protection of its cultural heritage. The law concerning the Folkekirke's church buildings and churchyards aims (1) to promote its church buildings as the best possible framework for services and other ecclesiastical activities of the congregation; (2) to ensure that there is enough space for burials in the churchyards and that they are well-kept; and (3) to secure that the cultural assets connected to church buildings and churchyards are not depreciated (Kirker og Kirkegårde 2001). It is the representatives of the Folkekirke, that is, the Ministry of Ecclesiastical Affairs and the dioceses, who have authority to decide whether the plans of a parish council for changes or restoration work on their church may be realized. But since the churches are considered to be historical buildings with great heritage value, the Ministry of Culture has since 1922 supported the work of the churches by placing the royal building inspectors and the experts of the National Museum at the disposal of the dioceses as professional consultants (Kjær, Søndergaard, and Trampedach 1998; Trampedach 2018). The advice of the building inspectors and the museum curators or conservators is therefore provided to the individual churches without charge.

The royal building inspectors are appointed on fixed-term state contracts and are attached to one or more dioceses, while the National Museum is a permanent adviser for all dioceses, covering all of Denmark as its field of responsibility, particularly concerning matters of conservation. Mural paintings and old church furniture demand special treatment, and specialists with the required technical knowledge are few in number. As incompetent treatment could have disastrous results, the responsible parish councils are in high need of professional assistance. The church laws therefore state that any restoration of mural paintings and furniture older than a hundred years can only take place through the National Museum and sanctioned by the diocese authorities. Such a case will typically begin with the emergence of a proposal in the parish council for a change, a repair, or a renovation. The proposal may spring from observations during the yearly inspections of the church, or it may come from a meeting in the parish council, to be followed by meetings involving the parish council, representatives of the diocese, the royal building inspector, and one member of the National Museum's staff. The parish council or the architect in charge of a project can ask for a visit by a professional conservator from the National Museum if the project involves restorations of mural paintings or furniture, new whitewashing, or changes involving the relocation of furniture or new colors. Such a visit will result in a report describing precisely how the mural paintings or the furniture must be treated from a conservation viewpoint. The report will be used as the basis for inviting tenders from experienced craftspeople and professional conservators (Trampedach 2018: 132).

When a detailed project is available, it must be sent to the diocese authorities for approval via the deanery, which is responsible for the distribution of local financial means. The diocese authorities will ask the opinion of their advisers, primarily the royal building inspectors and the National Museum. If the project concerns purely antiquarian heritage, only the National Museum must be consulted, while the museum will not be involved if the project concerns a church that is less than a hundred years old. The Ministry of Ecclesiastical Affairs has appointed some special consultants with expert knowledge about specific topics: churchyards, organs, bells, and heating, climate, and energy matters. If a project involves a plan for new art in the church, a committee appointed by the Royal Academy of Fine Arts is consulted. When the answers from all these consultants and advisers are at hand, the diocese will decide if the project can be approved directly, if it can be approved conditionally subject to some changes, or if it must be rejected. In spite of occasional situations of conflicting interests, in most cases the system succeeds in establishing a solution that is acceptable for all parties involved. Parish council, architect, craftspeople and conservators, church authorities, and the advisers and consultants collaborate to achieve the best possible treatment of the Danish churches and their mural paintings, furniture, and sepulchral monuments, and this has proved to be effective; although the churches are not protected by heritage law, they are in excellent condition, in line with their national importance.

The decisive principle for the National Museum is that the churches are not museums, but living houses of worship, which must be able to function as religious venues at the same time as they contain important traces of the past. When considering a change, the parties deliberate whether the new initiative is in accordance with what can be described as the "genius loci"—an expression originating in classical antiquity, meaning the "soul" of the place (Vadstrup 2018: 3). It is easy to dismiss something as being in bad taste or old-fashioned, but often it is only after the thing in question has been removed that people realize that a feature of value has gone. The National Museum strives to avoid such scenarios. In most cases old and new form a synthesis intended to inspire a deep awe, both religious and historical, in visitors to the churches. In other words, the management of the church buildings is predicated on a hybrid, religious-cum-heritage governance.

Danish Churches and the Danish People

The strong historic bond between the Folkekirke and the Danish state—whether as an absolutist kingdom or, after 1849, with a democratic government—is only one of the explanations for the unusual societal position of Danish state churches, going well beyond traditional religious significance. In comparison with other related European countries the churches in Denmark still maintain a remarkably strong position among the Danish population, due to the fact that daily church life encompasses cultural as well as religious activities. Following on from Denmark's nineteenth-century spiritual and national revival movement, personal and local identities have continued ever since to be connected closely to church and nation.

One of the constituent factors is the long tradition of historical research involving Danish churches or at least some of their elements. Seventeenth- and eighteenth-century antiquarians, such as the medical doctor and collector Ole Worm (1588–1654), would typically contact pastors in parishes all over Denmark in order to gather information concerning historical monuments (Jørgensen 1970, IX–X). The bishops and pastors were an obvious choice since they were educated people with knowledge of their local area and because of their previously mentioned status as state officials. Later antiquarian researchers used the same method (Jørgensen 1970: XXI–XXIII). In 1754 all Danish pastors were asked to supply answers to a detailed questionnaire from the architect Lauritz de Thurah for a planned topographic-historical description of Denmark, and the answers were incorporated into another large seven-volume topographic *Danske Atlas* by the bishop and historian Erik Pontoppidan (published 1763–81) (Weilbach 1924: 181).

In 1807 the newly established Royal Commission for the Keeping of Antiquities, the cradle of the National Museum, sent out questionnaires to all parish pastors in Denmark asking for information about historical remains in their parish, including runic stones, all sort of inscriptions in churches, all medieval pictures, and remains from the Catholic faith (Adamsen and Jensen 1995: 10–14). In some parishes the pastors read the questionnaire aloud from the pulpit to involve the parishioners in the antiquarian pursuit. The pastors' answers were incorporated in the still active antiquarian-topographic archive of the Danish National Museum, where all information is organized by parish. Even the prehistoric monuments and finds of ancient artifacts in Denmark were listed, until around 1984, in the so-called parish description (*sognebeskrivelsen*) kept in the Prehistoric Department of the National Museum, based on systematic surveys in the years 1873–1930 by the staff of the National Museum. An antiquarian system based on parishes seemed logical because the parishes with their medieval churches had been the most stable historical and administrative structures in Denmark.

The fact that the parish was for centuries the framework of historical-topographic studies went hand in hand with the equally old scientific acknowledgment that the churches themselves were sources of Danish history in the shape of inscriptions, pictures, gravestones, and epitaphs, that is, elements with inscriptions or heraldic information. The growth of nationalism and Romanticism in the nineteenth century spurred an interest in art-historical and architectural studies, giving the churches an enhanced scientific importance and drawing scholarly attention to the church buildings themselves as well as their furnishings. This scientific interest in churches combined with a much broader, popular movement peculiar to nineteenth-century Denmark: a steadily growing national awareness against a somber political background. After defeat in the Napoleonic Wars in 1814, the Danish king had to cede Norway to Sweden, and after the war against the combined forces of Prussia and Austria in 1864, Denmark lost the duchies of Schleswig-Holstein, including a large Danish population. The Denmark that remained was a small country with a very homogeneous population.

Since the beginning of the nineteenth century, artists and writers had worked to awaken an understanding of specifically Danish values, Danish landscape, and Danish history. An important figure was the author Bernhard Severin Ingemann (1789–1862), who in 1824–36 published a series of historical poems and novels dealing with Danish medieval history. His purpose was to raise the spirits of the Danish people with the help of national history. The poetic prologue of the first book, *Valdemar den Store og hans Mænd* (Valdemar the Great and his men; 1824), describes how Denmark had seemed to be on the edge of destruction once before but had arisen. It was possible to be inspired and uplifted by history (Ingemann 1824). The books were extremely popular and widely read, and they spread Ingemann's view of Denmark as a nation based on the Danish people, regardless of class and rank (Martinsen 2012). And since their plots made the Middle Ages come alive, they awakened an interest in historic monuments from that period, primarily the medieval churches that were to be found close at hand by readers all over Denmark.

Even more important for promoting historical and national awareness was the inspiration from the Danish pastor, poet, historian, and politician Nicolai F. S. Grundtvig (1783–1872). Grundtvig was a spokesman for enlightenment, but in his own fourfold interpretation: individual enlightenment, enlightenment for the people, the enlightenment of life, and Christian enlightenment. Individual enlightenment was a question of raising the spirits of each person by awakening fantasy, curiosity, and an understanding of the historical perspectives of his or her life. The next step was the enlightenment of the people, aiming at establishing a sense of belonging to a community of Danes living in Denmark. The enlightenment of life implies an even broader view, making us citizens of the world, while spiritual enlightenment entails experiencing the light of Christ.[6] The first two of these types of enlightenment were furthered by the establishment of so-called high schools (*højskoler*) for ordinary young Danish men and women. In these schools, which had no exams or tests, the teachers taught history, old Norse mythology, and other subjects that could open the eyes of the pupils to broader perspectives in their lives, side by side with practical subjects like gymnastics or woodwork. The aim of Grundtvig and his followers was to change the self-understanding of the rural population as expressed in the first motto of the high schools: "From peasants to a people" (*Fra almue til folk*) (Korsgaard 2013: 23–24). The work succeeded, as the ideology of these high schools not only flourished among farmers, but became influential at other levels of society too, and helped "conquer" Danish history and its historical monuments from the educated elite and make them a kind of common possession.

The texts from the songbook used in high schools, and in many other situations where Danes gather together, reflect this understanding of Danish identity, nature, and history. The first edition appeared in 1892, the nineteenth and most recent in 2020. The poet Jeppe Aakjær (1866–1930) wrote in his *The Song of History* from 1916:

> Just as the deepest well has the clearest water / and the best drink comes from deeply hidden springs / so is the heritage of the family of child and man / strengthened by the heritage of the people and its deep and strong memories. / Your own day is short, but that of your stock is long; / place your ear humbly at its roots; thousands of years carry sound in tears and songs, / while the new growth beckons towards eternity! – We seek the traces of our stock in objects large and small / in the stone axe unearthed after the plunging plough / in the treasure finds, coarse and rude, from the peat-bog, / in the ashlars of the church, laid by strong hands. (*Folkehøjskolens Sangbog* 2020: no. 505)

Interestingly, in historical terms this is a very early expression of "heritage of the people" (*folkets arv*) as being the property collectively of the nation, understood as a homogeneous people. Put simply, the nineteenth-century territorial contraction of Denmark evoked a strong sense of a unified and homogeneous nation undivided by class—a people who were the rightful heirs to a common material history, as evidenced and promoted in literature, song, pictorial media, and schools.

So the Danish churches are not only interesting historical sources, but they are still to the large majority of the Danish population a part of their family history. They are primarily seen not as aristocratic buildings but as something created by the Danish people for the Danish people, construed as the collective owners of this cultural heritage. And it is in the churches that one can meet the spirit of one's ancestors most directly. This sentiment has been popularized in many postwar publications, which extol the place of the village church as "the fixed center of the life of the village and of the whole parish" (Hastrup 1941: 9; cf. Exner and Finsen 1961: 14; Smedegaard Andersen 2013: 15; Fischer Møller 2013: 5). The statement is still valid. A comprehensive statistical survey from 2020 asked the respondents for their main motivations for being members of Folkekirken. The five most important arguments for membership were (1) I am a member because my parents had me baptized (65 percent), (2) I want to preserve the historical church buildings (60 percent), (3) I wish to have the right to use the services of the church if I want to (60 percent), (4) I want to support the Christian cultural heritage (58 percent), and (5) Being a Danish citizen I consider it a natural thing to be member of Folkekirken (51 percent). Only 43 percent answered that they were motivated by Christian faith (Poulsen et al. 2020).

Conclusion

Denmark has an unusual but efficient system for preserving its church heritage, at least with regard to the buildings belonging to the Danish state church. The Folkekirke is entwined with the Danish state, as the Danish monarch heads both church and state and as the Ministry of Ecclesiastical Affairs of the Danish government exercises authority over certain nontheological aspects of church administration. Via the church taxes that it collects from all official members of the Folkekirke (i.e., three-quarters of the population), the state also bankrolls salaries, operations, and maintenance of the churches. But the flow of decision-making is more complex than this top-down governance model might suggest; it is combined with a grassroots governance predicated on the autonomy of local congregations, which exercise substantial authority over the parish churches. Furthermore, all older church buildings of the Danish Lutheran Church are considered cultural heritage and hence are subject to oversight from experts of the Ministry of Culture and the National Museum, who act as advisers regarding heritage aspects. While all Folkekirke churches dating from more than one hundred years ago are considered cultural heritage, their preservation is mostly funded from the religious stream of state funding for the Folkekirke. Hence, the advice of heritage experts has limited scope, predicated on the idea that churches are living places of worship as well as cultural venues, where the local congregations enjoy primacy.

Church buildings embody something of real value to most Danes intellectually as well as emotionally. The great majority do not attend churches for weekly services, but occasionally they participate in baptisms, confirmations, weddings, and funerals, the important turning points in human life. Such emotionally laden moments tie most Danes and their churches together.

In addition to this, the parish churches act as the material reminders of common history and culture. This situation is an outgrowth of a specifically Danish Romanticist nationalism stemming from the nineteenth century, in which the nation came to be construed as homogeneous and unified.

Although the pattern of use of Danish churches shows the internationally recognizable development from obligation to individual choice, there is no obvious difference between younger and older age groups as consumers of what Danish churches have to offer, as one might have expected. It seems that all age groups seek cross-generation connections, cultural values, and personal experiences in their use of churches. To paraphrase Grace Davie's characterization of European religiosity as "believing without belonging" (Davie 1994), it is considered quite acceptable to "belong without believing" (Leth-Nissen 2018), thereby emphasizing the—perceived and enacted—singular unity of people, nation, state, and church in Denmark.

Ulla Kjær received her PhD in art history from the University of Copenhagen in 1988; doctoral degree (Dr.phil) in art history at the University of Copenhagen in 2010; and master's in education and human resource management from Roskilde University in 2010. She was editor at the scientific publication *Danmarks Kirker* (1988–94) and head of collection at the National Museum (1995–98). Since 1999, she has been curator / senior researcher at the National Museum, with responsibility for the statutory consultant service to the National Church. She has published about two hundred books and articles focusing on cultural history, Danish churches, museum history, and historic architecture, especially neoclassicism.

Poul Grinder-Hansen graduated in history from the University of Copenhagen in 1984 and in medieval archaeology from Aarhus University in 1986. In 1988, he became curator at the Collections of Middle Ages and Renaissance at the National Museum of Denmark. Since 2001, he has been curator and senior researcher. He has published about two hundred books and articles, both scientific and popular on a wide range of subjects, including mentality, iconography, museology, material culture, Renaissance history, and architecture as well as the cultural history of Danish churches.

NOTES

1. http://www.lutheranchurch.dk/faith-and-church-order/church-order/organisation-and-management/ (accessed 17 August 2019).
2. https://www.dst.dk/da/Statistik/emner/befolkning-og-valg/befolkning-og-befolkningsfremskrivning/folketal#, https://www.dst.dk/da/Statistik/emner/kultur-og-kirke/Folkekirken/medlemmer-af-Folkekirken (accessed 19 August 2019).
3. https://www.Folkekirken.dk/om-Folkekirken/organisation/sogn (accessed 19 August 2019).
4. Kommissionen for Mindesmærkernes Bevaring. The National Museum of Denmark, Antikvarisk-Topografisk Arkiv, Kasse IV, p.133.
5. *Dagbladet*, 30 January 1861.
6. U. Jonas, "Grundtvigs mange oplysninger," 2014, www.danmarkshistorien.dk/leksikon-og-kilder/vis/materiale/grundtvigs-mange-oplysninger (accessed 19 August 2019).

REFERENCES

Adamsen, Christian, and Vivi Jensen. 1995. *Danske præsters indberetninger til Oldsagskommissionen af 1807*, vol. 1. Højbjerg: Wormianum.
Agerbæk, Kirsten. 1984. *Høyen mellem klassicisme og romantik*. Esbjerg: Sydjysk Universitetsforlag.
Davie, Grace. 1994. *Religion in Britain since 1945: Believing without Belonging*. Oxford: John Wiley & Sons.
Exner, Johan, and Helge Finsen. 1961. *Kirken i landskabet*, Copenhagen: Gyldendal.
Fischer Møller, Peter. 2013. "Forord," in Leif Bahn, Kaj Bollmann, and Knud Munck (eds.), *Middelalderkirkens vedligeholdelse*. Roskilde: Roskilde Stift.
Folkehøjskolens Sangbog. 2020. 19th edn. Copenhagen: Forlaget Højskolerne.
Hastrup, Thure. 1941. *Vore gamle Kirker*. Copenhagen: Gyldendalske Boghandel Nordisk Forlag.
Hauge, Hans. 2013. *Danmark*. Aarhus: Aarhus Universitetsforlag.
Holm, Bo Kristian. 2017. *Reformationen*. Aarhus: Aarhus Universitetsforlag.
Ingemann, Bernhard Severin. 1824. *Valdemar den Store og hans Mænd*. Copenhagen.

Iversen, Hans Raun. 2015. "Kirkebygninger i religionsmodellens grænseflade," *Religionsvidenskabeligt Tidsskrift* 62: 29–44.
Jespersen, Knud J. V. 2011. *A History of Denmark*, 2nd edn. London: Palgrave Macmillan.
Jørgensen, Frank (ed.). 1970. *Præsteindberetninger til Ole Worm*, I. Copenhagen.
Kirker og Kirkegårde. En vejledning for menighedsråd. 2001. Copenhagen: Kirkeministeriet.
Kjær, Ulla. 2007a. "Oldnordisk Museum i felten," *Nyt fra Nationalmuseet* 114: 16–18.
Kjær, Ulla. 2007b. "Nationalmuseet i felten," *Nyt fra Nationalmuseet* 115: 4–7.
Kjær, Ulla. 2007c. "Opholdssted for statens samlinger," *Nyt fra Nationalmuseet* 116: 16–19.
Kjær, Ulla. 2013. *Roskilde Domkirke. Kunst og historie*. Copenhagen: Gyldendal.
Kjær, Ulla. 2014. "Kirker til salg – når kirker tages ud af brug," *Nationalmuseets Arbejdsmark* 2014: 252–65.
Kjær, Ulla, Kurt Søndergaard Nielsen, and Kirsten Trampedach. 1998. "Nationalmuseet i kirken," *Nationalmuseets Arbejdsmark* 1998: 167–183.
Kjærbøl, Helene. 2005. "Viborg domkirke nedrevet og genrejst," *Architectura* 27: 89–101.
Korsgaard, Ole. 2004. *En kristen stat. Kampen om Folket – et dannelsesperspektiv på dansk historie gennem 500 år*. Copenhagen: Gyldendal.
Korsgaard, Ole. 2013. *Folk*. Aarhus: Aarhus Universitetsforlag.
Kryger, Karin. 1977. "Restaureringen af romanske kirker i Danmark fra 1843 til ca. 1900." Unpublished manuscript, University of Copenhagen.
Leth-Nissen, Karen Marie. 2018. "Churching Alone: A Study of the Danish Folk Church at Organisational, Individual and Societal Levels." PhD dissertation, defended at the Faculty of Theology, University of Copenhagen, Det teologiske Fakultet.
Lockhart, Paul Douglas. 2007. *Denmark 1513–1660: The Rise and Decline of a Renaissance Monarchy*. Oxford: Oxford University Press.
Madsen, Hans Helge. 1983. *Meldahls rædselsprogram*. Copenhagen: Nyt Nordisk Forlag Arnold Busck.
Martinsen, Lone Kølle. 2012. "Bondefrihed og andre verdensbilleder. Idehistoriske studier af B.S. Ingemanns Danmarkshistorie 1824–1836," *TEMP. Tidsskrift for historie* 5: 75–104.
Mellon, James. 1992. *Og gamle Danmark – en beskrivelse af Danmark i det Herrens år 1992*. Viby: Centrum.
Molesworth, Robert. 1694. *An Account of Denmark as It Was in 1692*. London: Goodwin.
Mollerup, William. 1908. *Nationalmuseets anden Afdeling. Redegørelse for dens Virksomhed siden 1892*. Copenhagen: Thiele.
Olden-Jørgensen, Sebastian. 2005. "Robert Molesworth's 'An Account of Denmark as It Was in 1692': A Political Scandal and Its Literary Aftermath," in K. Haakonssen and H. Horstbøll (eds.), *Northern Antiquities and National Identities*. Copenhagen: Det Kongelige Danske Videnskabernes Selskab.
Østergaard, Uffe. 2012. "Danish National Identity," in M. C. Gertsen, A. M. Søderberg, and M. Zølner (eds.), *Global Collaboration: Intercultural Experiences and Learning*. London: Palgrave Macmillan, pp. 37–55.
Poulsen, Jais, Astrid Krabbe Trolle, Maiken Friischman Larsen, and Bjarke Schønwandt Mortensen. 2020. *Religiøsitet og forholdet til folkekirken 2020. Bog 1 – Kvantitative Studier*. Copenhagen: Folkekirkens uddannelses- og videnscenter
Salling, Emma. 1975. *Kunstakademiets Guldmedalje Konkurrencer 1755–1857*. Copenhagen: Kunstakademiets Bibliotek.

Smedegaard Andersen, Lisbeth. 2013. *Huset med de mange boliger*, Copenhagen: Kristeligt Dagblad.
Smidt, Claus M. 2018. "Fredning og bevaring før bygningsfredningsloven," in C. M. Smidt et al. (eds.), *Hele samfundets eje. Bygningsfredning i 100 år*, Copenhagen: Foreningen til gamle Bygningers Bevaring.
Sværke, Anne Grethe. 2010. *Nybygt af gammel art*. Århus: Skippershoved.
Trampedach, Kirsten. 2018. "Decision-Making Based on Dialogue: Preservation of Danish Churches under the Consultancy of the National Museum," in A. Heritage and J. Copithorne (eds.), *Sharing Conservation Decisions: Current Issues and Future Strategies*. Rome: ICCROM, pp. 131–41.
Vadstrup, Søren. 2018. *Genius loci. Bygningskulturens immatrielle værdier*. Aarhus and Copenhagen: Aarhus School of Architecture/Design School Kolding/Royal Danish Academy.
Vellev, Jens. 1981a. "Viborg domkirkes vestfront," *Hikuin* 7: 107–38.
Vellev, Jens. 1981b. "Professorens kirke," *Skalk* 1: 3–8.
Vellev, Jens. 1987. *Joakim Skovgaards fresco-malerier i Viborg Domkirke*. Viborg: Viborg Domkirke.
Weilbach, Frederik. 1924. *Lauritz Thura*. Copenhagen: Selskabet til udgivelse af danske Mindesmærker.

CHAPTER 4

World-Heritagization, Bureaucratization, and Hybridization in Two Religious Heritage Sites in Denmark

Sofie Isager Ahl, Rasmus Rask Poulsen, and Oscar Salemink

Introduction

In this chapter we explore how the authority of heritage and church policies are balanced in practice with the relative autonomy of individual Protestant congregations inside the Evangelical-Lutheran state Church of Denmark (Folkekirken), based on ethnography in two of the three World Heritage Sites with living church congregations: the Jelling Mounds, Runic Stones and Church (inscribed in 1994), and Roskilde Cathedral (1995).[1] We examine the multilayered and intertwined organization of the churches and their management as cultural heritage, as the growing number of visitors, who may not be primarily motivated by religious considerations, require the careful management of different uses of the churches. Well before World Heritage inscription, both Jelling and Roskilde were considered iconic sites in Danish history as monuments of the uniquely Danish convergence of state, nation, Lutheran state church, and royalty. As Lutheran churches, Jelling and Roskilde were since the Reformation subject to state governance in Denmark's undivided state-church nexus and were the object of cultural preservation policies since the nineteenth century.[2] Following their late-twentieth-century World Heritage status, both sites have been subject to different forms of what Chiara De Cesari calls "World-Heritagization" (2012: 409), which imposes additional layers of national and international heritage oversight to what are now considered heritage sites and hence complicates their management. As a complication of the simultaneous secularizing and sacralizing aspects of heritagization (see the introduction to this volume), the idea of World-Heritagization affords more analytical purchase than its companion term "UNESCOization," used by De Cesari (2012: 400) but also by David Berliner (2012: 776).

The growing literature on the relations between state, cultural heritage, and World Heritage shows how tensions arise when the grand ideals and costly requirements of UNESCO's World Heritage Committee are implemented locally in various political, social, and cultural contexts (Harrison and Hitchcock 2005; Waterton and Watson 2011; Brumann and Berliner 2016). A central topic in heritage studies is the relation between state authorities and local stakeholders, because, as formulated by Salemink (2016: 319), "heritage claims invariably bring in the state as the arbiter, guarantor, and protector of heritage. The global model for heritage practices is given by UNESCO, which assigns special responsibilities to the state." Given the appeal to national identity, states have a seeming institutional monopoly to both define heritage values and manage them based on present-day imaginaries of a national past (Herzfeld 2015: 531). Rosemary Coombe and Lindsay Weiss (2015) argue that the recent emergence of various local entities of authority complicates our view of heritage management as primarily an intertwined state-society or central-decentral relationship. Instead, local heritage management is an amalgamation of international policies of UNESCO and ICOMOS, national legislation about heritage preservation, and local practices and configurations. This casts nation-states as entities that distribute governmental powers over various local government agencies, boards, and joint or cooperative programs tasked with heritage management in what Coombe and Weiss (2015: 45–46) term "heritage governmentality." In this chapter, we operationalize this local-cum-global governmentality through the concepts of heritage purification, hybridization, and institutional proliferation.

In their chapter for this volume, Ulla Kjær and Poul Grinder-Hansen conclude that the management of the church buildings of the Danish state church is done through a hybrid institutional entwinement of (religious) church and (secular) state authorities, with simultaneous bottom-up self-governance by local congregations and top-down oversight and funding on behalf of the central state. In line with other scholars, they simultaneously emphasize the—perceived and enacted—unity of people, nation, state, and church in Denmark (Kjær 2013; Schütze 2013; Warburg 2013). This union represents a vision of national identity where, as Cecilie Rubow writes, "Christianity is an integral part of the foundational myth Danes live by, blossoming from time immemorial, the earth, and from the generations" (Rubow 2011: 98). This chapter takes these observations as points of departure while investigating in more ethnographic detail the church-congregation-state-heritage nexus in Jelling and Roskilde, respectively.

Purifying the Jelling Monuments

This section shows how the management of the Jelling Monuments resulted in a partial spatial cleansing motivated by heritage purification. In 1994 the Jelling site was inscribed on the World Heritage List as the first Danish site. It presents an example of the professionalization of heritage management against the backdrop of World Heritage inscription, drawing in not just state and church in Denmark, but also the local parish council and various religious and secular authorities as advisory or supervisory representatives on heritage management councils.

The Jelling site is a monument complex, which consists of Jelling Church, two runic stones, two large mounds, as well as the recently discovered remains of a stone ship setting and palisade wall, which in turn largely defines the perimeter of the monument site. Established in the late tenth century, the bigger runic stone marks the foundation of Denmark as a unified Christian nation and people, popularly known in Denmark as the "baptism certificate" of the Danish nation. The mounds and runic stones were erected by King Gorm the Old (c. 950) and his son King Harald Blåtand (c. 965). Nationally, the site holds unique value in Danish history because it monumentalizes the formation of the unified Danish nation under the rule of King Harald and because it marks the conversion from Norse Pagan religion to Christianity in Denmark. The site contains two almost identical mounds situated on either side of a twelfth-century Romanesque parish church built in limestone. By the entrance of the church, and coincidentally at the midpoint between each mound, stand the runic stone erected by King Harald and the one of King Gorm, which was moved there as well. Harald's stone heralds his achievement as the king who unified Norway and Denmark and who christened the Danes.[3]

Jelling town is administratively governed by Vejle Municipality, but the Agency for Culture and Palaces (Slots- og Kulturstyrelsen) under the Ministry of Culture is responsible for the protection of the ancient monuments, while the National Museum of Denmark conducts research, advises, and operates the Kongernes Jelling (Home of the Viking Kings) visitor center adjacent to the monuments. The heritage site is in principle open to the public, and visitors are not charged admission fees for the site nor for the visitor center. The center offers tourists various modern exhibits on Jelling's history, the Viking Age, and the monuments' central position in Danish history, as well as—for a fee—professional guided tours and lectures for visitors. The visitor center on the site receives a growing number of tourists, now over two hundred thousand per year, many of whom also visit the small church, but as a regular parish church it also holds regular religious services and cultural events for the local congregation.[4] However, the cost of hosting the church visitors falls to the parish, even though the usage by tourists dwarfs the use by local parishioners. In cooperation with Kongernes Jelling, the parish council has arranged for daily guided tours within the church around noon for a sum of DKK 30 (EUR 4), facilitated by the visitor center. This arrangement to secure a balance between the interests of tourists and parishioners has meant that private guided tours are not allowed within the church, in order to alleviate tension between religious uses (local churchgoers seeking peace) and secular uses (as a tourist attraction). The balance between different uses of the church is maintained by the church sexton, who stops tourists in the church portal who try to enter during Sunday service, but on at least one occasion we observed tourists visiting the church during a baptism.

During the twentieth-century revaluation of Jelling as the birthplace of the Danish nation, antiquarian preservation resulted in attempts to make the monuments stand out and hence more conspicuous in a process of what we call heritage purification—that is, the removal from a designated heritage site of everything that detracts from an undisturbed heritage gaze by reminding of other human activity. This purification was physically enacted by clearing a large number of houses in the immediate environment of the mounds, including some of the oldest in the town and one listed building (Christensen 2016), through what Michael Herzfeld called spatial cleansing:

> This term incorporates an intentional allusion to the notion of ethnic cleansing, since . . . both entail the disruption of fundamental security, and especially of ontological security, for entire groups of people. Spatial cleansing means the conceptual and physical clarification of boundaries, with a concomitant definition of former residents as intruders. (Herzfeld 2006: 142)

A series of archaeological excavations from 2006 and onward led to significant discoveries around the UNESCO site. A team of archaeologists uncovered remnants of a stone ship structure, a burial form from the Viking Age, and of a surrounding wooden palisade wall, which suddenly enlarged the perimeter of the monument area to twelve hectares (see figure 4.1). These discoveries led to a concentrated effort to present the existing World Heritage Site within an enlarged setting of the palisade, stone ship, and Viking dwelling remnants (Jessen et al. 2014). By 2009 a steering committee was founded by Vejle Municipality along with church authorities, the influential A. P. Møller Foundation,[5] the Jelling Tourist branch, the Agency for Culture and Palaces, the National Museum, and local museums. It sought to develop and improve the visitor experience of the site in order to live up to its World Heritage status. This resulted in a large-scale spatial clearing of the monument site and surrounding areas and the visible marking of the underground archaeological remains, lasting several years. Its completion coincided with the 2015 reopening of the Kongernes Jelling visitor center. The emergent

Figure 4.1. View of a field cleared of houses (left of the footpath) next to the northern mound, on a so-called Jelling Music Day, which brought together many spectators. In the distance one can see the white poles that follow the contours of the former palisade wall. © Sofie Isager Ahl, 2017.

professionalization of the Jelling site was cemented in 2013, when UNESCO asked that a site manager to be appointed. In line with official Danish church governance, this position was to be filled by the parish council.[6]

Management of the Jelling Monuments is formally organized between a steering committee, a cooperation council, and the UNESCO site manager. The last position is filled by the parish clerk of Jelling Church, employed by the Jelling parish council, who acts as the daily caretaker and monitor of the site. Thus, the daily management rests with Jelling parish council, as one of two primary site owners, along with Vejle Municipality. Supervision of the World Heritage Site therefore rests with church authorities (deanery and diocese) in cooperation with the National Museum. The reason for the divided supervision has to do with the composite nature of the monument complex, with both (secular) cultural-historical and religious (church) elements. The central non-church authorities that the site manager deals with are the Danish Agency for Culture and Palaces, Kongernes Jelling, and Vejle Municipality, all three government entities, while the Danish Lutheran Church remains undivided from the state as well. While the local parish council enjoys a great deal of autonomy, the church is largely funded by the taxes paid by its members and some additional state funding and is institutionally governed by the state, through the Ministry of Ecclesiastical Affairs. And as Kjær and Grinder-Hansen make clear elsewhere in this volume, buildings of the Danish Lutheran Church are subject to a system of preservation directed by the church authorities, with input from the National Museum when it comes to heritage preservation.

In short, World Heritage management of Danish churches is divided into three levels of governance. Nationally, the general responsibility for protection and management rests with the Danish Agency for Culture and Palaces, which coordinates relations between the site, the national state, and UNESCO. Locally, the site itself is managed by the parish council in Jelling and by Vejle Municipality in consultation with the National Museum (which operates the local visitor center), church authorities, the local municipality, and local museum authorities. Due to the nature of the site as an active church, a churchyard, and a national monument, the daily monitoring happens by the site manager employed by the parish council, in cooperation with staff at the local visitor center operated by the National Museum. Lastly, management is further formalized as a partnership in two different councils, for whom the site manager act as secretary and liaison. In 2013 the previous steering committee for the restoration of the monument site was transformed into the Cooperation Council (Samarbejdsgruppen), with local, regional, and national partners, also known as "the primary partners" of the UNESCO site. This council is made up of representatives from state and government institutions: Danish Agency for Culture and Palaces, the National Museum, Vejle Municipality, the Vejle Museums, Jelling local council, and church authorities from Jelling parish and Vejle deanery. The role of this co-operative council is to coordinate general management of the monument area. The council revises the management plan every four years and distributes information about events and construction projects relevant to the UNESCO site. In practice, the council negotiates and coordinates all the various practical issues that emerge because the monuments are a World Heritage Site, including answering inquiries about the usage of the monument site. Officially, these sorts of questions from the public are the resort of the local government, Vejle Municipality, but in order to lessen bureaucracy this was subsumed in the council's area of competence.

In 2017, the Cooperation Council was supplemented by a new steering committee consisting of representatives from the same organizations but with specified representation from the National Museum, Vejle Municipality, a local council, and the Haderslev diocese, but without the A. P. Møller Foundation (as the major funder). The new Steering Committee strove to manage the World Heritage values of the Jelling site according to the management plan, which is continually revised and approved. In this sense, the group overlooks the *big-picture* aspects of Jelling as a UNESCO site. The group discusses potential nomination alterations and is responsible for the strategic development of the site (such as a plan for sustainable tourism management) as well as construction projects in the surrounding area. Together with the Cooperation Council and the Steering Comittee, the site manager seeks to manage the Jelling Monuments according to the standards of UNESCO. In effect, these groups represent an amalgamation of interested parties from local, regional, and national levels of government, church, and civil society. In spite of this institutional proliferation, the core of everyday management, the practical and operational unit of running the Jelling Monuments as a World Heritage Site, rests with an employee of Jelling parish council, in line with the Danish law on church buildings and churchyards; the parish council is an autonomous, locally elected body. In other words, the only way that local citizens of Jelling could exercise any influence over the World Heritage Site in their backyard was through the parish council, and that naturally applied only to members of the Danish state church (*Folkekirken*), who make up almost 75 percent of the national population.[7] As we shall see in the next paragraph, the institutional proliferation was a way to deal with mounting local tensions over the management of the rising tourist numbers.

Localizing World Heritage

In this section we will show how these conflicts occurred against the backdrop of the inevitable professionalization and bureaucratization attending the World-Heritagization, resulting in a sense of underrepresentation and disenfranchisement among many local residents. Since the reopening of the Kongernes Jelling visitor center, many Jelling residents felt that the town was overrun by tourists and that something had to be amended in the local management of the World Heritage. Indeed, in 2016, 2017, and 2018 a number of conflicts erupted involving the relations between parish and local citizens over the use of the church and the heritage area. In 2016, Vejle Municipality and the local council (*lokalrådet*) of Jelling town proposed the establishment of a Viking-themed playground near the site of the remains of the palisade wall, now marked with concrete poles. This was then rejected by the parish council which—as a local chapter of the state church—is responsible for the church and partly for the World Heritage. The chair of the parish council offered that "the ancient palisade walls of Harald Blåtånd should not be plastered over with a theme park. . . . When you own land that is World Heritage you have to be careful, and then you should build a playground somewhere else." In a similar vein, the UNESCO site manager, who is also the secretary of the parish council, opposed plans for a solar panel plant in town, saying, "We think ICOMOS might have something against that, so we raised an objection against the local development plan." This upset local citizens who protested, "Why would the parish council interfere in that?" A group of local citizens expressed frustration with this "church meddling" in what they saw as a "living town," which was made possible by the key role of the parish council in managing the World Heritage. These citizens felt that their town had become World Heritage without their input, while they had to bear the consequences of living in a site governed according to ICOMOS standards. In order to gain decision-making influence, they decided to take the—in the Danish context—unusual step of politicizing the local parish council elections by contesting all eight seats. In the end, six of the eight incumbent parish councilors stepped down, and a new council was elected without vote. However, no Viking-themed playground has been built yet.[8]

In 2017, a series of meetings were held over the management of the town, the heritage, and the church, as many local residents thought that the site was overrun by tourists. A parish council meeting in August sought to deal with the increased numbers of tourists and the interference with services and ceremonies in the church and graveyard. In line with the parish council's official role in the management of the World Heritage Site, this meeting exuded a "can do" attitude by proposing a new management plan (*Forvaltningsplan*) plan for the area. A public meeting for town residents in October 2017, on the other hand, was characterized by a more gloomy atmosphere, where attendants kept on talking past each other, failing to resolve the strained relations between parties. While the frame of reference for officials in charge of the World Heritage Site, the visitor center, and local museums were the UNESCO and ICOMOS guidelines, local residents asked hard questions about what the UNESCO inscription had brought local residents and wanted to know whether the World Heritage is equally concerned about local residents as about tourists: "What is being done for the Jelling residents rather than for the tourists? We have only lost things, and you're only talking about tourists. What about traffic issues?" The chairperson of the parish council admitted that "it's as if we have a really nice piece of meat, but the plate is just a bit too small." In April 2018, a town meeting was convened over a plan to build new houses on the fringe of the monument area (*randbebyggelse*), right where years previously houses were razed in order to beautify the heritage area. Under the title "Revolt against local council: citizens want to be heard too" (*Oprør mod lokalråd: Borgere vil også høres*), the local daily *Vejle Amts Folkeblad* reported that some angry residents spoke out against the plan, some referring to its putative unacceptability to UNESCO. The local councilors were re-elected without contestation, however. During a second meeting in May 2018, the UNESCO site manager assured that the building plans would not violate UNESCO rules, but the chairperson of the parish council expressed protest against the plans. The resulting distrust led to the local council's chairman stepping down in August 2018.[9]

These meetings show that there was some local discontent over the lack of influence of Jelling citizens over the World Heritage and its impact on the town; over the strong role of the parish council in heritage management in comparison with that of local residents; over the importunity of the massive increase of tourists in the church and town and the lack of shared benefits; and over planning decisions made by outside agencies that have the interests of the heritage and its visitors at heart, but allegedly not those of local residents. The difference of the relative bargaining strength of local citizens in comparison with the local parish council in heritage matters was palpable. After a recent, post-UNESCO restoration of the church (in combination with archaeological and art-historical research), the church was also thoroughly renovated, with the laying of a new, modern tile floor and new stained glass windows. This reflects the respect of the Danish heritage authorities for churches as living sites of worship, but in UNESCO World Heritage Sites it is unusual to modernize crucial elements of the site. How this was justified to UNESCO is unclear, but this is testimony to the limits of World-Heritagization in the face of the fundamental hybridity of the church as, at once, heritage site and living site of worship. The institutional strength of the parish as an autonomous unit and hence of the local congregation stands in stark contrast with the cleansing of the heritage "buffer zone" of houses, no matter how old and valuable they are; even in the highly secularized Danish society, the local parish is strong, but the local community less so. That difference can be explained through the combination of top-down heritage preservation according to UNESCO guidelines, with practical heritage management by a site manager employed by a local church body that enjoys a high degree of autonomy.

This section provided a snapshot of some of the tensions evoked by the management of a Danish church as World Heritage. The increase in bureaucracy with external representation from church and government authorities in recent years shows how the recent World-Heritagization of Jelling has added more layers of professionalization and bureaucratization of heritage management and more lines of upward accountability, against the backdrop of local discontent with growing tourist numbers encroaching on the town and the church. Still, professional responsibility for management is anchored in the local parish council as the officially appointed steward of World Heritage, resulting in a hybrid religious-cum-heritage management setup entangled in a web of secular heritage bureaucracy. Some local town residents, on the other hand, feel underrepresented in the various management bodies, with little influence over the heritage impact on their town outside the parish council. The following section on Roskilde Cathedral will dwell on the combined institutional proliferation and hybridization against the backdrop of World-Heritagization.

Religious Propagation and Heritage Communication at Roskilde Cathedral

Founded in its current form in the late twelfth century, Roskilde Cathedral was Denmark's second site to be inscribed in the World Heritage List, in 1995. The cathedral was inscribed to the World Heritage List because it is deemed an outstanding example of the earliest Christian church complexes in northern Europe built in brick and for the successive architectural styles that have been added to the church through the centuries. This can be seen in the various ancillary chapels and porches of the cathedral, which since the sixteenth century has been the national burial grounds for the Danish royal family. The continuing addition of burial chapels makes this grand cathedral a place of national importance as the royal burial monument. Together with Jelling, the Roskilde Cathedral thus monumentalizes a union between Christianity, the Danish nation, and its royal family (Kjær 2013; Schütze 2013; Warburg 2013). In this sense, the two sites represent a historically rooted combination of secular (cultural, national) and religious interests and values. Like the Jelling parish, Roskilde Cathedral is also a functioning parish church within the Danish state church and is governed by the parish council and the diocese.

As an outstanding architectural monument, Roskilde Cathedral has for a long time been a listed heritage site in Denmark and a tourist attraction just outside the greater Copenhagen area. Within the past decade, the World Heritage label has emerged as an increasingly important part of the Cathedral's iconicity as a national heritage site and as a tourist attraction. A curious but telling indication of this World Heritage boom in Roskilde is the fact that it was not until 2015, twenty years after its World Heritage inscription, that an official UNESCO plaque was put up next to the main entrance of the cathedral. This hesitant World-Heritagization of the cathedral is also brought out by a conflict and subsequent solution over the proper way of funding a visitor center at the cathedral. This section shows how the case of a proposed visitor center in Roskilde in response to World Heritage requirements amplified the ambiguity that exists where church and cultural heritage converge in the religion-as-heritage complex in Denmark.

In line with the state-mandated governance of church and heritage in Denmark, the management of Roskilde Cathedral as a World Heritage Site resembles that of Jelling in that the local parish has a large degree of autonomy and local sovereignty, which in Roskilde is compounded by the fact that the cathedral is also the site for the Roskilde deanery (*provsti*) and diocese (*stift*). There are also important differences in how the Roskilde site is managed, the most significant one being that the parish council of the cathedral has set up neither an external steering committee nor a management group. In a periodic report to UNESCO, this sort of an external representational organ for management and supervision was "not considered relevant."[10] This means in practice that, like in Jelling, the main responsibility for management of the cathedral as a World Heritage Site rests with the parish council, as stated in church law. While maintenance and preservation of the church's structure in terms of its World Heritage value and as a cathedral of national importance are the responsibility of the parish council and employees of the church, the National Museum and local Roskilde museums are periodically consulted.

Apart from the regular funding and supervision structure for all church buildings in Denmark, Roskilde Cathedral annually receives specialized funding by the Danish state because of its national-historical importance. Thus, the state provides earmarked funds for restoration projects in the cathedral each year, where the Ministry of Ecclesiastical Affairs has been responsible for covering expenses for ordinary maintenance and restoration of the royal burial chapels inside the cathedral, which are subsidized annually through the state budget along with funding for extraordinary projects.[11] This continued government funding and the special supervisory arrangement regarding heritage aspects show us that already before World Heritage inscription, the management of Roskilde Cathedral entailed a certain degree of cooperation with various church and government agencies on cultural heritage preservation.

During a quiet first decade following the inscriptions of the Jelling (1994) and Roskilde (1995) sites, not much importance was attached to World Heritage status. This changed in the mid- to late 2000s, when interest in World Heritage began to set in among tourists, locals, and state agencies alike. In line with the global "heritage fever" since the mid-2000s, interest and pride in World Heritage status surged in Denmark, in part encouraged by UNESCO via the Danish Agency for Culture and Palaces. In line with this emergent interest and with formal requirements on the part of UNESCO, Roskilde parish council presented in 2010 the first plans for an underground visitor center to the public. The church stated that when built, the center would accommodate the standards expected of a World Heritage Site from tourists and heritage agencies (which at the time was deemed inadequate by UNESCO), with an estimated price tag of DKK 68 million (EUR 9 million).

Figure 4.2. A special section cordoned off for religious worshipers in Roskilde Cathedral. © Oscar Salemink, 2018.

However, the project of the visitor center was complicated because of the intricate organization and legislation regarding Danish churches and their responsibility for cultural heritage preservation. The heart of the matter was a concern about what kind of public funding of churches within the Danish state church could legally be used or not used for this purpose. As part of the Danish state church, the cathedral is primarily a religious site intended for worship, which implied that it cannot use church funds for a visitor center, which services tourists rather than worshipers, and hence serving cultural rather than religious purposes. The debate surrounding the visitor center at Roskilde Cathedral reveals a core tension between heritage communication (*formidling*) and religious propagation (*forkyndelse*) when churches in Denmark become World Heritage Sites (Figure 4.2). As described in detail by Lisbeth Christoffersen, professor of law and religion at Roskilde University, the initial plan for the funding was to collect church taxes, admission fees to the cathedral, and private grants as funding for the establishment of a modern underground visitor facility situated near the cathedral (Christoffersen 2015). The parish council had requested about DKK 500,000 (EUR 67,000) of church funds (*ligningsmidler*) to partially support the project, but the Roskilde deanery committee forwarded the request to the diocesan authority of Roskilde diocese. The deanery and diocese proved skeptical about the proposed model of using church taxes for a heritage-related visitor center servicing tourists—that is, for heritage communication rather than religious propagation—and asked the bishop of Roskilde and a state-employed regional director of the diocese to assess the legal framing of subsidizing such a project via church taxes.

In 2013 the diocese determined that a sum of about DKK 300,000 (EUR 40,000) could be allocated from admission fees from the cathedral to the fund, as these were not part of the subsidies collected from church members (Christoffersen 2015: 83). This resolved the dispute about whether the visitor center required by UNESCO could be funded by the church, with the outcome that income from commercial activities like admission fees to the cathedral could be allocated to the project, but not church funds. An expert on church law, Christoffersen calls this a "clarification of competence" between the religious (*forkyndelse*) and heritage (*formidling*) responsibilities of the cathedral, in the form of a demarcation of the parish council's authority over and autonomy to dispose its given (church) budget (Christoffersen 2015: 85). Talking about the project, the UNESCO site manager in charge of the cultural heritage expressed this responsibility and budgetary divergence as follows:

> The church is primarily a religious institution and cultural heritage dissemination is not its main responsibility. Some churches experience it as a challenge to balance these two things (i.e., heritage and church functions).... A church like

Roskilde Cathedral, which has this big, heavy heritage, assumes responsibility for heritage promotion and education, but the primary task of a church is religious and running the church as a place of worship.

Here, the UNESCO site manager clearly prioritizes *forkyndelse* (religious propagation) over *formidling* (heritage dissemination), showing the double bind in which he found himself.

The situation was compounded by disagreement in the parish council over the question whether entrance fees should be imposed. In November 2013, the vice-chairwoman who was in favor of free entrance—and hence on the side of *forkyndelse* rather than *formidling*, predicated on the idea that the church should be open to all—was deposed.[12] But entrance fees were not enough to fund the project, and despite initial hopes, no church funds could be allocated to the project within the current funding scheme framework for parish councils within the Danish state church, even though ultimately the source is the same, namely taxes collected by the Danish state. Yet, a parish council under the Danish state church has to consult with its respective deanery committee over the disposal of its funding and can potentially be assessed by church authorities, thus revealing its limited financial autonomy. The case of the funding of a UNESCO-mandated visitor center attached to Roskilde Cathedral shows that even though church and heritage funds ultimately come from the state, funds from church taxes are earmarked for religious activities under the rubric of *forkyndelse* and hence cannot be used for nonreligious purposes like servicing tourists.

Institutional Proliferation and Hybridization

In 2013, after funding for the visitor center proved harder to acquire than initially thought, control of the project was transferred from the parish council to an external foundation, the Fund for Communication of Cultural Heritage in Roskilde (Fonden for formidlingen af kulturarven i Roskilde). In 2015 another external foundation was constituted, namely the Development Fund for a Communication Center of the Cultural Heritage of Roskilde Cathedral (Anlægsfonden Formidlingscenter Kulturarven Roskilde Domkirke), whose purpose was to support the first foundation by acquiring the funds needed for the visitor center project. The UNESCO site manager and director of communication for Roskilde Cathedral was initially employed by the parish council, but the formal employment relationship was transferred when he became the director of both foundations, while both boards of trustees count the same representatives from the Danish Agency for Culture and Palaces, the National Museum, Roskilde parish council, and Roskilde Municipality:

While nobody disagreed with the plan to establish a visitor center, one encountered a bit of resistance against *fundraising* for the construction of a visitor center. There was concern that private foundations would not be willing to support such a project if it was managed by a church organization. Therefore it was decided to establish an independent commercial foundation, with the task to disseminate the cultural heritage of Roskilde Cathedral and to raise funds for the establishment and manage a visitor center. I was employed by the parish council, but I am now transferred to the foundation. That means that the dissemination tasks were separated from the parish council, but there is still close collaboration with the parish council. And so the Agency for Culture, the National Museum, the parish council, and Roskilde Municipality appoint the five members of the board, for which I am director and secretary. And they have now more dissemination-professional access, but there is still a link with the parish council in the sense that a parish council member sits on the board of the foundation. And some agreements were made on how to practically handle an organization next to a church organization. And that functions really smoothly.

Thus a potential conflict over funding for the visitor center required by UNESCO was externalized by setting up additional bureaucratic layers with representation from the same agencies through the same people, resulting in a process of institutional proliferation and simultaneous hybridization against the backdrop of the World-Heritagization of Roskilde Cathedral. As we will elaborate below, this hybridization stands in contrast to the heritage purification of the environment of the heritage site, as in Jelling.

In 2016 and 2017, two other World Heritage–related institutions were added by Roskilde Cathedral's parish council, thereby further hybridizing responsibility for cultural heritage management. The first of these was the World Heritage Committee (Verdensarvsudvalg) set up in 2016 as an internal committee to the parish council tasked with handling all World Heritage affairs. The other, the World Heritage Council (Verdensarvsråd), was set up in 2017 with internal representation from the parish council itself and external representation from relevant local organizations in Roskilde, including Roskilde Municipality, local museums, local tourist organizations, local businesses, Roskilde University, and local schools and colleges. The purpose of this external council was to improve the dissemination of information about the World Heritage Site and to involve interested parties from the area in order to handle common and diverging interests emerging in Roskilde over its World Heritage Site.[13] With the addition of the World Heritage Council made up of representatives from secular society (experts and state authorities), most matters of promoting Roskilde Cathedral as a UNESCO World Heritage Site have been formally removed from the parish council's sphere, marking a further "clarification of competence" between what the church authorities can and cannot do regarding the cultural heritage aspect of the cathedral. As Ulla Kjær and Poul Grinder-Hansen make clear in their chapter to this volume, the church already carries a legal responsibility to maintain its cultural heritage. In practice, the separation between religious and heritage functions and the consequent clarification of competence (cf. Christoffersen 2015) seem primarily to be a question of how church funds are handled, but ultimately the funding comes from the state, regardless whether it is channeled via religious or cultural institutions. Yet, handling this state funding requires a clarification of competence between religious and heritage interests in the cathedral, which is achieved through institutional proliferation.

Our research began in January 2017—that is, after most of the organizational and institutional changes had taken place—with a meeting that took place in the office building next to the cathedral, which is in use by the priests, the parish council, and also by the UNESCO site manager. The site manager emphasized the close working relationship between the church and heritage officials at the cathedral:

> It's quite important to say that I do not have any formal division between me and my colleagues. You can look in there, I am sitting in the same room as all the others. My paycheck just comes from another place and my superiors are someone else than the parish council. . . . In practice, I rarely do anything that is not in close collaboration with the church.

In other words, the UNESCO site manager extolled the smooth collaboration with the church and the parish council made possible by the separation of religious and heritage functions and his transfer from the first to the latter. Unfortunately we could not triangulate the interviews through ethnographic research at Roskilde Cathedral, hence our findings about the process of clarification of competence between religious and heritage management interests are limited.

The proliferation of the site manager's formal affiliations reflects the organizational changes needed for developing a visitor center in Roskilde, resulting in increased involvement of external government and nongovernment parties in the professionalization, bureaucratization, and institutionalization of heritage management. In effect, the autonomous existence of the parish council has become increasingly bureaucratized, as decisions about heritage management were hybridized through institutional proliferation involving the very same agencies and people. It is clear that this worked, for in the early spring of 2018, the foundation to establish the visitor center announced that, eight years after the project was first presented to the public, it would open in 2022. Plans include exhibition facilities, a café, and other amenities for the approximately 150,000 annual visitors to the cathedral, for an estimated price of DKK 115 million (EUR 15.8 million).

The development in Roskilde Cathedral from lacking interest in UNESCO World Heritage status to an increased interest coincided with a development from relative autonomy of the parish council to increased bureaucratization against the backdrop of its World-Heritagization. The resolution and aftermath to the deliberations over the visitor center reveal a bureaucratic tension over the overlapping competencies between the local autonomy of the parish council and the centralized authority of state and church. This tension was defused through the institutional proliferation of various boards and foundations with their shared purposes in relation to World Heritage, with the same agencies and the same people taking part in these various committees in Roskilde. This illustrates how the ongoing World-Heritagization of Roskilde Cathedral is predicated on institutional proliferation and their simultaneous hybridization, as these twin processes make it virtually impossible to practically distinguish between church and heritage interests and lines of accountability. Thus, by creating more hybrid entities responsible for the World Heritage Site and the visitor center, the so-called clarification of competence occurred within the very same circle of agencies and people, creating a specific hybrid context for the management of religious heritage as part of the Danish state church and as World Heritage.

Conclusion: World-Heritagization and Its Discontents

Both the Jelling and Roskilde sites were already considered national heritage before they were listed as World Heritage and therefore did not generate much attention in terms of regulation or publicity during the first decade after World Heritage inscription. This only began to change when these two sites began to experience the effects of the UNESCO label as an international brand in the tourist market and as a "quality control" device requiring adherence to specific regulations and "best practices." In both cases, World-Heritagization added other bureaucratic layers in response to UNESCO professional management requirements, in particular regarding the establishment of visitor centers at both sites. Given the articulation of specifically Danish legislation regarding state church property with UNESCO requirements, the heritage site managers in Jelling and Roskilde are formally affiliated with the local parish councils, meaning that institutionally cultural heritage values are superseded by the religious values of the churches—in the internationally unusual situation of non-separation of church and state in Denmark. Thus, the religious heritage sites that are part of the Danish church retain considerable say over their heritage, as the local parish councils employ the UNESCO site managers.

In both Jelling and Roskilde, the professional and institutional demands of World-Heritagization entailed bureaucratization and institutional proliferation. World-Heritagization compounded existing heritage management structures that conformed to Danish legislation privileging local parishes as the rightful owners of the churches, including of cultural heritage property. The different—religious and heritage—management requirements of the churches generate tensions that demand careful treading, something resolved through intertwined processes of heritage purification, hybridization, and institutional proliferation. Global and national heritage governmentality (cf. Coombe and Weiss 2015) is geared toward the purification of heritage sites, but where these sites are simultaneously under some form of religious sovereignty, the resulting tension is in the two Danish cases discussed here, distributed through the establishment and proliferation of hybrid institutions. These consist of largely the same actors but have slightly different purposes and mandates, so as to defuse any tensions. This might seem like a classic church-versus-state equation, but the Danish irony is that financially, both the cultural heritage and church streams of funding come largely from state coffers, albeit channeled through different agencies.

In conclusion, World-Heritagization of religious sites in Denmark generates changes in the management through the twin processes of institutional proliferation and hybridization and, in the case of Jelling World-Heritagization, even generates changes on the ground, in the environment (cf. Brumann and Berliner 2016). Whereas the exact nature and direction of these processes depend on local specifics, the churches in both Jelling and Roskilde are part of the Danish state church, in which the local parish councils exercise local sovereignty. The local parish council employs the heritage site manager and hence exercises a considerable say over the management of the cultural heritage site—sometimes to the detriment of nonreligious local residents, as in Jelling. In other words, in the context of World-Heritagization, local Danish congregations deploy various tactics such as institutional proliferation and hybridization with more or less success in order to deal with tensions and with potential threats to their local autonomy.

Sofie Isager Ahl received her doctoral degree from the Department of Anthropology at the University of Copenhagen, based on research on regenerative agriculture in Scandinavia. She has previously done fieldwork at religious World Heritage Sites in Denmark as scientific assistant in the HERILIGION: The Heritagization of Religion and the Sacralization of Heritage in Contemporary Europe research project and worked with the Danish delegation to UNESCO. She is the author of *Naboplanter* (2018), coeditor of *Ny Jord—Tidsskrift for naturkritik 1* (2015), and translator of Eduardo Kohn's *Soul Blindness* (2016).

Rasmus Rask Poulsen is a PhD fellow in the section for European Ethnology at the SAXO-Institute at the University of Copenhagen and the Danish Folklore Archives at the Royal Danish Library. His PhD project examines the (world) heritagization of three affiliated religious communities of the Moravian Brethren (Herrnhuter) and their eighteenth-century settlements in Denmark, Germany, and the United States. In 2017, he attained an MA in social anthropology from the Department of Anthropology at the University of Copenhagen, specializing in the fields of cultural heritage and religion.

Oscar Salemink is professor of anthropology at the University of Copenhagen. Between 2001 and 2011 he worked at Vrije Universiteit Amsterdam, from 2005 as professor of social anthropology, and from 1996 through 2001 he was responsible for Ford Foundation grant portfolios in social sciences and arts and culture in Thailand and Vietnam. He received his doctoral degree from the University of Amsterdam, based on research on Vietnam's Central Highlands. He is currently working on global projects on heritage and contemporary arts. He has published two monographs, ten edited volumes, and eight themed issues of journals.

NOTES

The research for this article took place in the framework of the European project HERILIGION: The Heritagization of Religion and the Sacralization of Heritage in Contemporary Europe (2016–20), funded by Humanities in the European Research Area (HERA) grant # 5087–00505A.

The fieldwork in Jelling and Roskilde was conducted by Sofie Isager Ahl (2017–18), and all of the quotations of informants come from her fieldnotes. Both Ahl and Rasmus Rask Poulsen (2018–19) were research assistants in the HERILIGION project that constitutes the basis for this volume. All three coauthors contributed substantively and substantially to this chapter.

1. In Denmark, four out of seven cultural World Heritage Sites contain Protestant church buildings. These are, in order of adaption to the World Heritage List, Jelling Mounds, Runic Stones and Church (1994), Roskilde Cathedral (1995), Kronborg Castle (2000), and Christiansfeld, a Moravian Church Settlement (2015). The church in Kronborg Castle is a chapel rather than a parish church with a congregation, as is the case in the other sites. Because Christiansfeld's Moravian congregation is outside of the Lutheran state church, it is both theologically and in terms of heritage preservation governed differently from the Danish mainstream, and hence not representative for the Danish case.
2. See the chapter by Kjær and Grinder-Hansen in this volume.
3. Translated into modern English the inscription says, "King Harald bade this monument be made in memory of Gorm his father and Thyra his mother, that Harald who

won for himself all Denmark and Norway and made the Danes Christians" (Hvass 2011).
4. "Vi er vilde med vikinger: Museum slår ny besøgsrekord," *Vejle Amts Folkeblad*, 2 January 2019, https://vafo.dk/artikel/vi-er-vilde-med-vikinger-museum-sl%C3%A5r-ny-bes%C3%B8gsrekord (accessed 24 August 2020).
5. The A. P. Møller Foundation is the majority shareholder of the global Mærsk shipping empire. The full name of the foundation is A. P. Møller og Hustru Chastine Mc-Kinney Møllers Fond til almene Formaal.
6. See the chapter by Ulla Kjær and Poul Grinder-Hansen in this volume.
7. See the official statistics here: https://www.km.dk/folkekirken/kirkestatistik/folkekirkens-medlemstal/ (accessed 1 September 2020). Many church members are token members who hardly ever visit church or engage in religious activities.
8. Fieldnotes by Sofie Isager Ahl. See also "Stor udskiftning i menighedsråd," TV Syd, 14 September 2016, https://www.tvsyd.dk/artikel/stor-udskiftning-i-menighedsraad; Seks af otte forlader Jelling Menighedsråd, *Vejle Amts Folkeblad*, 14 September 2017, https://vafo.dk/artikel/seks-af-otte-forlader-jelling-menighedsr%C3%A5d; "Opgør om nationalarv er slut i Jelling" *Kristeligt Dagblad*, 1 October 2016, https://www.kristeligt-dagblad.dk/kirke-tro/opgoer-om-nationalarv-er-slut-i-jelling (all accessed 24 August 2020).
9. "Oprør mod lokalråd: Borgere vil også høres," *Vejle Amts Folkeblad*, 21 April 2018, https://vafo.dk/artikel/opr%C3%B8r-mod-lokalr%C3%A5d-borgere-vil-ogs%C3%A5-h%C3%B8res; "Der kommer et nyt møde om randbebyggelsen," *Vejle Amts Folkeblad*, 7 May 2018, https://vafo.dk/artikel/der-kommer-et-nyt-m%C3%B8de-om-randbebyggelsen; "Brat farvel til lokalråd: Formand blev træt afmistilliden," *Vejle Amts Folkeblad*, 19 August 2018, https://vafo.dk/artikel/brat-farvel-til-lokalr%C3%A5d-formand-blev-tr%C3%A6t-af-mistilliden (all accessed 24 August 2020).
10. Periodic Reporting Cycle 2, section II, 2013: 5, see https://whc.unesco.org/en/list/695/documents/ (accessed 1 September 2020).
11. Finansloven 2018a §22.11.02. From 2005 to 2011, the state budget furthermore awarded extraordinary funds to restorations of the royal burial chapels and the cathedral's roof. From 2011 to 2017, the budget also covered expenses for the establishment of Queen Margrethe's sepulchral monument in a chapel of the cathedral at an estimated price of DKK 31.4 million (EUR 4.2 million) (Finansloven 2018b §22.11.15; see also Christoffersen 2015: 81–82).
12. "Intriger i domkirkens menighedsråd," *SN.dk*, 22 November 2013, https://sn.dk/Roskilde/Intriger-i-domkirkens-menighedsraad/artikel/371042 (accessed 24 August 2020).
13. "Menighedsrådet kom på plads," *Roskilde Avis*, 22 November 2016, p. 76, http://www.e-pages.dk/roskildemidtuge/555/78; Roskilde Kommune, 2017 Ansøgning om støtte til lokale erhvervs- og turismeprojekter: Verdensarvsdag i Roskilde lørdag den 10. marts 2018, http://roskilde.dk/sites/default/files/fics/DAG/3404/Bilag/Indkomne_ansoegninger_UVEG_oktober_2017.pdf (pp. 1, 13–15); "Nyt råd skal gøre unge bevidste om domkirkens verdensarv," *Dagbladet Roskilde*, 13 May 2017, sec. 1, p. 2, https://sn.dk/Roskilde/Nyt-raad-skal-vaerne-om-domkirkens-verdensarv/artikel/654884 (all accessed 1 September 2020).

REFERENCES

Berliner, David. 2012. "Multiple Nostalgias: The Fabric of Heritage in Luang Prabang (Lao PDR)," *Journal of the Royal Anthropological Institute* (N.S.) 18: 769–86.

Brumann, Christoph, and David Berliner. 2016. "Introduction: UNESCO World Heritage—Grounded?," in Chistoph Brumann and David Berliner (eds.), *World Heritage on the Ground: Ethnographic Perspectives*. Oxford: Berghahn Books, pp. 1–34.

Christensen, Leif Baun. 2016. *Jelling—byen der forsvandt*. Jelling: Lokalhistorisk forening for Jelling, Kollerup-Vindelev og Hvejse.

Christoffersen, Lisbeth. 2015. "Roskilde Domkirke. Styring af sognekirke og turistattraktion," *Religionsvidenskabeligt Tidsskrift* 62: 77–89.

Coombe, Rosemary J., and Lindsay M. Weiss. 2015. "Neoliberalism, Heritage Regimes and Cultural Rights," in Lynn Meskell (ed.), *Global Heritage: A Reader*. Hoboken, NJ: Wiley-Blackwell, pp. 43–69.

De Cesari, Chiara. 2012. "Thinking through Heritage Regimes," in Regina Bendix, Adytia Eggert, and Arnika Peselmann (eds.), *Heritage Regimes and the State*. Göttingen: Universitätsverlag Göttingen, pp. 399–413.

Harrison, Rodney, and Michael Hitchcock. 2005. *The Politics of World Heritage Negotiating Tourism and Conservation*. Bristol: Channel View Publications.

Herzfeld, Michael. 2006. "Spatial Cleansing: Monumental Vacuity and the Idea of the West," *Journal of Material Culture* 11(1/2): 127–49.

Herzfeld, Michael. 2009. *Evicted from Eternity: The Restructuring of Modern Rome*. Chicago: Chicago University Press.

Herzfeld, Michael. 2015. "Heritage and Corruption: The Two Faces of the Nation-State," *International Journal of Heritage Studies* 21(6): 531–44.

Hvass, Steen. 2011. *Jelling-Monumenterne—deres historie og bevaring*. Copenhagen: Kulturarvsstyrelsen.

Jessen, Mads Dengsø, Mads Kähler Holst, Charlotta Lindblom, Niels Bonde, and Anne Pedersen. 2014. "A Palisade Fit for a King: Ideal Architecture in King Harald Bluetooth's Jelling," *Norwegian Archaeological Review* 47(1): 42–64.

Kjær, Ulla. 2013. *Roskilde Domkirke*. Copenhagen: Gyldendal.

Rubow, Cecilie. 2011. "Religion and Integration: Three Danish Models for the Relationship between Religion and Society," in Karen Fog Olwig and Karsten Paerregaard (eds.), *The Question of Integration: Immigration, Exclusion and the Danish Welfare State*. Newcastle upon Tyne: Cambridge Scholars, pp. 94–110.

Salemink, Oscar. 2016. "Described, Inscribed, Written Off: Heritagisation as (Dis)Connection," in Philip Taylor (ed.), *Connected and Disconnected in Vietnam*. Canberra: ANU Press, pp. 311–46.

Schütze, Laura Maria. 2013. "Myten om Danmarks dåbsattest. Civilreligion i kongernes Jelling," in Margit Warburg, Signe Engelbreth Larsen, and Laura Maria Schütze (eds.), *Civilreligion i Danmark. Ritualer, myter og steder*. Højbjerg: Univers, pp. 55–76.

Warburg, Margit. 2013. "Dansk civilreligion i det store og Små, in Margit Warburg," in Signe Engelbreth Larsen and Laura Maria Schütze (eds.), *Civilreligion i Danmark. Ritualer, Myter og Steder*. Højbjerg: Univers, pp. 7–54.

Waterton, Emma, and Steve Watson (eds.). 2011. *Heritage and Community Engagement: Collaboration or Contestation*. London: Routledge.

PART III

THE RELIGIOUS CITYSCAPE OF KRAKÓW, POLAND

 CHAPTER 5

Challenging or Confirming the National Sacred?
Managing the Power Place at Wawel Hill in Kraków

Anna Niedźwiedź

Introduction

Wawel Hill—in Polish usually simply called Wawel—is a limestone plateau, surfacing seven and a half hectares (eighteen and a half acres) and picturesquely overlooking the Kraków's Old Town, with the Vistula River widely bending on its west side.[1] Since the early history of Polish statehood, which goes back to the tenth and eleventh centuries, Wawel has been dominated by the princely (and later royal) residential building and the Roman Catholic cathedral (see Carter 1994: 5). For ten centuries, these two edifices—changing and developing their material form—have overlooked the city. Today Wawel Hill, with its castle and cathedral, creates the city's picturesque landmark. Poles regard Wawel as "the most sacred monument of national heritage" (Kubik 1994: 95), since it is connected with the history of the Polish state and the formation of the modern national identity during the nineteenth century (Purchla 2018: 64). The cathedral is recognized as an important Catholic shrine—one of the oldest pilgrimage centers in the country (Witkowska 1984: 78; Jackowski 1999: 139). It also serves as the "Polish Pantheon"—a national necropolis with historic royal sarcophagi and tombs of national heroes and poets (Nungovitch 2019). In 1978, as part of the "Historic Centre of Kraków," Wawel was listed as a UNESCO World Heritage Site. Since the fall of the Iron Curtain in 1989 and the opening of Poland to a free-market economy and an expanding international tourist industry, Wawel has been promoted as a "must-see" attraction and has become the most visited tourist place in the country (Kruczek 2014: 30).[2]

Situating this chapter within the range of questions proposed by the editors of this volume, I treat Wawel as an example of a national-religious heritage site where one can observe various ways in which heritage is managed through both top-down and bottom-up processes (see introduction to this volume). The concept of heritage regime is a useful starting point here, as it turns our attention toward the processual and multidimensional character of heritage, its relations with power dynamics, politics, economy, and identity (Geismar 2015: 72). Haidy Geismar also indicates the complex role of institutions (including the nation-state) in "mediating and producing heritage, both as a form of governance and as an experiential domain for citizens on the ground" (2015: 72). Drawing on this perspective, I aim to demonstrate that what is called and experienced as "heritage" at Wawel should be seen as an effect of official power relations, cultural politics, and institutionally implemented managerial strategies, as well as the result of a constant cultural production that refers to people's interactions with both: heritage discourses and a particular space and its material form. "Experiential domain on the ground" or, to use another phrase, "an experiential way of knowing" (van de Port and Meyer 2018: 4) is, as Geismar points out, strongly shaped by institutional regimes that control visitors' movements, influence guides' narratives, design the layout of exhibitions and select their contents, or even create a particular ambience in heritage spaces to trigger distinct emotional responses. Indeed, two managerial institutions that share a stewardship over Wawel—namely, the Royal Castle state museum and the Royal Cathedral Chapter—play a central role in these processes. Using official narratives and designing visitors' practices, they cultivate a national and Catholic-oriented conceptualization of Wawel and its heritage (see Nungovitch 2019). Even in discourses aimed at foreigners, Wawel is depicted as the "essence of Polishness," and references to cosmopolitan, UNESCO-endorsed "universal values" are rather rare. The castle is promoted as a symbol of the history of the Polish statehood. It is also depicted as intimately connected to the cathedral as a place of royal coronations and burials (up to the eighteenth century). The cathedral is publicized as both a religious and national shrine, where national identity is expressed through Catholic symbols.

It is important to understand that due to the specific historical trajectory of east central Europe, Poles (like some other nations in the region) developed a modern national ideology in the absence of an independent nation-state (Johnson 1996: 134–36). Since Poland was partitioned between 1795 and 1918 by Russia, Prussia, and Austria, Polish identity was expressed not through state symbols and rituals, but through religious—mostly Catholic— ones (Zubrzycki 2010: 613). In the Polish case, the concept of "the migration of the holy"—originally coined by historians to describe the trajectory of many Western nation-states and then applied by social scientists in the secularization thesis (see Isnart and Cerezales 2020: 2)—does not seem very suitable because nationalism and Catholicism were seen as two sides of the same coin. During the nineteenth and twentieth centuries, the fusion of "national identity and Catholicism" (Zubrzycki 2010: 613) served as basis for "Christian patriotism" (Kotwas and Kubik 2019: 440) and the ideal of the "Pole-Catholic" (see Porter-Szücs 2011: 328). Even though in the last three decades these concepts have been questioned and debated in the quite polarized postcommunist Polish political and social scene, the official management of Wawel—as the most important national heritage site—remains strongly entangled with religious meanings as defined by institutional Catholicism. Wawel can be analyzed then as a "religious heritage complex" (Isnart and Cerezales 2020) where relations between what is perceived as "religion" and "heritage" are "far more complicated, intricate, and multi-layered" than suggested by a religio-secularism paradigm (6). Additionally, affordances of space and its material dimension need to be taken into account as active components constructing Wawel as a "religious heritage complex" where "religious" and "heritage" realms are rather enmeshed than separated (2). For instance, the physical proximity of the cathedral and the castle, due to the specific topography of Wawel, naturalizes the fusion of religious and national associations. The Catholic life of the cathedral, where sarcophagi and memorabilia of the royals are exhibited in a context of explicitly religious art and rituals, corresponds with the interiors of the neighboring castle, where the same royals are recalled through museum objects that refer to their governing power and the history of the Polish statehood.

While acknowledging the deep entanglement between the concept of a national heritage site and the Catholic aura of the cathedral, I will, however, go beyond analyzing the dominant heritage regime promoted by the state and church institutions that share stewardship over Wawel. My focus in this chapter will be on alternative discourses and bottom-up holistic spiritual practices that associate Wawel with one of the "Earth's chakras"—a sacred spot and energy knot, believed to radiate mystical and healing powers. This contemporary alternative spirituality is linked with rather unorthodox and heterogeneous narratives about Wawel as well as energy practices that are performed publicly at the very center of the hill. The focus will be on how these narratives and practices influence, change, promote, but also eventually—through a bottom-up experiential domain—manage what is perceived as "heritage" at Wawel as the most important Polish national heritage site.

First, I will turn toward the managers of the hill and analyze how the emergence of chakra spirituality and the physical location of the energy practices at Wawel were seen by the castle and the cathedral officials as a challenge to the institutionally canonized and cherished concept of a national heritage site. I will also show that the behaviors and narratives associated with the chakra were seen as a challenge to the dominant Christian notion of the sacred. Second, I aim to go beyond these conflicting discourses and see the chakra development as a new interpretation and a bottom-up form of managing the concept of the national heritage site. This form attempts to navigate beyond the official control surrounding Wawel and is applied on the ground by a range of people—Kraków tour guides as well as individuals who seek to access the Wawel chakra energy. I will refer to the latter as "the Wawel chakra energy drawers," since this denotes simply "those who draw energy at Wawel" and directly refers to how it is expressed in Polish.[3]

This chapter draws on ethnographic research conducted mostly between September 2018 and February 2020 that included participant observation at the Wawel chakra site, many informal discussions in the castle courtyard with people drawing energy as well as with casual visitors, and in-depth ethnographic interviews with the regular chakra energy drawers and Kraków tour guides.[4] I also refer to the few publications that have popularized the chakra story among a broader public within Poland. These books were written in the form of popular historical publications on sensational topics. The first publications that made chakra popular among a broader public were authored by a historian, Michał Rożek (1991), and a journalist, Zbigniew Święch (2000). There is very little social scientific scholarly interest in the chakra and its believers. I should mention here an article by the Cracovian ethnologist Róża Godula-Węcławowicz (2008) based on her observations of the chakra energy drawing practices around the turn of the millennium, as well as few rather popular and very general publications published by scholars connected with Kraków's Historical Museum.[5]

Like bottom-up spiritual beliefs, knowledge about the chakra has spread mostly through word of mouth and—more recently—through the internet. It is impossible to point to one "canonical version" of beliefs and practices related to the chakra, since people who draw energy are very diverse and build their own concepts and theories. In the following section, I will present the most significant aspects of chakra beliefs and practices as they appeared during ethnographic research. However, it needs to be stressed that due to the scarcity of space and the specific scope of this chapter, I am unable to focus more exhaustively on the fluidity, creativity, and individualization of chakra beliefs and practices or explore the complexity of the dynamics between various energy drawers.

Energy Spirituality

The Wawel chakra—by some also referred to as the Wawel stone or the magnetic Earth gland—is said to be located at the center of the hill, between the castle and the cathedral. The word "chakra" refers to a Sanskrit term as well as Hindu and Buddhist ideas about energetic centers located in the human body. The term is also widely adopted in a variety of Western holistic, esoteric, and syncretic spiritual movements. It describes not only energetic centers in the human body, but also—as in the case of Wawel—energetic centers connected with particular geographic locations. The Earth's chakras, like other "power places," are said to create "a worldwide web formed by energy lines spanning across the globe" (Fedele 2018: 112). Wawel, as a site where one of the Earth's chakras is believed to be located, is seen as part of a global transnational and trans-religious energetic network that includes such famous sacred places as Mecca, Jerusalem, Rome, Glastonbury, and Giza.

Every day for almost forty years the Wawel chakra energy drawers have visited a courtyard at the Wawel castle in order to connect with the chakra energy. The wide Renaissance arcaded courtyard is one of the most iconic sites at Wawel, and tourists stop here on their way to the castle's exhibitions or simply stroll leisurely, making pictures and admiring the harmonious design of the historic royal residence. The energy drawers can usually be spotted performing their practices in the northwest corner of the courtyard, under an arcade, where an exit from the castle exhibition, a luggage room, and a souvenir shop are located. An approximately fifteen-meter-long section of the wall is believed to be a spot where the strongest energy waves—emanating from the chakra—are felt. Here people lean toward the wall, many with closed eyes and deeply concentrating. They touch the wall with their backs or foreheads, sometimes stretch their arms along the wall, or stroke it with their open palms and fingers to draw more energy (see Figure 5.1). Some people stand barefoot on the pavement; others sit by the wall in a lotus position and meditate. I also heard stories about individuals who bring items and touch them on the wall to "catch the energy" (e.g., postcards, scraps of paper), a woman who performed rituals that included a Tibetan singing bowl, someone who "charged" water bottles with the chakra energy, and a student who in the 1980s brought his typewriter to the wall to get energetic support when writing his master's thesis. Often, those who visit the Wawel chakra spot search for physical or emotional healing and individual empowerment.

The chakra beliefs absorb various, sometimes very complex and even contradictory theories. For instance, they include alternative interpretations of Polish and Slavic history (usually relating to pre-Christian and Pagan traditions; see also the chapter by Kamila Baraniecka-Olszewska in this volume), esoteric and oriental spiritualities, natural healing and ecological holistic approaches, elements from various established religious traditions (e.g., Catholicism, Orthodoxy, Buddhism, Hinduism, and Paganism), and scientific discourses on physics, astronomy, etc. The fluid and heterogeneous character of theories and practices related to the chakra resembles other con-

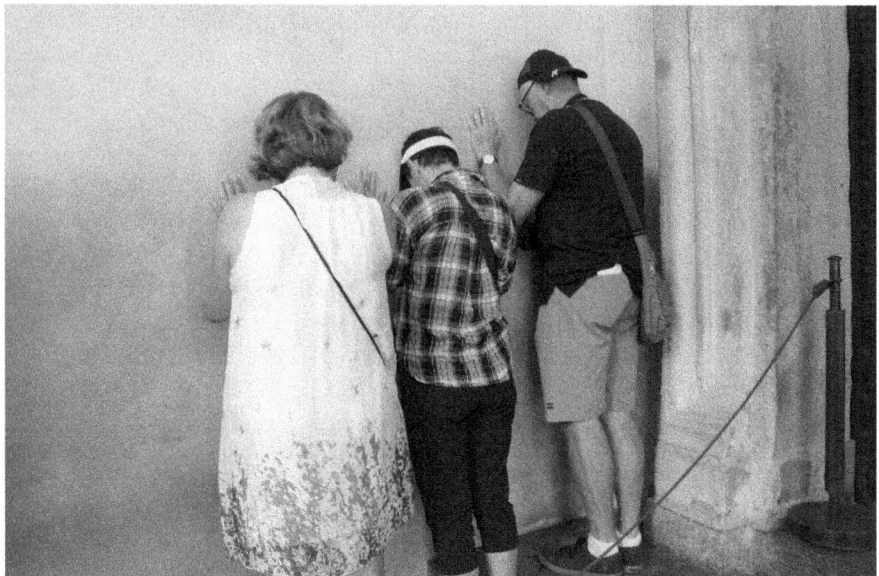

Figure 5.1. Drawing energy at the roped-off wall at the Wawel castle courtyard, September 2016. © Anna Niedźwiedź.

temporary spiritual movements, especially popular in western Europe and North America and described by scholars in terms of "religious creativity" (Weibel 2001), "invented religions" (Cusack 2010), "holistic spirituality" (Harris 2013), "alternative spirituality" (Fedele 2013), or more recently "energy pilgrims" (Fedele 2018).[6] The term "energy pilgrims" is particularly helpful, since it points to the concept of energy as central and shared within these multifaceted and fluctuating contemporary spiritual currents. Energy ties various spiritual narratives together through an inclusive, transnational, and trans-religious "energy grammar" (a term proposed by Anna Fedele) offering "a language that goes beyond religious affiliation" (Fedele 2018: 114). "Energy grammar" seemingly responds to "a desire for a more malleable notion of the divine" (114) than in conventional religious contexts and operates beyond established traditional institutional mainstream religiosity.

Energy is also central for individual spiritual practices. In the case of the Wawel chakra, energy creates an intimate relation between people's bodies and an exact location at the hill and its material tissue. Many people who touch the wall at the Wawel castle courtyard to draw energy from the chakra describe their experiences as physical sensations felt inside their bodies (e.g., "a wave going through the spine," "tingling in foot or fingers," "warm feeling," "something similar to an electric current going through the body"). Usually, direct physical contact with the chakra energy is perceived as a significant, sometimes powerful, and even transformative personal experience. It creates intimate bonds between individuals and Wawel, perceived as a concrete geographic location.[7]

I suggest that this bottom-up, noninstitutional, alternative, and hardly controllable type of relations between the chakra energy drawers and Wawel should be interpreted as belonging to what Geismar calls the "experiential domain on the ground" (2015: 72), because it has an impact on the production and perception of Wawel as a heritage site. Although silenced by institutional management strategies, and for many years officially resisted by the museum and condemned by the cathedral, the chakra energy drawers have been persistently present and visible at the very center of the hill since at least the early 1980s. As I will reveal in the final part of this chapter, for many of the energy drawers, the chakra beliefs and practices are not at odds with official national and Catholic heritage discourses about Wawel. Similarly, outside the officially promoted heritage narrative, the chakra stories confirm the outstanding value, sacrality, and uniqueness of Wawel as an important Polish historic site. However, at the same time, the energy drawers' use of "energy grammar" opens the hill up to a transcultural and trans-religious network of beliefs and theories. The chakra introduces a contemporary global spirituality to the experiential domain of the most important Polish national heritage site and indicates its more universal and cosmopolitan dimensions.

Powers over the Place of Power

In this section, I will present the objections that the castle and the cathedral management have against the energy spirituality developing at Wawel. To do so, I will return to events that happened almost twenty years ago, when on 25 May 2001 the "war" against the chakra was openly proclaimed. On that morning, before the first visitors would walk into the courtyard, metal poles and a thick rope were placed in the northwest corner, blocking access to the wall. The appearance of this spatial arrangement was clarified in an official announcement—printed out and placed on a big stand near the rope—and signed by representatives of the castle and the cathedral.

To evaluate the significance of the proclaimed message, it is necessary to make a short digression concerning the management structure of Wawel. As mentioned, the castle and the cathedral share the stewardship over the entirety of Wawel and are devoted to the promotion of a national and Catholic-oriented vision of its heritage. However, the collaborative action directed against the chakra drawing, performed in the area of the hill officially managed by the castle, was rather unusual given the managerial divisions between the two institutions. On a daily basis the castle and the cathedral manage their own parts of the hill separately, especially when organizing visitors' access. For instance, the castle sells tickets to all the exhibitions that are part of the Royal Castle state museum and are scattered all over the hill, while the church manages ticketing of tourists who visit the cathedral and the adjacent Cathedral Museum.

The lines between the two bodies are clear and connected with land ownership. Most of the hill is state-owned and managed by the castle museum. The section owned by the Roman Catholic Church is concentrated on the northern embankments and is managed by the Cathedral Board. Apart from the cathedral, these properties include a few other historic buildings, which are home to the Cathedral Museum, the Cathedral Archive, and the residence that accommodates some of the canons belonging to the Cathedral Chapter. To some extent, however, the church properties fall under the control of the museum. Due to their status as national monuments and as an integral part of the UNESCO World Heritage Site, the Wawel Hill conservator, who has a state-funded position at the castle museum, is in charge of approving any maintenance or alteration of the church-owned buildings.

The announcement and spatial arrangement that blocked access to the wall of the courtyard was, therefore, an exceptional top-down managerial act initiated by two institutions that were united in opposing the beliefs and practices associated with the chakra. It seems that the bottom-up, trans-religious, and heterogeneous spirituality developing at Wawel challenged established power dynamics and was seen as an ideological threat to a heritage regime authorized by the state and religious institutions in conjunction. As I will demonstrate, several expressions used in the announcement are crucial for interpreting Wawel as the religious heritage complex where national understanding of heritage is fused with references to a religious realm represented by Catholicism.

The announcement went as follows (layout and emphasis as in the original):

Management Board of the Royal Wawel Castle and the Board of the Kraków's Cathedral
warn against believing in rumors
about the existence of a miraculous stone (chakra) at Wawel Hill.
These rumors are not based on any scholarly or religious premises.

We are informing people that

– at Wawel Hill no extraordinary powers exist, especially none of those that would be able to have any positive influence on the psychological or physical condition of a human being;

- performing occult practices is incompatible with the grandeur of Wawel Hill; Wawel Hill is a special place related to the highest historic and religious values;
- participation in occult practices is contrary to the principles of the Catholic faith.

We cordially ask you not to gather at the courtyard's arcade, as this causes trouble by stopping the flow of tourists and leads toward the dilapidation of an ancient castle's wall.

According to the text, Wawel is a place whose significance is related to both "the highest historic and religious values," where "religious" is clearly defined as "the Catholic faith." The further reasoning follows this twofold pattern. The museum seems to be in charge of scholarly, reason-based, and rationalizing arguments against "rumors" about the existence of the chakra and any "extraordinary powers." The authority of the Roman Catholic Church is used as a decisive tool to draw a clear line between the chakra-related activities and religion. In this context it is worth pointing out that the word "rumors" appears twice, as does the phrase "occult practices" (described as "contrary to the principles of the Catholic faith"). Both expressions clearly seek to discredit the energy practices as neither "scholarly" nor "religious." Of a different character, yet of equal relevance, is the final argument about "the dilapidation of an ancient castle's wall." This practical argument directly relates to the efficient management of people's movement at a popular tourist place as well as to concerns about how to preserve the material tissue of this valuable heritage site, suggesting that by touching and leaning against the wall the energy drawers make it dirty and could possibly even damage the historic monument. This argument insists that the chakra practices at Wawel are out of place and do not fit within the museum regimes and "normal" behaviors in a heritage site, especially one possessing such a high national and religious (Catholic) importance.

The announcement and new spatial arrangement at the castle courtyard not only unpleasantly surprised those who visited Wawel on that May morning with the aim of drawing energy at the wall, but also made it to the local and national news. In the days and weeks that followed, the media pondered over Wawel energy, usually giving some general information about the chakra beliefs and commenting on the dispute. While some newspapers reported that "in the name of rationalism and faith the director of the Royal Castle at Wawel Hill and the parish priest of the Wawel Cathedral blocked people from accessing the wall,"[8] others wondered "why the managers of Wawel decided to slaughter a hen laying golden eggs" and "resign from this huge tourist attraction."[9] Comparisons with other globally famous "energy places" appeared, and even the Loch Ness monster was recalled as an example of a successful marketing strategy that Wawel managers should learn from in order to attract tourists. Even though most of the news described energy spirituality rather indulgently, the media cover of the 2001 chakra dispute made the Wawel chakra nationally famous.

Paradoxically, in the end rather than stopping the energy spirituality, the managerial operation conducted by the castle and the cathedral stirred a growing interest in the chakra. Over the summer of 2001 many casual tourists asked about the chakra when visiting Wawel and tried to gain access to the wall. The regular energy drawers did not give up their practices either. When stopped by the castle guards and kept away from the roped-off wall, they drew energy by leaning against other walls nearby or simply sat in the courtyard. As a result, the Wawel managers reformulated their restrictive measures, hoping that the fame of the chakra would weaken with the passing of time. They removed the controversial announcement but retained the rope and poles. Additionally, large stands partially covering the wall were installed, creating an open-air exhibition dedicated to the history of the castle restoration.

Nevertheless, the energy drawers and tourists regularly violated the rope not only by stretching their hands over it and touching the wall with their palms, but also by jumping over the rope and performing the energy drawing practices directly at the wall. Over the following months, the managers

Figure 5.2. A group of tourists at the northwest corner of the Wawel castle courtyard and a person sitting and performing his meditation at the chakra spot. Next to him are the exhibition stands, rope, chain, and poles erected by the museum managers around the chakra site, June 2019. © Anna Niedźwiedź.

started to turn a blind eye to these practices, keeping the rope at the wall but not chasing away those who did not respect it. Hence, it soon became quite usual to see a castle guard walking along the rope but not reprimanding those who jumped over it to draw energy directly from the wall. In recent years, when we were doing our research at the courtyard, the castle guards were usually not even present in the vicinity of the chakra site. If they happened to pass by, they either observed the energy drawers with some sort of curiosity but without any reprimands or simply pretended not to see them. When the guards were accosted by tourists searching for the chakra spot—a situation I observed a few times at the courtyard—they gave rather evasive replies saying that "they know nothing" and avoided any closer involvement with people eager to draw energy. In practice, in recent years not "war" but a "ceasefire" prevailed at the castle courtyard, with energy drawers continuing their activities usually undisturbed by representatives of the museum.

The 2001 chakra dispute and events that followed revealed that controlling the place of power is much more complex than what was assumed at the institutional level. The top-down vision by the management of Wawel as "a special place related to the highest historic and religious values," as stated in the announcement, was confronted by bottom-up practices and projections of meanings that did not fit the officially promoted national and Catholic-oriented heritage regime. The uses of Wawel by the energy drawers were seen by the managers as abuses of a national heritage site. Nevertheless, the chakra appeared to resonate well with a broader audience and attracted new practitioners and tourists, who were not stopped by roping off the chakra wall.

Managing Tour Guides

As sweeping away the chakra followers from the castle courtyard appeared to be rather like tilting at windmills, the museum managers decided to target another potential category of persons: the city tour guides. The tourist industry that boomed in Kraków in the 1990s led to the emergence of a thriving city tour guide community. In the last thirty years, many people found employment in the tourist sector and have treated guiding as their main source of income. Until 2014, Kraków had a very strict licensing policy for all tour guides—only state-licensed guides were allowed to lead walking tours through the city and visit various tourist attractions with groups. Gaining a license meant a significant time-consuming and expensive effort involving a several hundred hours' course, which consisted of lectures (mostly dedicated to the history of Kraków and Poland and art history) and practical classes in various museums, followed by a rather challenging state exam.

Tour guides who had gained their licenses before the 2014 act that opened up the profession[10] recall that they were warned during courses dedicated specifically to Wawel and led by the museum not to tell the chakra story to visitors. If guides were overheard at the Wawel courtyard referring to the chakra—even as a legend or local titbit—they could lose their license or at least be permanently banned from taking groups into the courtyard.

For years the most audible mouthpiece advocating institutional hostility toward the chakra was the Royal Castle museum director, a renowned professor of art history who held this post from 1989 until the end of 2019, when he retired. His public comments on the chakra followed the announcement he signed in May 2001 and were without exception aggressively negative. He usually referred to the chakra in a very cursory manner, describing it as a "rumor," "superstition," or "rubbish" and not even worth mentioning any further. In 2012, in one of the newspaper's interviews dedicated to his broader policy as the director of the museum, he focused on the grandeur of Wawel and positioned it within the context of Polish national identity and history. In his opinion, the Royal Castle museum served, first of all, as "a symbol of Polish statehood." When he was asked by the journalist about the chakra, he called it "a pseudoscience that damages Wawel's reputation and compromises us."[11] In his opinion, the chakra did not fit with a heritage site, which is represented through the ideals of "high culture," "art," and a "national past" for Polish and international visitors. Interestingly, the museum director did not even acknowledge the chakra story as "a legend." "Dragon yes, the chakra no!" was his usual response. Here he was referring to the "old legends," that is, the story about the Wawel dragon that was written down in a thirteenth-century chronicle. For him, the chakra was "new rubbish," a story created in the twentieth century that had nothing to do with legends or heritage.

Quite a different attitude toward the chakra emerges from the ethnographic material collected among tour guides. In interviews many of them pointed out that "the chakra is already a part of Wawel," hence it cannot be expunged. One tour guide described it as follows:

> I myself felt outraged about the ban on mentioning the chakra during tours. If people ask me, it means that they have heard something about the chakra and want to know more. So, it is my duty as a tour guide to relate the story! Of course, it is important to explain that scholars do not take the chakra seriously, but that there are people who believe in it, and so on. But banning it totally? It was outrageous! If one manages such a place as Wawel one needs to tolerate this kind of legends and customs. They have a function here. Wawel is a "cult place," and I do not mean only "religious cult," but it is a sort of a broader "cult place," for our broader culture. One cannot ban things like that, cannot ignore them. If people talk about it, transmit the story, we cannot ignore it. (Interview, 16 December 2019)

Since professional licenses were opened up during 2014, tour guides have been freed from submitting to the museum's rules. However, many still do not refer to the chakra story and its location when leading tourists around the castle courtyard. One guide explained that it is not only due to the negative attitude of the museum, but also due to the scarcity of time. "It is simply not possible to talk about everything when I typically have only one or two hours with a group to see Wawel—the cathedral and the castle—and after that we run to visit the Old Town" (interview, 18 December 2019). So, as this guide points out, priority is usually given to historical narratives about "kings, coronations, and graves." They are seen as "more serious" and more crucial stories to be narrated at "the national heritage site" within the limited time spent on the visit.

However, the chakra might appear in the guides' narratives during the Wawel tours through spontaneous interaction with a group. Usually, the topic is initiated by a question from those visitors who have already heard or read about the chakra. Additionally, questions emerge when tourists see some energy drawers performing their practices at the wall. The guides we talked with admitted that the majority of tourists are positively curious about the chakra, and many visitors upon hearing the story decide to stop for a few minutes to touch the wall and "feel the energy" themselves. Some treat these practices as a tourist attraction and are surprised that the story is not marketed more widely. Many tourists make selfies when touching the wall and loudly comment about "the energy," while others try to focus, close their eyes, and approach the spot with a serious look and comment on the "healing waves" they are feeling.

These usually very short stops at the chakra wall are sometimes managed by tour guides in a telling way. For instance, one guide described how she used to recall the chakra story when her group seemed to be tired or bored by a solemn narrative about Wawel:

> Especially when I bring schoolchildren and I see that they are tired, I make a break here and encourage them to touch the wall and draw energy to have enough strength for further visiting. They start interacting, feel curious, there is some laughter and comments, and they wake up. The same with adult visitors. For instance, when I see that my group has drunk too much alcohol last night, I tell them the chakra story and we joke that touching the wall can help them with a hangover. (Interview, 6 December 2019)

Another guide commented in a similar manner, treating the chakra as a handy tool to catch the visitors' attention because "this is such an interesting legend, much lighter and it is something different than all this grand history of Wawel" (interview, 18 December 2019).

Hence, the tour guides, who work on the ground and interact with various visitors, provide quite a different perspective on Wawel than the one promoted by the castle managers. In anthropological literature, tour guides have been described as pathfinders, animators, mediators, and communicators (see Cohen 1985), who "make sites and societies accessible and interesting for visitors" (Feldman and Skinner 2018: 6). Many Kraków tour guides realize that the chakra can help to engage tourists personally and emotionally with Wawel. The chakra is potentially attractive for a variety of contemporary visitors; it has a mystical aura and combines romanticizing visions of the "remote past," orientalism, and concepts of natural healing with a trans-religious understanding of energy. It can be treated seriously but also with sheer curiosity or enjoyment. When skillfully narrated by a tour guide, it provides a feeling of something out of the museum routine as well as something local and authentic, even more so since it is not recognized officially and is described as secretly practiced by locals.

The perception of Wawel as a heritage site by tour guides is much more dynamic than the museum's official stance that sees it as a rather fossilized entity to be simply preserved. Guides, who interpret the heritage site directly for visitors, are usually eager to accept the chakra practices and stories as a bottom-up domain that co-constitutes contemporary meanings of Wawel, and they are quick to learn how to apply these meanings in their guiding strategies. However, as I will describe in the next section, the tour guides also need to navigate cautiously when dealing with the Catholic clergy and their negative attitude toward the chakra.

"The Church Will Not Allow . . ."

"Are they not chasing people away today?" asked a middle-aged woman, a note of surprise in her voice, when standing to my right and leaning against the wall in the courtyard at the chakra energy spot. "Pe-re-stroi-ka! Didn't you hear? Things have changed, they're gonna open the chakra!" expressively responded the man on my left, with whom just few minutes before I was discussing the new, more tolerant policy toward accessing the chakra spot introduced by the new museum director, who was appointed in January 2020.[12] "Ah, but the church will not allow . . ." doubtfully answered the woman on my right—while still leaning against the wall. She then told me the story about her previous visit to Kraków three years ago. During the drawing of energy at the chakra, she and other people were chased away by a Catholic nun. "She came here and started shouting, 'Heathens! Pagans! Superstitions!' Then she exclaimed that our behavior was out of keeping with 'the solemnity of the place!' and that we should not do anything 'like that' at Wawel."

This is not the only story about the Catholic religious clergy expressing their hostile attitudes toward the chakra beliefs and practices that we collected during our fieldwork. Probably the most famous is yet another nun, who—as described by people who regularly draw energy at the castle courtyard—used to sprinkle holy water over those gathering at the chakra spot, exorcising them from the "satanic practices." A valuable insight into the clergy's attitudes toward the chakra was also revealed during interviews and discussions with the tour guides. A few of them described in detail their collaboration with Polish groups often coming from smaller towns and villages, which are organized by Catholic parishes and led by priests. One person, who has been working as a professional Kraków tour guide for the last thirteen years and often leads tourists to Wawel, stated:

> When I have a group like that, it happens that a priest, who organizes the trip, calls me beforehand to discuss details of the visit to the city. And then, often I am asked not to mention any "nonsense, like that about the chakra" because "we arrive in Kraków as pilgrims and practicing Catholics." (Interview, 6 December 2019)

Another tour guide mentioned that a priest, who brought a group of children from his parish to visit Kraków and Wawel, wanted her to emphasize the story about Saint Stanislaus—a medieval martyr and a bishop of Kraków whose relics are exhibited in the cathedral—and to avoid talking about any "pagan beliefs, like the chakra, so they do not influence children's brains."

The contemporary criticism of the chakra by the Catholic clergy follows the pattern revealed in the 2001 announcement. First, the chakra beliefs are labeled as "superstitions," "nonsense," or "rubbish." They are deprived, thereby, of any "religious status," while the Catholic version of the sacred is presented as the "cultural norm," "religion," and a proper element of the grandiose national heritage site. Second, whenever the chakra's religious dimension is taken more seriously, it happens to be framed as a "foreign spirituality," described as "occult," "oriental," and "pagan." It is inappropriate and sinful for Catholics, even dangerous and "satanic," to draw energy and believe in the chakra.

When these hostile attitudes by the Roman Catholic clergy toward the chakra are analyzed, it is important to remember that the trans-religious and transnational spirituality expressed by the "energy grammar" generally poses a challenge to institutionally oriented religions (Fedele 2018: 114). In the Polish context, the development of chakra spirituality can be regarded as part of the challenge posed by various "new religious movements" to the hegemonic position of the Roman Catholic Church in postcommunist Polish society. Additionally, the chakra's connection with Wawel—as the most important national heritage site—potentially destabilizes the dominant concept of national heritage. The trans-religious and heterogeneous spirituality publicly practiced at the castle courtyard introduces new components to Wawel as a religious heritage complex. These components go beyond the sacralization of the national heritage through Catholic symbols and possibly question the Catholic monopoly in the sacralization of Wawel as a heritage site.

(In)Compatible Sacred?

Contrary to the top-down managerial perspective, most of the chakra energy drawers are convinced that the energy spot is fully compatible with Wawel and fits well into its symbolic dimension as national history and sacralized heritage. The chakra is usually recognized by them as not only an integral part of Wawel but even as its "core," which has a direct link with the history of the Polish nation and the history of Kraków as the old capital city. "It is because of the chakra that Kraków turned out to be such an important and renowned place," mentioned one interviewee (interview, 15 September 2018). His statement summarizes approaches and opinions popular among people who visit Wawel to draw energy. For instance, a woman from central Poland whom I once encountered at the chakra spot, after completing her energy drawing session, looked around, visibly admiring the beauty of the Renaissance courtyard, and spontaneously shared her feelings with me: "Look at this big history here! It is possible that it all happened because of the chakra, because of its power!"

Indeed, many people we talked with at the chakra site or during the ethnographic interviews eagerly interpreted various facts from Polish history as referring to the chakra's location at Wawel. In their accounts, the hill's national reputation is not challenged by the presence of the energy spot but is rather confirmed by it. Popular interpretations create links between the hill—seen as a "condensed reservoir of Polish history" (interview, 11 October 2019)—and the chakra. Hence, it is often said that the Wawel chakra enabled the Polish state to emerge and consolidate in its early stages (i.e., between the tenth and thirteenth centuries). Furthermore, Kraków's subsequent development as a royal seat and a capital city (i.e., the fourteenth to seventeenth centuries) is seen as proof that the city and country thrived because of the chakra's energy. Very popular is the belief that due to the chakra's protective powers Kraków was spared from any serious damage during and after World War II, unlike Warsaw's gruesome fate. Important historic figures connected with Wawel are also frequently mentioned as influenced by the chakra energy. Among them are not only royals who lived at the castle, but also national heroes and leaders who visited the hill or are buried in the cathedral's vaults, such as Marshal Piłsudski, the military commander and head of the Polish state after World War I. Even the late pope John Paul II appears in the chakra stories. Before he became a pope, Karol Wojtyła had lived in Kraków for almost forty years (1938–78) and served as an archbishop at the Wawel Cathedral. As one person asserted, "He must have been aware of this [the chakra] because he lived here, and he knew and often mentioned publicly that Kraków had this special meaning" (informal discussion at the chakra spot, 15 February 2020).[13]

Associating Pope John Paul II—a Catholic saint and a figure who in Polish popular discourses often appears as "a national hero", "the Polish Pope," or "the great Pole" (Niedźwiedź 2017: 84)[14]—with the chakra complements both the national and religious dimensions of Wawel. Although the chakra is opposed by the Roman Catholic Church authorities and its clergy, stories popular among the chakra energy drawers refer to an underlying correlation between the energy spot and a Christian aura emanating from the cathedral. This correlation is grounded in the hill's topography and its alternative interpretation. The courtyard's corner and the wall where people gather to draw energy is located right above the archaeological excavations that in the 1920s revealed the Romanesque church of Saint Gereon.[15] The church is on the exact site where people believe the chakra is located. Popular stories point out that the old Romanesque church was located between the cathedral and the castle and that this was not accidental. It is claimed that the masons constructing the church in the eleventh century knew about the "ley lines" and the "energy spot"; they had access to pre-Christian Slavic beliefs and ancient secrets that, in the Middle Ages, were embraced by Christianity. One of the interviewees, a promoter of the chakra's healing powers and a leader of an informal group, the Supporters of the Wawel Chakra, explained:

> There are no accidents here; these things are linked, even though they are impenetrable for us. It was an old place of cult, more than one thousand years ago. And then the church of Saint Gereon appeared—it was here first and functioned as the [original] Wawel Cathedral! Only later did they build the new cathedral and the castle. (Interview, 15 September 2018)

Attitudes toward the Christian aura and Catholic presence at Wawel vary among the chakra followers. Those who are practicing Catholics or feel spiritually connected with the Catholic tradition straightforwardly combine the

Catholic sacred of the cathedral with the powers of the chakra. Some people mention experiencing the chakra's energy when praying in the cathedral's Eucharistic chapel. The chapel is situated on the east edge of the ecclesiastical building, which makes it the closest point to the supposed location of the chakra inside the cathedral. Also other locations inside the building, especially those related to popular Polish saints and their reliquaries and mementos (like Queen Jadwiga and Pope John Paul II), are seen as imbued with a spiritual dimension, energy, or healing powers.

Generally, chakra energy drawers describe the cathedral as a "spiritual place" where the chakra's influence can also be felt by those who are not connected with Catholicism. Many enter the cathedral to meditate or to "sit and feel the energy." For some, the cathedral is a reminder about links between the chakra energy and historical events. While attitudes toward the cathedral as an edifice filled with "spiritual energy" are mostly accepted, attitudes toward the managers of the cathedral are much more negative. Often, they are considered to be "the enemies of the chakra" who "do not like any competition at Wawel" and are blind to the power of the energy spot. Some energy drawers also detect a secret recognition of the chakra's power by the Catholic priests and an appropriation of energy by the church for its own purposes from the Middle Ages up to the present.[16]

The belief that the chakra should not be seen as related to any exact religious tradition or religious institution prevails among the chakra followers, irrespective of their individual religious and ideological background. In this discourse, the chakra and its powers relate to a primordial and universal "energy" that is open to anybody and can be felt potentially by anyone. Even though "for the managers of Wawel the chakra is at odds with the national and religious order that dominates at this symbolic space" (interview, 18 December 2019)—as one of the tour guides recapitulated—a closer look at discourses about the chakra reveals that they all emphasize the symbolic importance of Wawel. Chakra practices and narratives in fact do not challenge but rather confirm the reputation of Wawel as an important sacred and national heritage site, framing it, however, within more universal, trans-religious, and transnational discourses than those advanced by the official managers. The stories about the chakra also extend the dominant national history that is usually narrated to visitors at Wawel and include the pre-Christian period while adding their own interpretation. Energy drawers emphasize that the chakra had been present before the cathedral and the castle were even constructed and before the Polish state emerged. In that sense, stories about the chakra extend the history about the sacredness of Wawel embracing pre-Christian Slavic beliefs into narratives about the contemporary religious heritage site.[17]

Conclusion

The chakra drawing practices present at the castle courtyard at least since the early 1980s, and contested by institutional managers of this most important Polish national heritage site, have been influencing perceptions about Wawel for four decades and have added new interpretations and narratives to popular discourses about the hill. Chakra beliefs generate close, often intimate and emotionally loaded physical interactions between visitors and Wawel. This "experiential domain on the ground"—an alternative to officially promoted practices and a dominant heritage regime—responds to various needs overlooked by the site's institutional managers.

The chakra functions as a rather inclusive and noninstitutional sacred spot that is open to various spiritualities and individuals. At the same time, it is also an attractive and lively new element of Wawel referred to by Kraków tour guides as a "local attraction" or a "legend." It allows various visitors to add a more personal or even lighter dimension to a grand historic monument. What is also important, the chakra's popularity grew in the moment when Polish society opened up to outside discourses and transnational contacts after the collapse of the Iron Curtain. On the one hand, the chakra has absorbed various new spiritual currents and introduced them to the national heritage site. On the other hand, the chakra has situated Wawel in a more universal network and multicultural context than national and Catholic-oriented discourses promoted by the official managers.

The chakra site can be interpreted therefore as a place where the bottom-up and informal production and management of meanings are created around the Wawel. Even though not recognized by official managers, the chakra practices and beliefs are already a part of the Wawel heritage dynamics, confirming the fluid nature of heritage, challenging ossified managerial approaches, and adding a trans-religous and transnational layer to the most important heritage site in Poland.

Anna Niedźwiedź is an associate professor at the Institute of Ethnology and Cultural Anthropology at the Jagiellonian University in Kraków. As a visiting professor, she taught in the United States at SUNY Buffalo (2006–7) and Rochester University (2011). Her research focuses on anthropology of religion, anthropology of space, and the heritagization of religion. She has conducted ethnographic fieldwork in Poland and Ghana. Between 2016 and 2020, she served as a principal investigator of the Polish section in the international consortium HERILIGION founded by HERA and dedicated to the study of the heritagization of religion and the sacralization of heritage in contemporary Europe.

NOTES

1. I would like to thank Mariusz Meus for providing the estimates of the plateau's surface.
2. Over one million visitors annually enter the Royal Castle museum (ticketed entry), while it is estimated that around two million people visit the hill. See https://wawel.krakow.pl/en/the-castle (accessed 20 February 2020).
3. I use this descriptive term to avoid any connotations with a concept of any organized "group" or "community." While there are some emerging hierarchies and structures among those who draw energy at Wawel (e.g., an informal society named the Supporters of the Wawel Chakra), the term "energy drawers" embraces many independent individuals of varying ideological and religious backgrounds and varying levels of commitment to the chakra. On similar problems with labeling non-homogenous and non-organized individuals connected with spiritual movements, see Weibel (2001: 87).
4. The research was conducted as a part of the HERILIGION: The Heritagization of Religion and Sacralization of Heritage in Contemporary Europe research project, funded by Humanities in the European Research Area (HERA) grant # 5087-00505A, by myself and Jacek Skrzypek, who worked as a member of auxiliary staff. My preliminary research started in 2016 with participant observation and informal discussions at the chakra spot and with Kraków inhabitants who do not draw energy but heard about the chakra. More systematic participant observation and informal discussions about the chakra were undertaken between September 2018 and February 2020 (especially in the fall of 2018 and of 2019). Informal discussions involved the chakra energy drawers at the chakra spot, tour guides whom we met at Wawel, and people who sell souvenirs in shops located at the hill. Additionally, ten in-depth interviews with the chakra energy drawers were conducted and four in-depth interviews with tour guides who work as full-time, licensed city guides (interviews with tour guides were conducted by Jacek Skrzypek in October and December 2019). Internet research was also included because some chakra energy drawers are very active online (some of them referred to their websites, YouTube channels, or Facebook groups during the interviews and discussions). In September 2018, Jacek Skrzypek also collected material during the Second Rally of the Supporters of the Wawel Chakra in Stare Olesno (this two-day meeting was organized mostly as a fair dedicated to alternative medicine and healing practices). Ethnographic materials used in this chapter were collected before the Covid pandemic and epidemiological restrictions announced in Poland in March 2020. In this chapter I do not refer to these events.
5. These publications include a popular book on "legends and mysteries of Kraków" prepared by an ethnologist, Anna Szałapak, where she lists the Wawel chakra as one of the "legends" (2005: 158–63), and a brief description of various narratives about the chakra collected by a historian, Andrzej Szoka (2019).
6. Like many of these authors I prefer not to apply the term "New Age" as an analytical concept, debated recently in social sciences and questioned by social actors. See Fedele 2013: 16.
7. There is no space in this chapter to discuss these intimate relations in detail. But it is important to realize that many people we met at the chakra spot develop strong

emotional bonds with Wawel. There are people who experienced healing or found support in difficult moments (for instance, when a closed one was dying, or after the loss of a child). I also met a person for whom the relationship with the chakra became so important that he decided to move to Kraków to be able to draw on the chakra energy every day.

8. Olga Szpunar and Bartosz Mleczko, "Kłopoty z czakramem [Problems with the chakra]," *Gazeta w Krakowie*, 28 May 2001 (accessed 14 February 2020), https://krakow.wyborcza.pl/krakow/1,44425,291428.html.
9. Jarosław Knap and Agnieszka Sijka, "Energia negatywna" [Negative energy]," *Tygodnik Wprost*, nr 24 (968), 17 June 2001 (accessed 14 February 2020), https://www.wprost.pl/tygodnik/10305/Energia-negatywna.html.
10. The change of law was connected with a national deregulation of licenses and freeing occupations connected with tourism. However, the majority of Kraków city guides collaborate with tourist agencies that employ only those guides who completed a course to become a Kraków guide and passed all the exams.
11. Marek Bartosik, "Prof. Ostrowski hrabia z Wawelu [Prof. Ostrowski: the count from Wawel]," *Gazeta Krakowska*, 17 August 2012 (accessed 14 February 2020), https://gazetakrakowska.pl/prof-ostrowski-hrabia-z-wawelu/ar/638461.
12. Right after taking up office, the new director did not discuss the chakra issue per se; however, he moved the rope and the stands that had been blocking access to the wall (in his view "fighting with myths" makes no sense [personal communication]). About new developments, see endnote 15.
13. This is not an isolated opinion. The 1978 "election of the pope from Kraków" is frequently discussed as "a visible example of how emanations of the chakra influence us." See https://www.youtube.com/watch?v=diSqCypGmqQ (accessed 14 February 2020).
14. The popular image of John Paul II as a national hero does not limit itself to devout Catholics and relates not only to his religious activities but also to his role in political history (especially in the context of the fall of Communism in east central Europe in 1989–90). However, recently his popular reception in Poland has become more diverse—for instance, due to current debates on the sexual abuse scandals in the church that took place during his pontificate.
15. At the end of July 2020 (when the Covid pandemic restrictions were temporally loosened in Poland), a new tourist route was opened at Wawel. This route includes—among other attractions—a visit to archaeological sites at Saint Gereon church. This new arrangement is described by the chakra energy drawers as "the opening of the chakra," even though the museum is clear about disallowing drawing energy practices at Saint Gereon church and does not mention the chakra in its promotional materials (Saint Gereon church is described as a representation of the oldest Christian architecture in Polish lands). The castle controls the flow of tourist entering the new route (every day only a limited number of tickets is sold, and each group entering the route is led by a museum guide). This chapter draws on materials collected up to February 2020 and does not discuss this new tourist route, which is the subject of my continued research at Wawel.
16. A similar concept of the appropriation of the sacred by religious institutions is described by anthropologists working on alternative spiritualities and energy pilgrims present in various Christian shrines—for example, at Rocamadour (Weibel 2001),

Catholic shrines dedicated to Mary Magdalene (Fedele 2013), or Chartres Cathedral (Fedele 2018).
17. Many people connected with Paganism and Slavic traditions draw energy at the Wawel chakra. Due to scarcity of space in this chapter, I do not discuss it in detail.

REFERENCES

Carter, F. W. 1994. *Trade and Urban Development in Poland: An Economic Geography of Cracow, from Its Origins to 1795*. Cambridge: Cambridge University Press.
Cohen, Erik. 1985. "The Tourist Guide: The Origins, Structure and Dynamics of a Role," *Annals of Tourism Research* 12(1): 5–29.
Cusack, Carole M. 2010. *Invented Religions: Imagination, Fiction and Faith*. Farnham and Burlington: Ashgate.
Fedele, Anna. 2013. *Looking for Mary Magdalene: Alternative Pilgrimage and Ritual Creativity at Catholic Shrines in France*. Oxford and New York: Oxford University Press.
Fedele, Anna. 2018. "Translating Catholic Pilgrimage Sites into Energy Grammar: Contested Spiritual Practices," in Simon Coleman and John Eade (eds.), *Pilgrimage and Political Economy: Translating the Sacred in Chartres and Vézelay*. New York and Oxford: Berghahn Books, pp. 112–35.
Feldman, Jackie, and Jonathan Skinner. 2018. "Tour Guides as Cultural Mediators: Performance and Positioning," *Ethnologia Europea* 48(2): 5–13.
Geismar, Haidy. 2015. "Anthropology and Heritage Regimes," *Annual Review of Anthropology* 44: 71–85.
Godula-Węcławowicz, Róża. 2008. "Czakramu moc tajemna. Mit w akcji," in Róża Godula-Węcławowicz (ed.), *Miasto w obrazie, legendzie, opowieści*. Kraków: PTL, pp. 105–12.
Harris, Alana 2013. "Lourdes and Holistic Spirituality: Contemporary Catholicism, the Therapeutic and Religious Thermalism," *Culture and Religion: An Interdisciplinary Journal* 14(1): 23–43.
Isnart, Cyril, and Nathalie Cerezales. 2020. "Introduction," in Cyril Isnart and Nathalie Cerezales (eds.), *The Religious Heritage Complex: Legacy, Conservation, and Christianity*. London: Bloomsbury Academic, pp. 1–13.
Jackowski, Aleksander (ed.). 1999. *Miejsca święte Rzeczpospolitej. Leksykon*. Kraków: Wydawnictwo Znak.
Johnson, Lonnie R. 1996. *Central Europe: Enemies, Neighbors, Friends*. New York and Oxford: Oxford University Press.
Kotwas Marta, Kubik Jan. 2019. "Symbolic Thickening of Public Culture and the Rise of Right-Wing Populism in Poland," *East European Politics and Societies and Cultures* 33(2): 435–71.
Kruczek, Zygmunt. 2014. *Frekwencja w atrakcjach turystycznych*. Kraków, Warszawa: Polska Organizacja Turystyczna.
Kubik, Jan. 1994. *The Power of Symbols against the Symbols of Power: The Rise of Solidarity and the Fall of State Socialism in Poland*. University Park: Pennsylvania State University Press.

Niedźwiedź, Anna. 2017. "Framing the Pope within the Urban Space," in Victoria Hegner and Peter Jan Margry (eds.), *Spiritualizing the City: Agency and Resilience of the Urban and Urbanesque Habitat*. London and New York: Routledge, pp. 81–101.
Nungovitch, Petro Andreas. 2019. *Here All Is Poland: A Pantheonic History of Wawel, 1787–2010*. Lanham, MD: Lexington Books.
Porter-Szücs, Brian. 2011. *Faith and Fatherland: Catholicism, Modernity, and Poland*. Oxford and New York: Oxford University Press.
Purchla, Jacek. 2018. *Miasto i polityka. Przypadki Krakowa*. Kraków: TAiWPN UNIVERSITAS.
Rożek, Michał.1991. *Kraków czyli siódmy czakram ziemi. O tajemniczych osobliwościach tego miasta*. Kraków: Oficyna Cracovia.
Szałapak, Anna. 2005. *Legends and Mysteries of Cracow: From King Krak to Piotr Skrzynecki*. Kraków: Muzeum Historyczne Miasta Krakowa.
Szoka, Andrzej. 2019. "Czakram wawelski—centrum mocy ezoteryczno-patriotycznej," *Pauza Akademicka* 11(458), 14 February, p. 2.
Święch, Zbigniew. 2000. *Czakram wawelski: największa tajemnica wzgórza*. Kraków: Wydawnictwo Wawelskie.
van de Port, Mattijs, and Meyer, Birgit. 2018. "Introduction: Heritage Dynamics: Politics of Authentication, Aesthetics of Persuasion and the Cultural Production of the Real," in Birgit Meyer and Mattijs van de Port (eds.), *Sense and Essence: Heritage and the Cultural Production of the Real*. New York and Oxford: Berghahn Books, pp. 1–39.
Weibel, Deana L. 2001. "Kidnapping the Virgin: The Reinterpretation of a Roman Catholic Shrine by Religious Creatives." PhD dissertation, University of California, San Diego.
Witkowska, Aleksandra. 1984. *Kulty pątnicze piętnastowiecznego Krakowa. Z badań nad miejską kulturą religijną*. Lublin: Wydawnictwo Towarzystwa Naukowego KUL.
Zubrzycki, Geneviève. 2010. "Religion and Nationalism: A Critical Re-examination," in Bryan S. Turner (ed.), *The New Blackwell Companion to the Sociology of Religion*. Chichester: Wiley-Blackwell, pp. 606–25

 CHAPTER 6

Playing the Game of Truth
The National Heritage Regime in Poland and Contemporary Paganism
Kamila Baraniecka-Olszewska

Introduction

Just before midday on the first Tuesday after Easter,[1] great throngs of people came to the two neighboring hills in Kraków: the Lasota Hill and the Krakus Mound. They moved from one to another, flocking around the attractions. On the Lasota Hill, housing the annual indulgence[2] celebration called Rękawka, visitors looked inside the medieval church of Saint Benedict and bought sweets, toys, or religious paraphernalia from the stands set up in front of the church. On the Krakus Mound, where the "Traditional Celebration of Rękawka" was organized, they looked at a reconstructed early medieval Pagan[3] temple, watched food being offered as sacrifice for the souls of ancestors, and could take a peek into a diorama of "the Slavic Netherworld" built at the bottom of the Krakus Mound. For the duration of the afternoon, the audience moved freely between the Catholic church and the re-enacted early medieval world. Circumventing both hills and meandering between them, visitors were combining two religious realities: that of Roman Catholics, who believe in the dominant religion in Poland, and that of marginalized Pagans, who regard Rękawka as an opportunity to cement their place within public space. When I asked one of the re-enactors organizing the part of Rękawka taking place on the Krakus Mound how people could move between two religious realities so freely, reconciling a Roman Catholic indulgence celebration with a re-enactment of Pagan beliefs, he answered that "in Kraków we don't only have Catholicism. Not only that. Because that is not what the city grew from."

During my fieldwork, I often heard from re-enactors organizing the early mediaeval part of Rękawka that Kraków's history had its roots in the Pagan and not in the Christian past. Their strong conviction and determination to defend this view directed my research, prompting me to investigate the complex way in which contemporary Pagan heritage is constructed and introduced into the public sphere. Significantly, this whole process takes place in circumstances (political, social, and historical) that favor Christian heritage (Baraniecka-Olszewska 2019) and thus require some skillful management and assessment of potential gains and losses. In order to describe how the introduction of the contemporary Pagan heritage to Kraków's heritage-scape (see Winter 2016) is managed, I use the notion of the "game of truth," coined by Michel Foucault in his reflection on the "regimes of truth" (1995, 1997). I apply the term "regime of truth" to describe competing visions of national heritage and the role religion plays within it; the concept of the "game of truth" allows me to present how re-enactors lead their grassroots battle to challenge the dominant Roman Catholic heritage.

The organizers of the Traditional Celebration of Rękawka want to make the heritage they create recognizable in the public sphere, as "heritage has become a way of talking about and organizing the relationship between people and significant aspects of their culture, and between people and their environments" (De Cesari 2012: 400). However, due to its hegemonic nature and the tendency to undermine "alternative and subaltern ideas about 'heritage'" (Smith 2006: 11), it has begun to be perceived in terms of a "heritage regime" (Bendix, Eggert, and Peselmann 2012), a concept based directly on the Foucauldian regime of truth. Within one such regime, there are many games of truth, the rules of which are produced historically, socially, culturally, and politically (Lorenzini 2015: 5). In the game of truth, victory is principally achieved by claiming "the truth" and forcing other players to act according to it. In this case, re-enactors struggling to have the place of Pagan heritage recognized in the public sphere participate in the game of trying to undermine the dominant Christian heritage regime of truth by playing their own trump cards of locality and performativity. Thus, they demonstrate the connection Pagan heritage has to the place, to evoke the Pagan past in performances in order to offer a project of Kraków's heritage. Since these cards are not strong enough, contemporary Paganism undergoes a process of culturalization in the course of the game, because two different religious truths cannot be acknowledged by all players. As Michael Lambek noticed, various religious truths existing in parallel may remain incommensurable.[4]

Importantly, the truth produced by Roman Catholicism transcends the religious domain. In Poland, it also affects politics and, consequently, the formation of national heritage, since the relations between the Roman Catholic Church, national identity, and state politics are very close (Kubik 1994;

Porter-Szűcs 2011; Zubrzycki 2006; Pasieka 2015). This situation constitutes a specific context for the analysis of the position of non–Roman Catholic religions in Poland (Pasieka 2015) but also for the Catholic Church's investment in creating collective memory (Bogumił and Głowacka-Grajper 2019) and religious heritage (Baraniecka-Olszewska 2019). National heritage in Poland is state-governed, closely related to and inspired by the worldview embraced by the ruling right-wing Law and Justice Party[5] and the contemporary state historical policy.[6] Nowadays, the government actively strengthens this connection. The present heritage discourse in Poland is therefore built on Christian values and promotes an interpretation of Poland's past that is biased toward Roman Catholicism, which results in a specific combination of heritage and religious regimes of truth. Consequently, Roman Catholicism constitutes the main normative framework (Pasieka 2015: 217) for interpreting Polish heritage.

The complicated position the organizers of the Traditional Celebration of Rękawka occupy in the game stems from the privileged status of the Roman Catholic Church and thus from the constraints early medieval re-enactors and contemporary Pagans experience when participating in national heritage formation. Although Pagan heritage as such exists in the public sphere, it is represented in museums, cultural institutions, and school textbooks as a remote element of the Polish, pre-Christian past, portrayed in the limited and often folklorized form of legends and tales. Only rarely is it depicted as the heritage of a particular historical period that produced its own social structures, culture, and religion and provided the preliminary foundations for the emergence of the Polish state. Pagan religious heritage—understood both in terms of the past and as a contemporary religion—is excluded from the public sphere almost completely. The aim of the described game of truth is thus to present Pagan religious heritage and also the Pagan past as alternatives for the dominant vision of Roman Catholic heritage and the Christian history of Poland.

I analyze the grassroots management of Pagan heritage in terms of game of truths. In order to develop this concept further in the chapter, I present the scene of the game, the players, the stakes of the game, the two trump cards of locality and performativity used by the players, and finally the game result. Significantly, the notion of a "game" is not only a metaphor for organizing the description of the ethnographic material, but an analytical tool that, on the one hand, reveals the complex relations between various regimes of truth and their influence on bottom-up initiatives and, on the other hand, allows us to investigate how regimes of truths are challenged in social practice. As I will demonstrate, the stakes in the game are high, as is the price to pay for remaining in it. It becomes apparent that in the present circumstances, the very fact of being in the game is a win for contemporary Pagans.

Two Rękawka Celebrations

Rękawka is one of the most famous festivals in Kraków. Its participants and organizers, as well as ethnologists (Seweryn 1961; Pisarzak 1978; Oleszkiewicz 2016), describe it as an event deeply rooted in Kraków's history. Today Rękawka consists of two parts, one being a Roman Catholic indulgence celebration, the other an early medieval historical re-enactment of Slavic rituals and some martial skills. Both parts refer to the historical Rękawka celebration that, as sources confirm, was held on the Krakus Mound (albeit intermittently and with significant changes) at least since the sixteenth century (Seweryn 1961). The Roman Catholic part of Rękawka, taking place next to the Saint Benedict church, is organized by the Saint Joseph parish in the Podgórze district and remains an exclusively Catholic celebration. It consists of an indulgence holy mass and a small fair around the church, featuring carousels, stalls with sweets, and toys "made in China." Before 2001 it was the only Rękawka event, but it has since been overshadowed by the historical re-enactment fair called "the Traditional Celebration of Rękawka."

Both parts of Rękawka are held on the Tuesday after Easter, which binds the event tightly to the Christian ritual year. An interpretation developed (mostly) by nineteenth-century ethnologists states that the Rękawka fair is of Pagan origin and that the Saint Benedict church was erected in order to combat the Pagan cult on the Krakus Mound (Potocki 1861: X; Gloger 1903:

Figure 6.1. Saint Benedict church on the Lasota Hill, Rękawka, Kraków, 2018. © Kamila Baraniecka-Olszewska.

161). Despite the efforts of Christians, Pagan elements did, in time, appear within the Catholic ritual; according to ethnologists studying the Rękawka fair, they could be observed in the celebration until the entire event was banned by the Austrian authorities in the second half of the nineteenth century, during the partitions of Poland (Seweryn 1961; Pisarzak 1978). Nowadays, elements that were identified as Pagan in the nineteenth century have been reintroduced in the form of historical re-enactment.

The idea of bringing back Pagan elements to Rękawka lay at the very core of the organization of the event on the Krakus Mound. The initiative came from the Podgórze Cultural Center (Centrum Kultury Podgórze) and the "Krak" Vistulan Warrior Host (Drużyna wojów wiślańskich Krak) and was supported by the district authorities. This part of Rękawka is financed partially from the district budget, partially by sponsors solicited by the re-enactors (local bakeries, Podgórze entrepreneurs). The budget of the celebration is, however, quite limited, and the success of the whole fair—as with many other historical re-enactment events—strongly depends on the goodwill and involvement of the re-enactors, who come to Rękawka from various regions of Poland. For them, the event opens the annual re-enactment season (from April to October) and also provides a unique opportunity to re-enact early medieval Slavic rituals in the exact place where they are believed to have been performed. The Traditional Celebration of Rękawka is an example of an amalgam of grassroots and top-down initiatives. The city of Kraków officially takes patronage over the re-enactment part of the event, which grants it a certain level of recognition. Thus, accepting the city label is a conscious element of managing the celebration, since its organizers aim at advertising Rękawka to a wide range of audiences. The other part—held by the Saint Benedict church—is not financially supported by Kraków's authorities or mentioned in the advertisement campaign organized in the city. However, since the state national heritage policy is implicitly predicated on Roman Catholicism, the event next to the Saint Benedict church has become an element of Kraków's heritage-scape. The script for the Roman Catholic part of the event repeats the form of many other indulgence celebrations and consists of a solemn liturgy in the church and a small fair around it. The fair at the bottom of the Krakus Mound is much more complex. It is prepared by the Krak Host, whose members are granted full freedom in this respect. Each year, the event has a different theme; in 2018 it was the Slavic Netherworld.

Players in the Game of Truth

"After the anniversary of the Baptism of Poland two years ago, there appeared an idea to show more Slavic gods, to put more stress on it. You know,

Christianity was everywhere and our times [early Middle Ages] nowhere. So we had this idea to show it. This year we still continue realizing it, and we chose the Slavic Netherworld for this year." I had this conversation a day after the Rękawka fair, in a bar in the Podgórze district. My interlocutor was a re-enactor, tired after a long day of enacting the Pagan past and a night spent with his friends at the bottom of the Krakus Mound. The interview concerned the various leading themes of subsequent Rękawka celebrations. A few other meetings with members of the Krak re-enactment group confirmed that the general motivation for presenting Pagan religion is its almost complete absence in the public sphere. The organization of the Traditional Celebration of Rękawka remedies this situation to some modest degree, since—as one member of the group told me—"this is what we can do."

Although Rękawka is organized under the patronage of a local cultural center, the conceptual work remains in the hands of the Krak re-enactment group. Its members (with the help of fellow re-enactors from various parts of Poland) are the ones who organize and perform the Traditional Celebration of Rękawka. They constitute a group of very different people, unified in their interest in Kraków's early medieval history and their conviction that this history should be widely known. Thus, they dedicate their time and energy to promote it during re-enactment events and also through cooperation with museums and cultural centers. They describe themselves as a democratic group in which decisions are made collectively; unlike most re-enactment groups, they do not have a leader. The script for Rękawka celebration is the result of their collective efforts. Anyone can propose an idea for the leitmotif for next year's celebration, and—as one of the members of the Krak Host told me—this is the reason why it sometimes takes a lot of time to agree on a leading theme.

Although the group's members share an appreciation for the Pagan culture and work toward introducing Pagan heritage to the public sphere, not all of them are contemporary Pagans. Some members are Roman Catholics; some declare themselves as atheists. Nevertheless, they all participate in the kindling of the "sacred fire" at the top of the Krakus Mound and perform the pre-Christian past together. Other re-enactors who take part in Rękawka are also of different denominations. However, their engagement in early medieval history results in a very particular attitude toward Paganism, perceived both as a historical and contemporary religion.

These re-enactors endeavor to have Paganism acknowledged as the actual root (or at least one of the roots) of Polish culture. Connection to place and to its local history is crucial in understanding contemporary Paganism and the idea of its heritage. While there are religious movements in Poland that embrace beliefs like Celtic or Wicca, which are geographically and culturally foreign, what Rękawka's re-enactors refer to is a religion researchers of contemporary Paganism in Poland define in terms of ethnic Paganism (Filip 2011). It is exceedingly focused on the bond with the local—in this case Slavic—gods, with ancestors, and with links to the place in which these ancestors lived. Its believers call this religion Rodzima wiara, meaning "Native Faith," or Rodzimowierstwo, which stands for a particular Native Faith creed (see Simpson 2012). Scott Simpson, who investigated Rodzimowierstwo, noticed that "although nativeness is strongly linked to the past, it need not be frozen in time, but may be an element in an active process of indigenization of new influences" (2017: 66). Such an approach enables contemporary Pagans to regard the roots of Polish culture differently than in the official state-governed project of national heritage. Contemporary Rodzimowiercy "represent continuity with history, but this continuity attaches to a different set of anchor points than those emphasized by the Roman Catholic mainstream of Polish society" (Simpson 2017: 69).

Significantly, Rodzimowiercy understand contemporary Paganism as a continuation of the old faith, which provides them with a link with the past (Simpson 2017). It is a value contemporary Pagans share with early medieval re-enactors. These two groups—re-enactors and Rodzimowiercy—overlap to a significant degree, although not entirely (see Simpson 2012). Consequently, the group attempting to introduce Pagan heritage to the public sphere is not composed exclusively of Rodzimowiercy. It also includes historical re-enactors who dedicate their time and energy to the period of the early Middle Ages. The present work follows Simpson's practice of referring to the ones who do not follow the Pagan creed but feel a certain affinity with Pagan culture as *rodzimokulturowcy*. It is a term coined analogically to Rodzimowiercy but pertains to culture rather than faith. The author explains it as "Native Culture, following on the model of Native Faith" (Simpson 2017: 84); yet I would rather translate it as "cultural Rodzimowiercy." Sometimes it is also justified to use the broader notion of "cultural Pagans," since a certain reverence is quite often manifested by re-enactors toward other religions, such as Viking or Celtic. While cultural Pagans express general attachment to the pre-Christian past, cultural Rodzimowiercy also emphasize connections to places, evoking a particular space-time that embraces not only people from the past, but—through the link with locality—also in the present.

The First Trump Card in the Game: Locality

Locality is therefore the first card to play in the game of truth. Rękawka organizers ostensibly refer to Kraków's origins, since the Krakus Mound in the

Podgórze district is where the city's history (allegedly) began. This area of Kraków is located on the bank of the Vistula River opposite to its most popular tourist attractions: the Old Town and the Kazimierz district. At the end of the eighteenth century Podgórze was an autonomous town, and it was incorporated into Kraków's borders in 1915. The present district boundaries do not correspond to the former town borders, which encompassed the western part of the contemporary district. The history of the area is a troubled one, especially in the twentieth century. In the early 1900s, Podgórze was a prosperous industrial district inhabited by a large Jewish community. During World War II, Kraków's ghetto was established there, together with the nearby Konzentrationslager Plaszow. Consequently, Podgórze became a recognized Holocaust site. The postwar Communist era was not particularly propitious for the district either, and in the first years after the political transformation, Podgórze remained in the shadow of other rapidly developing tourist sites in Kraków. Very recently, however, the district underwent a thorough transformation (Niedźwiedź 2007) and has since become a tourist attraction, a fashionable location featuring museums, restaurants, and bars. The growing popularity of the district has also encouraged the development of Podgórze's own identity and the construction of its heritage, based on certain (though not complete) autonomy from the heritage-scape of Kraków in general.

The results of Kraków's official conceptualization of Podgórze's heritage are apparent in the recently opened (in April 2018) exhibition in the Podgórze Museum.[7] The exhibition is entitled *The City under the Krakus Mound*, and although it presents the history of one district, the title could also refer to Kraków as a whole: the Krakus Mound is the alleged place of the burial of Kraków's legendary ruler Krakus, who is believed to have founded the city. The hill has become a symbol of Kraków and remains one of the places connecting the city's present to the remote past and its legendary beginnings. In spite of the mound's close association with Paganism, this religion is ignored in the above-mentioned museum exhibition; the pre-Christian religion is only presented as a clouded past, so distant and blurred that it escapes historical knowledge and belongs to the mythical realm of Krakus. The Pagan history is presented simply as a period preceding the Christian era, which began Kraków's "actual" history and continues until today. The Jewish history of Podgórze is also treated as a mere addition to the dominantly Roman Catholic historical narrative. The exhibition thus reflects the premises of the national heritage project, which situates Roman Catholicism at its very center. There is even a short animated movie shown in the historical part of the exhibition, with the Saint Benedict church appearing from the shadows at Podgórze's landscape and a huge, bright sun shining all over the screen when the whole temple finally emerges at the foreground of the picture. Interestingly, the role of Roman Catholicism is not particularly emphasized in heritage events organized in Podgórze outside of the museum, since it constitutes a default element of local heritage (Baraniecka-Olszewska 2019). It is the Jewish heritage that gains more and more attention in the district, and tour guides focus predominantly on the ghetto area, Oskar Schindler's Enamel Factory Museum, the former concentration camp in Płaszów, and other sites related to Jewish history. The Pagan heritage is only present in the public sphere during a single (if spectacular) event in the district: the Traditional Celebration of Rękawka.

Contemporary Pagans all over the world see their religion as the continuation of the faith of their ancestors (see Butler 2015). Therefore, the concept of nativeness seems to be crucial for the interpretation of present Pagan religions. Rodzimowiercy seek a connection with the elements of the landscape that they perceive as native. As Marion Bowman observed during her research in Glastonbury, contemporary spirituality is often strongly related to a particularly powerful place. She describes this phenomenon in terms of "topophilia" (Bowman 2000: 91). This notion helps to understand the importance the Krakus Mound holds for contemporary Pagans. They regard it as a meaningful place where their ancestors observed rituals and placed offerings for the gods. Rodzimowiercy also choose this place for the offering. Moreover, they built a sacred circle at the bottom of the hill, on the premises of an old quarry, which used to be a labor camp during World War II. There they welcome the spring, celebrate the summer solstice, and perform rituals to honor the dead. Although there are no historical sources describing local Pagan rituals, and scholars as well as believers try to reconstruct them using comparative methods and referencing other religions of the time, contemporary Pagans feel that the very act of performing rituals (different as they may be from the old ones) in the same place is enough to establish a connection with the past. Topophilia is thus closely related to the idea of nativeness in Rodzimowierstwo—it connects the faithful to a local place, to the local spirits of ancestors. As one of the re-enactors put it, "You know, there are medieval cemeteries, here, under the Krakus Mound, there in Płaszów, you see. They have been discovered by archaeologists, investigated. And they are our ancestors, they rest here, here . . . You ask me if the place is important. For me yes, it is, you have all these people here, they were living here, they died here, so . . . yes." As we were talking in Podgórze, each word "here" was emphasized by a move of his hand pointing to the vicinity of the Krakus Mound. Furthermore, "here" has a long history that needs to be re-created and performed in order to be recognized as local heritage.

The Other Card to Play: The Performativity of Rękawka

Re-enactors who organize the Traditional Celebration of Rękawka are aware that the event will not gain recognition in terms of an actual religion. Moreover, such festivals are only seldom visible in the public, overshadowed by the omnipresent Roman Catholicism. This situation does not prevent re-enactors from endeavoring to make the Pagan religious heritage more popular. They therefore devote their time to create an attractive and memorable event evoking interest in the early medieval past. Re-enactors choose a very powerful tool to be noticed: performative enactments of the past. Presenting Pagan religious heritage in the form of historical re-enactment may be interpreted as another element used to gain an advantage in the game of truth.

Each year, the space around the Krakus Mound is organized in a similar fashion. The hill can be accessed only from one direction, which is why, before visiting the reconstructed early medieval encampment, visitors need to walk between stalls with contemporary products—folk jewelry, souvenirs, toys, food. Although the event's organizers select the vendors and try to invite folk artists or craftspeople, the products offered there have nothing in common with the Middle Ages. Visitor information points set up by the festival's organizers and their partner institutions (the Podgórze Cultural Center and Kraków Archaeological Museum) distribute leaflets with the event's program and a brief history of Rękawka. Beyond the stalls begins the re-enactment of the early medieval past. Its organization changes a bit each year, depending on the leading theme of the event.

Since the 2018 theme was the Slavic Netherworld, upon entering the festival grounds visitors passed through the "gate to Nawia"—a place inhabited by gods and demons, where human souls were said to dwell after death. Visitors could choose to ignore the gate, but those who decided to walk through it entered the re-enactors' vision of a Slavic sacred ritual. The supreme god Weles, accompanied by the goddesses of winter (Marzanna) and spring (Dziewanna), welcomed the "new souls" into Nawia and threatened them that they would stay in the realm forever, serving them, unless they made an offering. The new souls were guarded by demonic creatures known from nineteenth-century Slavic bestiaries—Żmij, Bies, and Południca—who prevented newcomers from leaving the Netherworld too quickly. Although all interactions between the re-enactors and the visitors were playful, some of the latter felt a bit upset with the re-enactors' behavior and escaped "Nawia"; others played along, asking Weles for mercy. Those who managed to leave the Netherworld safely could go further and visit a re-created Pagan temple.

The structure was erected at the outskirts of the re-enactors' encampment. It featured a light wooden frame and walls made of red fabric, which

Figure 6.2. Weles with goddesses Marzanna and Dziewanna in Nawia—Slavic Netherworld, Rękawka, Kraków, 2018. © Kamila Baraniecka-Olszewska.

sheltered a wooden figure of Światowid, a four-faced deity. The figure was a replica of a historical artifact found during archaeological excavations and displayed in the Kraków Archaeological Museum. Since the identification of the god represented on the statue is still a matter of a heated dispute, re-enactors used the example of the figure to explain to visitors the complexities of research pertaining to Pagan religion. Re-enactors of various denominations of Rodzimowiercy, Roman Catholics, and also nonbelievers took shifts in front of the temple to inform the audience about Pagan religion. Some spectators snuck curious peeks inside the reconstructed Pagan temple, asking questions about the figure, the rites that were observed in such temples, and Slavic gods. Some visitors passed by indifferently, heading directly toward the early medieval encampment re-created at the bottom of the hill, where for a single day re-enactors could try to live as their ancestors had in the past. They set up tents and placed simple furniture (wooden tables and stools) in front of them; later they lit fires to cook food and cleaned weapons and sets of armor, preparing for the afternoon battle. All of them, including small children, wore historical attire sewn by hand and made of handwoven fabrics, in line with the fashions and technologies known in the early Middle Ages. Some items of clothing, tools, and ornaments made in that manner could be bought in Rękawka, available both to the audience members and to re-enactors. Craftspeople displayed their work, mostly fabrics, pottery, jewelry, and leather accessories such as belts, pouches, and armor elements. Since handicraft products are not cheap, only a small group of visitors decided to buy historical souvenirs; re-enactors, in turn, saw the fair as an opportunity to add new items to their historical equipment and thus shopped eagerly. Visitors moved between tents, stopping to touch handwoven fabric or to try some flatbread baked over an open fire, as some re-enactors were selling food made on the premises. Spectators could hold a sword or a shield in their hands and take photographs with re-enactors. Some of them asked questions about the artifacts they saw or about life in the past; others were too timid and just looked on from a distance. For the entire day, visitors were moving along the bottom of the hill, visiting certain sections many times and just passing through others. The time they spent at the Traditional Celebration of Rękawka varied, from thirty minutes to several hours.

Like every year, the 2018 Rękawka fair started at noon with the kindling of a sacred fire at the top of the Krakus Mound. First, a procession of men and women in historical attire climbed the mound, carrying food offerings—some to be placed at the top of the hill, some to be rolled down from it. This time the fire was lit by a Jagiellonian University scholar, since the Pagan priest who usually performed the rite could not attend due to health issues. After the offerings for ancestors were complete, the event officially began. Short performances were enacted in front of the audience throughout the day. Three of them were related to the main theme of that Rękawka fair and represented legends connected to Slavic beliefs. The first performance told the story of the goddesses of winter and spring. One year Marzanna (winter) did not want to leave the human realm. Since people were starving because of the long winter, they needed to place offerings for her to persuade her to go back to Nawia and allow her sister Dziewanna (spring) to come. They were forced to make offerings from their very last supplies, risking death by starvation to make Marzanna go away. Eventually they succeeded, and spring finally arrived, bringing hope for a brighter future. The second play was presented in front of the reconstructed temple. It told the story of a female temple servant, called Siuda Baba, who ended her service performed in isolation and solitude and needed a young apprentice to replace her. After capturing a young girl and condemning her to a sad and lonely existence in the temple, Siuda Baba came back to her community expecting to live happily among people, only to be murdered as a person belonging to the nonhuman world. The third play presented the story of a cruel princess from the Lasota Hill, who managed to maintain her youthful appearance by killing men who courted her and absorbing their vital energy. One of them finally outsmarted the princess and saved his life, leaving her to perish.

Each of these stories was taken from folk legends told or read to children; members of the Krak Host rewrote and edited them to draw more emphasis to their relation to the actual Slavic religion, presenting them as possible elements in its canon. This, however, does not mean that the performances were enacted in a serious, solemn way, as a kind of religious drama. On the contrary, the rather gruesome tales of murder, sacrifice, and humankind's dependence on the whim of the gods were presented with a dose of situational humor, in a manner suitable for children (who were among the audience). As Rękawka is an event organized for families, the representation of the more cruel beliefs and the difficult living conditions of early medieval people is not possible; the only form that re-enactors can assume is the ludic one.

Other performances are shown to the audience during the Rękawka fair on a recurring (yearly) basis, although with a varying level of spectacularism. The first one is a warriors' race around the mound. Historical sources pertaining to Rękawka celebrations inform that it involved various games and competitions; the present-day races were conceived by the re-enactor organizers as a way to present how such games may have looked like (see Baraniecka-Olszewska 2016). The competition held in 2018 was a rather modest one, as only a dozen warriors decided to enter. Moreover, none of them was particularly determined to win, and the whole race appeared a bit slow. Another annually organized event involves a divination to foretell Kraków's fortunes for the coming year. In 2018 it was performed next to the re-created temple. A "priest" (one of the re-enactors) hid behind a huge loaf, asking three times whether he could be seen from behind the bread. The answer was no, which augured a prosperous year for the whole city. Interestingly, the prophecy was received by the vice-mayor of Kraków.

The most popular event among the audience members is the re-enacted battle staged next to the mound. Several dozen re-enactor warriors take part in it every year. Since no actual historical sources describe battles fought in the vicinity of Kraków in the tenth century, re-enactors invent them and perform before the audience, providing a short introduction, which justifies the historical probability of such an event. In 2018 the battle was entitled "Vistulan warriors against their invaders" and presented how the Vistulan tribe may have defended its territory from enemy raids. The closing event of the 2018 Rękawka fair was an anti-vampire burial, during which a faux corpse wrapped in a black shroud was pierced with a wooden stick through the heart before being buried. The organizers of the celebration explained that such a funeral rite corresponded with the idea of the Slavic Netherworld as a place full of demonic creatures that struck fear in our forebears, prompting them to invent ways to prevent such horrors from interfering with their daily lives. All performances were preceded by brief introductions given by re-enactors, to provide the audience with a historical and religious context for the presented stories.

Performances often prove a successful means of transmitting knowledge about the history of groups that are silenced or oppressed, granting such history a certain agency to act within the society (Taylor 2006: 193). History performed in re-enactments thus holds a potential for affecting the present (Schneider 2011). This performative potential is used by re-enactors who bring the past back into play in order to influence contemporary social reality and help them construct Pagan religious heritage. Performed history not only strengthens the bond that contemporary Pagans or cultural Pagans build with the past, but also enables a transformation of the Christian-biased vision of Kraków's history as the city of John Paul II (Niedźwiedź 2017, 2019).

Materializing the Pagan past in the form of performance gave re-enactors an opportunity to confront their audience with the vision of Kraków's history they propose. The form of the event assumed by the organizers of the Traditional Celebration of Rękawka promote this idea effectively, as the event gains more popularity with every passing year. Furthermore, it has already overshadowed the Roman Catholic part of the festival and became an emblem of Rękawka for its visitors. The festivities held next to the Saint Benedict church are visited by fewer people, and the visitors tend to spend less time at the site. As one of Podgórze district's inhabitants in her mid-twenties told me, she has been coming to Rękawka for as long as she remembers. She has always visited the fair around the church, since this is what Rękawka was when she was little. However, she really looks forward to the event on the Krakus Mound, because something interesting is always going on and she meets more friends there. In this respect, the event's organizers have succeeded in finding a niche for introducing Pagan heritage to the public sphere in a ludic fashion and were granted a place there, acknowledged, and recognized by the municipal and district authorities.

By Way of Conclusion: In Order to Win, You Have to Make Sacrifices

Performing the Pagan past in a playful way, reinvigorating folk legends in order to show their roots in the actual pre-Christian religion, and referring to the Pagan past as the actual history of Kraków are what re-enactors are allowed to present in the public sphere. The entire event is partially financed by the district authorities; it is given official city patronage and the permission to be organized within urban space. However, to keep all these resources, the organizers of the Traditional Celebration of Rękawka cannot fill this local heritage project of enacting the Pagan past with contemporary Pagan religion. Managing this situation prompts re-enactors to self-culturalize the religious aspects of Rękawka. The price re-enactors need to pay in order to stay in the game is the outcome of certain secularization practices involving non-Christian religions. These practices are imposed by the dominant role of Roman Catholicism within the national heritage project.

As contemporary anthropological research on the subject has demonstrated, secularization is neither comprehensive nor homogenous, and there are many variants deriving from specific cultural and historical backgrounds (Asad 2003; Cannell 2010). Moreover, it is important to look at secularism as just one of many possible attitudes toward religions. As Lambek writes, "Although secularism (by definition) recognizes and perhaps produces transcendent religion, something we might call immanent religion continues unremarked and unbidden, or is seen as vaguely threatening insofar as it cannot be pinned down and governed" (2013: 25). When we focus on the "pinning down and governing" religion as enacted by the Roman Catholic regime of truth, the secularization practices appear a political tactic: an attempt to govern non-Catholic religion and deprive it of its worship dimension in the public sphere. Understood in this manner, secularization is easily recognized in top-down, state-governed practices limiting the access contemporary Pagan religions in Poland have to the public sphere. Thus, the culturalization of Rodzimowierstwo is a result of secularization tactics.

Although the notions of culture and religion are inseparable, focusing on the process of culturalization enables us to grasp what happens with religion when in political or legal discourses it is presented as culture (Joppke 2018) and not as—to use Michael Lambek's (2013: 25) term—an "immanent religion." The organizers of the Traditional Celebration of Rękawka would like to operate within the "immanent" frame, gain recognition for both historical and contemporary Paganism as an actual religion, and consequently use this credit to build a Pagan religious heritage. However, it is the strategy of culturalization of Rodzimowierstwo that allows them to stay in the game, since the trump cards they hold in their hands are too weak to secure them the ultimate victory. Although the performativity card allows the ludic past to materialize on stage through attractive historical re-enactments and stories full of legendary creatures, gods, and goddesses, the event is perceived in terms of leisure, a pastime not to be taken entirely seriously. The locality trump card allows the Traditional Celebration of Rękawka to be inscribed into Kraków's heritage-scape, but situates the event among the city's other traditions, entangled in an unbreakable connection with the Roman Catholic Rękawka.

Significantly, many participants of both Rękawka celebrations do not perceive the Roman Catholic and the Pagan events as incommensurable.

Visitors go from one hill to another, commenting that after having a look inside the Saint Benedict church, they go to see the medieval encampment. Standing on one hill, some say to their family members and friends, "Now let's see another part of Rękawka." When I asked passersby both on the Krakus Mound and on the Lasota Hill a question that many found a bit annoying—"Where is the actual Rękawka?"—people were pointing to one hill and then the other, saying, "You see here and there," or "Here, where you're standing and on the other hill." When I asked, "And what is worth seeing at Rękawka?" the answers were also very similar: "An old church and the re-enactors' performances on the mound." And when, standing on the Lasota Hill, I finally decided to ask if what I was witnessing was a single Rękawka fair or two separate events, one older lady got a bit irritated by too many repetitive questions: "Child, please. This is the old part, there is the new part. But you see that all people are going both ways, to see both parts. This is how Rękawka is now, see?"

Aside from the organizers of the Traditional Celebration of Rękawka, most visitors do not distinguish between the two Rękawka fairs, but participate in one event. Among the dozens of visitors with whom I spoke, there was only one person who was not planning to see the part on the Krakus Mound. She came to the fair around the church with her husband and said that the new part of Rękawka is not what she was used to and that she did not like the crowds there. But even though she was reluctant to see what was happening on the Krakus Mound, she was still referring to the events there as the "other part" of Rękawka. Spectators do not experience any incommensurability between the events because they do not recognize both of them as religious. When I asked what happens in the Saint Benedict church, even tourists who were not from Kraków answered that there was a holy mass. And when I asked if there were any rituals performed at the Krakus Mound, usually my interlocutors replied that the event involved some plays and shows presenting medieval times. I inquired of several people about the kindling of fire at the top of the Krakus Mound, asking if they knew that this rite was usually performed by a Pagan priest. A few of my interlocutors were very surprised, but notwithstanding the information I shared, they were describing this ritual as "just Rękawka tradition." Only the Roman Catholic event is seen as religious in nature; therefore the potential competition between the religious regimes of truth remains unnoticed.

The elements of pre-Christian religions performed and presented during the celebration remain pre-Christian in the chronological sense; in the eyes of the spectators, they are not related to contemporary Paganism and its heritage. The continuity between past and present religion—which constitutes the present-day core identity claim for Rodzimowiercy—remains unrecognized by the audience. Spectators perceive Rękawka as a theatrical reconstruction of a legendary folk realm. As a creed without any fixed theology or ritual canon, featuring many local variations and individual forms of cult, Rodzimowierstwo is rarely taken seriously or recognized as a religion (Simpson 2017: 69–70). Therefore, it is granted only the status of local folklore within the national heritage regime. In Poland, the heritage regime allows the Roman Catholic past to become a national value. As far as this religion is concerned, the processes of heritagization and culturalization do not entail secularization. There is room for Roman Catholicism as an "immanent religion" within the national heritage regime. Other religions operate within this heritage regime according to the structure deriving from the hierarchical pluralism of religions in Poland (see Pasieka 2015). In the case of Rękawka, a smartly played game of truth grants Pagan heritage entrance to the public sphere, but neither the actions re-enactors undertake nor the rituals they perform are perceived as an actual religion by the spectators of the event. The audience is more likely to interpret them as mere re-enactment of past rituals, deprived of the "lived" religious content. Rękawka organizers have succeeded in introducing Pagan heritage to the public sphere, but they have not been equally successful in representing it as religious heritage. This is, however, a sacrifice the event's organizers needed to make in order to stay in the game.

Kamila Baraniecka-Olszewska works at the Institute of Archaeology and Ethnology of Polish Academy of Sciences. She studied ethnology and Latin American studies. Her main areas of interest are the anthropology of religion and performance studies, and in particular forms of religious expression. In 2011 she received her PhD from the University of Warsaw with a dissertation on participation in Polish passion plays. She is the author of articles on contemporary religiosity and historical re-enactments and of the books *The Crucified: Contemporary Passion Plays in Poland* (2017) and *World War II Historical Reenactment in Poland: The Practice of Authenticity* (2021).

NOTES

1. My research on Rękawka was conducted for the HERILIGION: The Heritigazation of Religion and Sacralization of Heritage in Contemporary Europe project in 2018, funded by Humanities in the European Research Area (HERA) grant # 5087-00505A. It was a part of a broader study on Kraków's heritage, and my task was to investigate how contemporary Pagan religious heritage is constructed in the circumstances of overwhelming dominance of Roman Catholic and Jewish identities of the city—also researched within the HERILIGION project. I was accompanied in my efforts by Dr. Alicja Sośko-Mucha, who kindly shared her fieldwork data with me, for which I am deeply grateful.

2. Indulgence is a ritual in the Roman Catholic Church. Participation in it, in accordance with the rules established by the Church, might contribute to the reduction of the time a soul would spend in purgatory after death.
3. In the chapter I decided to use terms "Pagan" and "Paganism" both for the historical and contemporary religion, emphasizing, however, when I refer to modern times only. The notion of Neo-Paganism is severely criticized by believers, as it ignores the connection to past religion that is crucial for contemporary followers. Although they also reject the term "Paganism" that was introduced by Christians fighting with local beliefs, I have decided to use it—just as other scholars investigating contemporary Pagan religions—rather than referencing only the names of specific native religions, which would narrow the analysis too much.
4. Michael Lambek, "Facing Religion, from Anthropology," *Anthropology of This Century* 4 (2012), http://aotcpress.com/articles/facing-religion-anthropology/ (accessed 31 August 2021).
5. The Law and Justice (*Prawo i Sprawiedliwość*) Party formed a government in Poland in the autumn of 2015; however, its presence on the political stage has been felt for much longer. Thus, the particular historical policy supported by the party and incorporated into its political program has already started to become visible in the public sphere in the first decade of the twentieth-first century (Traba 2010).
6. On the current historical policy in Poland, see Korzeniewski 2008; Łuczewski 2017; Traba 2010; and Wolff-Powęska 2007.
7. A branch of the Museum of Kraków.

REFERENCES

Asad, Talal. 2003. *Formations of the Secular: Christianity, Islam, Modernity*. Stanford, CA: Stanford University Press.

Baraniecka-Olszewska, Kamila. 2016. "Re-enacting Historical Slavic Rites in Contemporary Poland: The Rękawka Fair in Cracow," *Anthropological Journal of European Cultures* 25(11): 118–35.

Baraniecka-Olszewska, Kamila. 2019. "The State Historical Policy and the Default Religious Heritage in Poland: On Introducing Pagan Heritage to the Public Sphere in Kraków," *Etnografia Polska* 63(1–2): 155–86.

Bendix, F. Regina, Aditya Eggert, and Arnika Peselmann (eds.). 2012. *Heritage Regimes and the State*. Göttingen: Universitätsverlag Göttingen.

Bogumił, Zuzanna, and Małgorzata Głowacka-Grajper. 2019. *Milieux de Mémoire in Late Modernity: Local Communities, Religion and Historical Politics*. Berlin: Peter Lang.

Bowman, Marion. 2000. "More of the Same? Christianity, Vernacular Religion and Alternative Spirituality in Glastonbury," in Steven Sutcliffe and Marion Bowman (eds.), *Beyond New Age: Exploring Alternative Spirituality*. Edinburgh: Edinburgh University Press, pp. 83–104.

Butler, Jenny. 2015. "Remembrance of the Ancestors in Contemporary Paganism: Lineage, Identity, and Cultural Belonging in the Irish Context," *Journal of the Irish Society for the Academic Study of Religions* 1–2: 94–118.

Cannell, Fenella. 2010. "The Anthropology of Secularism," *Annual Review of Anthropology* 39: 85–100.

De Cesari, Chiara. 2012. "Thinking through Heritage Regimes," in Regina F. Bendix, Aditya Eggert, and Arnika Peselmann (eds.), *Heritage Regimes and the State*. Göttingen: Universitätsverlag Göttingen, pp. 399–413.

Filip, Mariusz. 2011. "'Polityka tożsamości we wspólnotach neopogańskich. Przykład Zakonu Zadrugi 'Północny Wilk,'" in Wojciech Dohnal and Aleksander Posern-Zieliński (eds.), *Antropologia i polityka. Szkice z badań nad kulturowymi wymiarami władzy*. Warsaw: Komitet Nauk Etnologicznych PAN, Instytut Archeologii i Etnologii PAN, pp. 175–88.

Foucault, Michael. 1995. *Discipline and Punish: The Birth of the Prison*. New York: Vintage Books.

Foucault, Michael. 1997. *The Essential Works of Foucault 1954–1984: Ethics, Subjectivity and Truth*. Edited by Paul Rabinow. New York: New Press.

Gloger, Zygmunt. 1903. *Encyklopedia staropolska ilustrowana*, vol. 4. Warszawa: Druk P. Laskauer.

Joppke, Christian. 2018. "Culturalizing Religion in Western Europe: Patterns and Puzzles," *Social Compass* 65(2): 1–13.

Korzeniewski, Bartosz. 2008. "Wprowadzenie. Polityka historyczna—propozycje definicji i spory wokół jej zakresu w polskim i niemieckim dyskursie naukowym," in Bartosz Korzeniewski (ed.), *Narodowe i europejskie aspekty polityki historycznej*. Poznań: Instytut Zachodni, pp. 7–28.

Kubik, Jan. 1994. *The Power of Symbols against the Symbols of Power: The Rise of Solidarity and the Fall of State Socialism in Poland*. University Park: Pennsylvania State University Press.

Lambek, Michael. 2013. "What Is 'Religion' for Anthropology and What Has 'Anthropology' Brought to Religion?," in Janice Boddy and Michael Lambek (eds.), *A Companion to the Anthropology of Religion*. London: Wiley and Sons, pp. 1–32.

Lorenzini, Daniele. 2015. "What Is a 'Regime of Truth'?," *Le Foucaldien* 1(1): 1–5.

Łuczewski, Michał. 2017. *Kapitał moralny. Polityki historyczne w późnej nowoczesności*. Kraków: Ośrodek Myśli Politycznej.

Niedźwiedź, Anna. 2007. "Krakowskie Podgórze—dziedzictwo odkrywane," in Andrzej Stawarz (ed.), *Miasto po obu brzegach rzeki. Różne oblicza kultury*. Warsaw: Muzeum Historyczne m.st. Warszawy, Muzeum Niepodległości, pp. 187–200.

Niedźwiedź, Anna. 2017. "Framing the Pope within the Urban Space: John Paul II and the Cityscape of Kraków," in Victoria Hegner and Peter Jan Margry (eds.), *Spiritualizing the City: Agency and Resilience of the Urban and Urbanesque Habitat*. London and New York: Routledge, pp. 81–101.

Niedźwiedź, Anna. 2019. "Global Catholicism, Urban Heritage, National Politics: The 2016 World Youth Day in Kraków," *Etnografia Polska* 63: 185–203.

Oleszkiewicz, Małgorzata. 2016. "Storage of Rituals: The Traces of the Emmaus and the Rękawka Church Fairs in the Seweryn Udziela Ethnographic Museum in Kraków as the Examples of the Intangible Heritage in Museums," in Magdalena Kwiecińska (ed.), *Intangible Heritage of the City. Musealization, Preservation, Education*. Kraków: Historical Museum of the City of Kraków, pp. 153–66.

Pasieka, Agnieszka. 2015. *Hierarchy and Pluralism: Living Religious Difference in Catholic Poland*. United States: Palgrave Macmillan.

Pisarzak, Marian. 1978. "Obrzędowość wiosenna w dawnych wiekach w związku z recepcją 'święconego' w Polsce," *Lud* 62(1): 53–74.

Porter-Szűcs, Brian. 2011. *Faith and Fatherland: Catholicism, Modernity, and Poland*. New York: Oxford University Press.
Potocki, Leon. 1861. *Święcone, czyli pałac Potockich w Warszawie*. Poznań: J. K. Żupański.
Schneider, Rebecca. 2011. *Performing Remains: Art and War in Times of Theatrical Reenactment*. London and New York: Routledge.
Seweryn, Tadeusz. 1961. *Tradycje i zwyczaje krakowskie*. Kraków: Wydawnictwo Artystyczno-Graficzne.
Simpson, Scott. 2012. "Strategies for Constructing Religious Practice in Polish Rodzimowierstwo," in Adam Anczyk and Halina Grzymała-Moszczyńska (eds.), *Walking the Old Ways: Studies in Contemporary European Paganism*. Katowice: Sacrum Publishing House, pp. 11–36.
Simpson, Scott. 2017. "'Only the Slavic Gods': Nativeness in Polish Rodzimowierstwo," in Kathryn Rountree (ed.), *Cosmopolitanism, Nationalism, and Modern Paganism*. New York: Palgrave Macmillan, pp. 65–86.
Smith, Laurajane. 2006. *The Uses of Heritage*. London and New York: Routledge.
Taylor, Diana. 2006. "Performance and/as History," *TDR: The Drama Review* 50(1): 67–86.
Traba, Robert. 2010. "Polityka wobec historii: kontrowersje i perspektywy," *Teksty Drugie* 1–2: 300–319.
Winter, Tim. 2016. "Heritagescaping and the Aesthetics of Refuge: Challenges to Urban Sustainability," in William Logan, Máiréad Nic Craith, and Ullrich Kockel (eds.), *A Companion to Heritage Studies*. Chichester: Wiley Blackwell, pp. 189–202.
Wolff-Powęska, Anna. 2007. "Polskie spory o historię i pamięć. Polityka historyczna," *Przegląd Zachodni* 1: 3–45.
Zubrzycki, Geneviève. 2006. *The Crosses of Auschwitz: Nationalism and Religion in Post-Communist Poland*. Chicago and London: University of Chicago Press.

PART IV

PORTUGUESE HERITAGES AND LUSOTROPICALISM

 CHAPTER 7

Curating Culture and Religion
Lusotropicalism and the Management of Heritage in Portugal
Maria Cardeira da Silva and Clara Saraiva

Introduction: Heritage Making and Lusotropicalism

Like the rest of Europe, Portugal partakes in a global regime of heritage (Bendix, Eggert, and Peselmann 2012) and follows the general principles established by UNESCO and other transnational institutions, having signed the World Heritage Convention in 1979 and the Intangible Heritage Convention in 2008. But UNESCO's marked presence in heritage studies has contributed to the neglect of national and regional dynamics that, in a more lateral sense, explain the particular configurations of patrimonial regimes[1] and religion management in different countries. The origins of a modern heritage regime in Portugal precede global directives and followed the historical constitution and legal steps of the *patrimoine* in France. This lent it specific contours that reflect national historical and political specificities, different ways of managing mainland and empire, culture, territory, and people. Nowadays these specificities can be summed up in a reprocessing of heritage making and national curatorship toward what we can consider, at the same time, one of its most celebrated cultural legacies: that of lusotropicalism. Lusotropicalism was a narrative about identity imported from Brazil[2] and integrated by the Portuguese dictatorship preceding the 1974 Carnation Revolution—the Estado Novo—to accommodate and nationalize racial diversity and thus to legitimize Portugal's colonial mission in the post–World War II world, in the face of international criticism of Portugal's late colonialism. This national narrative is predicated on the idea that Portuguese colonialism was a soft one, promoting cultural and religious tolerance as well as miscegenation.

This discourse ties into a rhetoric of the magnificence of the "Portuguese Discoveries," which is still today another important vector for curating and displaying national identity.

While describing the Portuguese specificities of heritage management and religious diversity in the recent past, this chapter will analyze the endurance of the lusotropicalist national narrative, going beyond the self-congratulatory discourse that plays a major part in its persistence and that, ultimately, allows us to approach it as a sacralized heritage in itself. The discursive similarities between Portuguese lusotropicalism rhetoric and UNESCO directives (which both took shape after World War II) may partly justify the persistence of this discourse of Portuguese exceptionality of an assumed tolerance toward cultural and religious diversity (Cardeira da Silva 2013: 64–65). This was refined in the later Declaration on Creative Diversity (2001) and subsequent conventions that globalize liberal cosmopolitanism. But beyond its compliance with global norms and neoliberal politics, lusotropicalism as a vernacular discourse seems to smoothly enable bottom-up processes of cultural or even religious claims through heritagization, and this may be another reason for its resilience.

Vernacular lusotropicalism can be thought of as a way to think of and conceptualize the Portuguese colonial past as exceptional by laypeople who never read its inaugural text but have absorbed notions that have lingered in the national rhetoric for decades, based on an understanding of Portuguese colonialism as marked by great deeds and "natural" tolerance. This vernacular lusotropicalism is not explicitly or coherently articulated, but it is hidden in lusotropes (cf. Bastos 2018) that linger in people's thoughts, discourses, and actions, also with regard to heritage. Lusotropicalism can be considered a tentative whitewashing of Portuguese colonialism by formulating it as "exceptional," and it can be updated as a cosmopolitan rhetoric of national identity.

In order to test and justify contemporary lusotropicalist purification, resilience, and endurance (and, ultimately, sacralization), we present a concise overview of the entangling and disentangling of religion, culture, and heritage and their management throughout Portuguese recent history. We will also analyze the entanglements of state and religion in this process: behind a formal process of secularization, Portugal, allegedly a secular country, treats the Catholic Church with partiality behind a veneer of religious diversity and rights.

With this scenario as context, we will follow the path of heritage management in the emblematic sites of Sintra and Mértola, using data from fieldwork undertaken from 2016 to 2019.[3] We will look at these from (1) a diachronic perspective, which summarizes state and church attitudes concerning both heritage and religion in the country since the end of nineteenth century; and (2) a more ethnographic perspective by describing the present situation, including some tensions and contradictions between top-down and bottom-up approaches to heritage management.

From Heritage to Religion, or Portugal's Incomplete Disenchantment

The first heritage regulations in Portugal, while formulated during the monarchy, were already inspired by liberal movements and tainted, from the beginning, with the monumental and celebratory fashion that still infuses national display to this day. The first liberal historians (at the time of the late monarchy) created the *monumentos pátrios* (motherland monuments) with strong nationalist purposes and established the Conservation Society of National Monuments (1840). In a scenario already molded by anticlericalism, the extinction of religious orders, and the confiscation of their properties in 1834, the positions of Portuguese liberalists were, nevertheless, ambiguous regarding religion, as they declared the unequivocal importance of religious belief and Catholicism as a "network of affections" indispensable to freedom and social cohesion.[4] This relates to a heritage genealogy that legitimizes and crystallizes an unclear position—which, up to the present day, has not suffered much contestation—despite the formal separation between the church and the state proclaimed in 1911 by the republicans. In fact, it is leading up to the establishment of the Portuguese Republic in 1910 that the first associations for the study, conservation, and restoration of the national heritage are founded and the classification of emblematic national monuments begins. These are, mainly and significantly, convents and churches and confiscated religious goods; the dying monarchy in a last-ditch effort sought to outflank the Jacobin movement by enacting anticlerical measures of its own.

The Estado Novo dictatorship established by Salazar two decades later definitively ended the period of liberalism in Portugal. And while strategically maintaining the law of separation of church and state, the new regime's relations with the church were always close even if ambiguous. In 1940 a new concordat with the Vatican reinforced the relations between the state and the Catholic Church, using particular contexts, such as the recognition by both of the importance of Fátima (Vilaça 2006; Vilaça et al. 2016: 31; Fedele and Mapril, this volume). This agreement implied a regime of privilege awarded to the Catholic Church and a hierarchy of religions, which resulted in the persecution of different minority religious groups (Mapril et al. 2017). With a strong nationalist ideology, Salazar used and abused both heritage and religion as a form of propaganda, placing them at the service of the nation and its display, founding in 1929 the Directorate-General for National

Buildings and Monuments, which would be abolished only in 2007. The continued use of heritage—very often religious heritage—and the educational and aesthetic efforts of what came to be known as the "policy of the spirit"[5] led by the masterful hand of Salazar propagandists were indelibly printed on a collective, self-congratulatory image of the Portuguese.

By the end of the Estado Novo, the lusotropical rhetoric of a "soft colonization" was used to project a positive external image, especially among multilateral organizations where Portugal was viewed with suspicion for its racist policies in its colonies. After a brief strategic participation in UNESCO (1965-72) as a way of guaranteeing the right to respond to such accusations, Portugal ended up withdrawing, following the approval of a UNESCO resolution that, according to the Portuguese state, allowed the allocation of funds to anti-Portuguese terrorist movements (Rodrigues 2006). Only after the 1974 Carnation Revolution, and the subsequent independence of the colonies, would Portugal resume its place in UNESCO.

Two convergent narratives persisted until the end of the Estado Novo: one concerning the nation, and another one legitimizing the empire, with the latter—explicitly expressed through lusotropicalism—strongly impregnating conceptions of national identity and of heritage, even if not explicitly formulated in national heritage vocabulary. This dual narrative forced the regime to make, and exhibit to the world, some compromises—accepting, for instance, the category of Portuguese Muslims in the colonies (Vakil, Machaqueiro, and Monteiro 2011), while in the metropole maintaining the unescapable association of "Portugueseness" with Catholicism intact. The state and church invested in a strong heritagization and enshrinement of the Sanctuary of Fátima and promotion of other Catholic monumental sites under the auspices of the church, while strategically discarding Islamic remains in archaeological national policies.

After the Carnation Revolution, which brought democracy to the country in 1974, the postrevolutionary governments proclaimed the intention to, as formulated in the Fifth Government Program in 1975, "break the traditional separation between erudite culture, mass culture, and popular culture, institutionalizing means of commingling between these different layers and of overcoming the dichotomy between culture understood as legacy or acquired heritage and the living expressions of cultural creation of today."[6] The program proclaimed the support to the growing and pluralistic mobilization of cultural dynamics, mainly through the "active participation of local authorities, public-interest foundations, cultural, recreational, and youth associations, as well as schools and the media,"[7] and in 1980 the Portuguese Institute of Cultural Heritage was created. These were the first efforts for democratizing heritage, intended to be socially inclusive, although still lacking concerns for cultural diversity and religious integration.

The 1976 constitution reiterated the freedom of consciousness and religion, condemned all religious persecutions, and clearly separated the state from the church, but it was only in 2001—the very same year when the Basic Law for Cultural Heritage regarding policies and regimes for its protection and enhancement was passed[8]—that the Law for Religious Freedom was enacted (Vilaça 2006). Still, Catholicism kept a regime of privilege that was legitimized, emphasizing its primacy in the constitution and the essence of Portuguese culture and heritage.

As elsewhere in Europe, a real heritage fever broke out in Portugal from the 1990s on (Fabre 1996), largely due to European Union incentives for regional development following Portugal's entry into the European community. By this time there were already several local and regional heritage and development associations, many of which had sprung from a post-revolution impetus for decentralization and subsequent impulses for regionalization.[9] Some of these promoted heritage as resource for local development inspired by laic utopias and, paradoxically, played a fundamental role in the preservation and restoration of religious heritage, as was the case in Sintra and Mértola.

A progressive criticism regarding the exaltation of national identity based on the idea of the Portuguese Discoveries grew in many sectors. Nevertheless, in 1986 the National Commission for the Commemoration of the Discoveries was created, only to be dissolved in 2002. Similarly, more than a decade later, the 1998 Lisbon World Exposition had as its theme "The Oceans, a Heritage for the Future," which in fact commemorated five hundred years of the Portuguese Discoveries.

The persistence of colonial ideas alongside the presence of the Catholic Church in the national genealogy and its celebration is also evident in the number and type of Portuguese heritage sites nominated by UNESCO. Beyond these national sites, there are twenty-six other sites in eighteen different countries, all of them integrated in the Network of World Heritage of Portuguese Origin—and thus directly tied to the Portuguese colonial empire—managed by Portugal (Cardeira da Silva 2013: 63). Regardless of the progressive spread of a multiculturalist rhetoric that is well matched to liberal cosmopolitanism and suitably supported by lusotropicalism, Portugal diplomatic engagements continue to favor relations with former colonies and celebrating *lusophonie*—thus exalting its colonial roots—even today. This multiculturalist rhetoric continues to be strongly inspired by the lusotropicalist discourse tied into an alleged Portuguese pioneering globalization with its most positive effects (Cardeira da Silva 2013: 63, 2015), especially at the cultural level—the early flourishing of "creative diversity" that neoliberalism would later come to celebrate and that is still one of its proclaimed corollaries.

Being traditionally a country of emigration, Portugal started receiving new flows of immigrants in particular after integration into the EU, in 1986.[10] It thus became possible to find a diverse religioscape where Brazilian charismatic Catholicism coexists with Punjabi Sikh and Hindu temples, Jewish congregations, Islamic groups, Evangelical, Neo-Pentecostal, and African churches (Sarró and Blanes 2009), Afro-Brazilian religions (Pordeus Jr. 2009; Saraiva 2008, 2013, 2016), Orthodox, Buddhists, as well as Neo-Pagan, Neo-Shaman, and Neo-Druid groups (Fedele 2013; Roussou 2017). These new migrants are people who no longer follow the colonial routes, and this has definitively rendered the cultural and religious diversity of the country more complex. With the acceleration of neoliberal politics, different governments engaged in what we could call (with Vertovec 1996) a public space of multiculturalism, giving visibility, at last, to ethnic and religious "minorities" and displaying layers of religious heritages in harmonious (or not so harmonious) ways. Would lusotropicalism be resilient enough to accommodate this new and, for some, disruptive "superdiversity" (Vertovec 2010)?

In 2004, the Commission for Religious Freedom was eventually established, with the objectives of denouncing the violations to religious freedom and promoting the dissemination of issues and events pertaining to religious liberty, and remains active to this day. Most minority religious groups try to organize themselves as NGOs to achieve empowerment as official religious associations and then apply to become "official religious entities," recognized by this commission. Beyond the legal and economic advantages, what they really seek is official recognition as religious groups (Saraiva 2013). In spite of such achievement (since the creation of an official institution to handle religious diversity was discussed for decades before it was finally established) and the fact that the Portuguese religious universe is nowadays a plural one, the presence of the Catholic Church in the public sphere has by no means weakened. The incompleteness of an alleged disenchantment in Portugal is brought out by the over-presence of Catholic heritage in the public space (and in heritage nomination lists), which clearly overshadows the actual religious diversity of the country.

Sintra: Magic, Heritage, and Religious Freedom

On a hot summer day in July 2019, hundreds of visitors queue in front of the Pena Palace gate. Some of them take a *tuk-tuk* to reach the top of the hill, others even a carriage; coming from all over the world, they expect to see the grandiosity of the Romantic fairy-tale-like palace and later be able to still visit the Moorish castle, on the opposite side. They probably do not know enough of Portuguese history to see it as a testimony to the Portuguese Reconquest and early affirmation of nationality, but it is part of the tourist itinerary of Sintra and therefore "a must" for a selfie or a group portrait.

The enormous inflow of tourists who crowd the narrow streets of Sintra is considered very beneficial by shop and restaurant keepers, as well as by the enterprise that manages the site, Parques de Sintra-Monte da Lua (PSML), which uses the revenue from tourist entrance tickets to pay wages, restore monuments, take care of the landscape—and make a profit. It is considered detrimental by local inhabitants and Sintra aficionados (which includes the religious groups that use the mountain for their rituals), who feel such an invasion is overwhelmingly excessive and that the commodification of the site brought with it rules that are neither pleasant nor fair for them: there is hardly any traffic circulation, they have to pay to enter sites that are now fenced off and were previously open to all, and the surrounding landscape is also overrun, as Sintra loses its Romantic and elite touch.

In fact, known for its specific climatic location, with cool summers and mild winters, Sintra was the preferred space of nobility since the Middle Ages. But it was the Romantic period of the late eighteenth and nineteenth centuries that, making use of Sintra's long-standing mountain reputation as the sacred and magical "Moon Hill," glorified it as a privileged destination and a center of European Romantic architecture and spirituality. In the second half of the nineteenth century, the consort King Ferdinand II of the Saxe-Coburg-Gotha dynasty, created an Orientalist Sintra of great scenographic impact. He transformed a ruined Hieronymite monastery—the former monastery of Our Lady of Pena from the early sixteenth century, damaged by the 1755 earthquake and vacant since the 1834 extinction of

Figure 7.1. Tourists taking selfies in Sintra. © Left Hand Rotation.

religious orders—into a Romantic castle, built a park that mixed local and exotic tree species, and reforested the Sintra mountain. The aristocracy and high bourgeoisie followed this Romantic impetus, and the palaces, quintas, and villas multiplied. Sintra attracted artists, writers, intellectuals, and travelers from all over the world and was cited in Beckford's, Lord Byron's, and Richard Strauss's writings. As part of the Grand Tour of the Romantic era, it thus confirms itself as an Orientalist destination, maintaining the perfect corollary of the double position of Portugal, simultaneously object and subject of Orientalism (Vakil 2003; Cardeira da Silva 2005).[11]

The liberal and secular ideals of the late nineteenth century and the 1910 republican revolution, both quite influential in the Sintra area, did not stop the manifestations of popular religiosity, despite the anticlerical initiatives (Silva 1993). In 1929 the Estado Novo founded the General Directorate of National Buildings and Monuments. Sintra was advertised as a national destination, part of the Portuguese soul and identity, where kings and nobility left their marks, and a living trope, a material trace of the glorious past of the country and its overseas feats. The Moorish Castle was a testimony to the triumph of Christianity, and in 1947 an important ceremony took place at the Sintra Town Palace to commemorate eight hundred years since its conquest. In 1970 the European Year of Nature Conservation was celebrated, and the Serra de Sintra was classified as natural heritage. The years following the 1974 revolution, however, were not so auspicious for Sintra. The separation between institutions in charge of the monuments and those in charge of the parks and forests would lead to decades-long poor management.

From Local Associations to UNESCO Classification

The situation of mismanagement and neglect persisted after 1974, and in the words of the president of one of the local heritage associations, there is still nowadays a memory that the monuments were "very much uncared for during the years following the revolution, as heritage was considered as something Fascist, tied to the memory of the great deeds of the Portuguese nation and colonialism." Nevertheless, there was a local consciousness of the value of Sintra and its heritage, and this triggered the organization of several local civic associations, which preceded the official UNESCO heritage nomination: the Association for the Sintra Heritage Defense was founded in 1981; Veredas, the Cultural Cooperative of Sintra, in 1991; the Association of the Friends of Capuchos, the Association of the Friends of Monserrate, and the Association of the Friends of the Old Village all date from the 1990s; the Alagamares Cultural Association was created in 2005 but had as predecessors many others. All these associations were (and are nowadays) crucial to enhancing a heritage consciousness. Meanwhile, new state heritage regulations began to appear. The Monserrate Palace and park were classified as "public interest buildings" in 1975. The Pena Palace was restored in 1994 with its original colors: pink for the old monastery, ochre for the nineteenth century palace built by Ferdinand II. Environmental concerns arose, and the Sintra-Cascais Natural Park was created in 1994.

Sintra was inscribed as a UNESCO World Heritage Site in 1995, after UNESCO expanded the World Heritage categories and established the cultural landscape criteria. The nomination of a cultural landscape to the World Heritage List requires an exceptional mixture of natural and cultural sites within a distinct framework. The Serra de Sintra represents a model of Romantic landscaping and is also an index for different architectural periods and historical groups that inhabited the country. In 2000 the enterprise Parques de Sintra–Monte da Lua (PSML) was created to manage the UNESCO-classified area, to safeguard the main cultural and natural public goods located in the area covered by the World Heritage Site. In 2017, the parks and monuments under management of Parques de Sintra received close to 3.2 million visitors.

The description of Sintra as a model of Romantic monumental and natural heritage is reproduced in a 2013 Portuguese UNESCO Commission/Ministry of Foreign Affairs publication, to celebrate thirty years of good practices in World Heritage management in Portugal (CN 2014: 7). It is stated that the document's objective is "telling the Portuguese and our partners at UNESCO what Portugal has been doing to support the implementation of the World Heritage Convention and the projects that our World Heritage Sites have developed and which constitute good heritage practices" (CN 2014: 7). The enterprise Parques de Sintra–Monte da Lua is included in the list of acknowledgments, and under the title "The Virtuous Circle of Heritage Management," the text describes its cultural and natural heritage management model as generating revenues through regular inflows of visitors, while preserving the outstanding universal value of the property, and rehabilitating monuments and parks, as well as improving the visitors' experience.

Mass Consumption and Mysticism

One evening in 2018, after sunset, while tourists still shop for "typical" Portuguese artifacts, such as the renowned tiles (*azulejos*) or the famous Sintra pastries, another group gathers in front of one of the local coffee shops. They soon set off on a four-hour-long walk through the hills, as the guide says, "Relax and feel the special energy fill your body and soul, while you embrace a 200-year-old tree or climb up the hill." This group is one of the various religious groups that praise the mystical aura of Sintra, using the space for rituals, ceremonies, and contemplation. This has increased considerably in the last thirty years, in line with the increase in religious diversity in the country. Buddhists, Catholics, Pentecostals, Africans and Afro-Brazilians, Neo-Shamans, Neo-druids, Neo-Pagans, Masons, satanic groups, as well as many other New Age practitioners, all make use of this heritage site and claim the right to enjoy it. They support their claims by invoking the Portuguese Law of Religious Freedom (2001), their identities as religious groups, and the way their religious essences tie in with the "magic of Sintra" and how, as citizens, they are therefore entitled to benefit from a space that they postulate was used by their ancestors, practicing worship in the area for centuries. They therefore criticize the way PSML has fenced out many of the spaces previously used for rituals, as well as the way the enterprise has security guards patrolling the area throughout the night, thus constraining their practices. As Astor, Burchardt, and Griera (2017: 129) state for the Spanish case, what minority religious groups do when they try to acquire the status of official religions is that they use their counter-hegemonic discourses on freedom of religion rights and combine it with heritage discourses in order to challenge existing power relations.

In Portugal, as elsewhere in Europe, there has been an increase in public discussions on the proliferation of religious diversity as problematic and as an obstacle to modernization, democracy, individual liberty, and civic rights, in parallel with discourses that frame religion as cultural heritage (Astor, Burchardt, and Griera 2017: 127). On the one hand, several articles in the constitution proclaim religious freedom; on the other, individuals feel that their rights are under attack if they go for a walk in the Sintra park and find a *despacho*, an offering made by members of an Afro-Brazilian congregation. Such *despachos* often include unpleasant items, such as bones, blood, or daggers, which cause panic and discomfort, especially to individuals with a mainstream Catholic affiliation (Saraiva 2013). To reinforce this displeasure, the use of candles or fires in the rituals presents a real fire hazard. The question of whether the expansion of official heritage discourses to include minority heritages necessarily generates an expansion of minority rights (Astor, Burchardt, and Griera 2017: 130) is a suitable discussion to have in this case, as is the acceptance of religious heritage as a basis for collective recognition and group rights (Astor, Burchardt, and Griera 2017:132).

Besides the groups that have more religious or philosophical approaches, other such events, with stronger historical components, stress the exceptionality of Sintra and of the Portuguese. Various episodes involving "holy individuals" throughout the centuries, as historical or invented characters, come to life in the explanations of tour guides. For instance, in the words of one of them, "Here we are now in the cave where the holy man Friar Honório lived and died, a man unique in the world, and of course, Portuguese," or "This is the spot where king D. Manuel saw Vasco da Gama's fleet arriving from India, and so decided to build a monastery to thank Our Lady for this glorious accomplishment."[12] Such introductions lead to long stories based on the Portuguese feats, thus drawing on the "hidden" vernacular lusotropicalism and, by reiterating these lusotropes, adding a "layer of exceptionalism to the theme of the great early empire" (Bastos 2018: 257).

Besides the reactions to and criticism of PSML from the various religious groups, the other spheres that strongly oppose that management are the local heritage associations. They criticize the excessive commodification of Sintra, which takes away its magic and mystery, as well as their comfort and peace as residents.

Many local heritage associations are active, both promoting debates, seminars, public interventions, and various events and trying to balance the positive effects of the UNESCO classification—as the conservation and rehabilitation actions of PSML—with the negative consequences of the tremendous tourist flows that collide with the everyday lives of local inhabitants. One such association stopped the planned construction of a large parking lot in the village center and fights against the construction of new hotels, which, according to them, might take the UNESCO classification away.

It was also one such association that fought to preserve the Capuchos convent in the 1990s, when several Sintra monuments were not cared for by the local or national entities and were illicitly occupied by homeless people and others, resulting in fires that would actually destroy some of them. As one of the founders of the Association for the Defense of Capuchos stated, "That very same day I went there with the apostolic nuncio and saw all the burned candles, the empty bottles, and the still-warm fires; I knew we had to do something to preserve the space before it was too late. That very same day I and other local friends created the association."[13] In fact, many advocate that it was the role of this association that enhanced the awareness that something had to be done to prevent the destruction of both natural and monumental heritage and triggered Sintra's submission to UNESCO World Heritage classification.

Nevertheless, both religious groups and local associations make use of a discourse informed by vernacular lusotropicalism: a history invoking the lusotropes of religious and cultural tolerance and of the glorious Portuguese history, where notions of the past often suppress multiple constituencies (Geismar 2015: 72). New Age groups talk about the religious connection with nature already present in the prehistoric rites and medieval religious orders (as is the case with the Capuchos convent), while they invoke the law of religious freedom to highlight their right to worship and practice their rituals. Members of local heritage associations emphasize the Portuguese achievements, especially the way this is a pivotal region to observe the richness and diversity of national cultural stratigraphy (the various groups—Celts, Iberians, Romans, Muslims, etc.—that, for centuries, contributed to the formation of the Portuguese nation), which is ultimately the cement of lusotropicalism. When several associations defend different heritage regimes in opposition to that of the State (De Cesari 2013), they often end up doing the same and forgetting the multiple contributions from people who make up the country's present ethnic, cultural, and religious diversity. Even religious groups resort to (vernacular) lusotropicalism when they invoke Portuguese traditions and history and, very explicitly, lusotropical ideas of the importance of the Portuguese in the establishment of the relations between Africa, Portugal, and Brazil, which was in fact a colonial era slave route. While extolling the cosmopolitan diversity represented by the World Heritage Site, all such groups and associations forget that Sintra municipality—which includes a large area between Lisbon and the village, populated by working-class immigrant minorities—is the most diverse in Portugal in ethnic and religious terms; those immigrants hardly visit or feel connected to the nearby World Heritage Site. As Bastos (2018: 257) puts it, lusotropicalism "not only masked the harsh and bitter reality—past and present—it also continues to provide a language, an appealing evasion, that makes the speaker feel good and special." Even without consciously acknowledging it, this is what local guides, visitors, associations, and stakeholders do when they invoke Sintra's heritage as directly connected to the exceptional Portuguese past, thus repeatedly appealing to the lusotropical Portuguese trope of grandiosity and tolerance.

Mértola: Islam as Heritage, Resource, and Performance

A major flood of the Guadiana River in 1876 uncovered important ruins in Mértola, and the archaeologist Estácio da Veiga was sent by the government to implement the Recognition of the Antiquities of the Right Bank of the Guadiana, placing the village for the first time on the national heritage scene. Estácio da Veiga's heritage conceptions corresponded to those of a positivist archaeology at the service of national but also regional ethnogenesis,[14] criticizing earlier Romantic para-archaeological initiatives that lacked systematic and methodological organization (Veiga, in Cardoso 2007: 350). And his vision led him to the systematic and intensive collection of all traces of "antiquity," including that of the Moors. His discoveries herald the archaeological treasure that would unfold in its splendor just a century later.

Looking at the list of monuments classified already in 1909, we see a topography that privileges the northern regions of the country, corresponding to an asymmetric conception of national history and typology of heritage: the North was (1) "the cradle of the nation" and (2) the landscape of Roman and Christian monumentality. This is an asymmetry that still exists today, and to confirm it, we have only to look at the maps of the distribution of the classification of built heritage.[15] However, in this map, Mértola was already under consideration, with its Roman Bridge and Mother Church. The church, in fact, was the mosque that, like other Islamic peninsular temples, was transformed into a church after the Reconquest.

From 1910 onward, and with the republican willingness to collect cultural resources, the first archaeological charts and monographs with ethnogenetic concerns came to stay, especially in areas neglected by the central power, such as the southern provinces (like the Alentejo, where Mértola is located). Thus, this period of patrimonialization can be summed up, with regard to the Arab and Islamic traces, as a set of heritage procedures (mostly restricted to inventorying and classification) that had the purpose either of spicing up national history or of displaying these regional ingredients with a view to moderately enhancing a southern autochthony. But in the ethnogenealogical narrative that presided over this positivist period—in which archaeology was the scientific warranty of the national roots, authenticity, and heritage—religion was subsumed under the idea of *civilization,* just as beliefs and traditions were neglected in favor of more material and monumental remains, which gave body and substance to the emerging idea of modern heritage.

With the advent of the Estado Novo led by the dictator Salazar, local pride and regional fervor were neglected in favor of a nationalist, centralist, and authoritarian spirit. Although medieval heritage exalted by the Romantics fitted well with the Estado Novo nationalist perspective, the Islamic and Arab vestiges were not archaeologically explored, in order to better exhibit the previous Roman roots or the Reconquest that led to the nation's creation. Even so, it was not until 1943 that the castle of Mértola, a Gothic castle erected in the late thirteenth century over an Arab *alcáçova* (fortified palace), was classified as a building of public interest. Only in 1951 did it become a national monument, and it was later included in the vast consolidation and restoration campaign of the General Directorate of National Buildings and Monuments. Indeed, although Mértola was included in the national heritage road map, the little that was exhibited and promoted during the Estado Novo was never its brilliance and prosperity throughout the Islamic period, but always the monumentality of the previous epoch or the military success of the Christian Reconquest that overcame Muslim rule, opening the doors to the constitution of the Christian Portuguese nation. Even when the rehabilitation works of the church in 1949 revealed an Islamic mihrab behind the Catholic altar, the true thickness and cultural continuity it testified was not acknowledged.

During the Estado Novo, the Alentejo was also a territory with a strong revolutionary symbolism, marked by the conflict between the rich landowners and the exploited rural workers. Contributing to its regional exaltation was therefore not in line with the regime's cultural and heritage policies, and much less the display of important traces of the impressive Arab presence. Paradoxically, as we have seen, the same regime would resort in its final phase to the lusotropicalist narrative to justify its late colonialism—a narrative that based part of its original genealogical argument on the Arab and Islamic heritage that the Portuguese had absorbed so well in the inaugural moment of the construction of the nation in the twelfth and thirteenth centuries.

From Left-Wing Utopia to Cosmo-optimism: Mértola Vila Museu

Following the 1974 Carnation Revolution, the Agrarian Reform would begin, in 1975, with the occupation of land by the workers and great revolutionary engagement. Cláudio Torres, a professor at the University of Lisbon, founded the Archaeological Field of Mértola (Campo Arqueológico de Mértola) and proposed to survey the Archaeological Charter of the Municipality. Due to the articulation of the Archaeological Field with the Heritage Defense Association and the city hall, Mértola became, in the 1980s, an example of the convergence of multidisciplinary academic practice that placed the material and immaterial heritage at the service of regional and local development. The archaeological and cultural stratigraphy of the village was explored to denounce previous nationalist history, recovering and integrating the Arab and Berber (Amazigh) presence in the past and displaying it in the present as a cultural and economic resource for the region. The label of Mértola Vila Museu (Museum Village) was created, and between the late 1990s and early 2000s several museological nuclei were founded. In the same period, contacts with North Africa (particularly Morocco) multiplied, and partnerships were developed with other similar developmental and regionalist projects in Spanish Andalusia, such as Almonaster, which already promoted an Islamic festival.

Beyond the revolutionary impetus that drove it, the breadth of regional development in Mértola was determined by Portugal's entry into the European Union. While on the one hand this made it possible to use the EU's structural funds for development, on the other it obliged leftist partisans—reticent to accept European integration—to politically affirm the roots and ties in and with the South and the consequent rehabilitation of the role of Muslims in national history and identity (Cardeira da Silva 2005). Paradox-

Figure 7.2. Islamic Festival, 2019. © CRIA.

ically, it is also the Mértola Archaeological Field that—leading its secularist local development project—collected, rehabilitated, restored, and today exhibits—one could say re-sacralizes—the scattered pieces of sacred art of Alentejo Catholicism formerly abandoned by the church and the state. One of its museums is dedicated to it and placed right in front of the Islamic Museum. Both were inaugurated in 2001.

From the 1990s—with particular emphasis on post-9/11—and until at least the first decade of the twenty-first century, Mértola fed into the national multiculturalist rhetoric and progressively got into what Geertz (1986: 257) designated as the "desperate tolerance of UNESCO cosmopolitanism." Both in diplomatic discourse on approaching Islamic countries and in formulations for inclusive citizen administration when it comes to Muslims, Mértola emerges as the undisputed icon of an atavistic Islamophilia, which finds its roots in the national foundation itself. The village epitomizes the old colonial lusotropicalist trope that Portugal recovered in the post-revolution era as a formula for national identity. The Islamic Community of Lisbon—the Muslims' privileged interlocutor with the government—adopted the same discourse and gave Mértola the same centrality (Cardeira da Silva 2005). This was especially useful at a time when Portugal redefined the Religious Freedom Act (2001). As a result of all the investments of the last two decades of academic, heritage, and museological venture, the scenographic conditions for the cultural spectacle are created: since 2001, and every two years, Mértola holds a so-called Islamic Festival.

The Way to Commodification of Heritage and Aesthetic Cosmopolitanism

Today, we can say that the Campo Arqueológico de Mértola has seen better days. Funds for local development and scientific research are scarce, and revolutionary impetus has faded since the first edition of the Islamic Festival. Margarida and José, who in their youth actively participated in conservation and the first museographic ventures and enthusiastically supported the first Islamic Festival, hosting artisans specially invited from Morocco, are now public servants at the municipality in different terms: it is more their technological skills than their integrated cultural knowledge that matters today. We have followed (and filmed) their engagement and work before, during, and after the preparation of the two last editions of the festival (2017 and 2019). They are the ones who currently lead the festival production (responsible for its curatorship, cultural programming, and scenography in all the details and often building and painting the sets themselves), but always with a nostalgic vision of the first editions back in 2001, when everybody participated, *genuine* artists and artisans came from Morocco, and science, economy, and culture merged together in a very egalitarian vein, according to them.

During the festival days it becomes increasingly clear how different political, religious, and economic projects converged over the years into a symbolically dense site, making use of different displays and scenographies, on different stages, to exhibit their often contradictory ideologies. With a resident population of no more than twenty-five hundred inhabitants, Mértola welcomed more than forty thousand visitors during the May festival in 2019, and when asked what the biggest pilgrimage in the region is, people often answer, "The Islamic Festival." Mértola quickly entered the circuit of commodification of heritage and aesthetic cosmopolitanism, and the municipal mode of production fulfills a calendar of regular fairs and festivals.

The Mértola Islamic Festival might well be seen as a mere commodity of the aesthetic cosmopolitism market. Like many other festivals and historical re-creations, it follows the pattern of re-enactment of the past and heritage claims and, like some of them, claims and commoditizes *authenticity* as a value and consumable good, while not refusing *replica* and *merchandizing*. Its vernacular and fluid Orientalism, mingling "vintage and antique" objects with "natural" goods and products of Andalusian inspiration or "Oriental" performances, endorses a deceptive apolitical scene that, in fact, overshadows different modern paradoxes under its festive and folkloristic atmosphere. Religion and heritage, faith and science, academic and vernacular Orientalism, relics and replicas, ritual and performance share the same stages, and this evinces the random character of all these categorization limits.

But the recent history of Mértola and its founding project of participative development grounded in archaeology are nowadays Mértola heritage in and of themselves. Those particular actors who strive to exhibit and safeguard this specific heritage are probably the main actors responsible for the success of the Islamic Festival. Beyond their expertise on restoration and cultural exhibition—which they had acquired in the 1980s from working at the archaeological site and now apply to the festival production—they actually act as the *living* (and *endangered*) *heirs* of that particular heritage, one that allows us to reach and re-create a deeper legacy: that of Al-Andalus and the cosmopolitan Mediterranean.

An "Islamic Festival"

After becoming the subject of some discussion, the 2019 edition of the festival was scheduled within the month of Ramadan. Commercial interests took precedence over religious obligations. Muslim participants—mostly immigrants working with Moroccan firms specialized in fairs and markets held all over Portugal and Spain—were tired and not happy; but then, "It was work, and we cannot refuse it," they said. Since the first Islamic Festival, alongside archaeologists and academics, suq vendors and municipality employees, different participants have conquered the scene. In a country where the Muslim community does not exceed fifty thousand, very few are Mértola residents. At first, the Islamic Community of Lisbon had a symbolic, merely sanctioning presence. In the last edition, only the Portuguese Ismaili Community was present, but merely through the performance of its choir group. However, since the first edition, the Almorabitun of Seville (and some others from Granada, all of whom are also participants in the Islamic Fair of Almonaster) have been protagonists of the festival, ensuring that all activities and goods stay within what they consider halal—demanding, for example, a ban on the sale of alcohol and pork inside the suq and leading the prayers around the church/mosque (demands that they did not achieve at the festival in neighboring Spain).

At the tenth edition of the festival in 2019, the members of the Islamic Junta de Sevilla participated as always, albeit after some hesitation due to Ramadan. At sunset they made the call for prayer to mark the end of fasting, just outside the mosque, with their backs to the mihrab and Mértola at their feet, a nice framing and photo opportunity that many tourists rushed to seize. The Andalusian scenario that the Campo Arqueológico team builds every two years is attractive for the exercise of *dikhr* (Sufi rituals) and *dawa* (Islamic predicament) of these neo-Andalusian communities, whose religious performances, in turn, provide extra authenticity to the stage. In Mértola's festival, religion, heritage, and market (the suq) seem to be detached, but only as much as necessary to better feed off each other, without apparent contamination. Nevertheless, the fact that its stage is mainly occupied by neo-Andalusian rather than by other Portuguese Muslim communities shows us that it is the patrimonialized scenario of Andalusia rather than the plot—its historical narrative of national and local culture, religious roots and their contemporary configurations—that is attractive here.

Conclusion

One historical reason for not being able to separate the concept of heritage from that of religion is the fact that it was, paradoxically, the impulse of secularization that enabled the constitution of the first large heritage collection: that which resulted from the destruction of religious orders and the nationalization of their properties. The first patrimonial assets were, in fact, of religious origin. As we see in the cases presented here, despite the separation of church and state, the Catholic Church has, for a long time, maintained ambiguous and close relations with the state and still holds, today, a dominant presence in national representations. Both seek to adapt to the basic values of human rights and to the liberal international norms of public policies in contexts of multiculturalism: the Catholic Church, with its relative autonomy in relation to the Portuguese state, using the discourse of ecumenical Christianity; the state, recycling the old lusotropicalist rhetoric, which in so many other historical and political occasions served as the nation's cement, first to legitimize its late colonialism, nowadays to declare and exhibit its "natural" and uncontested compliance with cultural and religious rights.

The celebration of the Mértola Islamic Festival from 2001 onward helps us to rethink the concerted action of various agents with different objectives in an arena of liberalization and commodification of multiculturalism, simultaneously marked by the calendar of a local production and the agenda of international agencies such as UNESCO.[16] The current narrative around Mértola, transcribed into the justification of its outstanding universal value, replicates effortlessly the lusotropicalist trope of national identity, as in the file of UNESCO's tentative list: "Knowledge of the past is indispensable for understanding current phenomena and it may be an important tool used in the service of awareness for such important values like multiculturalism, tolerance, and respect for others." In the case of Sintra, such multiculturalism, fully present nowadays in the municipality, is in the books, brochures, and discourses about the UNESCO classified site, transformed into an Orientalist and nationalistic scenario where conflicts over the recognition of various identities (Geismar 2015) are not present. Even local associations, with various ideas concerning what Sintra's heritage regimes should be, abide in the end to such consensual lusotropes.

With these examples, it could be said that, as in other matters, Portugal is a good follower of liberalization policies and that cultural and religious diversity is progressively celebrated in the public space, despite the evident centrality of the Catholic Church. The pervasiveness of heritage rhetoric is rooted in the continuous production of imagery, practices, discourses, and institutions that sustain its principles. Heritage places are used to perform and overlook the nation's conformity with universal cultural and religious rights. Better than spaces of "culture" or of "history," spaces of heritage, as *curated* culture and history, serve the purposes of an imagined transnational community and the normative cosmo-optimism of a global heritage regime (Geismar 2015; Von Oswald, Lidchi, and Macdonald 2017). On the other hand, "recognition is cheaper than representation or equality. Identity is a soft substitute for sovereignty" (Noyes 2005: 171), and the Portuguese cases presented in this volume show that what is celebrated is not necessarily the diversity or the experienced religiosity (much less by the believers of minority religions).

In Mértola, a village where hardly any Muslims live, an inclusive ethnogenesis is celebrated, with an Islam that does not relate to the different ways in which it is lived and celebrated in Portugal. In Sintra, a municipality that is one of the most culturally and religiously diverse in the country, a mere aesthetic Orientalism for the consumption of tourists is displayed, enhanced by a strong commoditization of heritage. In fact, in both cases, it is true that religion and diversity are promoted, but as heritage and hence as curated national history.[17] Looking back at a curated past and disregarding the actual present, vernacular lusotropicalism embedded in heritage practice persists as an inclusive and conciliatory myth of both nationalist and cosmopolitan conformity, with a value-added service for tourism (hospitality and safety) and for national conciliation, pacification, and self-esteem, as well as to justify (controversial) heritage management policies. Therefore, we may understand lusotropicalism as a sacralized heritage in itself. And yet, paradoxically, its endurance and omnipresence testify against what it claims to celebrate: its capacity to provide a place for other heritages and religions.

Maria Cardeira da Silva, professor at Universidade Nova de Lisboa and senior researcher at CRIA, is an anthropologist interested in Islam, gender, and tourism and heritage. She conducted ethnographic fieldwork in Portugal, Morocco, Mauritania, Brazil (Mazagão), and Senegal. Currently conducting fieldwork in Mauritania, she explores the local configurations of transnational feminisms and heritage global regimes. She is also interested in

Islamophobia and national and European public policies regarding Islamic heritage in Europe, focusing on the ways that Portuguese state, academy, and Muslim communities make use of Islamic heritage to assert and disseminate its religious and political identities and legitimacy.

Clara Saraiva is a social and cultural anthropologist and senior researcher at the Centre for Comparative Studies, Lisbon University. She was a visiting professor at the University of California, Berkeley (2013) and Brown University and a research fellow at the Watson Institute for International Studies at Brown (2001–2, 2008). She researches the anthropology of religion and ritual, also in relation with heritage studies, and has conducted fieldwork in Portugal, Brazil, and several African countries. She is coeditor (with Peter Jan Margry) of the Lit Verlag series on Ethnology of Religion. She is president of the Association of Portuguese Anthropology, and a board member of both the World Anthropological Associations (WCAA) and of the WCAA Ethics Task Force. She is also past vice president of the Society for Ethnology and Folklore (SIEF), where she is board member of the Working Group on Religion.

NOTES

1. The word "heritage" is established in UNESCO only in 1950 (Desvallées 2003), translating an allegedly consensual and transnational idea of what is understood as *cultural heritage* under a global heritage regime. To talk about "heritagization" before that may thus be misleading. The French word and semantics as an international driver in these matters prevailed until then. It is important not to assume that under this global regime all nations and people *perceive* heritage (or *patrimoine*) in the same ways or that all states make use of and manage it in similar forms. A politically shared world does not engender semantic homogeneity. See, among many others, Oulebsir and Swenson 2015 and Bendix 2011.
2. The lusotropicalist theory was engineered by Gilberto Freyre, a Brazilian sociologist, to inspire the idea of a Brazilian "racial democracy." This was subsequently imported by the Portuguese dictatorship (see, among others, Castelo 1998).
3. The text is based on archival research and fieldwork undertaken in the scope of the HERILIGION project The Heritagization of Religion and the Sacralization of Heritage in Contemporary Europe, funded by Humanities in the European Research Area (HERA), grant 5087-00505A), carried out from September 2016 to January 2020 by the Portuguese team. In Sintra, it was led by Clara Saraiva, with the participation of junior researchers Roberta Boniolo and Francesca di Luca. Besides participation observation with visitors, activities organized by associations, NGOs and other stakeholders, in-depth interviews were carried out with representatives of local associations, stakeholders, and various religious groups. In Mértola, the work was headed by Maria Cardeira da Silva. Interviews were undertaken with researchers (and former researchers) of the Campo Arqueológico de Mértola, mem-

bers of the Junta Islâmica de Sevilla, City Council employees, festival staff, and visitors. These were recorded and filmed with consent, with the support of Jonas Amarante and Virtudes Tellez. Visual and documental archives of Campo Arqueológico de Mértola, city hall, and National Museum of Archaeology were explored. Several field trips were carried out to follow the preparation of two editions of the (biannual) Islamic Festivals and three editions of the (annual) Jornadas Islâmicas de Almonaster.
4. This is particularly evident in the work of Alexandre Herculano (1810–77), a central figure of Portuguese Romanticism, regarded as the founder of both modern historiography and the development of the idea of heritage.
5. The *política do espírito*, created to shape and exhibit the national character through the arts, craft, and heritage, was led by António Ferro, responsible for the propaganda of the Salazar regime.
6. Fifth Government Program on Culture 1975, https://www.historico.portugal.gov.pt/pt/o-governo/arquivo-historico/governos-constitucionais/gc05/programa-do-governo/programa-do-governo-constitucional-5.aspx.
7. Sixth Government Program on Culture 1975, https://www.historico.portugal.gov.pt/pt/o-governo/arquivo-historico/governos-provisorios/gp06/programa-do-governo/programa-do-vi-governo-provisorio.aspx.
8. This was later followed by the signing of the UNESCO Intangible Heritage Convention in 2008.
9. Despite the complaints by academics about the lack of participation of civil society (and academia itself) in the processes of legislative definition regarding the definition of intangible heritage, it is in the register of this type of heritage that we find a greater social participation today, a definite bottom-up approach.
10. Among numerous studies on the condition of the country as a host nation see, for instance, Bastos and Bastos (2006), Vala (1999), and Machado (2002).
11. Both these authors, Vakil and Cardeira da Silva, discuss this issue, that is, the way Portugal was Orientalized—in the Said sense—as object but also subject of Orientalism: Portugal Orientalized the South but in turn was also Orientalized by central and northern European elites.
12. Examples taken during some of the organized walks through the site in 2019.
13. Interview with one of the association leaders in 2019.
14. We are talking about "ethnogenesis" and "ethnogenealogy" in the sense Díaz-Andreu and Champion (1996) and other historians of European archaeology and ethnography use them to describe the role of positivist archaeology, along with positivist ethnography, to legitimate the roots of "national" and/or "regional" cultures in the making of nationalisms and regionalisms in nineteenth-century Europe.
15. Something that replicates the asymmetry of UNESCO Word Heritage maps.
16. Mértola is now on the tentative list of UNESCO.
17. In 1995 there was an unusual flow of Iranian Shiite pilgrims to Fátima, triggered by a book that sought the origins of Portuguese religiosity in Muslim Fatimism. Called to intervene publicly as a representative of the Islamic Community of Lisbon, the imam of the Sunni mosque, having been surprised by the inclusion of Fátima in the itinerary of such an unusual visit, suggested the alternative diversion via Mértola: "There, yes, there is a clear Islamic heritage" (Cardeira da Silva 2005; Vale de Almeida 2004).

REFERENCES

Astor, Avi, Marian Burchardt, and Mar Griera. 2017. "The Politics of Religious Heritage: Framing Claims to Religion as Culture in Spain," *Journal for the Scientific Study of Religion* 56(1): 126–42.
Bastos, Cristiana. 2018. "Luso-Tropicalism Debunked, Again," in Warwick Anderson, Ricardo Roque, and Ricardo V. Santos (eds.), *Luso-Tropicalism and Its Discontents*. New York and Oxford: Berghahn, pp. 243–64.
Bastos, José P., and Susana P. Bastos. 2006. *Filhos Diferentes de Deuses Diferentes*. Lisbon: ACIME.
Bendix, Regina. 2011. "Héritage et patrimoine : de leurs proximités sémantiques et de leurs implications," in Chiara Bortolotto (ed.), *Le patrimoine culturel immatériel. Enjeux d'une nouvelle catégorie*. Paris: Éditions de la Maison des sciences de l'homme, pp. 227–29.
Bendix, Regina, Aditya Eggert, and Arnika Peselmann (eds.). 2012. *Heritage Regimes and the State*. Göttingen Studies in Cultural Property 6. Göttingen: Universitätsverlag Göttingen.
Cardoso, João Luís. 2007. "Vida e obras de Estácio da Veiga," *Xelb* 7. *Actas do Encontro de Arqueologia do Algarve* 4: 15–72.
Cardeira da Silva, Maria. 2005. "O sentido dos árabes no nosso sentido. Dos estudos sobre árabes e muçulmanos em Portugal," *Análise Social* 39(173): 781–806.
Cardeira da Silva, Maria. 2012. "Castles Abroad: Nations, Culture and Cosmopolitanisms in African Heritage Sites of Portuguese Origin," in Regina Bendix, Aditya Eggert, and Arnika Peselmann (eds.), *Heritage Regimes and the State*. Göttingen: Universitätsverlag Göttingen, pp. 61–78.
Cardeira da Silva. Maria (ed.). 2013. *Castelos a Bombordo. Etnografias de Patrimónios Africanos e memórias Portuguesas*. Lisbon: CRIA.
Cardeira da Silva, Maria. 2015. "Old Maps, New Traffics: Political Itineraries around Scattered Heritage of Portuguese Origin," in Laurent Bourdeau, Maria Gravari-Barbas, and Mike Robinson (eds.), *World Heritage Sites and Tourism: Global and Local Relations*. London and New York: Ashgate, pp. 308–17.
Castelo, Cláudia. 1998. *O Modo Português de Estar no Mundo O Luso-Tropicalismo e a Ideologia Colonial Portuguesa (1933–1961)*. Porto: Afrontamento.
CN—Comissão Nacional da UNESCO. 2014. *Portugal and World Heritage: 30 Years of Best Practices*. Portuguese Commission for UNESCO, Ministry of Foreign Affairs.
De Cesari, Chiara. 2013 "Thinking through Heritage Regimes," in Regina Bendix, Aditya Eggert, and Arnika Peselman (eds.), *Heritage Regimes and the State*. Gottingen: Gottingen University Press, pp. 399–413.
Desvallées, André. 2003. "De la notion privée d'héritage matériel au concept universel et extensif de patrimoine: retour sur l'histoire et sur quelques ambiguïtés sémantiques," in Martine Cardin, (dir.) *Médias et patrimoine*, Université de Laval/UNESCO, Chaire patrimoine culturel.
Díaz-Andreu, Margarita, and Timothy Champion (eds.). 1996. *Nationalism and Archaeology in Europe*. London and New York: Routledge.
Fabre, Daniel (ed.). 1996. *L'Europe entre cultures et nations*. Ethnologie de la France 10. Paris: Éditions de la MMSH, pp. 99–120.

Fedele, Anna. 2013. "The Metamorphoses of Neopaganism in Traditionally Catholic Countries in Southern Europe," in Ruy Blanes and José Mapril (eds.), *Sites and Politics of Religious Diversity in Southern Europe*. Leiden: Brill, pp. 51–72.
Geertz, Clifford. 1986. "The Uses of Diversity." Tanner Lectures on Human Values, delivered at University of Michigan, November 8, 1985.
Geismar, Haidy. 2015. "Anthropology and Heritage Regimes," *Annual Review of Anthropology* 44: 71–85.
Machado, Fernando. 2002. *Contrastes e Continuidades. Migração, Etnicidade e Integração dos Guineenses em Portugal*. Oeiras: Celta Editora.
Mapril, José, Ruy Blanes, Erin Wilson, and Emerson Giumbelli (eds.). 2017. *Secularisms in a Post Secular Age? Religiosities and Subjectivities*. London: Palgrave.
Noyes, Dorothy. 2005. "The Judge of Solomon: Global Protections for Traditional and the Problem of Community Ownership," *Cultural Analysis* 5: 27–56.
Oulebsir, Nabila, and Astrid Swenson. 2015. "Patrimoine: voyages des mots. Heritage, Erbe, Beni culturali, Turâth, Tigemmi." *Patrimoine et Architecture* 21–22: 10–23.
Pordeus, Ismael, Jr. 2009. *Portugal em Transe*. Lisbon: Imprensa de Ciências Sociais.
Rodrigues, Luís Nuno. 2006. "Da criação da UNESCO à adesão de Portugal (1946–1965)," *Relações Internacionais* 12: 167–81.
Roussou, Eugenia. 2017. "The Syncretic Religious Landscape of Contemporary Greece and Portugal: A Comparative Approach on Creativity through Spiritual Synthesis," in Stefania Palmisano and Nicola Pannofino (eds.), *Invention of Tradition and Syncretism in Contemporary Religions: Sacred Creativity*. Cham: Springer International, pp. 155–75.
Saraiva, Clara. 2008. "Transnational Migrants and Transnational Spirits: An African Religion in Lisbon," *Journal of Ethnic and Migration Studies* 34(2): 253–69.
Saraiva, Clara. 2013. "Blood, Sacrifices and Religious Freedom: Afro-Brazilian Associations in Portugal," in Ruy Blanes and José Mapril (eds.), *Sites and Politics of Religious Diversity in Southern Europe: The Best of All Gods*. Leiden: Brill, pp. 129–54.
Saraiva, Clara. 2016. "*Orixás* across the Atlantic: The Diaspora of Afro-Brazilian Religions in Europe," in Bettina Schmidt and Steven Engler (eds.), *The Handbook of Contemporary Brazilian Religions in Brazil*. London: Brill, pp. 320–32.
Sarró, Ramon, and Ruy Llera Blanes. 2009. "Prophetic Diasporas Moving Religion Across the Lusophone Atlantic." *African Diaspora* 2(1): 52–72.
Silva, Augusto Santos. 1993. *Tempos Cruzados: um Estudo Interpretativo da Cultura Popular*. Lisbon: Afrontamento.
Vakil, Abdookarim. 2003. "O 'Portugal Islâmico,' o 'Portugal Multicultural' e os Muçulmanos Portugueses: História, memória e cidadania na construção de novas identidades," in Guilhermina Mota (ed.), *Minorias Étnicas e Religiosas em Portugal: História e Actualidade*. Coimbra: IHES-FLUC, pp. 409–51.
Vakil, Abdoolkarim, Mário Machaqueiro, and Fernando Monteiro. 2011. *Moçambique: Memória Falada do Islão e da Guerra*. Coimbra: Almedina.
Vala, Jorge. 1999. *Novos Racismos: Perspectivas Comparativas*. Oeiras: Celta.
Vale de Almeida, Miguel. 2004. *Outros Destinos: Ensaios de Antropologia e Cidadania*, Lisbon: Campo das Letras.
Vertovec, Steven. 1996. "Multiculturalism, Culturalism and Public Incorporation," *Ethnic and Racial Studies* 19(1): 49–69.

Vertovec, Steven. 2010. "Towards Post-Multiculturalism? Changing Communities, Conditions and Contexts of Diversity," *International Social Science Journal* 61: 83–95.

Vilaça, Helena. 2006. *Da Torre de Babel às Terras Prometidas: Pluralismo Religioso em Portugal*. Coimbra: Afrontamento.

Vilaça, Helena, Enzo Pace, Inger Furseth, and Per Petersson (eds.). 2016. *The Changing Soul of Europe: Religions and Migrations in Northern and Southern Europe*. London: Routledge.

Von Oswald, Margareta, Henrietta Lidchi, and Sharon Macdonald. 2017. "Engaging Anthropological Legacies toward Cosmo-optimistic Futures?," *Museum Worlds: Advances in Research* 5: 97–109.

 CHAPTER 8

Between Catholic Nationalism and Inter-religious Cosmopolitanism
Religious Heritage in Fátima and Mouraria, Portugal
Anna Fedele and José Mapril

Introduction

This chapter is based on long-term ethnographic research in Portugal and explores the tensions between two tendencies present in the Portuguese governance of religious sites and heritages: on one hand, we find a desire of preservation of a Catholic, nationalist, "pure" Portugal and, on the other, the drive to affirm this country's international, inter-religious, and intercultural landscape. These two tendencies will be revealed in the context of two ethnographic case studies: the pilgrimage site of Fátima, and the Mouraria square project in Lisbon. We will argue that the tensions at the core of this chapter are linked to processes of (re)imagining national identity and belonging, through the mobilization of ideas about what constitutes Portuguese religious heritage and roots (see Salemink, Stengs, and van den Hemel, introduction).

As the editors of the present volume argue, "Religious heritage thus becomes implicated in narratives about who belongs and who does not, which religious sites and traditions should be funded, and who gets to decide what a cityscape has meant in the past, does mean in the present, and will mean in the future" (introduction, p. 4). Following this lead, we analyze "how heritage regimes are instrumentalized, adapted, changed, hacked, and turned inside out by different groups and societal actors that claim to have a stake in the cultural heritage and its management" (p. 10). As the other contributors to this volume, we focus on the intersections of religion and heritage and avoid reducing our case studies of heritagization only to a larger "regime" or stable power discourse imposed from above. Through our ethnographic approach we take into consideration the role of Catholic religion in heritage management not only from a top-down but also from a bottom-up perspective. We therefore analyze the frequent disconnections and disruptions existing between the dynamics of the management of religious sites and the uses people make of these sites from below. We also reflect on what these disruptions tell us about processes of political claims making and citizenship.

A second argument that comes through in this chapter is precisely how the aforementioned tensions are related to processes of domestication of non-Christian groups through the creation of "proper" places for religious minorities and its heritages that stand in contrast with religious majorities and their corresponding heritages. The cases of Fátima and Mouraria represent important examples because they can be seen as the core symbols of two important sources of heritage in Portugal: if Fátima stands for the nation's strong roots in Catholicism and its particularly fervent devotion to Our Lady, Mouraria stands for its Muslim past as well as for its large history of colonization.

Fátima is one of Europe's most important Catholic pilgrimage shrines and a good example of the changing meanings and competing discourses associated with pilgrimage sites (Eade and Sallnow 1991; Coleman and Eade 2018). Constructed as a patriotic altar during the military dictatorship until 1974 and as a bastion for an international "war against Communism," Fátima has also been creatively used by its international pilgrims as well as by Portuguese pilgrims who see Our Lady of Fátima first and foremost as "their" Mother (Fedele 2020a, 2020b). In the last decades, religious minorities such as Muslims, Hindus, New Agers, and others have made their own pilgrimages to Fátima, with or without the approval of local institutions or the support of advocates of inter-religious dialogue. There is a tension between a desire to maintain a sort of "pure," Portuguese, and Catholic Fátima and the need to demonstrate the country's modernity and openness, promoting a global Catholic Fátima that is also open to interculturality and in favor of inter-religious dialogue.

In a similar way, in the case of Mouraria square, one can observe two processes happening simultaneously. The first process could be described as the top-down heritagization of the Islamic past of Lisbon that relates to the current politics of religious diversity in Portugal and in Europe (Astor, Burchardt, and Griera 2017, Astor 2019; Hirschkind 2016). For city hall, the Moorish square, with its Al-Andalus reference and the presence of a mosque, is the recognition of an Islamic past of the city, an Islamic heritage that is more and more visible through several archaeological findings. This contemporary mobilization of ideas about religious diversity and heritage, past and present, is a major change in relation to the Estado Novo period (1933–74). During this dictatorship, the Mouraria quarter was seen as a morally decaying urban area that needed disciplining and in which several events promoted hegemonic representations of national identity in relation to Christianity, more generally, and Catholicism, in particular. This project produced a discourse that totally silenced nineteenth-century archaeological findings of the Islamic presence in the city and, simultaneously, reified the image, highly Orientalized, of the Islamic other, defeated in the twelfth century. Thus, the current recognition of the Al-Andalus past as something valuable is in radical contrast in relation to the Estado Novo period.

The second process, related to a bottom-up appropriation of Mouraria, is best exemplified by the relocation of a pre-existing mosque to the new square. This relocation is for Mapril's interlocutors—Portuguese-Bangladeshi Muslims—the recognition of their *right to the city* through the creation of a proper place to practice their religion—a claim of more than ten years. In this case, the heritage regime created the condition for the emergence of a distinct Muslim subjectivity (in relation to the main institutional representatives of Portuguese public Islam) and was appropriated (in a bottom-up process) to make a new place for lived Islam—albeit in a discretely visible place.

Although the case studies of Fátima and Mouraria may at first glance seem to be heritage sites with quite different characteristics, because the first is an explicitly religious place, while the other is a public square, only indirectly related to (Islamic) religion, the analysis of the ways in which their management, in terms of heritagization, takes place shows several elements in common. In both cases we have a tension between top-down processes of heritagization and a bottom-up appropriation of the space by religious actors. We also have two competing (and almost opposite) approaches, one emphasizing nationalist, purist discourses and the other focusing on intercultural and inter-religious discourses. Even if these tensions may seem specific for the Portuguese case, we will argue that similar processes are happening in other European contexts and more specifically in southern European societies. To understand such processes in Portugal, as in Italy and Spain, it is essential to pinpoint the role of the Catholic heritage in the definition of the "religious" in the public domain and ultimately in the construction of national identity and imaginaries.

To develop these arguments, we will firstly contextualize the relations between religion, heritage, and the public sphere in Portugal, in its historical and contemporary dimensions. This is essential to reveal the present and past relations between religion, patrimonialization processes, and hegemonic representations of Portuguese national identity. This section sets the scene for the two ethnographic case studies—Fátima and the Mouraria square project—that will be developed in the next two sections. We will then discuss these cases and proceed to the conclusions.

Religion, Heritage, and the Public Domain in Portugal

To understand some of the dynamics and processes around the two case studies of Fátima and Mouraria, it is essential to explore the role of the "religious" as practice and discourse in the Portuguese public domain and how it is connected with specific ideas about national identity and heritage, as it is analyzed in the chapter by Cardeira da Silva and Saraiva (this volume). As they explain, the construction of a national identity was, from the start, linked to Catholicism. When, in the twelfth century, the first Portuguese king proclaimed the independence from other Iberian kingdoms, this victory was also based on his achievements against the Muslims that occupied the peninsula. What Afonso Henriques proclaimed was a victory of Christianity, which was carried on by his successors in the following centuries. The main historical events of the country remained directly connected to the Catholic Church, and in spite of periods of tensions and ambiguities, the long-established relations between the monarchy and the church perpetuated the idea that Catholicism was the religion of the kingdom (Vilaça 2006). This situation lasted until the liberal revolution at the end of the nineteenth century, which brought about a proclaimed triumph of *laicité* (secularism) and the extinction of religious orders. The notion of a possible secular nation was further implemented with the proclamation of the republic in 1910 and a certain opening to religious pluralism during the First Republic (Vilaça and Oliveira 2019). In fact, during this period some new religious groups such as Protestant churches, Jehovah's Witnesses, Spiritists, and even Baha'i followers came to the country.

Under the Salazar dictatorship (1933), the ties between the state and the church were reinforced once again through a nonofficial but evident mutual support in many political and social decisions, as in the case of Portuguese Christian missions in the overseas colonies. Initially, the Estado Novo dictatorship proclaimed a national identity that was deeply Catholic, anti-Protestant, and suspicious, even if slightly tolerant, of other religious groups. The existence of an important Islamic heritage in Portugal was completely silenced, despite the numerous archaeological findings that proved its relevance (Cardeira da Silva 2005), thereby creating a nation imagined as Catholic and built against the presence of Muslims. Later, though, a lusotropical rhetoric was extensively adopted, with the desire to project "a positive external image" of Portugal that had important implications also on the ways in which heritage was managed (see Cardeira da Silva and Saraiva, this volume). It is in this context that during the liberation wars in Portugal's former colonial territories, the Estado Novo regime looked very suspiciously at Muslims in Mozambique and Guinea-Bissau and tried to create its own "brand" of Portuguese Islam (which could be used to show, according to the argument, the Portuguese "soft colonization"), a brand that met the resistance of some of the key Islamic figures (Vakil, Monteiro, and Machaqueiro 2011).

It was finally with the 1974 revolution that the social and religious scenario in Portugal underwent drastic alterations. In fact, although Portugal is still frequently described as a "traditionally" Catholic country, much has changed in the past decades due mainly to different types of mobilities (of people, ideas, and institutions). Even if Portugal is still usually perceived as an emigration country, in the last quarter of a century it has also become a country of immigration. The democratic transition, European integration, and implementation of the Schengen Agreement changed the position of Portugal regarding global migration flows (see, for instance, Castles and Miller 1997; King et al. 2000). These include the arrival not only of populations with historical/colonial connections with Portugal—such as Cape Verdeans, Guineans, and Angolans, to mention just a few—but also of populations with no prior links to Portugal. Chinese, Bangladeshis, Pakistanis, Senegalese, and populations from central and eastern Europe—Romania, Ukraine, Moldavia—are now part and parcel of Lisbon's sociocultural makeup. With these flows, which began in the 1960s but increased significantly from the late '80s onward, with its corresponding diversities, the religious landscape became much more complex (see Blanes and Mapril 2013; Cardeira da Silva and Saraiva, this volume).

Beyond the Catholic majority, Portugal nowadays has a large variety of Christian Orthodox, Protestants, Evangelicals and Pentecostals, Muslims, Jews, Mormons, Moonies, Buddhists, New Agers, Afro-Brazilians, and other religious minorities. It is also important to acknowledge that these more recent diversities were not opposed to a homogeneous (Catholic) past (Blanes and Mapril 2013). However, although religious pluralism and diversities were historically present in the country, it is also essential to acknowledge the current complexities and their relations with wider transformations in the past decades. Whereas in the discussion of the European Constitution the reference to the Christian roots of Europe stirred a considerable debate, the reference to a Portuguese heritage rooted in Christianity in general and Catholicism in particular did not cause too many conflicts. Nevertheless, discussions on religious pluralism were carried out in the Parliament in the 1990s, and the new religious law was approved in 2001, followed by, in 2004, the creation of the Commission for Religious Freedom.

It is in this scenario of contemporary religious variety that the two case studies of Fátima and Mouraria, which we will explore in more detail in the following two sections, come into play. These two examples allow us to address, from specific social locations, what constitutes the contemporary Portuguese public domain and its various concepts of heritage, focusing on its geographies of power and its ambiguities dealing with religion.

Although in Fátima the supremacy of Catholicism in terms of heritage becomes particularly evident, the authorities in charge of the management of the shrine also stimulate the development of a national and global devotion to Our Lady of Fátima that goes beyond the local cult. The result is a cult deeply engrained in a Portuguese national imaginary, and heritage, that is also open to the world and to other religions. However, as we will see, this openness has its rules and restrictions, resulting in what can be described as an ecumenism led by Catholicism.

The new Mouraria square, on the other hand, evokes the current changes in the Portuguese religioscape (Turner 2011), with different actors, projects, and heritages. This politics of religious diversities, though, is intimately connected with a public domain in which several segments, led by the Catholic Church, claim a new place for the "religious" (Mapril et al. 2017). Within these dynamics, the place of religious minorities (and by implication majority) is of paramount importance.

Fátima: From National(ist) Marian Shrine to Global Religious Heritage Site

A small Portuguese village clustered around a parish church, Fátima started attracting public attention after 13 May 1917, when three children reported having a vision that was later officially recognized by ecclesiastic authorities as an authentic Marian apparition. Fátima is currently a global Catholic pilgrimage site that also encompasses the village of Aljustrel and the area that is now the town of Cova da Iria-Fátima.

The processes of authentication and validation of this religious site as well as the gradual transformations of the meanings ascribed to Our Lady of Fátima during the last one hundred years are complex. They need to be understood not only in the context of the national political scenario in Portugal discussed above but also taking into account the increasing occurrence of Marian apparitions since the end of the nineteenth century and the gradual importance given to Marian apparition sites as well as to the figure of Mary within Catholicism (Christian 1996; Claverie 2003; Orsi 2010; Zimdars-Swartz 1991; Perry and Echevarria 1988). The following historical overview is therefore necessarily reductive and has the aim to provide the readers with the information necessary to follow Fátima's evolution from a national(ist) Marian shrine to a global religious heritage site. Thus the case of Fátima provides a privileged window upon the influence of nationalist discourses on heritage practices in Portugal.

On 13 May 1917, three children, Lucia Santos and Jacinta and Francisco Marto, now known as the three little shepherds (*os três pastorinhos*), reported having seen a lady dressed in white, which they soon identified as being Our Lady. As we have seen above, the First Portuguese Republic had a rather anticlerical attitude. The children grew up in a climate of worry and fear related to the international political situation, the separation of the state and the church, and increasing attacks against priests and proprieties of the church. After reporting their visions, the children were treated as liars by some and revered as visionaries by others; nevertheless worship in Fátima started to develop steadily, especially after the so-called Miracle of the Sun on 13 October 1917, when a large crowd assembled at Fátima reported seeing the sun move and shine in unusual ways, after a prophesy of the three children.

With the beginning of the military dictatorship in 1926, an auspicious period for the devotion in Fátima started. Eager to distance itself from the anticlerical positions of the republican period, the new government endorsed Fátima as a patriotic altar. This process became particularly evident when Our Lady of Fátima was crowned as queen of Portugal in 1942 with a golden crown made from jewelry given by Portuguese women as an offering for Our Lady's intercession to avoid Portugal's participation in World War II. Through the figure of the queen of Portugal (*rainha de Portugal*), a title used in what became the official hymn of Our Lady of Fátima, a strong link between Fátima, the Portuguese state, and the Portuguese population was created. This link was widely used to legitimize the dictatorship of Salazar as well as to encourage the colonial wars (e.g., Zimdars-Swartz 1991; Torgal 2011, 2017). Still today survivors of colonial wars go on pilgrimage to Fátima with their fellow soldiers to give thanks for coming home safe as well as to commemorate their participation in the wars. The crown of Our Lady, which is used only for the special celebrations held each year to commemorate the dates of the apparitions (see figure 8.1), gradually became a sacred object but also a piece that is jealously guarded and exhibited as part of the Portuguese heritage in the Museum of the Sanctuary.

Although it is clear that not all Catholics in Portugal, priests or laypeople, were in favor of the Estado Novo, Salazarism played an important role in the development of the devotion to Our Lady of Fátima in Portugal and in the consecration of Fátima as a patriotic altar. The link between Salazarism and Fátima remains a topic that has never really been clearly acknowledged by the exponents of the Catholic institutions in Portugal in the public space, and it is therefore still at the origin of fierce debates. While scholarship on Fátima has tended to focus on the analysis of the importance of this cult

Figure 8.1. The statue of Our Lady of Fátima during the crowded procession for the celebration of the centenary of the apparitions on 13 October 2017. Note the crown made of gold donated by Portuguese women. © Anna Fedele.

during Salazarism[1] and on its political dimension (e.g., Scheer 2006), other important aspects of this devotion have received little attention so far (but see Lopes 1989; Jansen and Kühl 2008; Pereira 2003; Fedele 2017, 2020a, 2020b; Gemzöe 2000). As we will show through our historical analysis, the cult to Our Lady of Fátima, with its top-down management as well as its bottom-up appropriations, is constantly changing. When Fedele was presenting her work in Portugal, she found that the audience almost always expected her to take sides, showing that she was in some way critical of Fátima devotion, linking it mainly to Salazarism, or that she was in some way "Catholic friendly" and therefore ready to minimize this political aspect. Fedele tried to explain that as an anthropologist she just wanted to understand devotion in Fátima, avoiding to reduce it only to its political dimension or only to one historical period, but this dichotomy was difficult to overcome.

Since the 1940s, replicas of the statue of Our Lady of Fátima conserved in the chapel of the apparition were created and sent out as pilgrimage statues, first to the rest of Portugal and then gradually to Spain, the rest of Europe, and the rest of the world. Pilgrim statues greatly increased international devotion, as did the activities of the Blue Army of Our Lady of Fátima. Founded in 1946 in the United States and later renamed the World Apostolate of Fátima, this organization fostered the association of Our Lady of Fátima with the devotion to the Immaculate Heart of Mary and as an important figure in the battle against the spread of communism.

After the revolution in 1974, the new government adopted a moderate position, as the nationalist aspect of Fátima was less emphasized and what Fedele describes below as the global Fátima discourse gradually became more and more important. Our Lady of Fátima increasingly became a symbol of international anticommunism through the pope's interpretation of his survival of an assassination attempt in 1981 as a consequence of the intervention of Our Lady of Fátima. In this context, the fall of the Berlin Wall in 1989 and the decline of the Soviet Union were interpreted as the triumph of Our Lady, and a piece of the Berlin Wall was displayed at the Sanctuary of Fátima and now forms part of its permanent heritage. In 2000 the pope preceded the ceremony of beatification of Jacinta and Francisco, who had died shortly after the visions. After Lucia's death in 2005, her case was granted by Pope Benedict XVI an accelerated process of beatification.

In 2016 and 2017, with the celebration of the centenary of the apparitions in Fátima, the visit of Pope Francis, and the sanctification of Jacinta and Francisco, the relevance of this site as a high place of global Catholicism and an important European heritage site was sanctioned once again. Through the constant attention of the Portuguese media and the celebration of the apparitions in 2016 and 2017 became a national event, implicating the president of the republic in the most important events. The national pilgrimages of 12–13 May 2017 paralyzed a part of the country and required the development of a huge apparatus of assistance and security measures.

Fátima is currently presented as a Catholic shrine of global religious significance but also as a national heritage shrine to be visited by tourists who wish to discover more about Portuguese culture and its religious traditions. In a brochure distributed by the local tourist office in 2017, Fátima was presented as an inter-religious site that increasingly attracted also non-Christian groups. This is not an entirely new phenomenon, since Hindus and Muslims living in Portugal have been visiting Fátima at least since the 1980s. It seems that with the turning of the new century, however, the visibility and public recognition of this phenomenon have become possible. The promotion of Fátima as a possible place for inter-religious worship, however, is still contested, as we will see in more detail below.

In Fátima we find two intertwined heritage discourses: a "nationalist Fátima" discourse, clearly influenced by a nationalist Portuguese imaginary, and a "global Fátima" discourse, which aims to reach through the entire world. These two discourses feed into each other. The importance of the worldwide cult of Fátima is used to endorse and demonstrate the international importance of Portugal worldwide, an association that emerged also from the discourse of the president of the republic on 13 October 2017. However there exist also tensions, especially when the global dimension of Fátima relates to its use by non-Christian religious groups living in Portugal. *Enciclopédia de Fátima* (Encyclopedia of Fátima) (Azevedo and Cristino 2007), written with the active participation of the Sanctuary of Fátima, recognizes the importance that Fátima had for Muslims living in Portugal. Hindus also visit Fátima regularly and often have statues of Our Lady in their shops and houses (Lourenço and Cachado 2018). Also, members of other religious communities visit Fátima and celebrate their rituals there—for instance, those related to alternative spiritualities (e.g.,New Age, Neo-Paganism, Neo-Shamanism), Afro-Brazilian religions, or groups practicing techniques more related to the culture of wellness such as meditation, mindfulness, or yoga. While some consider this inter-religious feature of Fátima an expression of the sacredness and powerfulness of the place, others feel the need to protect the "Catholicness" of Fátima. This tendency to protect Fátima from non-Christian religions became evident in 2004 after a Hindu priest was allowed to lead a ceremony at the chapel of the apparitions, which gave rise to fierce debates.[2] Those protesting against this inter-religious ceremony expressed through the Portuguese media their anger about the fact that the very heart of Portuguese Catholicism was being used to celebrate "pagan" rites.

These tensions between nationalist Fátima, seen as a religious heritage site that is only for the (Catholic) Portuguese, and global Fátima, seen as an international, even inter-religious heritage site, reflect the conflicting desires of preserving a Catholic Portugal and, alternatively, affirming its international, inter-religious grandiosity.

When we interviewed pilgrims, those coming from abroad were surprised to discover that non-Christian groups also visited Fátima. They usually saw this in a positive way, as a proof of the healing power of the shrines. Only those belonging to more conservative Catholic groups, such as the aforementioned Blue Army of Fátima, saw it as a potential threat and a silent takeover of Fátima by non-Christians. Many Portuguese pilgrims knew about non-Christian devotion in Fátima from the media and usually saw it as something obvious: since the healing power of Our Lady was great, other religious groups also wanted to ask for her help. Most of them also stated, however, that if other groups wanted to visit the shrine, they had to conform to Catholic norms and rituals (see also Fedele 2020a, 2020b). The pilgrims' Catholic-centered ecumenism mirrors also the overall management of the shrine by Catholic authorities. They are proud to show that other religious groups also recognize Fátima as an important and sacred place, as long as their ritual use of it happens under the control of Catholic authorities.

The Moorish Square and Its Quarter: Between Heritage and Lived Religion

In the past years, a project for the construction of a new square, named praça da Mouraria, literally the Moorish square, was approved by the city council of Lisbon. This project was proposed in 2012 as part of a larger initiative to regenerate the Mouraria neighborhood, the Moorish quarter, a working-class area in the center of the city, which is historically seen as an ambiguous place. The Moorish quarter, or bairro da Mouraria, is the current name of an area of the city where Moors (Mouros in Portuguese) were allowed to live, in the areas surrounding the walls, after the conquest of Lisbon in the twelfth century. The Lisbon Moorish quarters were partially autonomous in relation to the rest of the city, with several infrastructures such as mosques, madrassas, cemeteries, etc. (Gaspar 1985). By the end of the fifteenth century, Moors and Jews were expelled or forced to convert, and with this an erasure of the presence of Muslim institutions and symbols took place.[3] Despite these processes of expulsion and iconoclasm, and during all the major transformations in the following centuries, this area of Lisbon retained this Moorish reference up to the present.

Over the next centuries, the Moorish quarter went through a series of transformations. Throughout the sixteenth and seventeenth centuries it was the place of several crafts, such as ceramics and olive oil production, and references still linger to this day in the name of some of the streets in the area (Estevens 2018). In spite of its social marginalization, it was for a while attractive to members of the clergy, nobles, and rich members of the bourgeoisie, who built palaces in the upper side of Mouraria (Estevens 2018). By the late nineteenth century, and after remaining almost untouched by the earthquake of 1755, Mouraria became a working-class area, with a small bourgeoisie, and the place of unions, newspapers, associations, and several theaters. It was a republican area marked by the presence of several revolutionary and proletarian movements that criticized the increasing social inequalities and the monarchy (Estevens 2018).

During the Estado Novo dictatorship, Mouraria was perceived as the place of the "dangerous classes" and thus a place that needed disciplining. In this sense, several plans were developed to try to renovate the area, which had an effective component of urban space transformation, but also aimed at a larger moral transformation, via hygienist architecture (Bastos 2015). Although never finalized, these plans left a deep mark in the area because of the demolitions carried out in lower Mouraria, a condition that was aggravated by the fire and demolition of a central market in the vicinity.

At the same time, Mouraria was still thought of as a religious place, through the procession of Our Lady of Health, the oldest in the city (dating from 1570)—today considered a city heritage. Soon after the implementation of the republic, in 1910, the procession was interrupted and later resumed during the Estado Novo, in the 1940s, in a context in which the dictatorship was appropriating the Catholic identity of Mouraria (together with Fado and the Marchas populares). For the dictatorship, Mouraria was the place to continuously celebrate the connections between a national imaginary and the central role of Catholicism in it. This project produced a discourse that silenced nineteenth-century archaeological findings of the Islamic presence in the city and painted a highly Orientalized image of the Muslim "Other," defeated in the twelfth century.

After 1974 and until the twentieth century, Mouraria changed significantly once again. In the late 1970s, the aged buildings and the economic marginalization led to a sharp demographic decrease. It was frequently described as a place of margins and urban "problems," an image that, as we have seen, lingered throughout the twentieth century (Menezes 2004). Simultaneously, though, throughout the 1980s, several populations settled, commercially and residentially, in the area, coming from previous Portuguese colonies, in the context of postcolonial mobilities. From the 1990s, with the transformation of Portugal's position in relation to global flows, Mouraria was renewed with the arrival of new populations, which in the following decades transformed the entire area economically, culturally, and politically. In this context, Mouraria and Martim Moniz square saw their image transformed, now in a multicultural area and revealing the cosmopolitan and modern transformations of Portuguese society. At the same time, the whole area was the subject of new urban transformation projects—the creation of shopping centers (Mouraria shopping center in 1988 and Martim Moniz shopping center in 1992) and the opening of the square (1999). With the arrival of new populations, new expressions of cultural and religious diversity emerged in the public space, such as Todos: Caminhada de Culturas (Altogether: Walk of Cultures), Chinese New Year celebrations, International Mother Language Day (UNESCO), celebration of the anniversary of the recognition of the Sikh religion, and prayers concerning the two main feasts of the Islamic calendar—the feast of the end of Ramadan and the Feast of Sacrifice.

Thus, in the past decades, the image of Mouraria changed significantly, due to the arrival and settlement of migrants from China, Bangladesh, Pakistan, Guinea-Bissau, Mozambique, and many others; the statistics mention the existence of fifty-six different nationalities in this area (Fonseca et al. 2012). Mouraria is nowadays described as a place for cultural diversity, multiculturalism, and modernity. So, on one hand, this area of the city somehow evokes several moral panics and normative arguments about the proper urban environment, while at the same time, it is frequently celebrated by several segments as the place for multiculturalism and modernity of Portuguese society. On top of this, Mouraria is still one of the cheapest urban areas close to the city center, and therefore, it is subject to an increasing gentrification and touristic pressure. To understand the construction of this new square, it is imperative having this context in mind.

It is within this larger historical context that in 2012 the Moorish square project, or *praça da Mouraria*, was presented by city hall. The name of this new square is part of the aforementioned process of heritagization and patrimonialization of the figure of the Mouro and its role in Lisbon's history. In a wider sense, this patrimonialization of the Mouro relates to the increasing political and economic importance of the Al-Andalus heritage in contemporary Portuguese society, including for tourism (see Cardeira da Silva 2005), a process that has interesting comparative elements to what is currently happening in Spain (Astor, Burchardt, and Griera 2017; Astor 2019; Hirschkind 2016; Astor 2017). In Lisbon it is possible to find not only guided tours to Islamic Lisbon, organized by private companies, but also touristic plaques that are located in several parts of Mouraria indicating the presence of mosques and other Islamic facilities from the twelfth century (these plaques indicate several layers of history in old Lisbon—not only Islamic).

This architectural project is to be built in one of the main avenues close to Mouraria and includes a new square, a garden, a mosque, with sections for women and men, a multifunctional hall, and a cultural center that will be connected with the Lisbon Photographic Archive (just next door). The decorations of the mosque and the adaptation of the building for religious services will be funded by the Bangladesh Islamic Centre (BIC), an association created in 2004 to manage a mosque located in a small street in the Mouraria neighborhood that has been functioning for the past thirteen years. The transfer of this mosque to the new square means that it will function in one of the main avenues in the area, and thus increase its visibility. A protocol was thus celebrated between city hall and the Islamic Community of Bangladesh in which the funding is partially shared—city hall funds the construction of spaces of public use, including the square and the necessary expropriations, while the religious spaces, its management, and adaptations will be funded by the BIC.

For city hall, the Moorish square, with its reference to Al-Andalus and the presence of the mosque, is part of a larger process of transformation of a run-down area of the city. In this case, the mobilization of ideas about religious diversity and heritage is also a way of transforming an urban landscape that has a historically ambiguous image in the city. Simultaneously, for city hall, the transfer of this mosque to the future square means solving some previous safety issues and silencing some contestation and complaints from neighbors about the noise and the prayers in the middle of the street. It was also an opportunity to remove this mosque from the inner core of Mouraria and increase its visibility and control. Finally, for local authorities this project is also important, given the growing gentrification and touristic pressure that Lisbon has been facing in the past years.

On the other hand, though, this same project of the Moorish square is associated with more than a decade of negotiations and claims made by a specific segment of Sunni Muslims in the public sphere. The contemporary Baitul Mukarram Mosque in Mouraria began as a small apartment, in the early 2000s, adapted by a group of migrants from Bangladesh to function as a prayer room. This place of worship was created for daily prayer convenience. Simultaneously, it was also part of a larger process of bringing religious/moral order to a world of uncertainties and risks associated with their migration experience in Portugal and in Europe more generally. Over the

Figure 8.2. The Baitul Mukarram Mosque in Mouraria on its inauguration day. © José Mapril.

following years, and as this mosque grew in importance, its premises moved to a whole building and currently occupies a warehouse that serves five hundred to six hundred people per prayer service.

During the two most important prayers—at the end of Ramadan and the Feast of Sacrifice—an adjacent square is used, due to the size of the congregation. This mosque was eventually named after the Dhaka central mosque—Baitul Mukarram—and has been managed by the Bangladesh Islamic Centre (BIC), an association created and recognized by the Portuguese state since 2004. From the moment it grew in importance, the members of the executive committee began negotiations with the Lisbon city council for the creation of an adequate religious and ritual space for Muslims, Bangladeshis and others, in that area of the city.

For the executive committee, the relocation to the new square is essential, having in mind the reduced space for those attending and as a good deed (waqf) to all Muslims, but it is also their recognition as key actors not only locally, in Mouraria, but also within Portuguese public Islam (Salvatore and Eickelman 2004), which has been dominated institutionally by other segments of Sunni Muslims with longer established connections with Portugal through the colonial nexus (see Vakil 2003, 2004; Tiesler 2000; Mapril et al. 2017; Mapril 2014).

Finally, a word about the architectural project itself. The project was designed by a Lisbon architect and extensively presented in international architectural and art forums. Initially, the plan was to open a space between two of the main streets in the Mouraria area—bear in mind that Mouraria is one of the oldest areas of the city, marked by small and narrow streets and alleys. The main objective was, therefore, to foster communication and visibility. According to the architect, this idea of an empty space needed some confinement, some limits, and these were defined by the Moorish reference. Even before the inclusion of a mosque, the idea was to create a space that was evocative of an Islamic heritage. As Mapril's interlocutor argued:

> From the beginning, the Mouraria theme implied a reference to Muslim architecture. This was essential to me and that is why the square was designed as a patio. ... Thus, the idea of confinement, patio, a moment of silence or the creation of a small oasis was all about Muslim architecture. (Interview, Lisbon, 22 August 2019)

So, the initial plan was to build an open space that evoked an Islamic heritage present in the name of the square, but also in the contemporary configurations of the Moorish quarter. As soon as it was decided that an existing mosque in this area of the city would be transferred to the new square, the project was slightly changed. From then on, the architect collaborated closely with the president of the executive committee of the Bangladesh

Islamic Centre to adapt the space to the transfer of the Baitul Mukarram Mosque. Thus, the Moorish square project was eventually adapted to create an adequate ritual space for Muslims in central Lisbon, including ablution spaces and a minaret. After talks with the BIC, it was decided that the minaret would be slightly withdrawn from public view. The location of the minaret is quite interesting because, among other things, it reveals a kind of ambiguity between an aestheticized heritagized Islamic past, which can be mobilized to build a certain type of cityscape, and the acceptable visibility of lived religion, especially Islam (for comparative discussions, see Verkaaik 2013; Arab 2017). To put it differently, the location of the minaret in the project demonstrates a certain type of non-imposing visibility to Islam in the area. It is as if the idea was to make lived Islam visible but not too imposing or ostensible.

A final note about this case should be included here. This project has been highly discussed in the public sphere, with significant contestation coming from distinct segments but especially among extreme right movements and some segments of the Catholic Church. For the latter, in particular the local representative, local authorities are often criticized because they are abandoning the "proper" Portuguese heritage, namely Catholic churches, in favor of other religions that are not, and we quote, "Portuguese," such as Islam. So, for these segments of the local Catholic Church, Portuguese heritage is mainly Catholic, and this should be the one receiving all the funding and not others.

Between the National and the Global: Concluding Notes

Analyzing both cases from a historical perspective, we have seen that the presence of Catholicism as the main legitimate religion in the country has been, throughout the centuries, the rule. Portugal is making a strong effort to establish a dialogue with religious minorities in order to create an ecumenical society; however, the somehow "hidden" statement behind this religious and political agenda is that this ecumenism should happen under the benevolent supremacy of Catholicism. We believe that although this scenario may have some elements that are exclusive to Portugal, the influence of a Catholic-centered ecumenical discourse related to heritage making is present also in other European countries where Catholicism has played and often still has an important role, like France (Isnart 2012), Spain (Astor, Burchardt, and Griera 2017; Astor 2019), and Poland (see Niedźwiedź, this volume; Baraniecka-Olszewska, this volume).

In spite of their differences, both cases reveal the tensions within the Portuguese governance of religious sites and heritages, tensions that emerge from the efforts to preserve a Catholic, nationalist Portugal while affirming as well its international, interreligious, and cosmopolitan landscape. These two tendencies, we argue, are linked to the (re)imagination of national identity and belonging based on what constitutes Portuguese religious heritage and its relationship with lived religiosity. The stretching of the limits of what constitutes the "proper" Portuguese heritage is also the result of bottom-up appropriations of the space by religious actors, seen as minorities, that are making claims to citizenship through heritagization and religion.

As we have seen, these tensions of preserving a nationalist, "pure" Portugal while also opening up to other cultures and religions are also embodied in the ways social actors behave in these sites, feeling for instance that certain attitudes, gestures, and behaviors are appropriate and respectful while others are not. To fully grasp the complexities of such phenomena, it is important to pay special attention to the bottom-up appropriation of heritage and religious sites. With this text we hope to open the way for more ethnographic research that pays attention to the often hidden rules about appropriate and inappropriate rules at work at heritage sites and explores the more or less visible influence that Catholicism has on heritage management in Europe and in other countries with a strong Catholic past, such as in Latin America.

Anna Fedele works as an independent anthropological counselor and as a lecturer at the Free University of Bolzano. She is an associated researcher of the Center for Research in Anthropology at the Lisbon University Institute. Her research focuses on religion, ritual, and gender. Fedele is the author of the award-winning monograph *Looking for Mary Magdalene: Alternative Pilgrimage and Ritual Creativity at Catholic Shrines in France* (2013). She is cofounder and editor of the Routledge book series "Gendering the Study of Religion in the Social Sciences." With Kim Knibbe, she coedited *Secular Societies, Spiritual Selves? The Gendered Triangle of Religion, Secularity and Spirituality* (2020).

José Mapril is a PhD in anthropology from the ICS, University of Lisbon, with a thesis on transnationalism and Islam among the Bangladeshis in Lisbon. Currently, he is an assistant professor in the Department of Anthropology at the Universidade Nova de Lisboa and a senior researcher at CRIA NOVA. Since the end of 2018, José has been the coordinator of the executive committee of CRIA. Currently he is developing a project on onward migration, life course, and future among Bangladeshis in Europe and has just finished participation in the HERA project HERILIGION: The Heritagization of Religion and Sacralization of Heritage in Contemporary Europe.

NOTES

Anna Fedele's and José Mapril's research for this chapter was funded by the HERILIGION: The Heritagization of Religion and the Sacralization of Heritage in Contemporary Europe project, funded by Humanities in the European Research Area (HERA) grant # 5087-00505A and also by FCT/MCTES (the Portuguese Foundation for Science and Technology) as part of the strategic research plan of the Centro em Rede de Investigação em Antropologia (UID/ANT/04038/2013). Anna Fedele's research was also part of her activities as an FCT investigator (IF/01063/2014). We would like to thank Irene Stengs, Oscar Salemink, and the other members of the HERILIGION team for their useful comments and suggestions.

1. For a detailed discussion of the relationship between Fátima and the Estado Novo, see Barreto 2004; Cadegan 2004; Torgal 2011; Zimdars-Swartz 1991; and Simpson 2014.
2. For a detailed analysis of the Hindu cult in Fátima and the debates related to it, as well as an overview of Muslim devotion in Fátima, see Joaquim Franco's dissertation "Devotos improváveis: Hindus e Muçulmanos numa visão de Fátima," Universidade Lusófona, 2020.
3. Pedro Gésero, "Configuração da Paisagem Urbana pelos Grupos de Imigrantes: o Martim Moniz na migrantscape de Lisboa," master's thesis., Faculdade de Arquitetura, Lisbon, 2011.

REFERENCES

Arab, Pooyan Tamimi. 2017. *Amplifying Islam in the European Soundscape: Religious Pluralism and the Secularism in the Netherlands*. Oxford: Bloomsbury.

Astor, Avi. 2017. *Rebuilding Islam in Contemporary Spain: The Politics of Mosque Establishments, 1976–2013*. Brighton: Sussex Academic Press.

Astor, Avi. 2019. "Polarization and the Limits of Politicization: Cordoba's Mosque-Cathedral and the Politics of Cultural Heritage," *Qualitative Sociology* 42(3): 337–60.

Astor, Avi, Marian Burchardt, and Mar Griera. 2017. "The Politics of Religious Heritage: Framing Claims to Religion as Culture in Spain," *Journal for the Scientific Study of Religion* 56(1): 126–42.

Azevedo, Carlos Moreira, and Luciano Cristino (eds.). 2007. *Enciclopédia de Fátima*. Estoril: Princípia.

Barreto, José. 2004. *Religião e Sociedade. Dois Ensaios*. Lisbon: Imprensa de Ciencias Sociais.

Bastos, Cristiana. 2015. "Entre mundos: Thomaz de Mello Breyner e a clínica de sífilis do Desterro, Lisboa," in Gisel Sanglard et al. (eds.), *Filantropos da Nação: Sociedade, Saúde e Assistência no Brasil e em Portugal*. Rio de Janeiro: Editora FGV, pp. 77–94.

Blanes, Ruy. 2011. "Double Presence: Proselytism and Belonging in an Angolan Prophetic Church's Diaspora in Europe," *Journal of Religion in Europe* 4: 409–28.

Blanes, Ruy, and José Mapril (eds.). 2013. *The Sites and Politics of Religious Diversity in Southern Europe: The Best of All Gods*. Leiden: Brill Publishers.

Bondaz, Julien, Cyril Isnart, and Anaïs Leblon. 2012. "Au-delà du consensus patrimonial: Résistances et usages contestataires du patrimoine," *Civilisations: Revue i Internationale d'Anthropologie et de Sciences Humaines* 61(1): 9–22.

Cadegan, Una M. 2004. "The Queen of Peace in the Shadow of War: Fátima and U.S. Catholic Anticommunism," *U.S. Catholic Historian* 22 (4): 1–15.
Cardeira da Silva, Maria. 2005. "O sentido dos Árabes no nosso sentido," *Análise Social* 173: 781–806.
Castles, Stephen, and Mark Miller. 1997. *The Age of Migration*. New York: Guilford Press.
Christian, William A. 1996. *Visionaries: The Spanish Republic and the Reign of Christ*. Berkeley: University of California Press.
Claverie, Elisabeth. 2003. *Les Guerres de La Vierge: Une Anthropologie Des Apparitions*. NRF Essais. Paris: Gallimard.
Coleman, Simon, and John Eade (eds.). 2018. *Pilgrimage and Political Economy: Translating the Sacred*. Oxford and New York: Berghahn Books.
Eade, John, and Michael Sallnow. 1991. *Contesting the Sacred: The Anthropology of Christian Pilgrimage*. London and New York: Routledge.
Estevens, Ana. 2018. *A Cidade Neoliberal*. Lisbon: Deriva Editores.
Fedele, Anna. 2017. "Pellegrinaggio, Topografia Sacra e Religione Vissuta a Fátima," *Annali di Studi Religiosi* 18: 83–95.
Fedele, Anna. 2020a. "Walking Pilgrimages to the Marian Shrine of Fátima in Portugal as Democratic Explorations," in Graham Harvey et al. (eds.), *Reassembling Democracy: Ritual as Cultural Resource*. London: Bloomsbury, pp. 105–24.
Fedele, Anna. 2020b. "'God Wants Spiritual Fruits Not Religious Nuts': Spirituality as a Middle Way between Religion and Secularism at the Marian Shrine of Fátima," in Anna Fedele and Kim E. Knibbe (eds.), *Secular Societies, Spiritual Selves? The Gendered Triangle of Religion, Secularity and Spirituality*. London, New York: Routledge, pp. 166–83.
Fonseca, M., et al. (eds.). 2012. *Modes of Inter-ethnic Coexistence in Three Neighbourhoods in the Lisbon Metropolitan Area: A Comparative Perspective*. Lisbon: Colibri.
Gaspar, Jorge. 1985. "A cidade portuguesa na Idade Média. Aspetos da estrutura física e desenvolvimento funcional," in Emilio Satz, Margarita Cantera Montenegro, and Cristina Segura Graino (eds.), *La Ciudad Hispánica durante los siglos XIII al XVI: Actas del coloquio celebrado en La Rabida y Sevilla del 14 al 19 de septiembre de 1981*. Madrid: Editorial da Universidad Complutense, pp. 133–47.
Gemzöe, Lena. 2000. *Feminine Matters: Women's Religious Practices in a Portuguese Town*. Södertälje, Sweden: Stockholm University.
Hermkens, Anna-Karina, Willy Jansen, and Catrien Notermans (eds.). 2009. *Moved by Mary: The Power of Pilgrimage in the Modern World*. Burlington, VT: Ashgate.
Hirschkind, Charles. 2016. "Granadan Reflections," *Material Religion* 12(2): 209–32.
Isnart, Cyril. 2012. "The Mayor, the Ancestors and the Chapel: Clientelism, Emotion and Heritagisation in Southern France," *International Journal of Heritage Studies* 18(5): 479–94.
Isnart, Cyril. 2014. "Changing the Face of Catholicism in a Tourist Context: Heritage Care, Ritual Dynamics, and the Rhetoric of Transformation of a Religious Minority in Greece," *Journal of Tourism and Cultural Change* 12(2): 133–49.
Jansen, Willy, and Meike Kühl. 2008. "Shared symbols: Muslims, Marian Pilgrimages and Gender," *European Journal of Women's Studies* 15(3): 295–311.
King, Russel, et al. (eds.). 2000. *Eldorado or Fortress? Migration in Southern Europe*. London: Macmillan Press.
Lopes, Policarpo. 1989. "Le pèlerinage à Fátima: Une expression mystique du sacré populaire," *Social Compass* 36(2): 187–99.

Lourenço, Inês, and Rita Cachado. 2018. "Hindu Diaspora in Portugal: The Case of Our Lady of Fátima Devotion," in Pankaj et al. (eds.), *Hinduism and Tribal Religions: Encyclopedia of Indian Religions*. Leiden: Springer Netherlands, pp. 1–18.
Mapril, José. 2014. "'Aren't You Looking for Citizenship in the Wrong Place?' Islamic Education, Secular Subjectivities, and the Portuguese Muslim," *Religion and Society: Advances in Research* 5: 65–82.
Mapril, José, et al. (eds.). 2017. *Secularisms in a Post Secular Age? Religiosities and Subjectivities*. London: Palgrave.
Menezes, Marlucci. 2004. *Mouraria: Retalhos de um Imaginário*. Oeiras: Celta editores.
Orsi, Robert A. 2010. *The Madonna of 115th Street: Faith and Community in Italian Harlem, 1880–1950*. Yale University Press.
Pereira, Pedro. 2003. *Peregrinos: um Estudo Antropológico das Peregrinações a Pé a Fátima*. Lisbon: Instituto Piaget.
Perry, Nicholas, and Loreto Echeverria. 1988. *Under the Heel of Mary*. London and New York: Routledge.
Salvatore, Armando, and Dale Eickelman. 2004. *Public Islam and the Common Good*. Leiden: Brill.
Sarró, R., and Anne Mélice. 2011. "Kongo and Lisbon: The Dialectics of 'Center' and 'Periphery' in the Kimbanguist Church," in Sandra Fancello and Andre Mary (eds.), *Chrétiens Africans en Europe*. Paris: Karthala, pp. 43–67.
Scheer, Monique. 2006. *Rosenkranz und Kriegsvisionen: Marienerscheinungskulte im 20. Jahrhundert*. Tübingen: Tübinger Vereinigung für Volkskunde e.V.
Simpson, Duncan. 2014. *A Igreja Católica e o Estado Novo Salazarista*. Lisbon: Edições 70.
Teixeira, Alfredo. 2019. *A Religião na Sociedade Portuguesa*. Lisbon: Fundação Francisco Manuel dos Santos.
Tiesler, Nina. 2000. "Muçulmanos na margem: A nova presença islâmica em Portugal," *Sociologia: Problemas e Práticas* 34: 117–44.
Torgal, Luís Filipe. 2011. *O Sol Bailou ao Meio Dia: a Criação de Fátima*. Lisbon: Tinta-da-China.
Torgal, Luís Filipe. 2017. *Fátima, a (Des)construção do Mito*. Coimbra: Palimage.
Turner, Bryan S. 2011. *Religion and Modern Society: Citizenship, Secularization and the State*, Cambridge: Cambridge University Press.
Vakil, Abdoolkarim. 2003. "Muslims in Portugal: History, Historiography, Citizenship," *Euroclio Bulletin* 18: 9–13.
Vakil, Abdoolkarim. 2004. "Pensar o Islão: Questões coloniais, interrogações pós-coloniais," *Revista Crítica de Ciências Sociais* 69: 17–52.
Vakil, Abdoolkarim, Fernando Monteiro, and Mário Machaqueiro. 2011. *Moçambique: Memória Falado do Islão e da Guerra*. Coimbra: Almedina.
Verkaaik, Oscar. 2013. *Religious Architecture: Anthropological Perspectives*. Amsterdam: Amsterdam University Press.
Vilaça, Helena. 2006. *Da Torre de Babel às Terras Prometidas: Pluralismo Religioso em Portugal*. Coimbra: Afrontamento.
Vilaça, Helena, and Maria João Oliveira. 2019. *A Religião no Espaço Público Português*. Lisbon: INCM.
Zimdars-Swartz, Sandra L. 1991. *Encountering Mary: From La Salette to Medjugorje*. Princeton, NJ: Princeton University Press.

PART V

PERFORMANCES, RITUALS, AND RELIGIOUS HERITAGE IN THE NETHERLANDS

 CHAPTER 9

To Applaud or Not to Applaud? Bach's *Saint Matthew Passion* and Management of Sacrality in the Netherlands

Ernst van den Hemel

Introduction: A Slightly Awkward Moment

During a performance of Bach's *Saint Matthew Passion* in the Geertekerk (Geerte church) in Utrecht (the Netherlands, 30 March 2018), I witnessed someone committing a minor transgression. When the first part concluded, a young boy seated in the row in front of me started to applaud. He clapped his hands perhaps once before the father, who was seated next to him, placed his hand gently on his son's arm and whispered, "No applause." The boy acquiesced, the family stood up, and we all silently made our way to the area of the church where coffee and tea were served during intermission.

During my fieldwork into the popularity of passion plays in the Netherlands, I attended many performances of Johann Sebastian Bach's (1685–1750) musical rendition of the Gospel of Matthew.[1] At almost each performance an instance like this occurred. Whether it was through explicit hushes, stalwart glances, or mumbled comments, people reminded each other not to applaud. For reasons that will become apparent below, refraining from applause has become a central indicator of the special status of the *Saint Matthew Passion*. Therefore, at the end of this particular performance, it was surprising that something entirely different happened. After the final notes sounded, the conductor drew out the silence for a moment with a slight smile on her lips, before allowing, with a small nod of her head, the audience to applaud. The enthusiastic applause that followed turned into a standing ovation. The father and the son in the row in front of me got up and

Figure 9.1. Performance of the Sing-Along *Saint Matthew Passion*. Geertekerk Utrecht, 30 March 2018. © Ernst van den Hemel.

applauded. The boy even let out an audible "whoooo." Why was the young boy stopped from applauding after the first part, but not from letting out an excited "whoooo" after the second part?

These observations were made during a so-called *meezing-Matthäus*, a Sing-Along *Saint Matthew Passion*. This performance featured a choir of untrained singers, supported by a professional orchestra and soloists. The observations from the sing-along performance provide an entrance into the world of *Saint Matthew Passion* performances in the Netherlands. In this chapter, I want to show how in small gestures, such as the one by the father preventing the boy from applauding, a specific form of sacralization is upheld. The applause at the end of the performance is, as I will show, indicative of a development that gives new form to this sacrality. I will unpack this in two parts. First, I will sketch how, from the first performance in the Netherlands in 1870, Bach's *Saint Matthew Passion* became connected to notions of heritage and sacrality. Bach's *Saint Matthew Passion* offers a good illustration of how the category of heritage may be associated with a secularizing gaze. It takes elements of religion and places these in a seemingly secular heritage framework. At the same time, this case study shows how the inverse may also hold true—namely, heritage involving processes of sacralization. The *Saint Matthew Passion* and the conventions surrounding applause and silence thus form an interesting example of what Birgit Meyer and Marleen de Witte have called the "sacralization of heritage," providing an embodied and enacted illustration of how such sacralization takes shape in practices and gestures (Meyer and de Witte 2013: 277). Inspired by Haidy Geismar's concept of "ideologies of ownership" (Geismar 2015), I investigate how heritagization involves claims about who is seen as the beneficiary of heritage and who is involved in the setting up of "communities of care" (82) that concern themselves with how heritagized objects are handled, managed, and circulated: "Claims to ownership and care . . . constitute the foundational definitions of heritage and also form the ideological underpinnings of most heritage regimes" (76).

Second, by providing an ethnographic description of the performance and presenting findings from interviews with participants, I highlight how participation in the Sing-Along *Saint Matthew Passion* is indicative of the rise of new communities of care. Sing-along events can be productively interpreted as rebellious forms of performing music in which emotional participation is central. Far from being a vulgarization of the *Saint Matthew Passion*—an accusation frequently voiced by critics of the Sing-Along *Saint Matthew Passion*—I approach the Sing-Along *Saint Matthew Passion* as a new development in the contentious history of ideologies of ownership of the *Matthäus-Passion*, and, by extension, of heritagized religion in the Netherlands. To illustrate this, I will continue my description of how the sing-along *Saint Matthew Passion* in the Geertekerk unfolded.

Singing Along with the *Saint Matthew Passion*

Upon entering the church, I noticed that the audience was seated in close proximity to the choir, in crescent-shaped rows surrounding the orchestra and soloists. It was difficult for me to identify who was part of the choir and who was part of the audience. At other performances the distance between audience and choir was usually more formally indicated, for instance by a red velvet cord separating audience from performers. The opening of the sing-along performance also differed from the professional performances I attended. Madeleine Ingen Housz, director of the foundation Passieprojecten, who would also conduct the performance, addressed us shortly to outline the program. She introduced Ruud Bakhuizen, the speaker who was to provide the introduction, as a "businessman, philanthropist, and Bach fanatic." It was implied ("he is a great friend of the foundation") that Bakhuizen was also a sponsor of the event. In his speech, Bakhuizen presented historical facts about Bach's life and the history of the *Saint Matthew Passion*. He recounted how he traveled to the Thomaskirche (Leipzig, Germany) where Bach once performed the *Saint Matthew Passion* and described it as his "pilgrimage" (*pelgrimstocht*). He subsequently focused on the capacity of Bach to provide comfort in trying times, both in professional and personal life. After the introduction, Ingen Housz lit a candle, which, as she told us, was in commemoration of a board member of the foundation Passieprojecten who had recently passed away. After a moment's silence, the performance began.

As the performance progressed, I noticed that some of the singers, whom I later found out were novice participants, skipped some parts of the chorales, rejoining when the piece reached a more accessible section. Others participated with more apparent self-confidence. Eye contact and small winks exchanged between singers seemed to indicate camaraderie and support. It struck me how well the performance sounded. In preparation for my attendance, I had wondered how the genre of the sing-along event, which I associated with playful popular culture, would turn into perhaps *the* symbol of high-brow identification in the Netherlands. To be sure, a difference in quality was noticeable, but it sounded to my, admittedly untrained, ears like a convincing and impressive performance. As I found out during the interviews with some of the participants (as I will outline in more detail below), the performance was the culmination of many hours of solitary rehearsals. Moreover, many of the singers had prior experience with singing in choirs in the past.

After the performance came to its end and the applause and cheers died down, the singers made their way to their loved ones in the audience. One of them, who turned out to be the wife and mother of the father and son in front of me, approached them and received hugs, flowers, and warm compliments on her performance. Some singers idled in the church for about an hour, waiting in line to embrace the conductor. I overheard a first-time participant thanking Ingen Housz for helping her overcome her anxiety for the piece. There was no collective closing event or evaluation. Most people disbanded afterward, going their own way with family or friends.

The sing-along performance on the one hand combined well-known elements concerning the *Saint Matthew Passion*, like the policing of the applause and the framing of the *Saint Matthew Passion* as a source of inspiration for everyone. On the other hand, the burning of the candle, the applause at the end, and the use of the sing-along format do not fit expectations of a traditional performance of the *Saint Matthew Passion*.

In order to better understand how the Sing-Along *Saint Matthew's Passion* provokes and reinterprets hitherto dominant ideas about how the sacrality of the *Saint Matthew Passion* should be managed, I will first outline how silence and applause have become constitutive elements of the sacralization of the *Saint Matthew Passion*. Thereafter, I will return to the sing-along performance to present in more ethnographic detail how this sacrality takes on new forms.

Bach Is One of Us! The *Matthäus* in the Netherlands

For the non-Dutch reader, it may be a bit puzzling to understand why and how a work by a German Lutheran composer became so deeply engrained in the Dutch cultural landscape. Of course, Bach has been synonymous with accomplishments of Western culture for a long time, as indicated by the inclusion of Bach's works on the golden disc shot into space on the *Voyager* spacecraft in 1978 to acquaint unknown alien races with the miracle of music (Scott 2019). The "Bach mythos," the idea that Bach embodies the best of what humankind can produce, is an international phenomenon (Geck 1999). But in the Netherlands, Bach, and in particular attending or performing his *Saint Matthew Passion*, has become a particularly popular and well-known tradition.

In 2017 alone, the Netherlands saw nearly two-hundred performances of the *Matthäus*. For decades now, it is voted the most popular piece of classical music;[2] many Dutch families cherish the tradition of attending a performance of the *Saint Matthew Passion* once a year. What is more, a veritable "Bach industry" has developed. The Dutch broadcast radio station Concertzender started a daily radio program during which only pieces by Bach are broadcasted, entitled *Geen Dag Zonder Bach* (Not a day without Bach). This title also became the basis for a fashion collection, which has been selling

210 • *Ernst van den Hemel*

Figure 9.2. Performance of the *Saint Matthew Passion*, Grote Kerk Naarden, 22 April 2011. Dutch prime minister Mark Rutte and other cabinet members in attendance in the first row. Public domain.

Bach-themed hoodies, T-shirts, and romper suits for babies since 2011.[3] Numerous travel agencies offer "pilgrimages" to the Saint Thomas Church in Leipzig, where Bach composed and performed the *Matthäus-Passion*.

Annually, the performances of the *Matthäus* at the towns of Naarden and Leiden attract the elite of Dutch cultural and political high society, with sometimes the entire government cabinet in attendance in the first rows. The prime minister of the Netherlands, Mark Rutte, opened a major interview on national Dutch television just before the 2017 elections with the statement that attending the Naarden *Matthäus-Passion* is one of the highlights of his job:

> I get to go to see the *Saint Matthew Passion* every year. That's a tradition in the Netherlands. You sit there for three hours and you are washed away by waves of the most divine music imaginable. . . . When you listen to Bach, you know, I think that, even when you see all the misery in the world, all the horrors and wars, we are also capable of the highest good.[4]

Moreover, in the unruly political climate of the twenty-first century, it has become a common trope for Dutch nationalist politicians to invoke the brilliance of Bach and his *Passion* as a contrast to the allegedly inferior culture of Islam. Especially for the populist right-wing parties, it has become a mainstay to refer to Bach when one wants to illustrate the superiority of Western or Dutch culture.

In short, the *Matthäus* is not just an example of classical music in the Netherlands; it became a tradition in which experiencing Bach's composition is connected to matters of national and cultural identity. In order to understand how these affects became attached to the *Saint Matthew Passion*, it is helpful to trace the development of the popularity of Bach's *Passion*.

Applauding Jesus and the Sacralization of Heritage

When Bach composed the different versions of his *Saint Matthew Passion* between 1727 and 1736, it functioned as an integral part of the liturgical year, to be performed during Lent. Such liturgical pieces were oriented toward emotional participation of the congregation in the service. Bach's *Saint Matthew Passion* did not have a monumental reputation as a cultural accomplishment or the work of a genius, as these categories simply did not exist. Moreover, it was not common practice to perform compositions of composers after their death.

About a century later, the way in which music was staged and perceived changed drastically. The rise of Romantic nationalism (Leerssen 2013), multifaceted as it was (cf. Berlin and Gray 2013), contained one of the main programmatic goals to construct national identities based on a particular vision of the past (Leerssen 2013). This was paired with an emphasis on the capacity of art to give affective expression to the idea of communal identities (Leerssen 2013: 16). In Germany, intellectuals used Romantic cultural ideas to argue for the novel idea of one culture, one nation, and one state.

Instead of a composer firmly anchored in church life, Bach was now seen as of immense national value, whose work should be catalogued, performed, and preserved. In the works of poets, philosophers, and musicologists, art was presented as a sacred affair and as monuments commemorating the cultural roots of the nation. An early example can be found in the preface of musicologist Johann Forkel's (1749–1818) 1802 biography of Bach:

> Bach's works are a priceless national patrimony [*Erbgut*]; no other nation possesses a treasure comparable to it. Their publication in an authoritative text will be a national service and raise an imperishable monument to the composer himself. All who hold Germany dear are bound in honour to promote the undertaking to the utmost of their power. I deem it a duty to remind the public of this obligation and to kindle interest in it in every true German heart. (Forkel 2020: xxvi)

As indicated by the emotional admonishments to "all who hold Germany dear," Forkel provides a strong normative address to a national community that is expected to care. This citation expresses the tendency in early nineteenth-century Germany to embrace artists, writers, and composers as artistic geniuses, the faithful understanding and preservation of whose work should kindle an affective bond between the individual and the national community (Jensen et al. 2010; Leerssen 2013). Keeping in mind that this takes place before the unification in Germany (1871), it becomes apparent that such invocations of art and nation played a role in the ideological construction of the nation-state.

This citation is also an early example of how the idea of heritage is connected to a Romantic ideology of national identity. The word *Erbgut*, literally "inherited goods," was initially used to describe the inheritance of material things within familial law. Frans Grijzenhout points out how in Germany the word *Erbgut* was used earlier than in other contexts to describe "the most fleeting of art forms, music" as an inheritance of immense cultural value (2007: 11). It shows how the modern notion of cultural heritage, as it emerged in the mid-twentieth century, was preceded by the embrace of cultural objects as *Erbgut* and as monuments of a national community. Against the backdrop of this Romantic vision, the *Saint Matthew Passion* was restaged for the first time since Bach's lifetime. Organized in 1829 by Felix Mendelssohn Bartholdy (1809–47), the first performance took place in the concert hall of the Berlin Sing-Akademie. Founded in 1791, the Sing-

Akademie was modeled after the London Academy of Ancient Music. These academies were themselves part of a late eighteenth-, early nineteenth-century drive in which music from the past was seen as something that needed to be maintained and performed (Little 1991).

Mendelssohn's performance of Bach's *Saint Matthew Passion* was an event in which a sizable part of the elite of the time were present, including the Prussian king and Romantic intellectuals such as the poet Heine and philosophers Schleiermacher and Hegel (Applegate 2005). Though the objective was to revive Bach's work, Mendelssohn adapted Bach's *Saint Matthew Passion* to the spirit and the demands of his time. The performance, for which Mendelssohn altered the score by shortening it by ten arias, among other adjustments, aimed to downplay certain baroque elements deemed to be outdated and too difficult to perform (Marissen 1993). Mendelssohn's *Passion* was literally framed by nineteenth-century developments. These included the emphasis on emotional connection rather than historical accuracy, the rise of the concert hall and the notion of "classical music," and an emphasis on cultural objects of the past as monuments to the artistic genius of the nation.

A wealth of scholarship has been devoted to Mendelssohn's 1829 *Passion* and its aftermath. I want to highlight how the rediscovery of Bach involved the mobilization of explicit religious terminology. Felix Mendelssohn himself wrote to a friend, "The choir sang with such devotion, as if they were in church" (Marissen 1993). Bach-specialist Martin Geck states in his monograph on the rise of the Bach mythos that the "rediscovery" of the *Saint Matthew Passion* took place against the backdrop of a profound reorientation of the role of art in German society. Art was imbued with a collective mythologizing, which before then was reserved for religion. Geck describes it as follows: "[It was a period in which] traditional authorities of church and state were losing their, until then self-evident, legitimacy. A new mythology was needed to unify the splintered bourgeois society. Art became the vehicle for this new mythology" (Geck 1999: 154). Aesthetic experience and nationalist fervor were brought together in an affective plea to experience religious objects of the past (and Christianity in general) as cultural roots of the nation. The *Saint Matthew Passion* arose in this framework as the miracle wrought by the German genius Bach.

This brings into view an early illustration of the double effect of heritagization as outlined by Meyer and de Witte (2013). First, the staging of Bach's *Saint Matthew Passion* in concert halls illustrates how heritagization can be seen as a form of secularization. As argued by Crispin Paine in connection to museum practices, setting a religious object apart as heritage usually means uprooting it from its religious context (Paine 2013). The same can be argued for Bach's *Saint Matthew Passion*. Originally intended as liturgical object, it was, metaphorically speaking, unearthed and performed in the nineteenth century in the concert hall as German *Erbgut*, or heritage. Religious elements remained at play, however. Again, returning to Meyer and De Witte's argument, in the very process of heritagization itself there is "some kind of sacralization" at work (2013: 275). As *Saint Matthew Passion* moved from church to concert hall, it changed from fulfilling a liturgical function to being an object of artistic genius and national heritage. This can be adequately described as a process of re-sacralization. The re-sacralization orients itself not primarily to God, but to art as a human accomplishment and to a national community.

By setting cultural forms apart and lifting them up, heritagization involves dimensions of sacralization and secularization that can occur dynamically and simultaneously. It is, for instance, very well possible for religious objects to be displayed as heritage in churches, to be enjoyed by visitors of a church as heritage *and* congregants, who see the same church as predominantly a place of worship (cf. Ahl, Poulsen, and Salemink, this volume). Heritagization also frequently means that practices, such as rituals or performances, are turned into spectacles, disconnecting the communities from the practices they themselves have brought forth (Salemink 2016: 339). These dimensions might also lead to tensions, as religious communities might resist heritagization of religious objects and practices because of the perceived secularizing effect it has. Conversely, communities that embrace objects or practices as cultural heritage that were or are religious in origin might not acknowledge religious communities as primary stakeholders of said heritage and even experience their claims as burdensome (Timothy and Olsen 2006).

This affords a better understanding of how Bach's *Saint Matthew Passion* and the notion of applause became significant issues in the Netherlands. It shows how the *Saint Matthew Passion* became sacralized and how this sacralization expressed an intense concern for, and management of, audience behavior.

The *Saint Matthew Passion* in the Netherlands

In 1870, the *Saint Matthew Passion* was performed for the first time in the Netherlands. Organized by the Maatschappij tot Bevordering van de Toonkunst (Society for the Promotion of the Performing Arts) in a concert hall in Rotterdam and directed by Woldemar Bargiel, a German director with close ties to Mendelssohn, the performance was heavily influenced by the way in which Bach was rediscovered in Germany. This was, for instance, also a truncated version, adapted both in length and in setting to the audience of its time. The discourse surrounding the performance was equally influenced by Romantic notions of art, national culture, and the importance of its past. The booklet described the performance as follows: "May now the doors of the heavenly kingdom built by Bach in music be opened for our fellow inhabitants of this city, may many enter there and enjoy its splendor" (Dinglinger 1999: 23).

The quote is an example of how religious terminology is used, but there is an ambiguity whether this language concerns the heavenly kingdom built by Bach or by God, whether the enjoyment of it benefits the community ("the inhabitants of this city") or the eternal salvation of the individual. We see here how religious and secular notions of sacrality mutually reinforce each other. Bach built a heavenly kingdom in music, the booklet states, and whether that is primarily Bach's or God's accomplishment is not (yet) a divisive issue. Bach's *Saint Matthew Passion* is, so states the booklet, a sacred affair that should be venerated and cherished by all.

The number of performances of the *Saint Matthew Passion* increased in the decades that followed. In Rotterdam, performances were staged in 1871 and 1872. In 1874, the first performance was organized in Amsterdam, followed by performances in 1878, 1881, and 1883. Raving reviews in newspapers followed. Take for instance the following review that appeared in *Algemeen Handelsblad* about the 1874 performance:

> We have witnessed Bach in all his greatness. All of us in our nation's capital, this evening in March, admired his genius and experienced his powerful influence and holy solemnity came over us when the eternal beauties of the colossal work [*reuzenwerk*] appeared to our inner mind. (Dinglinger 1999: 25)

All of these performances took place in concert halls. The newly built concert hall of Amsterdam (Het Concertgebouw), opened in 1888, became a stage for *Saint Matthew Passion* performances. In 1899 conductor Willem Mengelberg (1871–1951) started the tradition of annually performing Bach's *Saint Matthew Passion* in the Concertgebouw. Steeped in the vision of Mendelssohn, Mengelberg also presented his Passion in truncated form (Giskes 1999: 31). According to the conductor himself, the *Saint Matthew Passion* should only be performed "in the spirit and technique of the times in which it is performed" (Mengelberg, quoted in Giskes 1999: 37). With regard to Mendelssohn's choices, he stated approvingly that Mendelssohn liberated the work from its past:

> Mendelssohn has liberated the power of Bach's art from the connection with liturgy and staged it according to completely different technical insights than were dominant at the time when the work originated. . . . This made Bach's creation come to life again, it opened the eyes of contemporaries for the universal beauty of the work. (Mengelberg, quoted in Giskes 1999: 37–38)

This was also the period in which audiences were disciplined into behaving according to the new status of high art in the concert halls.[5] Concerts in the early nineteenth century were noisy events during which people openly socialized, were called away publicly by carriage drivers, and or were making a late and dramatically enacted entrance or early exit. As outlined by Cas Smithuijsen in his history on the emergence of an expectation of silence in concert culture, the second half of the nineteenth century saw the rise of a new protocol for audiences of "classical music":

> The plea [for a change in attitude of the audience] was addressed to listeners who let their emotions dominate their reactions to the music. Audiences have to listen with the ears of an erudite, critically informed lover of music, not with the ears of a pious church-goer. (Smithuijsen 2001: 112)

Smithuijsen highlights how silence became a dominant symbol for this new attitude: "Characteristic for this cerebral reception of music is that the audience display a silence that can be characterized as goal-oriented: more silence means one can better scrutinize the music" (113).

In the Concertgebouw, this had the following practical consequences. In 1890, the director of the orchestra ordered the doors to be closed during performances. Not long after, in 1893, the chairs were bolted to the floor to prevent unwanted noisy mingling, and the serving of food and drink during performances was banned (Smithuijsen 2001: 114). Applause was allowed, but not until after the end of the entire performance. Applause served as a means for the cultured audience to express its appreciation in a controlled manner (94). Helped by the furious glances of conductors toward transgressive audience members, audiences were, slowly but surely, silenced.

The way in which Bach's *Saint Matthew Passion* was taken up in this process soon gave rise to criticism. Critics objected to the way in which Mengelberg's style, criticized for being extravagant and bombastic, detached the *Passion* from piety and introspection. Take for instance the following scathing article printed in the newspaper *De Telegraaf* on 30 March 1920:

> This is why the *Saint Matthew Passion* belongs in a church. It pains the heart to see a mystery performed without anyone seemingly thinking about the consequences, it pains the heart to see sincerity feigned in matters of faith, hope, and love, to see them pass as vain sounds of which one expects nothing more than aesthetic appreciation. I know of no dilettantism more horrific.[6]

According to critics like these, the popularity of the *Saint Matthew Passion* in concert halls was nothing more than "aesthetic appreciation." The fact that the *Saint Matthew Passion* was performed in concert halls where also mundane music was performed was seen as victory of entertainment over religion. According to the reviewer, Bach's *Passion* should be performed with fidelity to the religious framework in which it was composed, including pious reflection on the mystery of salvation and faith.

In the 1920s, a movement emerged that stressed the importance of a more modest, more authentic, and pious performance of the *Saint Matthew Passion*. Proponents of this view stated that Bach's *Saint Matthew Passion* should be performed in a manner reminiscent of how Bach had intended it. Such performances should be held in a church, not a concert hall; it was to be unabridged, performed with the instruments used in Bach's time; and, naturally, there was to be no applause (Wennekes 1999: 103). These were at least the principles of the Netherlands Bach Society (Nederlandse Bachvereniging), which was established in 1921. Where the Concertgebouw version followed the style of Mengelberg, the Bach Society pleaded for a performance that resembles elements seen as characteristic of Bach's time. Take, for instance, these words of the first president of the society, J. H. Gunning (1859–1951), professor of pedagogy, in 1925:

> A falsification [*vervalsching*], it is not an exaggeration to state that that is what is presented to the audiences of our concert halls, and regretfully, the most accomplished conductors often give the worst example! (Gunning, cited in Wennekes 1999: 100)

The Bach Society did not advocate for a return to the liturgical function of the *Saint Matthew Passion*. Instead, what we see is a quarrel not about *whether* Bach's *Saint Matthew Passion* is heritage or liturgy, but about *what to prioritize* in the performance of heritage. This meant that performances should approximate and commemorate a vision of a Lutheran church service as sober, modest, and characterized by pious silence.

This, however, is a biased vision of what a church service and piety may sound like. Not only can church services be noisy, participatory affairs, the historical record of church services in Bach's time show that Mass was firmly planted in everyday life. Innovations in secular music spilled over into religious services and vice versa (Schoenbohm 1943). What is more, Lutheranism (and Protestantism in general) prided itself in the participation of the congregation in the singing of hymns, which was seen as a return to the pure Christianity of the early church (Blume 1975). In Bach's time, though people did not sing along with Passions, collective singing of hymns was common. In short, far from being an accurate record, the Bach Society's vision of what a religious service sounded like in the past should be seen as a projection onto the past of an idealized notion of Protestantism that arose in the nineteenth century.

The Bach Society held its first *Saint Matthew Passion* church performance in 1922, in the Grote Kerk in the town of Naarden. This return of the *Saint*

Matthew Passion to the church can be seen as an early version of what has been called the "authentic method" (*authentieke uitvoeringspraktijk*), which would lead to increasingly detailed re-creations of what the *Saint Matthew Passion* sounded like (Grijp and Bossuyt 2001). This is also an early version of the emphasis on authenticity in the maintenance and performance of heritage (Labadi 2010). The original drive of the society, a strong moral emphasis on how the *Saint Matthew Passion* should be performed, continues to this day. The society continues to stage the most well-known performance of the *Saint Matthew Passion* and has developed into an institution that emphasizes the importance of promoting Bach scholarship and "preserving and disseminating Bach's heritage . . . as well as investing in a future filled with inspiration and emotion."[7] A small anecdote serves to illustrate how this mission continues to translate into policing practices of the audience. In 2020, on an internet forum devoted to Bach, a member of the Netherlands Bach Society relates how the society enforces its anti-applause stance:

> As a long-standing member of the Bach Society, I went to Naarden each year. After every performance we immediately reserved our tickets for the next year. Every year your seat changes and normally your seats improve each year. Until a friend . . . joined our small group one year. After the performance, he stood up and started to applaud loudly. The next year, our seats were all the way in the back, behind these enormous pillars. Life is fickle, even with the Bach Society![8]

The transgression committed by the friend was swiftly and ruthlessly penalized by the Bach Society. The Bach Society regulates the correct behavior of its audience both in its outreach activities as well as in its allocation of less desirable seats to unruly applauders.

Secular Sacralization of the *Saint Matthew Passion*

Though there was disagreement about location and behavior of the audience, the conviction that the *Saint Matthew Passion* is something to be treated with care by the Dutch audience became widely accepted and cited in the second half of the twentieth century. This is indicated by how explicitly secular atheist public figures speak of the *Saint Matthew Passion* as sacred. An exemplary illustration of this is the booklet *Zijn bliksem, zijn donder: Over de Mattheus-Passie van Johann Sebastian Bach* (His lightning, his thunder: about Johann Sebastian Bach's *Saint Matthew Passion*) by Martin van Amerongen (1997). Martin van Amerongen (1941–2002) was an influential Dutch journalist and public intellectual in the second half of the twentieth century. As he outlined in interviews before his death in 2002, he had always been a self-professed atheist: "I don't feel any need for God because I have accepted art as a replacement of religion. For me religion is Mozart, Nabokov, Shakespeare. I can draw comfort from art like a believer does from religion."⁹ He describes the *Saint Matthew Passion* as "an undeserved gift [given by Bach] to humanity" to which the most suitable response is "respectful silence" (van Amerongen 1997: 63). Throughout the book, he aims to set Bach's *Passion* apart from "profane" popular culture. Against this backdrop, applause remains the symbol of blasphemous transgression:

> Of course, people didn't applaud. To applaud when seated at the foot of the cross would be highly inappropriate. This point of view is slowly disappearing in our secularized society. The Dutch audience has become increasingly eager to applaud. Everyone, moved to tears, loves to sound his approval from Protestant Dokkum to Catholic Monnickendam. Recently the first person who shouted "bis" [Latin for "twice," used to request an encore] has been heard in Arnemuiden [a village known for the orthodoxy of its inhabitants]. (66)

To van Amerongen, applauding the *Saint Matthew Passion* is a sign of barbarous secularization. Yet in contrast with confessional critics of secularity who lament the decline of belief in God, he laments the decline of belief in Bach.

Works like these are part of the construction and maintenance of a community of care. Through the idealization of Bach's *Saint Matthew Passion* as a miracle and through the shaming of transgressions, performances of the *Saint Matthew Passion* became more than a concert among others; it became a tradition to be safeguarded—it became cultural heritage. Here is how the *Saint Matthew Passion* is described in the national register for Dutch Intangible Heritage:

> The Dutch *Saint Matthew* tradition [*de Matthäustraditie*] is unique in the world. Nowhere is it entrenched so deeply [*diep verankerd*] in society as in the Netherlands.... De *Matthäus* in Naarden became an annually recurring ritual of reflection [*bezinning*] and, for many, a family tradition.¹⁰

Two things stand out here. The Dutch word *bezinning* (which I, imperfectly, translated as "reflection") contains spiritual connotations, indicating that the *Saint Matthew Passion* is connected to reflection on existential questions. Secondly, the tradition of performing the *Saint Matthew Passion* in Naarden, including its emphasis on silence and sacrality, is presented as a national ritual, deeply rooted in Dutch society. It shows how the Romantic discourses I outlined above, in which sacred art is connected to the cultural past and present of national societies, have resulted in and are perpetuated in the heritagization of the *Saint Matthew Passion* in the Netherlands.

The Rise of New Forms: The Sing-Along *Saint Matthew Passion*

The history of sacralization and heritagization I outlined above is present in the hand placed on the arm of the young boy with which I began this chapter. But what of the applause that sounded after the sing-along performance? In order to understand this, we need to sketch how new forms of performing the *Saint Matthew Passion* arose. The Sing-Along *Saint Matthew Passion* has its roots in a series of performances that challenge traditional views of how the *Saint Matthew Passion* is supposed to be performed. Starting in the 1990s, new forms of performing the *Saint Matthew Passion* began to appear. In 2003, a "DJ-*Matthäus*" was performed; in 2006, a popularized Dutch translation premiered; in 2011, a television program with the title *Matthäus Masterclass* was aired in which celebrities tried to sing arias from Bach's *Passion*; in 2012, a children's version of the *Saint Matthew Passion* was performed. Perhaps the first and most successful of these new forms of staging the *Saint Matthew Passion* was the sing-along version.

A sing-along event enables an untrained audience to participate in singing a piece of music. This differentiates a sing-along event from, for instance, a recital by an amateur choir. It is also what differentiates a sing-along event from a concert in which participating in singing might be a by-effect of its popularity. A sing-along event is also differentiated from karaoke, which generally does not involve communal singing but rather offers a stage for individuals (or duos) to perform in front of smaller audiences as a technologically informed mode of escapism (Zhou and Tarocco 2007). Yet, under different monikers, participation by untrained singers in the performance of pieces of music are as old as amateur choirs, folk music performances, religious revivals, or even church services of the early Christian church in the first centuries CE (Alikin 2010). Though sing-along events can be seen as continuations of such practices, it is nonetheless productive to highlight the effect of this new name. By calling something a "sing-along" event, a semblance of newness is evoked, allowing people to appropriate musical objects in new ways, often in provocative contrast with more established traditions.

This rebellious mode of audience participation under the name "sing-along" events arose in the 1990s. The Sing-Along *Sound of Music* (1998) is credited to be the first sing-along event, although screenings of musicals like *The Rocky Horror Picture Show* or *Jesus Christ Superstar* are also mentioned as early examples of the phenomenon.[11] During the performances, audiences, often dressed up in drag as characters of the movie, sang along with screenings of the musicals. This was a stark contrast with the mainstream reception of the musical, which tended to see (and still sees) *The Sound of Music* (1965) as a mainstream family-friendly box-office hit. David Johnson, organizer of the Sing-Along *Sound of Music*, stated in an interview with the *New York Times*:

> It was sacrilegious, but great fun.... Within a few weeks, the largely gay audience was balanced out by Julie [Julie Andrews, lead in *the Sound of the Music*] worshipers of all ages, genders and sexual orientations. It was clear we had a hit.¹²

The genre of sing-along events developed from subcultural playful subversion into a popular (and lucrative) phenomenon. It has since 1998 developed into large-scale sing-along festivals, cinema festivals, and official sing-along editions released by movie studios and Broadway production companies. Sing-along events of more high-brow objects have appeared. Today it is not uncommon to see sing-along performances of Mozart, Händel, or Beethoven.

In the Netherlands, the first sing-along concert of classical music, a performance of Bach's *Saint Matthew Passion*, took place in 1998. Composer and conductor Huub Kerstens and journalist Huib Schreurs in collaboration with *De Groene Amsterdammer* opened a call for a "Sing-Along *Saint Matthew Passion*: no experience needed." Kerstens is a composer who has predominantly worked on contemporary classical music. Huib Schreurs is a pop musician and journalist. The organizers were not interested in debates about concert halls or churches at all. As they stated in an interview in 1998:

> "We wanted to see what we could do with a big group of people, and we wanted to see what was left of religion," says Schreurs after the final choir ended in blistering silence followed by applause and cheers, which would normally be seen as desecration of the *Matthäus*. "And that seems to be more than we thought!"¹³

In 1999, one year after the first Sing-Along *Matthäus*, the phenomenon was further developed by Passieprojecten (Passion projects), the foundation introduced in the opening of this chapter, which has organized Sing-Along *Matthäus* performances since then. The slogan used by this foundation is "Everybody can sing." The slogan reflects the motivations of director Madeleine Ingen Housz. Ingen Housz has a history herself as singer in the professional official Bach choir of the Netherlands Bach Society. According to her, dominant forms of staging the *Saint Matthew Passion*, including both those by the Bach Foundation and those organized in the main concert halls, prevent people from experiencing "fun and freedom."¹⁴ Ingen Housz aims at lowering the threshold for the audience to maximize the emotional connection with the piece through participation. The Sing-Along *Matthäus* is, in Ingen Housz's words, aimed at freeing Bach's *Saint Matthew Passion* from "the straitjacket" it was placed in. She experienced considerable pushback from both sides in the debate between church and concert hall. As she indicates, "I was criticized by everybody in the classical music world because it was supposed to be impossible to have untrained singers perform the *Saint Matthew Passion*. Now, you see sing-along concerts all over the place."[15]

Ingen Housz attributes the success of sing-along events to "freedom and fun." But this does not yet fully answer the questions we have asked above. How does the sing-along performance relate to the registers that have influenced how the sacrality of the *Saint Matthew Passion* is managed or regulated? The answer to this question can be found in the motivation of the participants of the Sing-Along *Saint Matthew Passion*.

In the words of Tine, a 72-year-old retired doctor and experienced amateur choir singer, "Pfah. These people, the Bach Society or the church, they want to tell us how to enjoy the *Passion* narrative. I have had enough of that." Tine made it clear that after a religious upbringing, she left religion behind and that her participation in the *Matthäus* has little to do with the religion of her childhood: "Look, I was born a Catholic. But the Catholic Church is an empty shell and no one goes there anymore. But people like me still want to experience spirituality in a community, and that is what they, or I should say I, find in the *Matthäus*." This communal experience, according to Tine, is "so much more important than theological bickering [*theologische scherpslijperij*]." She finds it refreshing to sing with people with little or no experience: "We help each other, you see people grow into their role in the choir. When you see someone become one [*samensmelten*] with the piece, that's really something special."

Tine's reflections on religion were similar to the reflections of other participants I spoke with, like John, fifty-eight years old. John is a trained musician, who has participated in a variety of orchestras, usually supporting amateur choirs in the performance of classical music. The religious dimension of the *Passion* is of no interest to him: "The text is highly outdated. I mean come on, Lutheran theology dating back three centuries? Hardly a source of wisdom for today's world." John was raised in a religious household; his father was a Protestant preacher. John left the church when becoming an adult. He described his own interest in the Sing-Along *Saint Matthew Passion* as more "horizontally oriented than vertically." When I asked him to explain this, he stated that he values his participation more because of the shared experience with other people rather than because of any higher spiritual reflection. His participation reminded him of what "is good about church, a sense of community and connection with your fellow human beings [*medemensen*] but without the brainwashing and mumbo jumbo [*poespas*]." When I asked him whether he had a preference for concert halls or churches, he scoffed, "No, it works everywhere."

Whereas John and Tine referenced their religious upbringing, Frederique, forty-two, was raised "without religion" and has never really "felt the urge" to believe. She has had some prior experience with singing in choirs; she joined a choir two years ago but did not always like the repertoire: "I like a challenge, and singing the Andrews Sisters with a bunch of old ladies doesn't really do it for me." But she considers herself nonetheless a novice (*nieuweling*). The status of the *Saint Matthew Passion* was attractive to her: "I thought to myself, could I do this? Should I do this? I thought it was terribly scary [*doodeng*], but exciting." She admitted she did not sing all parts but enjoyed participating in the overwhelming sound: "When we sang the part *Sind Blitze, sind Donner*, you know, we were really hitting it off [*we gingen echt los*], it gave me chills." Asked about whether the ideal location is a church or concert hall, Frederique answered carelessly, "Oh, I don't really care. As long as the acoustics are good." When we talked about the religious dimension of the piece, she indicated that for her the *Matthäus* is about "what religion is meant to be about." She specified that religion should be about "sharing emotions with each other; that is why music was such a big part of church services, I guess."

These three sing-along *Matthäus* participants spoke about the capacity of *Saint Matthew Passion* to recover something that, in their experience, used to be or should be part of religion. This also implies that to them religion has become something less geared toward emotional participation. It is worth mentioning here that the negative image of religion that is projected by Tine, John, and Frederique arises out of reflections on mainstream Christianity in the Netherlands. As I concluded above, the idea that applause seems to be anathema to religious piety hails from mainstream reformed Christianity in the Netherlands. However, within Pentecostal or Charismatic forms of Christianity, emotional participation including the clapping of hands is quite common. Though it would be imaginable that a sing-along performance would be associated with forms of religion in which emotional participation is allowed or stimulated, all three of them see the *Saint Matthew Passion* as a sort of substitute for religion.

The participants are also critical of the way in which the heritagized sacrality is managed by the Bach Society. Participants even lumped "the church" together with the Bach Society. As Tine said, "Pfah. These people, the Bach Society or the church, they want to tell us how to enjoy the *Passion* narrative. I have had enough of that." The moniker "sing-along" enables a mode of participation that appropriates the sacrality of the *Matthäus* in new ways. It rebels against the nonparticipation enforced in the heritagized performances in church and concert hall. It also rebels against the code of conduct that connects the sacrality of the *Saint Matthew Passion* to pious silence and abstaining from applause. As a result, the applause at the end of the performance in the Geertekerk is to be understood not as anathema to the sacrality of the *Saint Matthew Passion*, but as a new incarnation of it.

Conclusion

Since Mendelssohn's rediscovery of Bach's *Saint Matthew Passion*, its value has been described in terms of heritage and sacrality. This chapter illustrates the idea, formulated by Birgit Meyer and Marleen de Witte, that heritagization involves secularization as well as sacralization. As the *Saint Matthew Passion* moved from church to concert hall, it was secularized in that it was taken out of the liturgical context, but it was simultaneously re-sacralized as a monument that commemorates the cultural roots of the national community and as a communal experience of cultural identity in the present. This chapter further builds on Meyer and de Witte's work in that it zooms in on the contestations that arise out of such processes of sacralization.

This chapter shows a perpetual process of contestation: Bach's *Saint Matthew Passion*, originally a part of liturgy, was performed in concert halls as a sacred work of genius, expressive of the cultural roots or accomplishments of a nation. This led to a backlash from people who disagreed with the role of religion in such processes of heritagization. The resulting tradition, characterized by secular performances in churches, where silence and sober style are dominant, in turn encountered criticism from those like Madeleine Ingen Housz who feel that the *Saint Matthew Passion* was placed in a straitjacket. The sing-along performance is, in that sense, the latest installment in a process in which heritagization and sacralization give rise to new contestations and new forms.

Applause has functioned in this history as an example of how audience behavior is managed, disciplined, and self-imposed. Whether it was seen as indicator of vulgar emotional enthusiasm or as cultured appreciation of the concert hall audience, applause was and remains part of how the emotional participation of the audience is managed. For the participants of the Sing-Along *Saint Matthew Passion*, however, applause took on new meaning. The sing-along format and the applause that sounded at the end can productively be read as a reappropriation of sacrality. Participants affirm the status of the *Saint Matthew Passion* as sacred and inscribe themselves in the tradition that sees emotional participation in Bach's *Passion* as an important source of spiritual inspiration and communal identity. But for them, this sacrality of the *Saint Matthew Passion* entails a justification to perform and participate in new ways.

As outlined in the introduction to this volume, heritagization can be (and has been) seen as a top-down process, involving the official recognition of and management by (inter)national organizations. This chapter shows how top-down processes can lead to bottom-up reappropriations. As illustrated by this chapter (and others in this volume), a focus on how heritagization takes shape and is managed "on the ground" can productively add to our understanding of how heritagization sets up communities of care for whom the experience of sacralized heritage is the impetus for reappropriation and creative innovation.

Ernst van den Hemel is a researcher at the Meertens Institute. He defended his dissertation about Calvinism and political emotions at the University of Amsterdam in 2011. He was postdoctoral researcher in the HERA-funded HERILIGION: The Heritagization of Religion and the Sacralization of Heritage in Contemporary Europe project. In 2019 he joined the interdisciplinary research group NL-Lab, at the Humanities Cluster of the Royal Netherlands Academy of Arts and Sciences. In his research, he combines ethnographic fieldwork, social media analysis, and historiography and focuses on religion, heritage, and national identity. His publications include *The Secular Sacred: Emotions of Belonging and the Perils of Nation and Religion* (Palgrave, 2020; coeditors Markus Balkenhol and Irene Stengs).

NOTES

1. This chapter is based on ethnographic fieldwork, conducted in the Easter periods of 2017–20. I attended eleven performances of Bach's *Saint Matthew Passion* and held seven interviews with participants of the Sing-Along *Saint Matthew Passion* and two interviews with its organizer. Besides ethnographic fieldwork, I conducted archival research and social media analysis. This research was conducted in the context of the HERILIGION: *The Heritagization of Religion and Sacralization of Heritage in Contemporary Europe* project, funded by Humanities in the European Research Area (HERA) grant # 5087-00505A. See www.heriligion.eu.
2. "Matthäus Passion op 1 in Hart & Ziel Lijst NPO," *Reformatorisch Dagblad*, 10 November 2019.
3. https://www.muziekweb.nl/Muziekweb/Kledinglijn_(accessed 8 October 2020).
4. VPRO, *Zomergasten*, 4 September 2016, https://www.vpro.nl/programmas/zomergasten/kijk/afleveringen/2016/Mark-Rutte.html. Min. 04:30–04:45 (accessed 30 November 2020). All translations by Ernst van den Hemel.
5. This development mirrors the work done, for instance, by Tony Bennett on the role of the museum as a disciplinary institution (Bennett 2013).
6. Mattijs Vermeulen, "Die Matthäus-Passion," *De Telegraaf*, 30 March 1920.
7. See https://www.bachvereniging.nl/en/support (accessed 7 October 2020).
8. https://www.nederlanders.fr/profiles/blog/show?id=3295325%3ABlogPost%3A991738&commentId=3295325%3AComment%3A991927 (accessed 7 October 2020).
9. Arjan Visser, "Martin van Amerongen," *Trouw*, 15 August 2005.
10. See the entry "*Matthäus Passion* Door de Nederlandse Bachvereniging in de Grote Kerk Naarden" on the website of the Dutch Center for Intangible Heritage, https://www.immaterieelerfgoed.nl/en/page/5581/matth percentC3 percentA4us-passion-door-de-nederlandse-bachvereniging-in-grote-kerk (accessed 28 November 2020).

11. The "Sing-A-Long-A-*Sound of Music*" was introduced at London's 1998 Gay and Lesbian Film Festival. It was continued by the London Prince Charles Cinema, which had been showing participatory screenings of *The Rocky Horror Picture Show* since 1991. See Kristin Hohenadel, "The Hall Is Alive with the Sound of Music," *Los Angeles Times*, 14 May 2000, https://www.latimes.com/archives/la-xpm-2000-may-14-ca-29768-story.htm (accessed 7 October 2020).
12. Thomas Vinciguerra, "Do You Really Call That Sound Music?," Week in Review, *New York Times*, 20 August 2000, https://www.nytimes.com/2000/08/20/weekinreview/do-you-really-call-that-sound-music.html (accessed 7 October 2020).
13. See Cultuur & Media, *De Volkskrant*, 23 March 1998.
14. Marieke Van Willigen, "Madeleine Ingen Housz: Ik had heel lang geen houvast," Voorpagina, *Trouw*, 31 December 2017, https://www.trouw.nl/gs-b22cd56e (accessed 7 October 2020).
15. Ibid.

REFERENCES

Alikin, Valeriy A. 2010. "Singing and Prayer in the Gathering of the Early Church," in *The Earliest History of the Christian Gathering, Origin, Development and Content of the Christian Gathering in the First to Third Centuries*. Leiden: Brill, pp. 211–54.

Applegate, Celia. 2005. *Bach in Berlin: Nation and Culture in Mendelssohn's Revival of the "St. Matthew Passion."* Ithaca, NY: Cornell University Press.

Bennett, Tony. 2013 [or. 1995]. *The Birth of the Museum: History, Theory, Politics*. New York and London: Routledge.

Berlin, Isaiah, and John Gray. 2013. *The Roots of Romanticism*, 2nd edn., ed. Henry Hardy. Princeton, NJ: Princeton University Press.

Blume, Friedrich. 1975. *Protestant Church Music: A History*. London: Gollancz.

Dinglinger, Wolfgang. 1999. *De "Matthäus-Passion": 100 jaar passietraditie van het Koninklijk Concertgebouworkest*. Bussum, Amsterdam: Thoth.

Forkel, Johann Nikolaus. 2020. *Johann Sebastian Bach: His Life, Art, and Work*. New York: Harcourt, Brace and Howe.

Geck, Martin. 1999. *"Denn alles findet bei Bach statt": Erforschtes und Erfahrenes*. 60 Notenbeispieleth Edition. Stuttgart: J. B. Metzler.

Geismar, Haidy. 2015. "Anthropology and Heritage Regimes," *Annual Review of Anthropology* 44: 71–85.

Giskes, Johan. 1999. "De weg naar Mengelbergs monumentale creatie van de Matthaus-Passion," in Wolfgang Dinglinger (ed.), *De "Matthäus-Passion": 100 Jaar passietraditie van het Koninklijk Concertgebouworkest*. Bussum, Amsterdam: Thoth, pp. 22–40.

Grijp, Louis Peter, and Ignace Bossuyt. 2001. "De Opkomst van de Historische Uitvoeringspraktijk in Nederland en Vlaanderen," in Louis Peter Grijp and Ignace Bossuyt (eds.), *Een muziekgeschiedenis der Nederlanden*. Amsterdam: Amsterdam University Press, pp. 765–22.

Grijzenhout, Frans. 2007. *Erfgoed: de geschiedenis van een begrip*. Amsterdam: Amsterdam University Press.

Jensen, Lotte Eilskov, et. al. 2010. *Free Access to the Past: Romanticism, Cultural Heritage and the Nation*. Leiden: Brill.

Labadi, Sophia. 2010. "World Heritage, Authenticity and Post-Authenticity: International and National Perspectives," in Sophia Labadi and Colin Long (eds.), *Heritage and Globalisation: Key Issues in Cultural Heritage*. London and New York: Routledge, pp. 66–84.
Leerssen, Joep. 2013. "Notes towards a Definition of Romantic Nationalism," *Romantik: Journal for the Study of Romanticism* 2(1): 9–25.
Little, William, A. 1991. "Mendelssohn and the Berlin Singakademie: The Composer at the Crossroads," in R. Larry Todd (ed.), *Mendelssohn and His World*. Princeton, NJ: Princeton University Press, pp. 65–86.
Marissen, Michael. 1993. "Religious aims in Mendelssohn's 1829 Berlin-Singakademie Performances of Bach's *Saint Matthew Passion*," *Musical Quarterly* 77(4): 718–26.
Meyer, Birgit, and Marleen de Witte. 2013. "Heritage and the Sacred: Introduction," *Material Religion* 9(3): 275–80.
Paine, Crispin. 2013. *Religious Objects in Museums: Private Lives and Public Duties*. London and New York: Routledge.
Salemink, Oscar. 2016. "Described, Inscribed, Written Off: Heritagisation as (Dis)connection," in Philip Taylor (ed.), *Connected and Disconnected in Vietnam: Remaking Social Relations in a Post-Socialist Nation*. Canberra: Australian National University Press, pp. 311–345.
Schoenbohm, Richard. 1943. "Music in the Lutheran Church before and at the Time of J. S. Bach," *Church History* 12(3): 195–209.
Scott, Jonathan. 2019. *The Vinyl Frontier: The Story of NASA's Interstellar Mixtape*. London: Bloomsbury.
Smithuijsen, C. 2001. *Een verbazende stilte: Klassieke muziek, gedragsregels en sociale controle in de Concertzaal*. Amsterdam: Boekmanstudies.
Timothy, Dallen, and Daniel Olsen. 2006. *Tourism, Religion and Spiritual Journeys*. London and New York: Routledge.
van Amerongen, Martin. 1997. *Zijn bliksem, zijn donder: Over de "Mattheus-Passie" van Johann Sebastian Bach*. Baarn: Ambo.
Wennekes, Emile. 1999. "Over traditie en vernieuwing, romantische vervalsing en liturgische soberheid," in Wolfgang Dinglinger (ed.), *De "Matthäus-Passion": 100 Jaar passietraditie van het Koninklijk Concertgebouworkest*. Bussum, Amsterdam: Thoth, pp. 100–110.
Zhou, Xun, and Francesca Tarocco. 2007. *Karaoke: The Global Phenomenon*. London: Reaktion Books.

CHAPTER 10

Moral Management and Secularized Religious Heritage in the Netherlands
The Case of the Utrecht Saint Martin Celebrations
Welmoed Fenna Wagenaar

Introduction

Every year, on the Saturday evening before 11 November, the center of the Dutch city of Utrecht provides the stage for a spectacle of moving light sculptures, music, and performance art. Over the course of two hours, thousands of people watch or walk along in the participatory Saint Martin Parade, bringing paper lanterns or other light sources with them. Little children look around in wonder as local communities carry light sculptures or wear costumes made from white rice paper and willow branches, forming abstract representations of animals, human-shaped figures, and a wide range of objects, all illuminating the medieval city streets. Along the route, the sounds of brass bands, choirs, and church bells ring. So-called beggar clowns play their part being "alone," "sick," or "homeless," made explicit via signs carried around their necks. There is a lot to see, but the true eye-catcher is the light sculpture of a figure on horseback, about four meters tall, raised high above the public (see figure 10.1). Used since the parade's first edition in 2011, the sculpture depicts a young Martin during his time in the Roman army. Although abstract like the other sculptures, he visibly wears a plain helmet and the cloak he famously gave away to a beggar at the city gates of the French town of Amiens.

The Saint Martin Parade is the ritual highlight of the Utrecht Saint Martin celebrations, an annual event dedicated to the city's patron saint, Saint Martin of Tours. Over the past twenty years, Utrecht's celebration of Saint

Figure 10.1. The light sculpture of Saint Martin, just before passing the cathedral Dom Tower in Utrecht, 2018. © Welmoed Fenna Wagenaar.

Martin's Day has changed significantly. As in other places in the Netherlands where Saint Martin is celebrated,[1] Utrecht's Saint Martin feast had been primarily an evening of excitement for young children; comparable to Halloween, the Dutch Saint Martin tradition consists of kids going door-to-door on the evening of Saint Martin's Day, carrying paper lanterns and singing Saint Martin songs in exchange for candy or fruit. In Utrecht, however, this generally localized ritual practice transformed and expanded into a weeklong, citywide event called the Feast of Sharing. Taking place in the days leading up to 11 November, the Feast of Sharing is composed of a variety of rituals and practices that exhibit a local identity of inclusiveness and charitability. In addition to the still-existing lantern walking of children, festivities include guided Saint Martin tours, lantern and musical workshops, theatrical performances and storytelling events, concerts, dialogue sessions, lectures, solidarity awards, a debate competition for schoolchildren, a meal for the homeless, a collection campaign for local food banks, the ringing of the Martin bell in the famous Dom Tower, and the Saint Martin Parade with its spectacular, festival-like opening, the Fire of Saint Martin.

In 2012, the Utrecht Saint Martin celebrations became inscribed on the UNESCO-associated Inventory Intangible Cultural Heritage in the Netherlands, thus being officially recognized as cultural heritage. The appreciation of the Saint Martin feast as cultural heritage fits a broader trend in Europe in which religious objects, practices, and places are attributed specific historical, cultural, and identity value as heritage. With regard to Saint Martin for example, there have been parallel instances of renewed interest in the feast both in the Netherlands and in Europe at large, resulting among other things in a Dutch Saint Martin Network (since 2018) and the European Reseau Européen des Centres Culturels Saint Martin, formed in 2012 to bring European Saint Martin cities together to exchange ideas on how to safeguard the heritage of Saint Martin. An ethnographic analysis of the Utrecht Saint Martin celebrations provides insight into what these processes of heritagization entail locally and how religious components and histories may play a role in it.[2]

In this chapter, I demonstrate the significance of the management involved in making a celebration like Saint Martin be recognized and appreciated as heritage. The case of the Utrecht Saint Martin celebrations presents remarkable developments with regard to religious heritage management. Although the Saint Martin feast originated as a Catholic name day celebration, it has long since lost its religious character in the Netherlands; religious elements are (and have been for a long time) absent from the secularized Dutch Saint Martin tradition. It is striking, therefore, that religion turned out to be an important issue in the management of the Utrecht Saint Martin celebrations, its position being a topic of ongoing concern to the feast's key stakeholders. How is it that religious connotations surrounding Saint Martin—connotations long gone in the Netherlands—have re-emerged as relevant factors in the management of the feast as heritage? How can we understand religion's surprising reappearance on the (back)stage? Who are the key players and what are the contexts that shape the management practices with regard to Saint Martin's, apparently sticky, Christian provenance?

Using the notions of the culturalization of citizenship (Duyvendak et al. 2016) and sacralization of heritage (Meyer and de Witte 2013), I first paint a picture of the current Dutch heritage landscape. I show how, in the Netherlands, religious rituals and celebrations have been lifted up and set apart as symbols of national identity and how because of that they have increasingly become part of public contestations. This contextualizes the specific ways in which stakeholders have revitalized Utrecht's Saint Martin tradition and manage the meanings surrounding Saint Martin. Specifically, I argue that as a result of interactions with broader heritage regimes and politics, religious interpretations and symbols get "veiled" in the Utrecht Saint Martin celebrations. This "veiling" should be understood metaphorically, in that religion is relegated to the background, to establish a secularized frame of inclusive universality that has contributed to and upholds Saint Martin's status as cultural heritage. Before turning to this, however, let us briefly take a look at Saint Martin's historical background.

Saint Martin's Day

Saint Martin of Tours (c. 316–397) is a Christian saint who was widely worshiped in Europe during the early and High Middle Ages. He is likely best known for the legend of him giving away half his cloak to a beggar in front of the city gates of Amiens, when he was stationed there as a young soldier of the Roman army. According to Saint Martin's hagiography *Vita sancti Martini*, written by his contemporary Sulpicius Severus, Jesus revealed himself to Martin in a dream the night after this act of charity, wearing the half-cloak Martin had given away. As a result of this experience, the young Martin had himself baptized and left the army. The story goes that in the years that followed he traveled through Europe to convert people to Christianity and destroy pagan temples and imagery. After a while, he settled as a monk in the area of Poitier, established several monasteries, and became bishop of Tours around 370, which he would remain until his death on 8 November 397. His name day would be celebrated for centuries to come in various European countries on or around the date of his burial, 11 November.

Saint Martin's charitable practices and humble nature made him a symbol of Christian virtue and earned him, among other titles, the title of patron saint of the poor. As a result, Saint Martin celebrations were popular among the people and have always involved (symbolic) elements of generosity. Next to masses and processions, medieval Saint Martin feasts involved the poor going door-to-door to collect alms. There were also rites related to the change of seasons, such as bonfires, market fairs, and the first slaughter. Nowadays, European Saint Martin celebrations may still entail forms of these earlier rituals. Depending on local tradition and interpretation, church services,[3] bonfires, market fairs, processions, and lantern walking (derived from the practice of collecting alms) may be part of Saint Martin's Day (Nissen and Rose 1997: 22–23). In countries such as Denmark and Germany, "Saint Martin's goose" is part of festive Saint Martin menus, based on the legend of Saint Martin hiding among geese to avoid his appointment as bishop (Lauvrijs 2004: 262).

The lantern walking, lantern processions, and bonfires became typical of the Dutch Saint Martin tradition. Moreover, the celebration of Saint Martin as Catholic name day gradually made way for a notion of Saint Martin's Day as an innocent children's feast. In 2007, ethnologist John Helsloot concluded that in the Netherlands, Saint Martin is mostly meant to "give children a couple of exciting hours, with the chance to obtain a lot of candy." The feast "does no longer seem to be ideologically colored," he adds, apart from some "general references to the symbolic of light and darkness" and "a call to forms of charity here and there."[4]

The Culturalization of Religious Feasts in the Netherlands

Almost fifteen years after Helsloot's statements, it seems as if some things are changing. The interest in Saint Martin's Day as an authentic, "truly Dutch" tradition—often contrasted with Halloween, celebrated just short of two weeks earlier but still relatively new in the Netherlands—has increased. The official heritage status of the Utrecht Saint Martin celebrations forms the strongest evidence of this. It indicates that Saint Martin has become more than "just" an innocent children's feast, which is a development that does not stand on its own nor is it ideologically void.

In the Netherlands, similar to the popular Sinterklaas (or Saint Nicholas) feast, the religious character of Saint Martin early on made way for an interpretation of the feast as essentially non-confessional (Balkenhol and van den Hemel 2018: 9–10; Boer 2009). During the Reformation, Protestant ministers sought to bring a halt to all Catholic celebrations but failed miserably in their attempts, as popular feasts continued to be celebrated among the common people. The Saint Martin feast was one of them, its denominational character quickly fading in exchange for a notion of Saint Martin as a feast of the poor. Like Saint Nicholas, Saint Martin came to be understood as a "saint of the people" (*volksheilige*) rather than a Catholic figure (Helsloot 2001: 508). In the first decades of the twentieth century, folklorists used this status to fully redefine Saint Martin as part of Dutch folklore. Saint Martin songs and the lantern walking, preferably with hollowed beets instead of paper lanterns, were viewed as authentic folk practices that had nothing to do with religion, being meaningful and worthy of respect because of their long history (503).

Parallel to the folklorization of feasts like Saint Martin, cultural elements increasingly became symbolic of national identity after World War II. This process has been described by sociologist Jan Willem Duyvendak and associates as the "culturalization of citizenship": citizenship has become less understood in terms of political and social rights and more as being about cultural norms, values, and practices (Duyvendak, Geschiere, and Tonkens 2016: 2). This reinforced the ability of ritual practices and holidays to become powerful tools for establishing group identity and defining the boundaries of said group (Stengs 2012: 11–13). In the Netherlands, for example, culturalization becomes apparent in how religious holidays like Christmas and Easter are lifted up as "(Judeo-)Christian heritage," obtaining special status as foundations of Dutch society. Birgit Meyer and Marleen de Witte refer to such processes as the "sacralization" of heritage (Meyer and de Witte 2013), pointing to the ways in which heritage formations can transform religious sacrality into secular sacrality.[5]

Because of the culturalization of citizenship and religion, the Netherlands sees a broadly shared sense of protectiveness toward Christian holidays as well as a growing anxiety about people no longer knowing their "true meanings" (a development that spurred the Dutch HERILIGION research program). Moreover, religious rituals of any denomination have become central to the debate on social integration (see, e.g., Balkenhol 2015; Stengs 2012; van den Hemel 2017). Due to the increased uncertainty about who or what constitutes a society—due to the arrival of immigrants, for example—cultural practices have become claimed as heritage and are not seldomly mobilized to draw boundaries between cultural selves and others. The case of the heritagization of the Sinterklaas feast, admitted to the Inventory Intangible Cultural Heritage as reaction to the backlash on the feast's controversial Black Pete figure, is an example (Stengs 2018: 8–9).[6]

Thus, the religious character of Saint Martin's Day disappeared early on in exchange for a view of Saint Martin as Dutch folk practice and—as of recently—cultural heritage. Crucially, the management of Saint Martin as heritage should be understood within the context of this folklorization and culturalization in the Netherlands. Saint Martin celebrations belong to and need to position themselves within a society where religious feasts and holidays have become increasingly controversial and where celebrations with a Christian history have become part of exclusionary, nationalist discourses. Inevitably, this has shaped the heritagization of the Utrecht Saint Martin celebrations and the ways its custodians manage its meanings.

The Heritagization of the Utrecht Saint Martin Celebrations

Due to Saint Martin's travels and his role as patron saint of the Franks, many villages, monasteries, and churches in Europe have been named after him or have him as their patron saint. This includes the Dutch city of Utrecht. Utrecht was historically the bishop's town of the Lower Countries, its main church being the thirteenth-century Gothic Saint Martin's Cathedral, also known as the Dom Church. References to Saint Martin can be found throughout the city; there are statues and depictions on buildings, and the colors of the city's flag and football club (red diagonally on white) refer to the saint's tunic and cloak. The city is also home to several Saint Martin relics, currently on display in Museum Catharijneconvent, the national museum for the art, history, and culture of Christianity in the Netherlands. However, despite how much Saint Martin is ingrained in Utrecht, for a long time the city's Saint Martin celebrations were no different from those in other places in the Netherlands familiar with the tradition. In some neighborhoods, children would go door-to-door with paper lanterns or walk in small processions, but these activities remained localized and depended on if something was organized by local churches, schools, or parents.

This started to change in 2001, with the arrival of a working group called the Saint Martin's Assembly.[7] The assembly started organizing special Saint Martin events, such as the raising of a Saint Martin city flag by the city's mayor and schoolchildren on 11 November, and it began promoting Saint Martin activities that still existed in the city. The assembly also approached other organizations to join the celebrations and develop their own activities. Slowly but surely, different parties picked up on the feast, including two music centers that organized a small parade in one of the city's districts in 2007.[8] This event formed the basis of the Saint Martin Parade as the city now knows it. In 2011, a broad range of city institutions—cultural institutions, the municipality of Utrecht, various museums, the Utrecht Archives, and the Saint Martin's Assembly—cooperated in organizing the parade's first official edition. In the years that followed, the Saint Martin Parade grew in prominence and turned the Saint Martin celebrations into a central event on the city's annual festivities calendar,[9] exemplifying ritual's inclination to magnify and multiply and make something the topic of special attention (Stengs 2018: 17).

In light of these developments, the Saint Martin's Assembly managed to successfully admit the Utrecht Saint Martin celebrations to the Inventory Intangible Cultural Heritage in the Netherlands in 2012. The Inventory is a list of cultural practices, rituals, and events, each of which has been applied for admission by its own practitioners together with a safeguarding plan. Whether a practice becomes (and remains) listed is decided by the Dutch Centre for Intangible Cultural Heritage (Kenniscentrum Immaterieel Erfgoed Nederland [KIEN]), the organization that by order of the Dutch Ministry of Education, Culture and Science is responsible for putting into practice the 2012 UNESCO Convention for the Safeguarding of Intangible Cultural Heritage. In other words, the KIEN coordinates on a national level the composition of the Inventory and monitors the safeguarding of the listed heritage, the actual safeguarding being done by the heritage communities themselves. In practice this task is often taken up by specific individuals (Köbben 1983), which in the case of the Utrecht Saint Martin celebrations are the people behind the Saint Martin's Assembly. The assembly is therefore the official custodian of the heritage titled "Utrecht Saint Martin celebrations."

Although the admission of the Utrecht Saint Martin celebrations to the Inventory Intangible Cultural Heritage does not seem to have had a direct effect on people's perception of the feast (i.e., apart from the assembly and its closest partners, no one I spoke to brought up its official status as cultural heritage on their own), the admission does inevitably link the celebrations to existing heritage regimes. That is, its heritagization takes place in interaction with a framework of specific registers, vocabularies, and discursive rules (Bendix 2009; Bendix, Eggert, and Peselmann 2013; Van de Port and Meyer 2018: 12). As the editors point out in the introduction to this volume, this may also result in stakeholders having to translate various aspects of a heritage into terms of their value for broader societal or even global frameworks. As I will show, the Saint Martin's Assembly and its closest partners continually engage with heritage regimes and cultural politics in their management of what the Utrecht Saint Martin celebrations (are supposed to) mean. What is more, in the management of the meanings surrounding Saint Martin, religion makes a comeback.

Saint Martin's Assembly and the "Reinvention" of a Heritage

As the above paragraph has shown, the Saint Martin's Assembly has been crucial to the transformation of Utrecht's Saint Martin feast and is a key stakeholder in its management. The assembly was founded by a Catholic pastoral worker, Chris van Deventer (1938–2016), with the aim to "stimulate, enthuse and coordinate" Saint Martin practices in the city of Utrecht so as to "bring the century-old tradition of Saint Martin back to public life."[10] Despite van Deventer's Catholic background and the personal, religious connection he felt to Saint Martin, his attempt to bring back to life the Saint Martin tradition was focused on what the assembly views as the "cultural side" of the Saint Martin celebrations: those elements that twentieth-century folklorists designated as authentic folk practices. According to van Deventer, Saint Martin had lost its meaning in Utrecht because the majority of inhabitants no longer knew who Saint Martin was. It was his conviction that cultural practices like lantern walking and singing Saint Martin songs would hold the most power to breathe new life into the feast and keep the memory of Saint Martin alive.

In other words, an important reason why the Saint Martin's Assembly was founded was to ensure people would not forget about Saint Martin, making this case an example of the aforementioned anxiety surrounding the lack of knowledge about Christian holidays in the Netherlands.[11] Even so, van Deventer's anxiety did not result in an attempt to claim Saint Martin for a particular kind of people or strictly preserve its current form. As van Deventer passed away in 2016, I spoke to a friend of his about the early motivations and goals of the assembly. This friend, Rien Sprenger, is now one of the key members of the assembly and has been an essential figure in the organization of especially the first editions of the Saint Martin Parade. Sprenger told me that the assembly deliberately set out to "reinvent the tradition" (using this exact English terminology) of Saint Martin, which he explained as the current celebrations "drawing on what was and adjusting it to what has changed and giving new meaning to it again." Take the mission statement of the assembly:

> The goal is to preserve the tradition and philosophy [*gedachtegoed*] of Saint Martin and translate them to contemporary, modern society.... [The Saint Martin's Assembly Utrecht] translates the philosophy of Saint Martin, sharing the cloak, to social and cultural goals: sharing together in solidarity and peace. [The assembly] wants to broaden and renew the tradition and practices surrounding Saint Martin and deploy them as unifying element in modern, pluriform society.[12]

For the Saint Martin's Assembly, preservation of the tradition and ideas of Saint Martin go hand in hand with "translating," "broadening," and "renewing" the practices surrounding Saint Martin to "modern, pluriform" society. Similar sentiments are expressed by one of the assembly's closest partners, the Sharing Arts Society (SAS). Since 2014, this community art center has taken most of the responsibility in organizing the Saint Martin Parade under the artistic leadership of theater-maker Paul Feld. Their website reads:

> The Saint Martin Parade is formed by a multicolored network of participating organizations and initiatives from all districts of the city that grows each edition. ... This deliberately includes locations for refugee reception (asylum centers), homeless people, care homes, and schools for mentally and physically disabled children. Saint Martin is a powerful plea for a society that no one gets excluded from. It is a Feast of Sharing, a feast of the whole city, with all its cultures, generations, and differences.[13]

In reinventing the Saint Martin celebrations, the Saint Martin's Assembly and the SAS have put forward an interpretation of Saint Martin as an inclusive and diverse heritage for all. This move was more than just a "reinvention." It has been part of a careful navigation of existing heritage regimes and politics. Saint Martin is explicitly framed in terms of broad societal value that speaks to a diverse public, making the exact kind of translation referred to in the introduction to this volume. Most notably, the presentation of a fiercely inclusive narrative surrounding the heritage of Saint Martin has become a way for the assembly and the SAS to react to cultural politics surrounding religious feasts and holidays. The Sinterklaas feast in particular, and how particular groups lay claim to it due to the Black Pete controversy, was often brought up in conversations as an example of what Saint Martin should *not* become. In addition, the overall openness toward contemporary renewal, as found in both quotes, is one of the requirements for admission to the Inventory Intangible Cultural Heritage; the KIEN states that heritage should be "dynamic, meaning that it may change with time" and that custodians need to be "open to these dynamics and express this accordingly."[14]

The quotes above also show something else. In presenting Saint Martin as a heritage for all, the notion of "Feast of Sharing" is essential. In their attempt to (in Sprenger's words) "expand" and "broaden" the feast, the Saint Martin's Assembly focuses on what they understand to be the "essence" of Saint Martin and the foundation of his heritage. This essence, which can be considered the sacred core of the celebrations, is the moral value of sharing, as materialized in Saint Martin's act of sharing his cloak. Interestingly, this turns the spotlight on the ideological or moral component of Saint Martin that Helsloot back in 2007 noted was only "here and there" present: the call to charity and solidarity. This provides a stark contrast to previous decades and is, I believe, the reason why religion has reared its head in how the assembly manages the Saint Martin celebrations.

Sacralizing a Moral Framework and Confronting the Burden of Religious Heritage

The focus on Saint Martin's morality has contributed significantly to the appreciation and expansion of the feast. By emphasizing the value of sharing instead of letting the celebration of Saint Martin be "just" about children walking with lanterns for candy, the Saint Martin's Assembly has managed to present the feast as something that is not only meaningful because of its long history, but also because of its relevance to a society having to deal with issues like social isolation, integration, and economic inequality. As historian Willem Frijhoff points out, when heritage comes with a narrative that makes it meaningful for contemporary and future life, then people are able to identify with it and accept it as authentic heritage (Frijhoff 2011: 39). The same goes for the Utrecht Saint Martin celebrations. Many people attending (parts of) the celebrations told me that they appreciate the Saint Martin feast because it "brings the whole city together" and it "is really about something." Emphasizing the value of sharing has also opened the feast up to a wide range of stakeholders; as long as organizations or institutions manage to link their activities to this theme, the activities can become part of the Feast of Sharing and are taken up in its promotion. Whether an activity fits the theme is decided upon by the assembly. This not only makes them the architects of the renewed Saint Martin tradition, but also turns them into the gatekeeper of what the heritage of Saint Martin is supposed to stand for: the moral value of sharing, relatable to anyone from any background.

However, the renewed focus on the person of Saint Martin and the value of sharing has also resulted in something else: it centers a moral framework that increases the possibility of foregrounding the religious components that the Saint Martin tradition lost. Saint Martin's act of sharing his cloak can easily be interpreted as it was originally, namely as an act of Christian virtue. And Saint Martin himself remains a Christian saint who, according to his hagiography, had always been interested in Christianity, who approached others like one would Jesus Christ, who had an encounter with Jesus, and who traveled through Europe to convert pagans and dismantle their places of worship.

It is these Christian interpretations and elements of Saint Martin's heritage that both Sprenger and Feld referred to as an "obstacle" or "restriction" during interviews. This may seem odd in a context where Christian feasts are increasingly *appreciated* as Dutch national heritage, but if we take into consideration the goals of the Saint Martin's Assembly (i.e., to reinvent Saint Martin to be an inclusive heritage for all), the apprehension toward overtly visible religious elements and interpretations makes sense. First, the assembly and the SAS are afraid that Christian elements risk ostracizing nonreligious or non-Christian people. Dutch society is one of the most secularized societies in the world. Since the 1950s, there has been a steady decline of organized religion, with only 49 percent of the Dutch population today saying they belong to a religious group (including religions other than Christianity, like Islam) and just under one in six people attending religious services with regularity.[15] Part of this development has also been that a generation of people—particularly baby boomers, many of whom experienced the obligatory church attendance as a burden—understand "religion" to be institutional, dogmatic, moralistic, and restrictive. It has also led to the viewpoint that religion is, or at the very least has a serious inclination to be, exclusionary. This broadly shared Dutch conception of religion shapes the assembly's and the SAS's view on the matter. Sprenger explained, "If possible, then in this time and age, the patron should not only be there for a minority—namely those who go to church—but if possible, he should still and again be there for and belong to everyone." Religion understood in these ways works against the aim to turn Saint Martin into a heritage for all, which is why religious interpretations and elements become a potential risk.

Second, religious elements may also become a problem when obtaining funding. The Saint Martin's Assembly and its partners, the Sharing Arts Society especially, are dependent on subsidies obtained from institutions such as the municipality of Utrecht, the Dutch Cultural Participation Fund (Fonds voor Cultuurparticipatie), and local funding associations. To receive funding from these parties requires that events be accessible to a broad public or pay attention to cultural diversity. Religious activities, from the viewpoint that religion is exclusive and restrictive, do not match this criterion. Moreover, as religion is often equated with institutional religion, state-related institutions generally do not support religious activities, on the premise that it goes against the Dutch separation of church and state. This shapes what I call a "politics of funding": in order to receive money, stakeholders have to play it smart, in this case when it comes to the topic of religion. In other words, in order to obtain funding, the assembly and the SAS have to manage and contain the danger of being associated with or understood as (Christian) religious practice.

Paradoxically, this means that because of the emphasis on the figure of Saint Martin and his morality, religion—understood in the sense of institutional, non-culturalized Christianity—has returned through the back door, finding its way back into the Saint Martin celebrations *within* the management of stakeholders like the SAS and the assembly. In order to safeguard the broad societal relevance and financial resources of the feast, these stakeholders have to navigate existing viewpoints and criteria surrounding religion and the meanings Saint Martin may have. The last sections of this chapter analyze in detail how the assembly and the SAS do this. To this aim, I will zoom in on the management strategy with regard to Saint Martin's religious provenance and show how in the process of establishing the moral framework of sharing, religion becomes "veiled" in favor of a secularized gaze of universality.

Managing Meaning, Veiling Religion

In 2015, the Saint Martin's Assembly entered into an official partnership with not just the Sharing Arts Society, but also Museum Catharijneconvent, the aforementioned Dutch national museum for Christian heritage. As a national museum, Museum Catharijneconvent is a secular institution that aims to "safeguard, share, and extend the knowledge about Christian heritage."[16] As mentioned previously, the museum has several Saint Martin relics on display: a piece of Saint Martin's skull in a modern relic holder and the Hammer of Saint Martin, a secondary relic said to have been the object used by Saint Martin in his quest to destroy pagan places and objects of worship. According to the museum, the relics belong to the city and its people and form a valuable medium through which people can be taught about the history of Saint Martin. Therefore, they suggested them to be carried around or be otherwise included in the Saint Martin Parade.

Whereas one might expect the assembly and the SAS to be immediately enthusiastic about the museum's proposal, they turned out to be rather apprehensive. Of course, there were practical concerns: Is it worthwhile to incorporate such objects if you have to take extra precautions for them to be safe and visible? What to do with the Hammer of Saint Martin, which is too fragile to be carried around? However, there were also other considerations at play. Sprenger explained to me that the Saint Martin Parade is not meant to be a religious procession and that carrying relics is not the parade's purpose. Furthermore, he expressed concern that an openly Catholic practice within the parade might lead to "controversy"—a reference to the aforementioned worry surrounding the supposed exclusionary dimensions of religion.[17] In other words, the apprehension toward incorporating the relics was at least partly grounded in the explicitly Christian associations these objects might evoke.

During my fieldwork, I saw that a similar apprehensiveness kept emerging throughout the Utrecht Saint Martin celebrations. Take, for example, the description of the Saint Martin Parade on the Sharing Arts Society's website:

> The Saint Martin Parade is an atmospheric, annually recurring event full of light, lanterns, and music that wants to keep the memory alive of the legend of the Roman Martin, who cut his red cloak in half with his sword to help a beggar chilled to the bone.
>
> Martin is a worldwide icon with many faces that is inseparable from Utrecht. All legends surrounding Martin attest to a dynamic figure who was not afraid to take risks and make unexpected decisions. The impulsive act of sharing his cloak with a beggar in need is only one of the examples. The stubbornness [*eigenwijsheid*] of Martin attests to an open spirit who wants to give space to himself and others.[18]

The parade is described as an event in tribute to Martin the generous Roman soldier, "a worldwide icon." There is no mention of his saintly status, Jesus's appearance to him, or any other religious element. The parade's light sculpture of Martin also does not show any signs of Christianity, such as a cross or clerical clothing. Instead, it depicts a soldier with a cloak on horseback (see figure 10.2). As with the relics, which elements are incorporated and which are not are not coincidental but rather the result of deliberate negotiations. The story that gets foregrounded is that of the peaceful soldier who shared half his cloak with a stranger in need. This means, as Sprenger explained to me, that in the parade, "the cross doesn't go on the helmet, because for a moment, he [Saint Martin] belongs to and is there for everyone."

Moral Management and Secularized Religious Heritage in the Netherlands • 241

Figure 10.2. The light sculpture of Saint Martin, 2018: a soldier on horseback, deliberately without showing signs of Christianity. © Welmoed Fenna Wagenaar.

The Saint Martin's Assembly and the SAS were not the only stakeholders who carefully negotiated what parts of the narrative would find their way to the front stage. At a storytelling event in the Utrecht Archives, I spoke to an actor who refrained from telling the public that it was Jesus who revealed himself to Martin in a dream the night after Martin gave away his cloak. Instead, he spoke about "a voice," telling Martin he had done well. When I asked him about this afterward, he explained that the appearance of Jesus was "too Christian" for his taste. A tour guide of a Saint Martin children's tour at the Dom Tower explained that it is important to "not present certain things as fact" when telling kids and their parents about the history of the saint, because "you don't want to preach." At the first official meeting of the network of Dutch Saint Martin cities, representatives discussed tactics for applying for funding, concluding that it is sometimes more effective to refer to Saint Martin as a *"schutspatroon"* (a patron) rather than a *"beschermheilige"* (a patron saint) so as to avoid any associations with religion.

On all these occasions, Saint Martin is framed in a way that I would argue "veils" religious symbols and interpretations. The notion of veiling is helpful here because the strategy used to deal with Saint Martin's religious history does not fully dispose of religious elements, nor is it meant to do so. When asked, no one would deny Saint Martin's history as a Christian bishop or his status as a saint. Instead, as if there were a thin piece of cloth preventing us from looking at it directly, religion gets concealed just enough to keep it confined to the background. The question that remains, then, is what this piece of cloth entails—what the veil is that religion gets hidden behind.

A Secular Veil of Universality

An essential part of reinventing the heritage of Saint Martin has been the act of translation; as we saw earlier, the Saint Martin's Assembly aims to "translate" Saint Martin's philosophy of "sharing the cloak" to a "modern, pluriform society." In an interview with magazine *Immaterieel Erfgoed*, van Deventer argued:

> Saint Martin was of course a Christian saint from the fourth century, long before the church split. But we believe his meaning transcends the religions. Saint Martin stands for the universal values of solidarity, peace, sharing together and is a feast of light. Feasts of light exist in many religions. We try to propagate that the spirit of Saint Martin goes beyond religions and politics. (Meier 2014: 47, translation by the author)

For the assembly and the SAS, the Christian dimension should never become primary to the Saint Martin celebrations. Sprenger and Feld both explained to me that the Utrecht Saint Martin celebrations are an "a-religious" feast—not anti-religious, as Christian communities are very much welcome to participate in and contribute to the celebrations, but supposedly neutral toward religion. Specifically, they view Saint Martin as an a-religious feast because the value of sharing is interpreted and presented as a *universal* value, contributing to the notion of Martin as "a worldwide icon" (as seen in the previous section).

The frame of universality put forward in establishing the meaning of Saint Martin does not stand on its own, but is—as is typical of many heritage formations—connected to a secular gaze. This gaze, viewed as a political and social neutrality rather than as anti-religious (Engelke 2012: 161), is grounded in the European post-Enlightenment separation of church and state, which seeks to confine religion to a private realm (in this case "the church") and views the public domain (in this case "the city") as the realm of the secular (Asad 2003; Casanova 1994; Salemink 2009). This is most apparent in the prominent connections between the Utrecht Saint Martin celebrations and secular initiatives and institutions. Every year, the Saint Martin Parade derives its theme from one of seventeen United Nations Global Goals. The Global Goals are the successors of the Millennium Goals: sustainable development goals that, according to the UN website, are meant to "build a better future for everyone."[19] In 2018, the theme of the parade was goal number sixteen: Peace, Justice, and Strong Institutions. The SAS translated this to the slightly less abstract "peace and safety for everyone," with the subtheme of "building bridges." This also provided an opportunity to connect the Saint Martin Parade 2018 to the one-hundred-year anniversary of the World War I Armistice, signed on 11 November 1918.[20] Practitioners were asked to create light sculptures related to peace and bridges, and the reused sculpture of a bird (in early editions of the parade meant to represent the Saint Martin's goose) functioned as a peace dove. The parade began with a brief speech by the Dutch minister of education, culture, and science, who, like other government officials before her, gave the parade's start sign.

The creation of a secular gaze also arises in how the current Saint Martin celebrations are legitimized and authenticated through references to the past. In minutes of a meeting between stakeholders of the parade, Feld was quoted as saying that the medieval Saint Martin feast was "the biggest annual outdoor feast [*outdoorfeest*]," "owned by the guilds, thus owned by the city and therefore secular."[21] Sprenger on several occasions referred to the work of cultural historian Llewellyn Bogaers to defend this viewpoint. Bogaers, who has written extensively about the city of Utrecht in the (late) Middle Ages, describes how the medieval Saint Martin feast included a market fair with bonfires, music, dance, and theater. Members of the city council, accompanied by musicians, walked through the streets in a torchlight procession, which because of the absence of clergy is described by Bogaers as "no actual procession" (Bogaers 2008: 297–99). Bogaers also writes that the Saint Martin feast included religious ceremonies where the city council was present and that religious purpose was an important motivation behind many medieval practices, including those performed by city councils, but the presence of a procession without clergy serves for the Saint Martin's Assembly and the SAS as proof that the Saint Martin feast has a legitimate origin as an a-religious celebration.

The explicit connections made between the Saint Martin celebrations and secular initiatives and institutions, linked to a discourse of universality, provide an effective alternative to Christian symbolics and interpretations.

They serve as the veil that confines religion to the background so as to keep in line with the custodians' aims to establish the heritage of Saint Martin as being of broad societal significance. Legitimizing the secular gaze by means of academic research, moreover, means that the Utrecht Saint Martin celebrations in their current form maintain their connection to the past and hence their label of authenticity, without risking being painted as a religious feast after all.

Conclusion

This chapter has demonstrated the significance of the management involved in making a secularized religious practice be recognized and appreciated as cultural heritage. Remarkably, while the Saint Martin tradition no longer holds religious connotations in the Netherlands, Saint Martin's religious provenance (re-)emerged as an important factor in the management of the Utrecht Saint Martin celebrations. In these celebrations, which have taken a completely new form over the past twenty years, the focus on the figure of Saint Martin and his moral values creates the possibility of foregrounding traditional religious interpretations and elements of Saint Martin's story. However, in a society where religious rituals and celebrations have become part of public debates on inclusion and exclusion and where heritage management inevitably involves a politics of funding in which accounting for diversity is a criterion, the potential foregrounding of religion becomes a risk that requires constant negotiation. In other words, if heritagization is to succeed, stakeholders continually need to make choices about where to position the heritage formation in the broader heritage landscape and where to position "religion" within the heritage's narrative framework. The heritagization of (secularized) religious celebrations in the Netherlands therefore not only involves an anxiety about people forgetting the "true meanings" of Christian holidays, it also involves an anxiety about the simultaneous aversion many Dutch people still feel toward institutionalized religion. This creates a tension that even the most proficient heritage custodians continue to struggle with, ultimately raising the issue of what it means to be truly inclusive and manage a heritage accordingly.

Welmoed Fenna Wagenaar is a PhD researcher at the Department of Comparative Study of Religion of the University of Groningen. Her project, funded by the Dutch Research Council, examines processes of ritual and sacralization in the everyday, online practices of media fans. Prior to this, she was a junior researcher at the Meertens Institute (KNAW), where she conducted research on the Utrecht Saint Martin celebrations as part of the

HERILIGION: The Heritagization of Religion and the Sacralization of Heritage in Contemporary Europe project. She received her MA cum laude in religious studies from the University of Groningen, specializing in the fields of ritual and popular culture.

NOTES

A word of thanks to the HERILIGION team, especially Irene Stengs, for valuable comments and suggestions on earlier drafts of this chapter. In addition, I am extremely grateful to all those who were willing to participate in this research by allowing me to interview them and/or participate in their events: our research partner Museum Catharijneconvent, Citypastoraat Domkerk Utrecht, Gilde Utrecht, the Sharing Arts Society, Sint Martinusparochie Utrecht, Stadslab RAUM, Stichting De Vrolijkheid, Stichting Zorg en Participatie, the Utrecht Archives, the Utrecht Public Library, Utrecht Marketing, De Voorkamer, and Wijkspeeltuin De Boog. I also want to sincerely thank the Saint Martin's Assembly, Rien Sprenger in particular, for their openness and help during this project.

1. Saint Martin's Day has traditionally been celebrated in the north and northwest of the Netherlands, as well as some places in the south. People who moved from these regions to other places often took the tradition of Saint Martin with them and (re)introduced it in their new neighborhoods (Helsloot 2001: 502).
2. This chapter is based on ethnographic fieldwork, conducted from September 2018 to August 2019, as part of the HERILIGION: The Heritagization of Religion and Sacralization of Heritage in Contemporary Europe project, funded by Humanities in the European Research Area (HERA) grant # 5087-00505A. The majority of the fieldwork was done in October and November, when (the preparations for) the Utrecht Saint Martin celebrations 2018 took place. In this period, I participated in a variety of activities and events, talked informally to practitioners and organizers, and conducted semi-structured interviews with key stakeholders of the celebrations (among which its custodians), several participants of the Saint Martin Parade, and representatives from two of the largest local church communities. I also analyzed policy papers and promotional material from stakeholders and other organizations related to the Saint Martin Celebrations, such as subsidy providers.
3. Special church services are not always part of Saint Martin celebrations. In the Netherlands, the Saint Martin tradition generally does not include religious elements, although there are places (like Utrecht) where local church communities celebrate their own Saint Martin Mass or another kind of church service.
4. John Helsloot, "Sint-Maarten," 2007, http://www.meertens.knaw.nl/cms/nl/?option=com_content&view=article&id=141193 (accessed February 2019).
5. Such a transformation has also been understood in terms of the migration of the holy, where the nation-state has become the new object of devotion (see Cavanaugh 2011).
6. Black Pete is a blackface character that plays the role of Saint Nicholas's servant during the Dutch annual Sinterklaas feast. Due to its connections to slavery and racist stereotypes, the character has become strongly criticized and the subject of a heated public discussion about racism, national identity, and tradition in the Neth-

erlands. The sentiment that people "from other backgrounds" threaten the culture and identity of "actual Dutch people" plays an important role in this debate (see, e.g., Balkenhol 2015). It is within this context—more specifically, in reaction to a lawsuit that proclaimed Black Pete to contain negative stereotyping of black people—that the association Stichting Sint en Pietengilde decided to apply the Sinterklaas celebration, including "black petes," for admission to the Dutch Inventory Intangible Cultural Heritage in 2014. As Stengs has pointed out (2018: 9), this admission is not just aimed at safeguarding the feast's position on the annual calendar (which is not under scrutiny). It rather serves as a way to establish how the feast, albeit with some room for change, is "supposed to be" celebrated.

7. Initially, the Saint Martin's Assembly consisted of representatives of different cultural and religious organizations, such as the Utrecht Archives, the Tourist Information Office, and Protestant and Catholic church parishes. Over time, this model disappeared, and currently the assembly is run by eleven volunteers, many of them with personal religious backgrounds but primarily active in the city's cultural sector. The assembly is part of the Association Saint Martin, a (slightly) broader organization that also organizes the annual Open Garden Day Utrecht.

8. Specifically, this initiative came from music centers Muziekhuis Utrecht and Fort van de Verbeelding, made possible via a national funding program titled Volkscultuur en Immaterieel Erfgoed.

9. This centrality is, for example, apparent in the upcoming celebration of the city's nine-hundred-year anniversary of its city rights: the Saint Martin celebrations will form the finale of the anniversary activities. The willingness of the municipality to include Saint Martin in large city events is partly due to smart storytelling on part of the Saint Martin's Assembly and its foremost partners, as they are able to present Saint Martin in a way that matches the city's recent brand of "creativity and connecting," which also involves being "welcoming" ("Meerjarenplan 2017–2020," Utrecht Marketing, p. 8, https://www.utrechtmarketing.nl/wp-content/uploads/2017/11/UTM-17-015-Meerjarenplan.pdf, accessed May 2019).

10. "Organisatie," Sint Maarten Utrecht, https://sintmaartenutrecht.nl/organisatie (accessed June 2019). Translation by the author.

11. Hence being part of the Dutch HERILIGION research program.

12. "Organisatie," Sint Maarten Utrecht, https://sintmaartenutrecht.nl/organisatie (accessed June 2019). Translation by the author.

13. "Sint Maarten Parade," Sharing Arts Society, http://www.sharingartssociety.com/sint-maarten-parade/ (accessed June 2019). Translation by the author.

14. "Procedure and Criteria," Kenniscentrum Immaterieel Erfgoed Nederland, https://www.immaterieelerfgoed.nl/en/procedure/ (accessed July 2019).

15. "Meer dan de helft Nederlanders niet religieus," Centraal Bureau voor de Statistiek, 2018, https://www.cbs.nl/nl-nl/nieuws/2018/43/meer-dan-de-helft-nederlanders-niet-religieus (accessed February 2019).

16. "Kennisplan 2015–2020," Museum Catharijneconvent, https://www.catharijneconvent.nl/documents/19/Kennisplan_2015-2020_oyoeaRH.pdf (accessed December 2018).

17. The apprehension toward including historical objects from the museum in the Saint Martin celebrations is especially remarkable knowing that objects from the contemporary celebrations did move *into* the museum. In what is perhaps the most telling

example of the heritagization and subsequent status of the Utrecht Saint Martin celebrations, since 2017 Museum Catharijneconvent has included a light sculpture and video of the Saint Martin Parade in their permanent exhibition on religious feasts and holidays.
18. "Sint Maarten Parade," Sharing Arts Society, http://www.sharingartssociety.com/sint-maarten-parade/ (accessed June 2019). Translation by the author.
19. "The 17 Goals," Global Goals website, https://www.globalgoals.org/ (accessed May 2019).
20. The Saint Martin's Assembly and the Sharing Arts Society are not the first to link the WWI Armistice to Saint Martin. During the interwar period, the Dutch branch of the International Women's League for Peace and Freedom (Vrouwenbond voor Vrede en Veiligheid) set out to give the Saint Martin feast "new content" by linking it to Armistice Day. Together with progressive Protestant groups and schoolteachers, they organized processions where children carried peace emblems, slogans, and symbols like doves and peace angels. Back then, the makeover received criticism: the general public opinion was that it destroyed "the character" of Saint Martin (Helsloot 2001: 505–6). I am not sure the assembly and the SAS were aware of this connection; if they were, they did not mention it.
21. It may come as no surprise that when the minutes of this meeting were sent around, Museum Catharijneconvent—rightfully—commented on this statement by saying, "This is factually incorrect; in the Middle Ages the concept 'secular' did not yet exist—everyone and everything (thus also the city) was Christian." Feld agreed to remove the "and therefore secular" from the minutes; the "statement without the conclusion" would be fine.

REFERENCES

Asad, Talal. 2003. *Formations of the Secular*. Stanford, CA: Stanford University Press.
Balkenhol, Markus. 2015. "Zwarte Piet, racisme, emoties," *Waardenwerk* 62/63: 36–46.
Balkenhol, Markus, and Ernst van den Hemel. 2018. "Zwarte pieten, moskeebezoek en zoenende mannen. Katholiek activisme van Cultuur onder Vuur en de culturalisering van religie," *Religie en Samenleving* 14(1): 5–30.
Bendix, Regina. 2009. "Heritage between Economy and Politics: An Assessment from the Perspective of Cultural Anthropology," in Laurajane Smith and Natsuko Akagawa (eds.), *Intangible Heritage*. London: Routledge, pp. 253–69.
Bendix, Regina, Aditya Eggert, and Arnika Peselmann (eds.). 2013. *Heritage Regimes and the State*, 2nd edn. Gottingen: Universitätsverlag Göttingen.
Boer, Eugenie. 2009. "Sint Nicolaas, een levende legende," in Willem Koops, Madelon Pieper, and Eugenie Boer (eds.), *Sinterklaas verklaard*. Amsterdam: SWP, pp. 11–34.
Bogaers, Llewellyn. 2008. *Aards, betrokken en zelfbewust. De verwevenheid van cultuur en religie in katholiek Utrecht, 1300–1600*. Utrecht: Levend Verleden Utrecht.
Casanova, José. 1994. *Public Religions in the Modern World*. Chicago: Chicago University Press.
Cavanaugh, William T. 2011. *Migrations of the Holy: God, State, and the Political Meaning of the Church*. Grand Rapids, MI: Eerdmans.

Duyvendak, Jan Willem, Peter Geschiere, and Evelien Tonkens (eds.). 2016. *The Culturalization of Citizenship: Belonging and Polarization in a Globalizing World*. London: Palgrave Macmillan.

Engelke, Matthew. 2012. "Angels in Swindon: Public Religion and Ambient Faith in England," *American Ethnologist* 39(1): 155–70.

Frijhoff, Willem. 2011. *De mist van de geschiedenis. Over herinneren, vergeten en het historisch geheugen van de samenleving*. Nijmegen: VanTilt.

Helsloot, John. 2001. "An Element of Christian Liturgy? The Feast of St Martin in the Netherlands in the 20th Century," in Paul Post et al. (eds.), *Christian Feast and Festival: The Dynamics of Western Liturgy and Culture*. Leuven: Peeters, pp. 493–518.

Hemel, Ernst van den. 2017. "The Dutch War on Easter: Secular Passion for Religious Culture and National Rituals," *Yearbook for Ritual and Liturgical Studies* 33: 1–19.

Köbben, André J. F. 1983. *De zaakwaarnemer*. Deventer: Van Loghum Slaterus.

Lauvrijs, Bart. 2004. *Een jaar vol feesten: oorsprong, geschiedenis en gebruiken van de belangrijkste jaarfeesten*. Antwerpen: Standaard.

Meier, Elise. 2014. "In het voetspoor van Sint Maarten: Twee jaar op de Nationale Inventaris," *Immaterieel erfgoed* 3(3): 46–49.

Meyer, Birgit, and Marleen de Witte. 2013. "Heritage and the Sacred: Introduction," *Material Religion* 9(3): 274–80.

Nissen, Peter, and Else Rose. 1997. Introduction to Sulpicius Severus, *Het leven van de heilige Martinus*, trans. Peter Nissen and Else Rose. Kampen: Kok, pp. 9–25.

Salemink, Oscar. 2009. "Afterword: Questioning Faiths? Casting Doubts," in Thomas D. DuBois (ed.), *Casting Faiths: Imperialism, Technology and the Transformation of Religion in East and Southeast Asia*. Basingstoke and New York: Palgrave Macmillan, pp. 257–63.

Stengs, Irene. 2012. "Inleiding. Nieuwe Nederlandsheid in feest en ritueel," in Irene Stengs (ed.), *Nieuw in Nederland: Feesten en rituelen in verandering*. Amsterdam: Amsterdam University Press, pp. 9–24.

Stengs, Irene. 2018. "Gepopulariseerde cultuur, ritueel en het maken van erfgoed." Inaugural Lecture, Vrije Universiteit, Amsterdam, 9 November 2018.

Van de Port, Mattijs, and Birgit Meyer. 2018. "Introduction: Heritage Dynamics; Politics of Authentication, Aesthetics of Persuasion and the Cultural Production of the Real," in Birgit Meyer and Mattijs Van de Port (eds.), *Sense and Essence: Heritage and the Cultural Production of the Real*. New York and Oxford: Berghahn Books, pp. 1–39.

AFTERWORD

Heritage as Management of Sacralities
Oscar Salemink

On Monday evening of 15 April 2019, the images of a burning Notre-Dame Cathedral shocked Paris and the world. As usual these days, part of the news coverage in the early hours of the fire consisted of interviews with stunned onlookers about what the church and its partial destruction meant to them. Many Catholic faithful were aghast and spent the evening and night praying for the salvation of this most holy church in France. Also beyond Paris and the flock of the faithful, many people expressed their absolute horror about the ravage, for Notre-Dame meant many things to many people and institutions around the world. Being one of the earliest and finest materializations of Gothic church architecture in the European Middle Ages, Notre-Dame is part of the World Heritage Site "Paris, Banks of the Seine." In addition, Notre-Dame is a touristic icon of Paris and France known throughout the world. Finally, it is a focal point for local or national identification. These four aspects—as a major religious site, as cultural heritage, as icon, and as focus point for ontological identification—involve dimensions of religious and/or secular sacralization, and involve—often paradoxical—overlaps and *connections* with other fields: geographic, economic, cultural, social, political. Let me unpack these four aspects with their entangled dimensions here.

Notre-Dame is undeniably a religious site. At the time of the fire, some onlookers reportedly prayed or chanted hymns, but some of the mediated interviews start with "I am not Catholic/religious, but...." Unsurprisingly, Pope Frances tweeted, "Today we unite in prayer with the people of France," as the Vatican News site emphasized the religious importance of Notre-Dame:

> The Bishops of France said Notre-Dame's influence "extends beyond the capital" and that it would remain "a major symbol of the Catholic faith." They also

invited Catholics around the world to "be living stones of the Church," especially as the faithful journey through the Holy Week and look to the hope of Christ's Resurrection.¹

Beyond the Catholic Church, there was public sympathy from non-Catholic religious leaders in the world. The grand imam of Al-Azhar (the highest religious authority in Sunni Islam) tweeted, "I feel so sorry for the massive fire at the historical architectural masterpiece "Notre-Dame Cathedral' in Paris, our hearts go out to our brothers in France, they deserve our full support." This public expression of inter-religious sympathy is couched in surprisingly secular terms (in Talal Asad's [2003] sense of the term) when the grand imam characterizes the church not as a site of worship but as a "historical architectural masterpiece"—which arguably voids the site of religious meaning.

Much of the interest in Notre-Dame is predicated on its cultural heritage status. UNESCO director-general Audrey Azoulay said, "We are all heartbroken. . . . Notre-Dame represents a historically, architecturally, and spiritually, outstanding universal heritage." The director-general also announced that a rapid damage assessment would be carried out as soon as possible. "UNESCO stands by France in safeguarding and rehabilitating this invaluable heritage," she said.² Here, the characterization of Notre-Dame as heritage of outstanding universal value is combined with the epithet "invaluable" (which I take to mean that its value cannot properly be measured). Yet, such calculations were made when the day after the fire French president Macron pledged to rebuild Notre-Dame "more beautifully than before" within five years.³ Even before that, during the time of the fire, estimations for rebuilding started to be made, and la Fondation du Patrimoine launched a national collection campaign while donations started to pour in immediately—even temporarily crashing its website.⁴ The fire started a competition in donations by two of the richest people in France, François-Henri Pinault (owner of Gucci), promising €100 million, and the Arnault family of Louis Vuitton, promising €200 million. In three days, French billionaires publicly committed almost €600 million, but three months later that money had not yet come in.⁵ Donations also poured in from the United States to what across the Atlantic is regarded as the capital of romance.⁶ So the heritage is considered invaluable, but its restoration is at the same time financially measurable; there is a political economy undergirding the invaluable heritage. The use of words like "invaluable" and "outstanding / universal value," however, rhetorically places Notre-Dame as heritage beyond the realm of the material, thereby emphasizing its spiritual value, which is arguably a form of secular sacralization.

In *The Tourist: A New Theory of the Leisure Class*, Dean MacCannel argues that the transformation of a site into a major tourist attraction—what he calls "sight sacralization"—involves the mechanical and social reproduction of the "sacred object" (1999: 43–45).[7] In other words, the site becomes sight becomes icon. Many commentators commented on Notre-Dame as an icon—for Paris, for France, for humanity. The Dutch prime minister Mark Rutte tweeted, "Paris and France were hit hard by a scorching fire in Notre-Dame, one of the most iconic buildings on our continent. This destructive fire is felt throughout Europe. Just wished Emmanuel Macron a lot of strength with this enormous catastrophe."[8] The iconicity is buttressed by connections with other fields of cultural valuation, like literature and popular culture, as captured in the words of UNESCO director-general Audrey Azoulay that "Notre-Dame . . . is also a monument of literary heritage, a place that is unique in our collective imagination." The iconicity is made possible by the recognizability of the simplified form or shape of Notre-Dame (just like, in Paris, the Eiffel Tower and the Arc de Triomphe), making it an exquisite material sign for Paris, both for Parisians and for tourists. In one of the many mini-interviews during the fire, an aging American couple who had booked a tour in Notre-Dame for the day after the fire professed to be deeply moved and shocked at its partial disappearance, even before they had the chance to see and experience it. And the day after the fire, British novelist Ken Follett flew to Paris and wrote within ten days *Notre-Dame: A Short History of the Meaning of Cathedrals* (2019), which he described as a declaration of love for Notre-Dame and the proceeds of which go 100 percent to its restoration.

Azoulay's literary reference, however, is to Victor Hugo's *Notre-Dame de Paris* (*The Hunchback of Notre-Dame*), whose original publication in 1831 triggered a sense of shame in France over the state of the church and spurred on official restoration efforts. Many interviewees and commentators referred to the novel, but also to the Disney films and the musical. And the media picks it up when iconic people make that connection—for example, when the Brazilian football player Neymar, who plays for Paris Saint-Germain football club, tweeted the Disney cartoon figure of the "hunchback" Quasimodo to express his grief.[9] Not only football players, but other sports figures like the Tour de France organizer ASO tweeted a photo of cyclists passing by Notre-Dame. What is relevant here is that iconicity is predicated on instant visual recognizability based on formal simplicity—in Paris brought out by Notre-Dame, the Eiffel Tower, and the Arc de Triomphe—making Notre-Dame an exquisite material sign for Paris, both for Parisians and for tourists. The reconizability of the sign is at the very least enhanced by such "cross-sectoral" recognition and "social reproduction" (cf. MacCannell 1989: 45) by iconic figures, like artists, sports heroes, and even politicians, as sources of iconic authority themselves.

Speaking of political figures, former president Trump tweeted (while attending, rather ironically, a roundtable at *Burns*ville, Minnesota), "God bless the people of France!"[10] which brings me to the issue of ontological identification. Many mini-interviews with onlookers in the various media expressed that the sight of the burning felt not just as if Paris was losing its heart, but indeed as if they were losing part of their body—a limb or something very essential to their being. On stormy Twitter, many outsiders felt compelled to use words that are normally reserved for the loss of a person—perhaps not exactly offering condolences, but wishing strength with the loss and recovery. Here the valuation of Notre-Dame is not just as heritage or icon, but as a part of self, which indeed is literally invaluable in the sense that its value is purportedly unmeasurable (although we know that there is a price and a limit to medical treatments, as human lives do have a price as well). During a visit to Notre-Dame three years after the fire, President Macron described its restoration "as a metaphor for the country pulling together as France reached the symbolic mark of 100,000 deaths from coronavirus."[11] This status of Notre-Dame as a site of ontological identification beyond its religious aspect as the main site of Catholicism in France is based on a secular valuation of human life as the ultimate value, if we are to follow Talal Asad in his "non-definition" of the secular as not just the absence of religion, but as productive of specific, this-worldly discourses, subjectivities, and sensibilities (e.g., absence of disease and pain, human rights, pursuit of pleasure; cf. Asad 2003). To put it in other terms: a nonreligious valuation of Notre-Dame is ultimately predicated on a sacralization of humanity.

These four aspects of the Notre-Dame—as a major religious site, as cultural heritage, as icon, and as focus point for ontological identification—entail different but entangled kinds of valuation that may be paradoxical—as brought out in the religious and secular forms of sacralization. But the catastrophic sight of the fire brought all these different religious, national, cultural, and popular together in a seemingly frictionless manner, thereby exemplifying—at least temporarily—the UNESCO discourse about "exceptional universal value." And in this exceptional case of near destruction, religious and secular heritage valuations reinforced each other.

However, the different valuations that adhere to religious heritage sites are not free-floating movements but are backed up by the authority of powerful institutions: the church, the state, experts, media, and—last but not least—both commercial and philanthropic capital. In Córdoba, the famous "mosque-cathedral" la Mesquita has been the arena for a long-running row between religious and political authorities over the ownership of the World Heritage Site, which was once known as the great mosque, but in which after the Christian reconquest in 1236 a cathedral was built. While the Catholic diocese claimed the site as an exclusive place of worship for Catholics, others operating since 2013 under the "Platform for the Mosque-Cathedral of Córdoba: Everyone's Heritage" argued that it was a place of worship for other religious groups as well as a cultural heritage site for everyone, regardless of religious affiliation. When in 2016 the church attempted to formalize and legalize their ownership claims, local authorities intervened: "Local authorities in Córdoba have dealt a blow to the Catholic church's claim of legal ownership of the Spanish city's mosque-cathedral, declaring that 'religious consecration is not the way to acquire property.'"[12] In other words, different valuations entail different—religious and secular—sources of institutional authority and may involve conflicting claims over sites and their interpretation.

The above simplistic binary of religious versus secular valuations and authorities in Córdoba becomes more complicated when we move to another recent event involving a religious edifice inscribed on the World Heritage List, namely the Hagia Sophia (Ayasofya in Turkish) in Istanbul. The rise and consolidation of power of the Justice and Development (AK) Party under Recep Tayyip Erdoğan in Turkey established a regime that Ayhan Kaya, in his *Populism and Heritage in Europe* (2020), characterizes as a form of Islamist populism. After the enforced secularism of Kemal Atatürk's laicist policies that converted historical mosques like the Hagia Sophia to secular museums, Turkey is culturally and religiously increasingly neo-Ottomanist in its harking back to the Ottoman self-understanding as a nation of Islam (*millet*) (Kaya 2020: 201–27). In the 2010s, there was a growing movement to reconsecrate the Ayasofya as a mosque—an effort that in 2019 received support from President Erdoğan. A court case brought before the Turkish Council of State by an Islamist historical society unsurprisingly allowed for the reconversion as a mosque on 10 July 2020, on the same day followed by a presidential decree by Erdoğan.[13]

The move was condemned by many cultural, political, and religious authorities outside Turkey. UNESCO's director-general expressed "serious concerns" in an official statement issued the same day under the heading "Hagia Sophia: UNESCO deeply regrets the decision of the Turkish authorities, made without prior discussion, and calls for the universal value of World Heritage to be preserved." The main concern was whether its (secular but sacred) "outstanding universal value" would be sufficiently upheld under a religious regime—a concern that does not seem to extend to Catholic sites like Notre-Dame or Vatican City, also a listed World Heritage Site. The move was also protested by political leaders, not just former US secretary of state Mike Pompeo, but closer in the region by Greece and Cyprus. The Greek Ministry of Culture referred to the Hagia Sophia's "international status" that would be violated, and the Greek culture minister, Lina Mendoni, called the decision an "open provocation to the civilised world," since "Hagia Sophia, located on Turkey's territory, in Istanbul, is a monument to all mankind, regardless of religion." More interesting than these contestations between political Islam and political and cultural secularism is the reaction of various Christian denominations. The patriarchs of the Greek and Russian Orthodox churches protested as well, claiming that altering the status quo of the Hagia Sophia "would fracture the eastern and western worlds." Even the Catholic Pope Francis confessed to be "very distressed" over the decision—a very different reaction from the unified support pouring in during the Notre-Dame fire.[14] Yet, as a mosque the Hagia Sophia remains eminently accessible to visitors and tourists, just like Notre-Dame, the Mesquita in Córdoba, and Saint Peter's Basilica in the Vatican.

Here a complicated picture emerges, characterized not just by the divergence of cultural heritage and religious valuations, but by the entanglement of various religious valuations imposed on this palimpsestic structure (Christian church—Muslim mosque—secular museum—mosque *annex* museum), in which Christian iconography must now be hidden behind veils during Muslim services. To compound matters further, the various religious denominations are localized in specific countries or regions, and the political authorities of some of these countries champion the cause of "their" religion with regard to the Hagia Sophia.

* * *

The three high-profile events at Notre-Dame in Paris, the Mesquita mosque-cathedral in Córdoba, and the Hagia Sophia in Istanbul provide a graphic illustration of the many angles and paradoxes pertaining to religious heritage. They speak to the various types of valuation—religious, cultural, political, also economic—that are projected to these prominent and historical religious structures; onto the different discourses and institutions that claim authority over such sites; onto the different constituencies—"heir" communities or congregations, cities, nations, and even global organizations (UNESCO) and publics—to whom such sites have meaning. How do these high-profile and highly politicized events in three prominent World Heritage Sites in Europe relate to the chapters in this volume? Also in the various chapters we see entanglements involving very different valuations, institutions, authorities, and publics, leading to vastly different figurations and outcomes.

In Denmark, the strong overlap of church, nation, state, and royalty in the conception of Danish heritage generates a strong discourse in which tensions and disagreement—if any—are backgrounded. In Jelling and Roskilde, the overlapping religious and cultural valuations are managed by the same institutions or by institutions that are deeply intertwined—and sometimes by people who combine religious and heritage responsibilities. The two English cases—Saint Peter Hungate in Norwich and the Abbey of St Edmund—testify in different ways to the divergence between religious and cultural valuations through the historical processes of reformation and de-churching.

At the same time, these cases show the incompleteness of secularization, as brought out in present-day attempts to reconquer "spiritual ground" in Saint Peter Hungate and the Abbey of St Edmund respectively. Thus, religious valuations and acts of sacralization make inroads in deconsecrated churches that have become cultural heritage sites.

The two Dutch cases showcase the trend in staging Bach's *Saint Matthew Passion* during Lent and the festival of Saint Martin in Utrecht, in a country that purports to be thoroughly secular—even more than Denmark and Great Britain. A sacral composition intended as a Christian service during Bach's times, the *Saint Matthew Passion* is performed as a musical concert for a highbrow audience of paying music lovers. Even when performed in a church, the *Saint Matthew Passion* is a hybrid affair in which secular-cultural and religious expectations intermingle. Such intermingling also takes place at Utrecht's Saint Martin festival, which is an originally Christian saint's day that became a secularized children's feast in the Netherlands. Church clergy and laypeople who are involved in the organization, however, seek to emphasize religious elements in the celebration, as if in a surreptitious religious "counteroffensive" in the children's feast. As in the English cases, the Dutch cases reveal somewhat hidden religious sensibilities and agendas against a secular heritage backdrop.

The Portuguese cases presented in this book offer a complex picture of four sites and more diverse religions and population groups, against the backdrop of Catholic nationalism and a state-mandated, cosmopolitanizing discourse of "lusotropicalism" that portrays Portugal as a benevolent, inclusive colonial power in past and present. The latter discourse is enacted through a careful curation of the past in cultural heritage sites like Sintra and Mértola, whereas Catholic nationalist discourses afford the backdrop for the famous pilgrimage site of Fátima and the rough Mouraria neighborhood in Lisbon. In all cases, diverging religious sensibilities are co-opted and domesticated through secularist heritage policies that offer space for celebrating diverse religious identities.

The two Polish cases, the "chakra" worship at the royal Wawel Hill, which is part of a World Heritage Site, and the Rękawka celebration on Krakus Mound—both in Kraków—reveal stronger acts of dissent against an authorized heritage discourse (cf. Smith 2006) that fuses Polish nationhood and Catholic religion in official assertions of cultural heritage. Wawel Hill is believed to be a nodal point of an "Earth chakra," publicly revered by a variety of different people in spite of official attempts at suppression. On nearby Krakus Mound, the Rękawka celebration just after Easter consists of reenactments of early medieval Slavic rituals—an occasion used by Polish Pagans to enact their rituals undisturbed by the religious and heritage authorities. So in contrast with the reconquest of spiritual ground in the two

English cases, the two Polish ones show how subaltern religious groups enact but simultaneously subvert and transform official, intertwined religious and heritage valuations.

Taken together, the case studies show how different (institutional) actors, interests, and valuations interweave through time. Sometimes, various religious and cultural heritage valuations work to reinforce each other, as most clearly brought out in official heritage discourses and practices in Denmark, Poland, and Portugal where religious heritage sites, objects, and practices are appropriated by the state as symbolic of the nation. As such, religious and heritage valuations can be seen as mutually reinforcing, much along the lines of the "religious heritage complex" as sketched by Cyril Isnart and Nathalie Cerezales: "The religious heritage complex illustrates how secularity and the sacred form a relational system that binds religious interests and lay motivations, allowing the actors to legitimate their own domain of activity" (2020: 216). For Isnart and Cerezales, such convergence of heritage and religious valuations supports their view that "the superposition of heritage and religious practices and values of conservation helps us to rethink what is deemed as a divide between religious and secular domains [and] permits us to reassess a simplistic explanation of heritage making referred to as the 'migration of the holy'" (209). In other words, in contrast with religious forms of sacrality, cultural heritage involves a sacralization of sites, objects, and practices that relate to secular principles that are most authoritatively promulgated by UNESCO, but Isnart and Cerezales interpret the eventual convergence of religious and heritage interests as offering an analytical argument for the conflation of the two.

The cases offered in this volume show that such valuations may converge at times, but they can also diverge, resulting in hidden or open tensions that may be irreconcilable but that nevertheless have to be managed. The management of such tensions might entail a wide variety of tactics, like hybridization and bureaucratic proliferation (in the Danish sites described in this book). They might evoke tacit expectations of how to behave during performances of Bach's *Saint Matthew Passion* in the Netherlands. They might involve overt curated narratives of the past, as in some Portuguese cases. They might involve official attempts to police heritage sites and cleanse them of undesirable religious practices, as in Sintra (Portugal) and on Wawel Hill (Kraków). In such religious heritage settings, the management of such tensions between religious and secular sensibilities and valuations is in fact a management of secular and religious sacralities.

To complicate the analytical angle offered by Isnart and Cerezales even more, cultural heritage can be an arena for differing religious claims from a variety of different religious groups. Unsurprisingly, in countries that by and large define themselves in terms of a dominant Christian denomination—

which in the five countries covered in this book would include Denmark, Poland, and Portugal—official cultural heritage is discursively, politically, and practically very much entangled with the material expression of that dominant religion. But precisely *because* of the principles by which cultural heritage is valuated, validated, and evaluated, it might afford opportunities for subaltern religious groups to assert their claims or at least to claim a presence, as we have seen in the case studies in Poland and Portugal and to a lesser extent also in Bury St Edmunds in the UK. In the de-churched context of the Netherlands, nationalist movements increasingly define Christianity as the leitmotif for Dutch culture and identity as part of a broader, supposedly "Judeo-Christian" civilization in Europe. This leads to new fault lines and new practices of in- and exclusion (van den Hemel 2014). In such situations, cultural heritage becomes an arena for tensions between multiple—secular and religious—sacralities that need to be managed in ways that at least pay lip service to the supremacy of cultural heritage within a heritage regime (cf. Geismar 2015). Ultimately, that heritage regime and its attendant "authorized heritage discourse" (Smith 2006) derive their authority from an international convention overseen by an intergovernmental organization, UNESCO.

UNESCO's definition of heritage in terms of "outstanding universal value," its criteria, and its list have been replicated in member countries, regions, and cities in staggered fashion (Askew 2010). The heritage values listed by UNESCO construe the value of any cultural heritage "property"—or in the case of cultural practices, "intangible cultural heritage"—against a global scale, with "humanity" at the top. In some cases, such valuation renders specific sites "invaluable," as is the case of Notre-Dame of Paris, the Mesquita mosque-church in Córdoba, and the Hagia Sophia in Istanbul. These are sacred sites from a religious vantage point, but also from a secular heritage vantage point predicated on criteria emanating from "humanity." The fire in Notre-Dame shows that invaluable heritage also has price tags attached to it, meaning that at least to some extent their value is measurable after all. In such religious heritage settings, then, this supposedly "invaluable" heritage valuation is comparable, and to some extent commensurate, with other valuations—not just financial but also religious.[15] These tensions may be subdued, subterranean even, but they are nevertheless real, and they refer to or derive from different—religious and secular—sacralities, as brought out in the various chapters of this volume no less so than in the more politicized tensions surrounding the high-profile World Heritage Sites mentioned above. The management of such religious heritage sites, objects, and practices is tantamount to managing the different sacralities involved and their mutual entanglements, disentanglements, and tensions, sometimes openly but more often subtly and in subdued manner—for example, by a parental nudge to a child to not applaud after the performance of Bach's *Saint Matthew Passion* in a church.

Oscar Salemink is professor of anthropology at the University of Copenhagen. Between 2001 and 2011 he worked at Vrije Universiteit Amsterdam, from 2005 as professor of social anthropology, and from 1996 through 2001 he was responsible for Ford Foundation grant portfolios in social sciences and arts and culture in Thailand and Vietnam. He received his doctoral degree from the University of Amsterdam, based on research on Vietnam's Central Highlands. He is currently working on global projects on heritage and contemporary arts. He has published two monographs, ten edited volumes, and eight themed issues of journals.

NOTES

The research for this article took place in the framework of the European project HERILIGION: The Heritagization of Religion and the Sacralization of Heritage in Contemporary Europe (2016–20), funded by Humanities in the European Research Area (HERA) grant # 5087-00505A.

1. See https://www.vaticannews.va/en/pope/news/2019-04/pope-francis-notre-dame-fire-closeness-prayers.html (accessed 15 October 2021).
2. See https://en.unesco.org/news/fire-notre-dame-cathedral-paris-unesco-stands-france-safeguard-and-rehabilitate-historic (accessed 15 October 2021).
3. See https://www.theguardian.com/world/2019/apr/17/notre-dame-fire-macron-promises-to-make-cathedral-more-beautiful-than-before (accessed 15 October 2021).
4. See https://www.express.co.uk/news/world/1114813/notre-dame-fire-paris-cathedral-news-update-Henri-Pinault-Bernard-Arnault; https://www.rtbf.be/info/monde/detail_incendie-a-notre-dame-de-paris-la-fondation-du-patrimoine-lance-mardi-une-collecte-nationale?id=10197206; the website https://www.fondation-patrimoine.org/ even briefly crashed the evening of the fire (all accessed 15 October 2021).
5. See https://www.theguardian.com/commentisfree/2019/jul/18/ruins-notre-dame-billionaires-french-philanthropy (accessed 15 October 2021).
6. See https://www.theguardian.com/lifeandstyle/2019/aug/08/notre-dame-paris-why-have-americans-given-so-much-money-to-restore (accessed 15 October 2021).
7. In *The Tourist* (1989: 44–45), Dean MacCannell distinguishes five stages in the "sight sacralization" of tourist attractions: the naming phase, the framing and elevation phase, enshrinement, mechanical reproduction, and social reproduction.
8. See https://nltimes.nl/2019/04/16/dutch-pm-wishes-france-strength-notre-dame-fire (accessed 15 October 2021).
9. See https://www.dailymail.co.uk/sport/football/article-6926099/Neymar-Paul-Pogba-express-grief-Notre-Dame-cathedral-fire.html (accessed 15 October 2021).
10. See https://twitter.com/realDonaldTrump/status/1117910111236681728 (accessed 15 October 2021).

11. See https://www.theguardian.com/world/2021/apr/15/notre-dame-cathedral-repair-is-a-metaphor-for-pulling-together-france-emmanuel-macron-says (accessed 16 October 2021).
12. See https://www.theguardian.com/world/2016/mar/13/cordoba-catholic-churchs-claim-mosque-cathedral; also https://www.theguardian.com/world/2014/dec/05/cordoba-mosque-cathedral-name-change-row-andalusia (accessed 16 October 2021).
13. See https://www.theguardian.com/world/2020/jun/30/ayasofya-the-mosque-turned-museum-at-the-heart-of-an-ideological-battle; and https://www.theguardian.com/world/2020/jul/10/turkey-court-ruling-paves-way-for-istanbuls-ayasofya-to-revert-to-mosque (both accessed 16 October 2021).
14. See https://en.unesco.org/news/unesco-statement-hagia-sophia-istanbul; https://www.vaticannews.va/en/pope/news/2020-07/angelus-pope-remembers-seafarers.html; and https://www.theguardian.com/world/2020/jul/12/pope-francis-very-distressed-over-hagia-sophia-mosque-move (accessed 15 October 2021).
15. The commensurability of such valuations might resemble Pierre Bourdieu's theory of the commensurability of the "four capitals" (including cultural capital), while the tension between these different valuations speaks to the relative autonomy of the fields (in this case the "art field") as sources of valuation (Bourdieu 1993).

REFERENCES

Asad, Talal. 2003. *Formations of the Secular: Christianity, Islam, Modernity*. Stanford, CA: Stanford University Press.
Askew, Marc. 2010. "The Magic List of Global Status: UNESCO, World Heritage and the Agendas of States," in Sophia Labadi and Colin Long (eds.), *Heritage and Globalization*. London: Routledge, pp. 19–44.
Bourdieu, Pierre. 1986. "The Forms of Capital," in J. Richardson (ed.), *Handbook of Theory and Research for the Sociology of Education*. New York: Greenwood, pp. 241–58.
Bourdieu, Pierre. 1993. *The Field of Cultural Production: Essays on Art and Literature*. New York: Columbia University Press.
Follett, Ken. 2019. *Notre-Dame: A Short History of the Meaning of Cathedrals*. New York: Viking Books.
Geismar, Haidy. 2015. "Anthropology and Heritage Regimes." *Annual Review of Anthropology* 44: 71–85.
van den Hemel, Ernst. 2014. "(Pro)claiming Tradition: The 'Judeo-Christian' Roots of Dutch Society and the Rise of Conservative National," in B. Blaagaard, R. Braidotti, Tobijn de Graauw, E. Midden, and T. Graauw. *Transformations of Religion and the Public Sphere*. London: Palgrave Macmillan, pp. 53–76.
Isnart, Cyril, and Nathalie Cerezales (eds.). 2020. *The Religious Heritage Complex: Legacy, Conservation, and Christianity*. London: Bloomsbury.
Kaya, Ayhan. 2020. *Populism and Heritage in Europe: Lost in Diversity and Unity*. London and New York: Routledge.
MacCannell, Dean. 1999 [or. 1976]. *The Tourist: A New Theory of the Leisure Class*, new ed. Berkeley: University of California Press.
Smith, Laurajane. 2006. *Uses of Heritage*. London and New York: Routledge.

Index

Aakjær, Jeppe, 84
Aastrup Church, 76
Abbey of St Edmund, 44, *45*, 46, 48–52
   tennis courts at, 57–58
Abbey of St Edmund Heritage Partnership, 44, 46–49, 51, 61, 62–63
   spiritual significance and, 53
absolutism, 71–72
An Account of Denmark as It Was in the Year 1692 (Molesworth), 69
aesthetic cosmopolitanism, 174
aesthetic Orientalism, 177, 179n11
Agency for Culture and Palaces, 92, 94
Agrarian Reform, 172
Alentejo, Portugal, 172
Alentejo Catholicism, 173
alternative spirituality, 115
Amerongen, Martin van, 218–19
ancestors, offerings for, 147
Ancient Monuments Act, 1882, 24
Al-Andalus heritage, 195–96
Andalusia, 176
Anglican cathedrals, 4
Anglican Church, 57
Anglicans, 57
anticommunism, Fátima and, 191
antiquarian questionnaire, 82–83
A. P. Møller Foundation, 95, 109n5
applause, *Saint Matthew Passion* and, 205, 207, 209, 216–17, 219, 223
appropriation
   bottom-up, 185, 199
   of the sacred, 130, 133n16
   of spirituality, 55

archaeology
   da Veiga, Estácio, 170
   excavations at Jelling, 93
   Prince Duleep Singh, 28
   research, 50
   Torres, Cláudio, 172
architecture
   Danish church, 70–71
   ecclesiastical, 22
   Gothic, 22, 77
   Gothic church, 249
   of mosque, 197–98
   Romantic, 165
Armistice Day, 247n20
artists, 77
Asad, Talal, 6
Association Saint Martin, 246
aura
   Christian, 129–30
   mystical, 168
authenticity, 39, 41n25
authentic method, of *Saint Matthew Passion*, 218
authorized heritage discourse, 5, 8
Ayasofya (Hagia Sophia), 253–54
Al-Azhar (imam), 250
Azoulay, Audrey, 250, 251

Bach, Johann Sebastian, 205, 208, 212, 215, 218
   in the Netherlands, 209–11
Bach industry, 209, 211
Baitul Mukarram Mosque, *196*, 196–97
   architecture of, 197–98

Bakhuizen, Ruud, 208
Bangladesh, Islamic Community of, 195
Bangladesh Islamic Centre (BIC), 195, 197
Bargiel, Woldemar, 214
Berger, John, 53
Berlin Sing-Akademie, 212–13
Black Pete controversy, 237, 245n6
Blue Army of Fátima, 192
Brazil, 159
Britain, 39n2
Bury St Edmunds, 47, 48

Carnation Revolution 1974, 159, 162
cathedrals, Anglican, 4. *See also specific cathedrals*
Catholic Church, 70, 120, 161
   colonialism and, 163
   indulgence and, 153n2
   Portugal and, 176
   Wawel and, 121
Catholicism, 7, 46, 137–38, 143–44, 150
   Alentejo, 173
   Fátima and, 188, 192–93
   heritage management and, 184
   nationalism and, 115, 255
   pilgrimage shrines, 184
   Portugal and, 163, 198
   Portuguese national identity and, 186, 199
   Rękawka celebration and, 139, 149
   Wawel Roman Catholic cathedral and, 113, 119–20
CCT. *See* Churches Conservation Trust
chakra
   dispute, 2001, 122–23
   practices, 130–31
   spirituality, 115–16, 127–28
Christian III (king), 71
Christianity, 4, 38, 54, 91
   Danish churches and, 70–71
   Danish nation and, 99
   Folkekirken and, 85
   Martin of Tours (saint) and, 240–42
   in the Netherlands, 223
   in Portugal, 187
churches, 3
   budget, 102–3

   buildings, management of, 82, 86
   churchmanship, 23
   closure of, 38
   commissioned reports, 25
   Copenhagen, 75
   Danish medieval, 78
   decline in attendance of, 7
   dilapidation of, 30
   dioceses, 74, 81, 100
   entry fees, 4
   Folkekirke, 73
   funding from, 102–3
   heritage and, 214
   inspection law, 78
   Lutheran, 90
   medieval, 75, *76*
   National Museum of Denmark and, 78–80
   of Norwich, 27
   objects, 79
   ownership of, 76
   preservation of, 24, 28–29
   Protestant, 108n1
   redundant, 21, 32
   restoration of, 23–24, 27–28, 77
   Saint Matthew Passion in, 217–18
   state and, 71–73, 91, 106, 186
   taxes, 74–75, 85, 102, 103
   as World Heritage Sites, 101
Churches Conservation Trust (CCT), 25
Church Going (poem), 38
Church of Denmark, 72–73, 90
Church of England, 22, 23, 24–25, 27, 46
   closure of churches and, 38
   Saint Peter Hungate and, 30
   spirituality and, 53, 55
City under the Krakus Mound, The (exhibition), 143
closure of churches, 38
colonialism, 159
   Catholic Church and, 163
   Mouraria and, 184
   Portuguese, 160
   Portuguese wars, 189
Commission for Religious Freedom, 164
communities of care, 207
concert culture, 216

Concertgebouw, 215, 216
consecration, 25
Conservation Management Plan (CMP), 49–52, 62
  spirituality and, 56
  spiritual significance and, 53
Conservation Society of National Monuments, 161
Córdoba, 252–53
cosmopolitanism, 160
  aesthetic, 174
cultural heritage. *See* heritage
culturalization, 150, 152
  of citizenship, 230–31, 233
  of religious feasts, 232–33
cultural stratigraphy, 170, 172
curators, 80–82

Danish churches, 72, 86
  architecture of, 70–71
  Christianity and, 70–71
  clergy, 71
  Danish people and, 82–85
  Danmarks Kirker documentation, 80
  funding and UNESCO, 103–4
  funding for Roskilde Cathedral, 100, 102, 104
  funding from, 102–3
  funding from state, 105
  fundraising, 104
  heritage category and, 75–78
  Lutheran Church, 16n5, 70, 74, 86
  Lutheran Reformation, 71
  medieval, 78
  parishes, 75, 83, 86
Danske Atlas (Pontoppidan), 82
dawa (Islamic preaching), 175–76
Dawson, Ann, 58–59
Dawson, Steve, 58–59
Declaration on Creative Diversity, 160
Denmark, 6, 16n5, 70, 108n1
  Constitution, 75
  Evangelical-Lutheran Church in, 73–75
  flag, 72, 72
  historic buildings in, 76–77
  history, 83–85, 92

identity, 69–70, 84
kings, 71–72
kirkeskat (taxes), 74–75
law, 75
legislation, 107
lejlighedskirker (occasional churches), 75
Lutheran Reformation, 71
  restoration and, 77
  Romanticist nationalism, 86
  Royal House, 69–70
  state, 82, 85–86
despacho offering, 168
Development Fund for a Communication Center of the Cultural Heritage of Roskilde Cathedral, 103
Deventer, Chris van, 235–36, 242
dikhr (Sufi rituals), 175–76
Dissolution of the Monasteries, 46, 55, 56
diversity
  ethnic, 170
  racial, 159
  religious, 168, 177, 187, 194
DJ-Matthäus, 220
dowsing, 58–60, 65n18–19
Dowsing Anglia, 58
Dutch Cultural Participation Fund, 239
Dziewanna (goddess of spring), 145, 147

Earth chakras, 115, 117
ecumenism, 198
Edmund (Saint), 44, 47–48, 49
  body of, 57–58
  bones of, 57–58, 59–60
Epoche: Suspension of Judgment (exhibition), 35
Elm Hill, 27, 30
energy drawers, 116–19, *118*, 121, 127, 132n3
energy grammar, 118, 119
energy pilgrims, 118
energy spirituality, 116–19, 122
English Civil Wars, 22
English Heritage Trust, 63n4, 64n9
Enlightenment, 4, 84
Estado Novo, 159, 161, 162, 166, 171
  Fátima and, 200n1

ethnogenealogy, 179n14
ethnogenesis, 170, 177, 179n14
Evangelical-Lutheran Church, in Denmark, 73–75

Fællesfonden (common fund), 74
Fátima, 179n17, 183
　anticommunism and, 191
　Catholicism and, 188, 192–93
　Estado Novo and, 200n1
　heritage discourses and, 192–93
　Hindu cult in, 200n2
　inter-religious feature of, 192
　Marian apparition, 188–89
　Our Lady of Fátima, 184, 188–89, *190*, 191
　pilgrimage to, 184
　Salazarism and, 190
Feast of Sacrifice, 194, 197
Feast of Sharing, 229, 236, 237, 238
Ferdinand II (king), 165
Ferro, António, 179n5
festival, Islamic, 174–75
Folkekirke churches, 73, 74–75, 79–80
　Danish state and, 82, 85–86
　membership of, 85
folklorization, 232–33
Forkel, Johann, 212
forkyndelse (religious propagation), 99–103
Frances (pope), 249–50
Frederique (singer), 222–23
Freyre, Gilberto, 178n2

game of truth, 137, 138, 140–42
Geck, Martin, 213
Geertekerk (Geerte church), 205, *206*, 207
General Directorate of National Buildings and Monuments, 166, 171
gentrification, 195
Germany, 212
Gorm the Old (king), 92
Gospel of Matthew, 205
Gothic
　church architecture, 249
　Revival, 23
　style, 77

Gothic architecture, 22, 77
Greenland, 74
Grundtvig, Nicolai F. S., 84
Gunning, J. H., 217

Hagia Sophia (Ayasofya), 253–54
Harald Blåtand (king), 92
Hazlitt, William, 33
Henry VIII (king), 46
Herculano, Alexandre, 179n4
heritage (including cultural heritage), 171, 178n1, 179n4
　Al-Andalus, 195–96
　assessment, 46
　authority of, 90
　churches and, 214
　commodification of, 99–103, 174
　Danish churches and category of, 75–78
　discourses, 114, 119, 192–93
　dissemination (*formidling*), 103
　Fátima and, 192–93
　fever, 100
　fluidity of, 131
　genealogy, 161
　governmentality, 91
　intangible, 179n9
　interpretation, 56
　Islamic, 184–85, 198
　Jewish, 144
　Kraków, 152n1
　making, 159–61, 256
　Muslim, 186–87
　national, 128, 138
　national identity and, 212
　nomination, 10
　Pagan, 137, 138, 141–42, 152
　performance of, 217
　Polish national, 138
　purification, 92, 93, 107
　regimes, 5, 8–10, 114, 137, 152
　regulations, 161, 166–67
　reinvention of, 235
　religion and, 9, 176, 183–84
　religious heritage complex, 39n1, 99–100, 115
　rhetoric, 177

sacralization of, 5–9, 207
Saint Martin's Assembly and, 235–37
shrine, 191
significance, 51
valuation of, 257, 259n15
volunteers, 35, 49
Heritage Assessment (HA), 49–52, 64n13
Heritage Lottery Fund, 35
heritage management
  authenticity and, 39, 41n25
  Catholicism and, 184
  England, 21–26
  hybridization of, 103–7
  local, 91
  parish councils and, 98
  in Portugal, 160–61, 198–99
  religious, 9–11
  sacred and, 38
  sites, 1–5, 24
  World, 95, 97
heritagization, 2–5, 46, 152, 178n1, 225
  Mouraria square and, 195
  process of, 10, 63n1
  of religion, 5–9, 207
  sacralization and, 213, 214, 224
  Saint Matthew Passion and, 213–14
  World-Heritagization, 90–91, 98, 104–6, 107
hierarchical pluralism, 8
Historic England guidelines, 51, 52, 63n2, 64n10–11
højskoler, 84
Holmes, Henry, 32
holy
  individuals, 168–69
  migration of the, 114–15, 245n5
  water, 127
Høyen, Niels Lauritz, 77–78
Hugo, Victor, 251
Hunchback of Notre-Dame, The (*Notre-Dame de Paris*) (Hugo), 251
Hungate Medieval Art, 34–39

iconoclasm, 22
identity
  cultural, 224
  Danish, 69–70, 84, 91

heritage and, 212
national, 4, 176–77
Portuguese, 163, 186, 199
religious, 36
Ingemann, Bernhard Severin, 83
institutional proliferation, 103–6
interculturality, 184
Inventory Intangible Cultural Heritage in the Netherlands, 234, 235
Iranian Shiite pilgrims, 179n17
Islam, 8, 171, 211, 253–54
Islamic Community of Bangladesh, 195
Islamic Community of Lisbon, 173, 175, 179n17
Islamic Festival, Mértola, 173, *173*, 174–76
Islamic heritage, 184–85, 198
Islamic Junta de Sevilla, 175, 178n3
Islamic Museum, 173
Islamic period, Portugal, 171
Islamic preaching (*dawa*), 175–76
Islamic re-enactors, 174
Islamophilia, 173

Jelling
  archaeological excavations, 93
  Church, 94
  Kongernes, 92, 93
  mounds at, 92, *94*
  parish councils and, 93, 94–95, 96–97
  public meeting, 97–98
  site, 90, 92–96, 106–7
  town council, 96
  World Heritage and, 96–99
Jewish heritage, in Poland, 144
John Paul II (pope), 129, 133n14
Judaism, 8

Kraków
  Easter in, 136
  heritage in, 152n1
  Krak Vistulan Warrior Host, 140
  locality and, 142–44
  Old Town, 113, 125
  Paganism and, 136–37, 149
  Podgórze district, 143–44
  tourism in, 123, 124

Wawel chakra energy and, 128–29
Krak re-enactment group, 141
Krakus Mound, 136, 139, 142–45, 147, 151

Lad's Brigade, 29, 30
Larkin, Philip, 38
Lasota Hill, 136, *139*, 147, 151
Law and Justice Party (*Prawo i Sprawiedliwość*), 153n5
Leicester Cathedral, 44
Leitkultur, 8
Lisbon
  Islamic Community of, 173, 175, 179n17
  Islamic past of, 184–85
  Martim Moniz square, 194
  Moorish quarter, 193, 197
localizing, World Heritage, 96–99
lusotropicalism, 163, 170, 177, 178n2
  Portuguese, 159–61
  vernacular, 160
Lutheranism, 217
Lutheran Reformation, Denmark, 71

Maatschappij tot Bevordering van de Toonkunst (Society for the Promotion of the Performing Arts), 214
Macron, Emmanuel, 251, 252
magnetism, 54
management. *See also* heritage management
  of church buildings, 82, 86
  of cultural heritage, 183–84, 244
  of heritage sites, 1–5, 24
  of Pagan heritage, 138
  plan, 97
  religious heritage, 9–11
  of secularism, 244
  of Sintra, 166–67
  tour guides, 123–26, 133n10
  of Utrecht Saint Martin celebrations, 230, 233, 235, 239
  of Wawel castle, 119–20, 121
  World Heritage, 95, 97
Marian apparition, 188–89

Martin of Tours (saint), 230, 233–34, 235, 239, *241*
  Armistice Day and, 247n20
  Christianity and, 240–42
martyrdom, 47
Marzanna (goddess of winter), 145, 147
masculinity, Christian, 29
mass consumption, at Sintra, 167–70
Matthäus Masterclass (television program), 220
Matthäus-Passion, 211
meezing-Matthäus (Sing-Along *Saint Matthew Passion*), *206*, 207, 208–9, 220–23
Mendelssohn Bartholdy, Felix, 212, 213
Mengelberg, Willem, 215
Mértola, 160, 172, 178n3
  Islamic festival, 173, *173*, 174–76
  Muslims and, 173, 177
  ruins in, 170
  Vila Museu (Museum), 172
Mesquita, 252–53
Michael and Mary lines, 59–60
Middle Ages, 142, 146
migration of the holy, 114–15, 245n5
Ministry of Ecclesiastical Affairs, 81, 85, 95
minorities, religious, 7–8, 164, 168, 184
Miracle of the Sun, 189
Molesworth, Robert, 69
monastic community, 63n3
monastic infrastructure, 45
monasticism, 54
monumentos pátrios (motherland monuments), 161
monument preservation, 63n4
Moon Hill, 165
motherland monuments (*monumentos pátrios*), 161
Mouraria square, 185, 188, 193–98
  colonization and, 184
  heritagization and, 195
  history of, 193–94
  multiculturalism and, 195
multiculturalism, 176, 195
Musée des Arts et Métiers, 31
Museum Catharijne convent, 239, 245, 246n17, 247n21

museums. *See also specific museums*
   benefits of, 64n16
   ecclesiastical, 31
   Islamic, 173
   in Norwich, 31
   Oude Kerk, 1–2
   Roskilde, 100
   Royal Castle state, 114
   Saint Peter Hungate as, 31–34
   secular ritual and, 33–34
Muslim heritage, 186–87
Muslims, 172
   Mértola and, 173, 177
   Portuguese, 162
   Sunni, 196
Muslim subjectivity, 185
mysticism
   auras and, 168
   Sintra and, 167–70

nationalism, 77, 83
   Catholic, 255
   Catholicism and, 115
   Danish Romanticist, 86
   Romantic, 211–12
National Lottery Heritage Fund, 51
National Museum of Denmark, 78–81, 82–83
Nawia, 145, 147
Neo-Paganism, 153n3
Netherlands, 6–7, 209–11, 244
   Christianity in, 223
   Inventory Intangible Cultural Heritage in the Netherlands, 234, 235
   religions in, 238
   religious feasts in, 232–33
   Saint Matthew Passion in, 214–18
   sing-along events, 221
Netherlands Bach Society, 217, 218, 223
New Age, 132n6
non-Christians, 51–52
non-separation, of church and state, 106
Norfolk and Norwich Archaeological Society (NNAS), 28, 29–30
Norwich, 26–28, 30–32
Norwich Historic Churches Trust (NHCT), 34

Notre-Dame Cathedral, 251
   burning, 249–50, 252
   donations for, 250
Notre-Dame de Paris (*The Hunchback of Notre-Dame*), 251

occult practices, 120, 121
offering, *despacho*, 147, 168
Oldnordisk Museum in Copenhagen, 79
Orientalism, aesthetic, 177, 179n11
Oude Kerk (Old Church), 1–2
Our Lady of Fátima, 184, 188–89, *190*, 191
Our Lady of Health, 194
Oxford Movement, 57

Pagan
   heritage, 137, 138, 141–42, 152
   rituals, 144
   site, 54, 64n13
   Vikings, 47
Paganism, 134n17
   Kraków and, 136–37, 149
   Neo-, 153n3
   Rękawka celebration and, 139–41, 145–49
   Rodzimowiercy, 142
Paris, 252
parish councils, 73–74, 103, 107
   heritage management and, 98
   Jelling site and, 93, 94–95, 96–97
   restoration and, 81
   Roskilde Cathedral, 100
Parques de Sintra-Monte da Lua (PSML), 165, 167, 169
Passieprojecten (Passion project foundation), 208, 221
passion plays, 205
patrimonialization, 195
patrimonial regimes, 159
Pena Palace, 167
performance of heritage, 217
performativity of Rękawka celebration, 145–49, 151–52
performed history, 149
pilgrimages, 113
   Catholic pilgrimage shrines, 184
   to Fatima, 184

pilgrims
  energy, 118
  Iranian Shiite, 179n17
Płaszów concentration camp, 144
pluralism
  hierarchical, 8
  religious, 46
Podgórze Cultural Center, 140
Podgórze district, Kraków, 143–44
Podgórze Museum, 143
Poems for Earthlings (art installation), 1–2
Poland, 7, 113, 116, 131, 255–56
  Baptism of, 140–41
  culture, 141–42
  history, 128
  Jewish heritage in, 144
  national heritage, 138
  Polishness, 114
  politics in, 153n5
  Roman Catholicism and, 137–38
  saints, 130
  state, 138
politicians, Dutch nationalist, 211
politics of funding, 239, 244
Pollock, Bertram, 32, 33
Pontoppidan, Erik, 82
Portugal, 7, 183, 255
  Alentejo, 172
  Catholic Church and, 176
  Catholicism and, 163, 198
  Christianity in, 187
  colonialism, 160
  colonial wars, 189
  disenchantment in, 161–64
  ecumenism and, 198
  Estado Novo, 159, 161
  ethnic diversity, 170
  Fifth Government Program, 162
  heritage management in, 160–61, 198–99
  heritage regulations in, 161, 166–67
  history of, 186
  immigration to, 164, 187
  Islamic period, 171
  Ismaili Community, 175
  Law of Religious Freedom, 168
  lusotropicalism and, 159–61
  national identity, 163, 186, 199
  Portuguese exceptionality, 160
  Portuguese Muslims, 162
  racial diversity and, 159
  Reconquest, 164–65
  Religious Freedom Act (2001), 173
  religious heritage in, 162, 185–88, 199
pre-Christian religions, 151
preservation
  of churches, 24, 28–29
  of cultural heritage, 79–80
  of tradition, 236
procession of Our Lady of Health, 194
Protestant churches, 108n1
Protestantism, 217
purification of heritage, 92, 93, 107

Quebec Declaration of ICOMOS, 53, 97
questionnaires
  antiquarian, 82–83
  spiritual significance, 52

racial democracy, 178n2
racial diversity, Portugal, 159
racism, 245n6
Ramadan, 175, 197
re-enactment, Rękawka celebration, 148–49
re-enactors
  Islamic, 174
  Rękawka, 141, 142, 145–48, *146*, 150
Reformation, 21–22, 26, 46, 232
  Lutheran Reformation, 71
  scholars, 61
regimes
  heritage, 5, 8–10, 114, 137, 152
  patrimonial, 159
  of truth, 137
Rękawka celebration, 136, 137, 150–52
  competitions, 148
  Paganism and, 139–41, 145–49
  performativity of, 145–49, 151–52
  re-enactments, 148–49
  re-enactors, 141, 142, 145–48, *146*, 150
  Roman Catholicism and, 139, 140, 149
  Saint Benedict church and, 139, *139*

religion, 222
  culture and, 150
  heritage and, 9, 176, 183–84
  heritage sites and, 3
  heritagization of, 5–9, 207
  in the Netherlands, 238
  pre-Christian, 151
  Saint Martin's Assembly and, 239–42
  Saint Matthew Passion and, 222–23
  secularism and, 150
  spirituality and, 54
  Utrecht Saint Martin celebrations and, 242–44
  veiling of, 242
religio-secularism paradigm, 115
religious diversity, 168, 177, 187, 194
Religious Freedom Act (2001), Portugal, 173
religious heritage, 8, 183, 254
  burden of, 237–39
  identity, 36
  leaders, 250
  managing, 1–5
  minorities, 7–8, 164, 168, 184
  pluralism, 46
  in Portugal, 162, 185–88, 199
  protecting, 80–82
  religious heritage complex, 39n1, 99–100, 115
  religious heritage management, 9–11
  religious propagation (*forkyndelse*), 99–103
  terminology, 215
  valuations, 254
  wars, 22
re-sacralization, 214
restoration
  of churches, 23–24, 27–28, 77
  of mural paintings, 80
  parish councils and, 81
  of Wawel castle, 122–23
Richard III (king), 44, 60–61
rituals
  Pagan, 144
  secular, 33
  Slavic, 139, 140–41, 145, 147
Rodzimowiercy, 142, 144, 151

Rodzimowierstwo, 142, 144, 150
Rojas, Adrián Villar, 1–2
Romanesque abbey church, 47
Romanesque churches, 70
Romanesque church of Saint Gereon, 129
Romantic architecture, 165
Romantic nationalism, 211–12
Roskilde Cathedral, 5, 90, *101*, 107
  deanery, 100, 102
  funding for, 100, 102, 104
  heritage communication and, 99–103
  visitor center at, 102, 103–6
Roskilde museums, 100
Royal Castle state museum, 114, 132n2
Royal Cathedral Chapter, 114
Royal Commission for the Keeping of Antiquities, 78–79, 82–83
Runic Stones and Church, 90

sacralization, 3
  of heritage, 5–9, 207
  heritagization and, 213, 224
  of humanity, 252
  moral framework and, 237–39
  re-sacralization, 214
  of *Saint Matthew Passion*, 209, 214, 224
  secular, 6, 44, 218–19
  sight sacralization, 251
sacred, 36, 50
  appropriation of the, 130, 133n16
  compatibility and the, 128–30
  migration of the, 6–7
  secular and, 44
  spirituality and the, 54, 56–57
Sacred and/or Secular (exhibition), 35, 36
sacredness, 55
Saint Benedict church, 139, *139*, 140
Saint Gereon church, 133n15
Saint Martin feast, 232–33, 235, 237–38, 243
Saint Martin Parade, 228–29, *229*, 234, 236, 240, 243
Saint Martin's Assembly, 234, 246n7
  heritage and, 235–37
  mission statement, 236
  religion and, 239–42
Saint Martin's Day, 229, 231–32, 245n1

Saint Matthew Passion, 211, 215, 224–25
  applause and, 205, 207, 209, 216–17, 219, 223
  authentic method of, 218
  in church, 217–18
  critics of, 216
  heritagization and, 213–14
  in Netherlands, 214–18
  performance of, *206*, *210*
  religion and, 222–23
  sacralization of, 209, 214, 224
  secular sacralization of, 218–19
  Sing-Along, *206*, 207, 208–9, 220–23
Saint Peter Hungate (church), 21, 26, *29*, *37*, 39
  on brink of destruction, 27–30
  Church of England and, 30
  medieval art, 34–38
  as museum, 31–34
Saint Peter Hungate Museum of Ecclesiastical Art, 31–36
Saint Peter Southgate church, 28
Saint Thomas Church, 211
Salazarism, 189–90
Salazar regime, 161, 179n5, 186
Samarbejdsgruppen (Cooperation Council), 95
sculptures, light, 228, *229*
secularism, 44–45, 219, 247n21
  management of, 244
  in Portugal, 186
  religion and, 150
  religio-secularism paradigm, 115
secularization, 3–4, 6–7, 30, 44, 150, 214, 224
secular ritual, 33
secular sacralization, 6, 44, 250
  of *Saint Matthew Passion*, 218–19
sense of presence, 56–61
Sharing Arts Society (SAS), 236–37, 239, 240
sight sacralization, 251
Sing-Akademie, Berlin, 212–13
sing-along events, 220–21
Sing-Along *Saint Matthew Passion* (*meezing-Matthäus*), *206*, 207, 208–9, 220–23

Sing-Along *Sound of Music*, 220–21
Sinterklaas (Saint Nicholas), 232
Sintra, 160, 164
  construction around, 169
  management of, 166–67
  mass consumption at, 167–70
  mysticism and, 167–70
  tourists at, 165, *165*
  UNESCO and, 166–67
  as World Heritage Site, 167, 169
Siuda Baba, 147
Skovgaard, Joakim, 78
Slavic rituals, 139, 140–41, 145, 147
Slavic stories, 147–48
Society for the Protection of Ancient Buildings (SPAB), 24
Soćko-Mucha, Alicja, 152n1
The Song of History (Aakjær), 84
Sound of Music, Sing-Along, 220–21
spirituality, 39, 46
  alternative, 115
  chakra, 115–16, 127–28
  Church of England and, 53, 55
  CMP and, 56
  contemporary, 144
  dowsing and, 60
  energy, 116–19, 122
  enlightenment, 84
  experience, 55
  practices, 118
  religion and, 54
  resonance, 36
  sacred and, 54, 56–57
  significance consultation, 52–56
  Sintra and, 165
  transnational, 127
  value, 51–52
Sprenger, Rien, 236, 240, 243, 245
Stanislaus (saint), 127
state
  church and, 71–73, 91, 106, 186
  Danish, 82, 85–86
  funding from, 105, 109n11
  Polish, 138
St Edmundsbury Cathedral, 48–49
Sufi rituals (*dikhr*), 175–76
Sunni Muslims, 196

Suppression of the Monasteries, 46
Światowid (diety), 146

Taylor Review, 25, 26, 40
Todos: Caminhada de Culturas, 194
topophilia, 144
tour guides
   interviews with, 132n4
   licensing policy for, 123–24
   managing, 123–26, 133n10
   Wawel chakra energy and, 124–25
tourism, 36, 99
   in Kraków, 123, 124
tourists, 93, 122, *122*
   Sintra, 165, *165*
   at Wawel castle, 125, 133n15
   Wawel chakra energy and, 125–26
tradition, preservation of, 236
Trump, Donald, 251–52

UNESCOization, 91
United Kingdom, 39n2, 45
United Nations Educational, Scientific and Cultural Organization (UNESCO), 5, 9–10, 63n1, 159
   funding and, 103–4
   Jelling site and, 98
   label for, 106
   multiculturalism and, 176–77
   Portugal and, 162
   Sintra and, 166–67
   site manager, 103, 106
   World Heritage Committee, 91
universality, 242–44
Utrecht Saint Martin celebrations, 228–29, *229*, 232, 237, 246n9
   church services and, 245n3
   heritagization of, 233–35
   management of, 230, 233, 235, 239
   religion and, 242–44

valuation of heritage, 257, 259n15
vandalism, 64n14, 79
Vanishing Point (exhibition), 35
Vejle Municipality, 94, 96
Viborg Cathedral, 78
Vikings, 47, 92
Viking-themed playground, 96–97

waqf (good deed), 197
Wawel castle, 117, *118*
   chakra dispute 2001, 122–23
   courtyard at, 119, 120, 121, 122, *122*
   emotional bond with, 132n7
   management of, 119–20, 121
   as place of power, 119–23
   restoration of, 122–23
   Roman Catholic Church and, 121
   royals at, 129
   tourists at, 125, 133n15
   wall at, 122, *122*
Wawel Cathedral Museum, 120
Wawel chakra energy, 116–19, 120–21
   avoidance of, 127
   ban on, 124–25, 133n12
   Catholic clergy and, 126–28
   chakra dispute 2001, 122–23
   energy drawers and, 128, 130–31
   Kraków and, 128–29
   research on, 132n4
   supporters, 129
   tour guides and, 124–25
   tourists and, 125–26
Wawel Hill, 113, 128, 131
Wawel Roman Catholic cathedral, 113, 119–20
   Christian aura and, 129
   Eucharistic chapel at, 130
Weles (god), 145
West Suffolk Council, 48
World Apostolate of Fátima, 191
World Heritage
   Committee, UNESCO, 91, 104
   Council, 104
   List, 99, 108n1
   localizing, 96–99
   management of, 95, 97
   maps for UNESCO, 179n15
   Sites, 5, 100, 120
World-Heritagization, 90–91, 96, 98, 104–5, 107
Worm, Ole, 82
Worsaae, J. J. A., 79
worship area, at Roskilde Cathedral, *101*

Young, Francis, 58

www.ingramcontent.com/pod-product-compliance
Lightning Source LLC
Chambersburg PA
CBHW051531020426
42333CB00016B/1882